ZINN & THE ART OF ROAD BIKE MAINTENANCE

2nd Edition

LENNARD ZINN

ILLUSTRATED BY TODD TELANDER

BOULDER, COLORADO

Zinn & the Art of Road Bike Maintenance, 2nd Edition
© 2005 Lennard Zinn

Printed in the United States of America

10 9 8 7 6 5 4 3 2 1

Distributed in the United States and Canada by Publishers Group West

Library of Congress Cataloging-in-Publication Data

Zinn, Lennard.
  Zinn & the art of road bike maintenance/Lennard Zinn. — 2nd ed.
    p. cm.
  Includes index.
  ISBN 1-931382-69-7 (pbk. : alk. paper)
1. Bicycles—Maintenance and repair. I. Title: Zinn and the art of Road bike maintenance.
II. Title.
  TL430.Z56 2005
  629.28'772—dc22

VeloPress®, a division of Inside Communications, Inc.
1830 N. 55th Street
Boulder, Colorado 80301–2700 USA
303/440-0601; Fax 303/444-6788; E-mail velopress@insideinc.com

To purchase additional copies of this book or other VeloPress® books, call 800/234-8356 or visit us on the Web at www.velopress.com.

Cover and interior design by Erin Johnson
Composition by Paula Megenhardt
Cover photo by Don Karle; bike built by Lennard Zinn.

To Ted, Lodema, and Chama

TABLE OF CONTENTS

Introduction 1

CHAPTERS

1   Tools 9

2   Basic Stuff 21

3   Emergency Repairs 35

4   The Chain 49

5   The Shifting System 69

6   Wheels and Tires 105

7   Brakes 139

8   Cranks and Bottom Brackets 165

9   Pedals 185

10   Saddles and Seatposts 203

11   Stems, Handlebars, and Headsets 215

12   Cycling Computers 251

13   Wheel Building 259

14   Forks 275

15   Frames 285

APPENDIXES

A   Troubleshooting Index 299

B   Gear Chart 305

C   Road Bike Fitting 309

D   Glossary 319

E   Torque Table 325

Bibliography 341

Illustration index 343

Index 353

About the author 357

A TIP OF THE HELMET TO ...

Todd Telander. A picture is worth a thousand words, adding up to hundreds of thousands of illustrative "words" from Todd's capable hand. Todd's drawings make my written words more intelligible and this book more useful and beautiful.

My everlasting appreciation goes to the late Bill Woodul for teaching me much of what I know about working on road bikes. I have learned tricks from thousands of other people too numerous to count, but remain grateful for suggestions from Scott Adlfinger, Paul Ahart, Saul Danoff, Skip Howat, Calvin Jones, Paul Morningstar, Andy Pruitt, Wayne Stetina, along with innumerable readers of my Q&A column on www.velonews.com who have written me with great tips.

Thanks to Mary Eberle, Iris Llewellyn, Ted Costantino, and Renee Jardine for their fine editing; to Iris, Renee, and, before them, Lori Hobkirk, for keeping this and all my VeloPress books moving smoothly through the editorial process, and to Charles Pelkey for his editing contributions and content suggestions. My appreciation to Amy Rinehart, Dave Trendler, Pete Hammond, and Rick Rundall for keeping the fires burning under this book and for their contributions, which make VeloPress such a fine organization to work for.

Thanks to Erin Johnson and Paula Megenhardt for putting together all the pieces into a great-looking package. And acknowledgment is due to Felix Magowan and John Wilcockson for establishing VeloPress in the first place.

And, lastly, thanks to my family for providing support and such a nice working environment for me at home.

Exploded road bike

INTRODUCTION

First things first, but not necessarily in that order.
—Doctor Who

ABOUT THIS BOOK

So, you want to maintain your road bike? Congratulations. You will be glad to have taken this step. Although it is nice to learn from the input of friends or shop employees who know more about bikes than you do, it is also important not to be dependent on them whenever anything happens. And the exhilaration of riding with the wind in your hair is enhanced by understanding the classical structure of the mechanical system upon which you are sitting and to which you are trusting your life.

Even the pure romantic can follow the simple step-by-step procedures and exploded diagrams in this book and discover a passion for spreading new grease on old parts. And, I hope, everyone will develop an appreciation for how infusing love into the work will guarantee more success at bike maintenance. If not, frustration will take over, you will use less care, and riding enjoyment will be compromised.

Zinn & the Art of Road Bike Maintenance is organized in such a way that you can pick maintenance tasks appropriate for you. Anyone can perform the repairs illustrated on these pages. It takes only a willingness to learn, as well as the appropriate tools.

This book is intended to be valuable for everyone from shop mechanics to those who only want to know about the most minimal maintenance their bike requires. Chapter 2 is for those only interested in the latter; the rest of the book is for those who choose to go to greater lengths to make everything work optimally and look clean and beautiful. Even for those who wish to focus on Chapter 2, the information in Appendix C on fitting your bike to you instead of the other way around will increase your riding pleasure and safety.

WHY DO IT YOURSELF?

There are a number of reasons why you would want to learn to maintain your bike. Obviously, if done correctly, it is a lot cheaper to fix a bike yourself than to pay someone else to do it. And home-based maintenance is a necessity for most racers and others who live to ride and have no visible means of support.

ı. ı The object of our attention (and affection), racing version

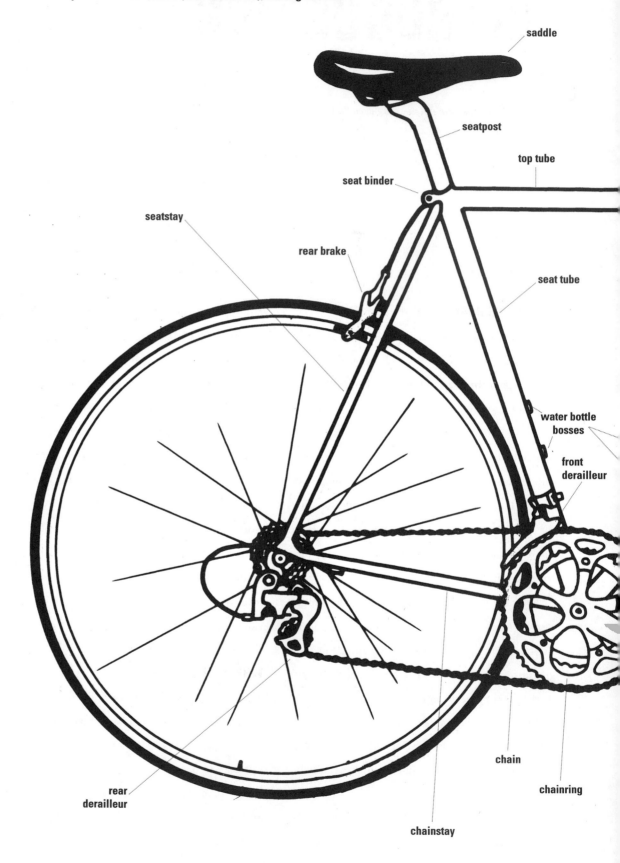

saddle

seatpost

top tube

seat binder

seatstay

rear brake

seat tube

water bottle bosses

front derailleur

rear derailleur

chain

chainring

chainstay

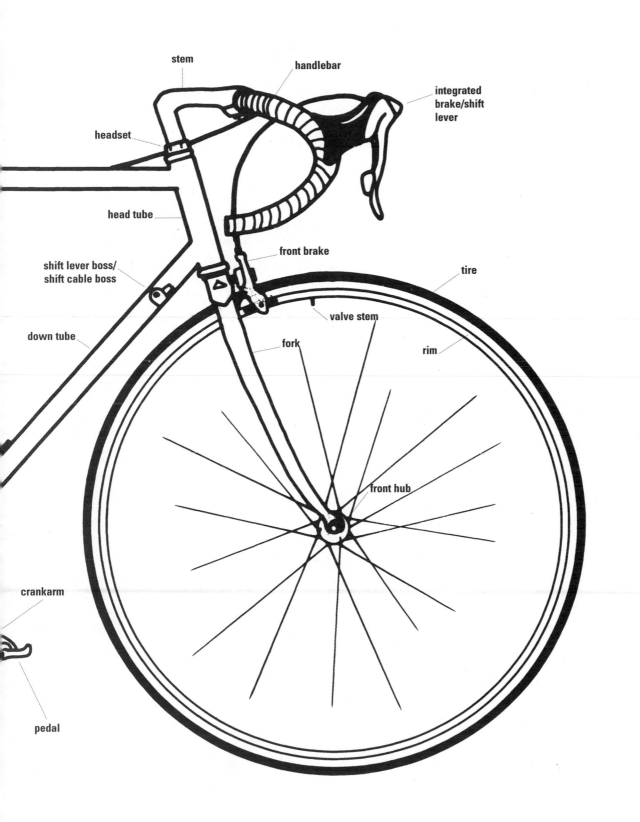

stem

handlebar

integrated
brake/shift
lever

headset

head tube

front brake

tire

shift lever boss/
shift cable boss

valve stem

down tube

fork

rim

front hub

crankarm

pedal

As your income increases, economic necessity ceases to be a significant issue. However, you may find that you enjoy working on your bike for reasons other than just saving money. Unless you have a trusted mechanic to whom you regularly take your bike, you are not likely to find anyone else who cares as much about your bicycle's smooth operation and cleanliness as you do. Furthermore, if you love to ride but have limited time to ride, you frankly need to be able to fix mechanical breakdowns that occur on the road. It may also be hard to find the time to drop off your bike and pick it up from the shop. Nor will you like missing a ride during beautiful weather while your bike sits in a shop that is backed up with repairs. Once you have finally taken your ailing machine to the shop, finding out that you can't just drop it off during high season and expect anything faster than a three-week turnaround on a minor repair can ruin your day. Even scheduling and adhering to a repair appointment can be a hassle. And sometimes, a shop slammed with summer work will return your bike in less-than-optimal condition because too little time was devoted to the repair or the time was sufficient but the mechanic was inexperienced. But you are not about to go through the wringer again and wait for them to fix it correctly. You decide to save the aggravation and do it yourself.

Working on your bike can be fun. Bicycles are the manifestation of elegant simplicity. Bicycle parts, particularly high-end components, are meant to work well and last a long time. With the proper attention, they can shine in appearance and performance for years to come. Satisfaction can be found in dismantling and cleaning a filthy, barely functional part, lubricating it with fresh grease, and reassembling it so that it works like new. Knowing that you made

1.2 Triathlon or time-trial bike

those parts work so smoothly—and that you can do it again when they next need it—is rewarding. You will be eager to ride hard and long to see how your work holds up, rather than being reluctant to get far from home for fear of breaking something.

There is also something very liberating about going on a long ride and knowing that you can fix just about anything that may go wrong. Armed with this knowledge and the tools to put it into action, you will have more confidence to explore new roads and go farther than you may otherwise have gone. You may also find yourself more willing to share your love of the sport with riders who are less experienced. You will enjoy riding with them more if you know that you can fix their questionably maintained bikes, and you will revel in their adoration of you after you have removed an annoying squeak or skipping chain from their bikes.

HOW TO USE THIS BOOK

Skim through the entire book. Skip the detailed steps, but look at the table of contents and the exploded diagrams, and get the general flavor of the book and what's inside. When it's time to perform a particular task, you will know where to find it, and you will have a general idea of how to approach it.

Illustrator Todd Telander and I have done our best to make these pages as understandable as possible. Exploded diagrams are purposefully used to show more clearly than a photograph could how each part goes together. Nevertheless, the first time you go through a procedure, you may find it easier to have a friend read the instructions out loud as you perform the steps.

Obviously, some maintenance tasks are more complicated than others. I am convinced that anyone

1.3 Touring bike

with an opposable thumb can perform any repair on a bike. Still, it pays to spend some time getting familiar with the really simple tasks, such as fixing a flat, before throwing yourself into complex jobs, such as building a wheel.

Tasks and tools required are divided into three levels indicating their complexity or your proficiency. Level 1 tasks need level 1 tools and require of you only an eagerness to learn. Level 2 and level 3 tasks also have corresponding tool sets and are progressively more difficult. All tools required are shown in Chapter 1, and all repairs described in this book are classified as level 1 unless otherwise indicated. At the end of Chapter 2 is the must-read section A General Guide to Performing Mechanical Work (§ii-16); it states general policies and approaches that apply to all mechanical work. Note that the symbol § denotes the section in the book.

Each chapter starts with a list of required tools in the margin. If a section involves more than basic experience and tools, there will be an icon designating the difficulty. Tasks and illustrations are numbered for easy reference.

A troubleshooting section is included at the end of some chapters. This is the place to go to identify the source of a certain noise or particular malfunction in the bike. There is also a comprehensive troubleshooting guide in Appendix A.

The appendixes contain other valuable information as well. Many tasks will be simplified or improved by using the information presented in the appendixes. Appendix B is a complete gear

I.4 Track bike

chart and includes instructions on how to calculate your gear with nonstandard-size wheels. Appendix C is an extensive section on selecting the proper size bike and positioning it to fit you. It includes information about setting up your bike for triathlons or time trials. Appendix D, the glossary, is an inclusive dictionary of bicycle technical terminology. Appendix E lists the tightening (torque) specifications of almost every bolt on the bike. I can't emphasize enough how useful it is to use a torque wrench to tighten bolts as tightly as the component manufacturer intended, but no tighter. Flag Appendix E so you can flip to it easily whenever you work on your bike.

The Internet can be a useful supplement to this book. For instance, www.bikeschool.com, www.dtswiss.com, and other sites have spoke-length calculators to use when you are building wheels. And exploded views of some parts can be found on component-company Web sites, such as www.campagnolo.com, www.shimano.com, and www.mavic.com.

THE ROAD BIKE

This is the creature (Fig. i.1) to which this book is devoted. All of its parts are illustrated and labeled. Take a minute to familiarize yourself with these parts now, and then refer back to this diagram whenever necessary.

The road bike comes in a variety of forms, from road racing (Fig. i.1) to triathlon or time-trial (Fig. i.2), to touring models, which are rigged for carrying luggage (Fig. i.3), to models with front—and even rear—suspension. Some distant cousins are track (Fig. i.4) and cyclo-cross bikes (Fig. i.5)

ı.5 Cyclo-cross bike

THIS MEANS YOU!

Because this book clearly spells out the steps necessary to properly maintain and repair a road bike, even those who see themselves as having no mechanical skills will be able to tackle problems as they arise. With a willingness to learn on your part and after a little bit of practice, you will find that your bicycle will suddenly transform itself from a mysterious black box, too complicated to tamper with, to a simple, understandable machine that is a delight to work on. Just allow yourself the opportunity and the dignity to follow along, rather than deciding in advance that you can't. All you have to do is follow the instructions and trust yourself.

So, if you think you are not mechanically inclined, set that opinion aside, along with any other factors that may stand in the way of rolling up your sleeves in the interest of improving your bike's performance.

CHAPTER 1

TOOLS

If the only tool you have is a hammer,
you tend to see every problem as a nail.
—Abraham Maslow

You can't do much useful work on a bike without a basic assortment of tools. And bicycles—like other evolved machines such as automobiles and watches—have specific fasteners and threads that require specific tools to fit them. This chapter will clarify which tools you should consider owning, on the basis of your level of mechanical experience and interest.

As I mentioned in the introduction, the maintenance and repair procedures in this book are classified by their degree of difficulty. Nearly all repairs are classified as Level 1, because most bicycle repair jobs are pretty easy to complete once you understand the principles involved. The tools for Levels 1, 2, and 3 are pictured in Figures 1.1, 1.2, and 1.3, respectively, and described on the following pages. In addition, the tools you may need for a specific repair are listed in the margin at the beginning of each chapter.

For the uninitiated, there is no need to rush out and buy a large number of bike-specific tools. With few exceptions, the Level 1 Tool Kit (Fig. 1.1) consists of standard metric tools, many of which you may already own. In a more compact and lightweight form, this is the same collection of tools I recommend carrying on long rides (Fig. 1.6)

The Level 2 Tool Kit (Fig. 1.2) contains several bike-specific tools, allowing you to do more complex work on the bike. Level 3 tools (Fig. 1.3) are extensive (and sometimes expensive) and ensure that your riding buddies will show up not only to ask your sage advice, but to borrow your tools as well. And if you are one to loan tools, you may consider marking your collection and keeping a list of who borrowed what, so as to help recover those items that may otherwise take a long time finding their way back to your workshop.

i-1 LEVEL 1 TOOL KIT

LEVEL 1

Level 1 repairs are the simplest and do not require a workshop, although it is nice to have a well-lit and comfortable work space. For easy repairs, you will need the following tools (Fig. 1.1):

- **Tire pump with a gauge** and a valve head to match your tubes (either Presta or Schrader valves; see Fig. 1.1B).
- **Standard slot-head screwdrivers:** small, medium, and large.
- **Phillips-head screwdrivers:** one small and one medium.
- Set of three plastic **tire levers**—if you have clincher tires.
- At least two **spare tubes**—or **tubulars**—of the same size and valve type as those on your bike.
- Container of regular **talcum powder** for coating tubes and the inner casings of tires.

  NOTE: *Do not inhale this stuff; it is bad for your lungs.*

- **Patch kit.** Choose one that comes with sandpaper instead of a metal scratcher. Every year, check that the glue has not dried up.
- One 6-inch **adjustable wrench** (a.k.a. "Crescent wrench," which is a brand name).
- **Pliers:** regular and needle-nose.
- Set of **metric Allen wrenches** (or "hex keys") that includes 2.5mm, 3mm, 4mm, 5mm, 6mm, and 8mm sizes. Folding sets are available and work nicely to keep wrenches organized. I also recommend buying extras of the 4mm, 5mm, and 6mm sizes.
- Set of **metric open-end wrenches** that includes 7mm, 8mm, 9mm, 10mm, 13mm, 14mm, 15mm, and 17mm sizes.

**LEVEL 1
TOOL KIT**

I.IA Level 1 tool kit

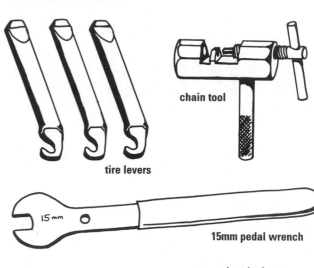

tire levers

chain tool

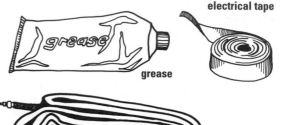

15mm pedal wrench

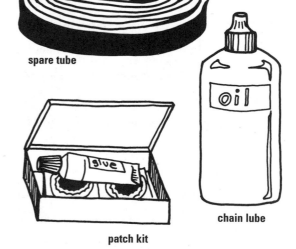

grease

electrical tape

spare tube

chain lube

patch kit

- A 15mm **pedal wrench.** This type is thinner and longer than a standard 15mm wrench and thicker than a cone wrench, to fit into the space between the pedal and crank.
- **Chain tool** for breaking and reassembling chains. If you have a nine-speed or ten-speed system, you may need a narrower chain tool to

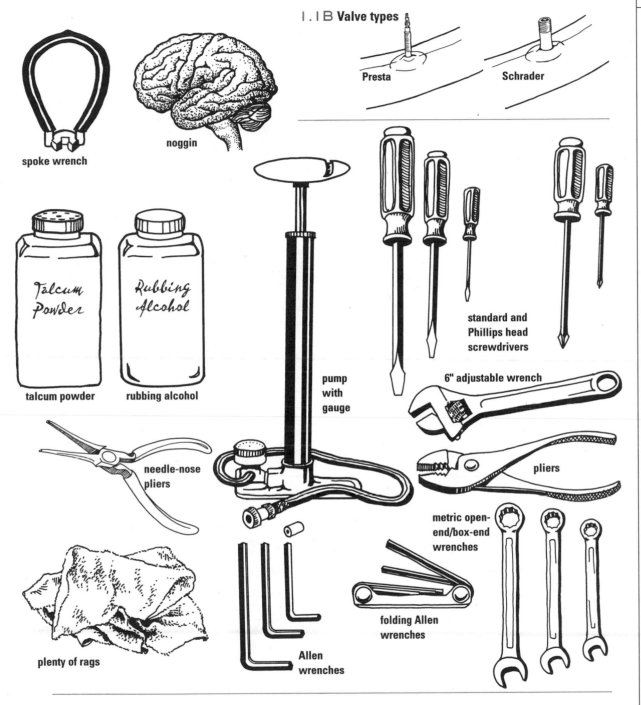

1.1B Valve types

Presta   Schrader

spoke wrench

noggin

talcum powder

rubbing alcohol

pump
with
gauge

standard and
Phillips head
screwdrivers

6" adjustable wrench

needle-nose
pliers

pliers

metric open-
end/box-end
wrenches

plenty of rags

Allen
wrenches

folding Allen
wrenches

avoid bending the center prongs of the tool. Shimano's TL-CN23 and TL-CN32 work for seven-, eight-, and ten-speed chains. Many other chain tools work as well.

- **Spoke wrench** to match the size of nipples used on your wheels.

- Tube or jar of **grease.** I recommend using grease designed specifically for bicycles, but standard automotive grease is okay.

- Drip bottle or can of **chain lubricant.** Please choose a nonaerosol; it is easier to control, uses less packaging, and wastes less in overspray.

- **Rubbing alcohol** for light cleaning, and for removing and installing handlebar grips, if you have them instead of handlebar tape.

- A roll of **electrical tape** for taping off the end of your handlebar and for marking your seat height.

- A lot of **rags!** Old T-shirts work fine, by the way. Also get safety glasses and rubber dish gloves or a box of cheap latex gloves. A bucket, large brushes and sponges, and dish soap also will serve you well for cleaning a dirty machine rapidly.

i-2 LEVEL 2 TOOL KIT

Level 2 repairs are a bit more complex, and I recommend that you attack them with specific tools and a well-organized workspace with a shop bench. Keeping your workspace well organized is probably the best way to make maintenance and repair easy and quick. You will need the entire Level 1 Tool Kit (Fig. 1.1) plus the following tools (Fig. 1.2):

- **Portable bike stand.** Be sure that the stand is sturdy enough to remain stable when you're really cranking on the wrenches.

- **Shop apron** (this is to keep your nice duds nice).

- **Hacksaw** with a fine-toothed blade.

- Set of **razor blades** or a sharp shop knife.

- **Files:** one round and one flat, with medium-fine teeth.

- **Cable cutter** for cutting brake and shift cables without fraying the ends.

- **Cable-housing cutter** for cutting coaxial-indexed cable housing. If you purchase a Shimano, Park, or Wrench Force housing cutter, you won't need to buy a separate cable cutter, because all of these cleanly cut cables as well as housings.

- Set of **metric socket wrenches** that includes 7mm, 8mm, 9mm, 10mm, 13mm, 14mm, and 15mm sizes.

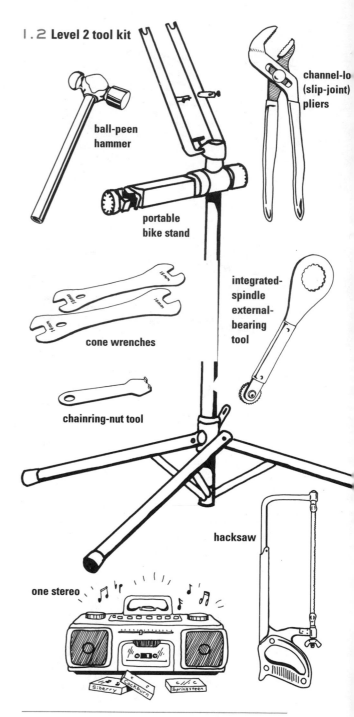

1.2 Level 2 tool kit

ball-peen hammer

channel-lo (slip-joint) pliers

portable bike stand

cone wrenches

integrated-spindle external-bearing tool

chainring-nut tool

hacksaw

one stereo

- **Crank puller** for removing crankarms. Its push rod is sized for either square-taper crankarms or ISIS/Octalink crankarms, so get the right one for your crankset.

- **Chainring-nut tool** for holding the nut while you tighten or loosen a chainring bolt.

- Medium **ball-peen hammer.**

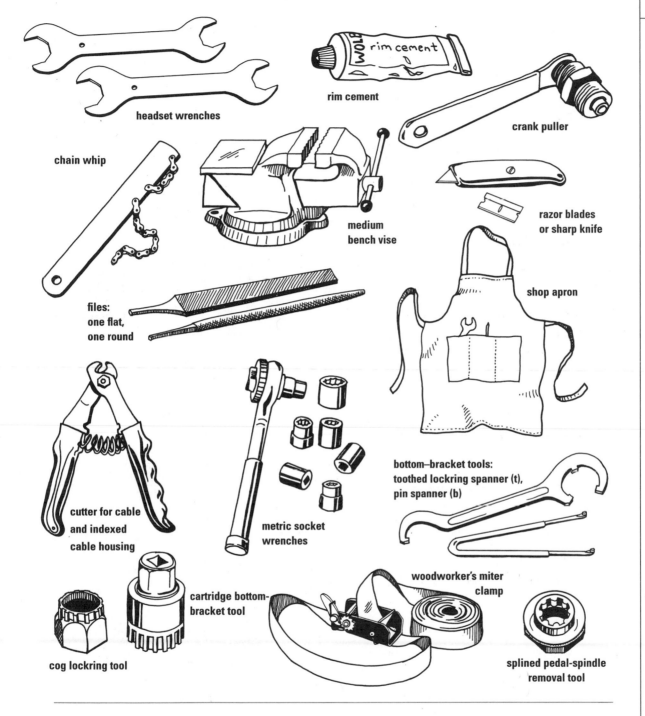

headset wrenches

rim cement

crank puller

chain whip

medium bench vise

razor blades or sharp knife

files: one flat, one round

shop apron

cutter for cable and indexed cable housing

metric socket wrenches

bottom–bracket tools: toothed lockring spanner (t), pin spanner (b)

cartridge bottom-bracket tool

woodworker's miter clamp

cog lockring tool

splined pedal-spindle removal tool

LEVEL 2
TOOL KIT

- Two **headset wrenches.** Be sure to check the size of the headset on your bike before buying these. This purchase is unnecessary if you have a threadless headset and plan to work on your own bike only.

- Medium-size **bench vise** (bolted to a sturdy bench).

- **Cog lockring tool** for removing cogs from the rear hub. Note that Campagnolo and Shimano cogs require different tools for this job.

- **Chain whip** for holding cogs while loosening the cassette lockring.

- **Bottom-bracket tools.** For Shimano or Campagnolo cartridge-bearing bottom brackets and clones of them, you'll need the splined cartridge bottom-bracket tool specifically made for this type of bottom bracket. Note that if you have an ISIS or Octalink splined-spindle bottom bracket, you need a tool with a bore large enough to swallow the fatter spindle. For recent **external-bearing integrated-spindle** cranks, you'll need yet another oversized splined wrench to remove the cups, which are larger and sit outboard of the bottom-bracket shell, and a little splined tool to tighten the left crank's adjustment cap. And for cup-and-cone bottom brackets, you'll need a lockring spanner and a pin spanner to fit your bottom bracket.

- **Cone wrenches,** if you have loose-bearing hubs. The standard sizes are 13mm and 14mm, but check what size you need before buying.
- **Channel-lock ("slip-joint") pliers.**
- **Splined pedal-spindle removal tool.** Note that the specific tool differs for Shimano and Look pedals.
- **Rim cement** for tubular tires, if you have them. Use Continental clear glue or Vittoria Mastik'One for aluminum rims, but stick to Mastik'One for carbon-fiber rims.
- **Woodworker's miter clamp** for gluing tubulars (optional).
- One **stereo** with **good tunes.** This is especially important if you plan on spending a lot of time working on your bike.

i-3 LEVEL 3 TOOL KIT

If you are an accomplished Level 3 mechanic, you are completely independent of your local bike shop's service department. You can even build up brand-new frames. By now, you have a well-organized, separate space intended just for working

1.3 Level 3 tool kit

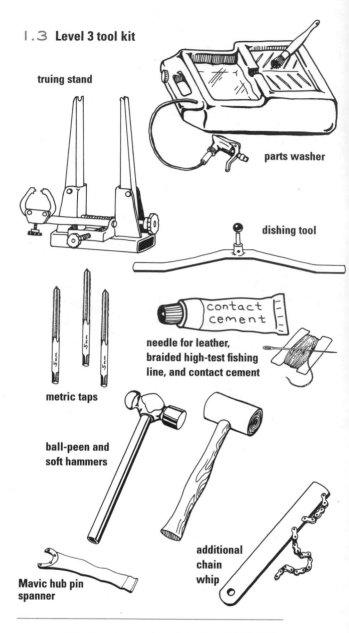

truing stand

parts washer

dishing tool

metric taps

contact cement

needle for leather, braided high-test fishing line, and contact cement

ball-peen and soft hammers

Mavic hub pin spanner

additional chain whip

on your bike. Some elements of the Level 3 Tool Kit (Fig. 1.3) are obviously heavier-duty replacements or substitutions for parts of the Level 2 Tool Kit.

- **Parts washing tank.** Please use an environmentally safe degreaser. Dispose of used solvent responsibly; check with your local environmental safety office.
- Fixed **bike stand.** Be sure it comes with a clamp designed to fit any size of frame tube.
- Large bench-mounted **vise** so that you can free stuck parts.

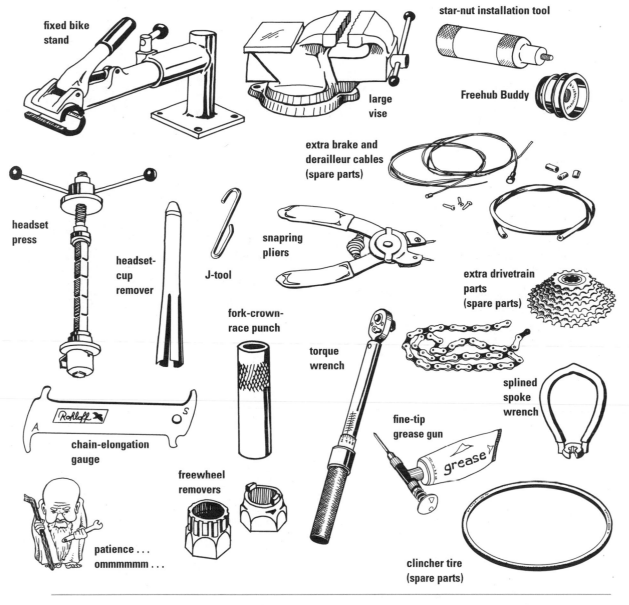

fixed bike stand

star-nut installation tool

large vise

Freehub Buddy

extra brake and derailleur cables (spare parts)

headset press

headset-cup remover

J-tool

snapring pliers

extra drivetrain parts (spare parts)

fork-crown-race punch

torque wrench

splined spoke wrench

fine-tip grease gun

grease

Rohloff

chain-elongation gauge

freewheel removers

patience . . . ommmmmm . . .

clincher tire (spare parts)

LEVEL 3
TOOL KIT

- **Headset press** used to install headset bearing cups. The press should fit all three cup sizes. Chris King and some other cartridge-bearing headsets need a press that does not contact the pressed-in bearing. Chris King sells inserts for regular headset presses to install his headsets.

- **Fork-crown-race punch** (a.k.a. slide hammer) for installing the fork-crown headset race. (Thin Shimano or Chris King crown races require a second support tool to protect the crown race during installation.)

- **Headset-cup remover.**

- **Star-nut installation tool** for threadless headsets.

- An **additional chain whip.** A second whip is handy for disassembling freewheels or old-style cassettes.

- **Freewheel removers.** If you will be working on retro stuff, you should get removers for Shimano, Sachs, and Suntour freewheels.

- Large **ball-peen hammer.**

- **Soft hammer.** Choose a rubber, plastic, or wooden mallet to prevent damage to parts.

- **Torque wrenches,** which are great for checking proper bolt tightness. Most component manufacturers recommend using one and thus provide torque specs; following them dissuades parts from stripping, breaking, or falling off while riding. There is a complete torque specification list in Appendix E of this book.

- Set of **metric taps** that includes 5mm x 0.8, 6mm x 1, and 10mm x 1. These work for threading bottle bosses, seat binder clamps, derailleur hangers, and cantilever bosses (on touring or cyclo-cross frames).

- Pair of **snapring pliers** for removing snaprings from pedals, suspension forks, and other parts.

- Fine-tip **grease gun** for parts with grease fittings and for Campagnolo headsets with grease holes.

- Morningstar **Freehub Buddy** for lubricating Shimano freehubs.

- Morningstar **J-tool** for removing Shimano freehub dust covers.

- **Chain-elongation gauge.** This handy little plastic item helps you quickly determine whether a chain needs replacing. An accurate 12-inch ruler will substitute adequately.

- **Truing stand** for truing and building wheels.

- **Dishing tool** for checking whether that set of wheels you just built is properly centered.

- A full range of **spoke wrenches** of various sizes, including splined ones.

- **Splined spoke wrench** for Mavic Zicral spokes.

- **Pin spanner** for adjusting Mavic hubs.

- **Needle** for leather, braided high-test **fishing line,** and **contact cement** for patching tubular tires.

- One healthy dose of **patience** and an equal willingness to work and rework jobs until they have been properly finished.

a. Other stuff

- **Spare parts** to save you from having to make a lot of last-minute runs to the bike shop for commonly used parts. Any well-equipped shop really requires several sizes of ball bearings, bolts, spare cables, cable housing, and a lifetime supply of those little housing ferrules (cylindrical caps) and cable-end caps. You should also have a good supply of spare tires, tubes, chains, and cogsets.

- **Various fluids.** Threadlock fluid, titanium anti-seize compound, outboard-motor gear oil, or specialty freehub lubricants are required for some jobs.

i-4 NOW, IF YOU REALLY WANT A WELL-STOCKED SHOP . . .

The following tools (Fig. 1.4) are not even part of the Level 3 Tool Kit and are rarely needed for bike repairs. That said, they sure do come in handy when you need them.

- **Bottom-bracket tap set.** This tool cuts threads in both ends of the bottom bracket while keeping the threads in proper alignment. English-threaded taps are required for most modern road bike frames. Most Italian frames, however, have Italian threads and will require appropriate taps. French threading and Swiss threading are different yet, but these threads are fortunately rare in modern road bikes.

- **Bottom-bracket facer.** Like a bottom-bracket tap, this tool cuts the faces of the bottom-bracket shell so that they are parallel to each other.

- **Head-tube reaming and facing tool.** This tool keeps both ends of the head-tube perfectly parallel and bored out to the right size.

I.4 Tools for the well-stocked shop

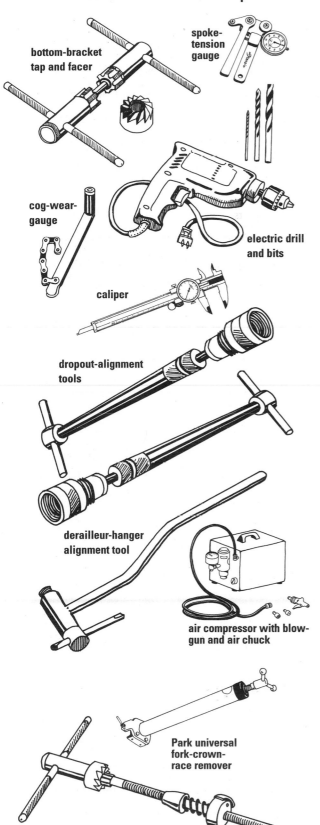

bottom-bracket tap and facer

spoke-tension gauge

cog-wear-gauge

electric drill and bits

caliper

dropout-alignment tools

derailleur-hanger alignment tool

air compressor with blow-gun and air chuck

Park universal fork-crown-race remover

head-tube reaming and facing tool

- **Electric drill** with drill-bit set for customizing.
- **Dropout-alignment tools** (a.k.a. tip adjusters).
- **Derailleur-hanger alignment tool** to straighten the derailleur hanger after you shift the derailleur into the spokes or crash on it.
- **Cog-wear-indicator gauge** to determine whether cogs are worn out.
- **Park universal fork-crown-race remover.** This hefty tool can remove a fork-crown race from any shape of fork without using a hammer and screwdriver and suffering consequent collateral damage to the fork.
- **Measuring caliper** with a vernier, dial, or electronic gauge to precisely measure parts.
- **Spoke-tension gauge** to check for proper spoke tension, resulting in stronger, longer-lasting wheels.
- An **air compressor** sure makes quick work of mounting tires.

i-5 SETTING UP YOUR HOME SHOP

Make your shop clean, well-organized, and comfortable, and you'll find that the speed and quality of your work will improve. Hanging tools on pegboard or slatboard, or placing them in bins or trays, are all effective ways to maintain an organized work area. Being able to lay your hand immediately on the tool you need will immensely increase the enjoyment of working on a bike. It is hard to do a job with loving care if you are frustrated by not being able to find the cable cutter. Placing small parts in a bench-top organizer, one with several rows of little drawers, is another good way to keep chaos at bay.

TOOLS

SETTING UP
YOUR
HOME SHOP

1.5 Tools to take on all rides

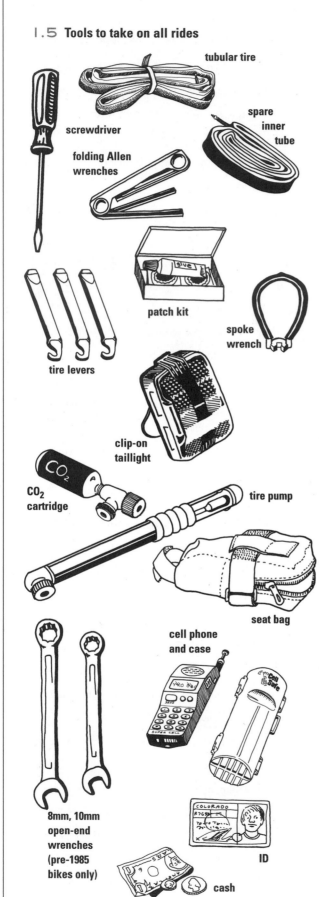

screwdriver

tubular tire

spare inner tube

folding Allen wrenches

patch kit

spoke wrench

tire levers

clip-on taillight

CO₂ cartridge

tire pump

seat bag

cell phone and case

8mm, 10mm open-end wrenches (pre-1985 bikes only)

ID

cash

i-6 TOOLS TO CARRY WITH YOU WHILE RIDING

a. For most riding

You can keep everything you need for light repairs (Fig. 1.5) in a **small bag under your seat**. Some people may prefer a fanny pack. As you stock this bag, look for tools and parts that are light and serviceable. Many of the tools are available in combination and sold as "multitools." Make sure you try all tools at home before depending on them on the road.

- **Spare inner tube** or **tubular.** Always carry one. Make sure the valve matches the ones on your bike. If rarely needed, keep it in a plastic bag to prevent deterioration.

- **Tire pump** or **CO₂ cartridge.** If a pump, the bigger the better (for pumping, but heavier for carrying), but road bike pumps need also to be thin to attain high pressures. Mini-pumps are okay, but they're slow. Make sure the pump has the right head for your type of valves. If you prefer "air" cartridges, get the correct size for the spare tube or tubular (probably 12g [grams], unless you are filling a huge touring tire, in which case you may need a 16g cartridge).

- At least two plastic **tire levers,** preferably three (for clincher tires only).

- **Patch kit.** You'll need something after you've used your spare tube. Check it at least every year to make sure the glue has not dried up. You can also bring glueless patches.

- **Small screwdriver** for adjusting derailleurs and other parts.

- Compact set of **Allen wrenches** that includes 2.5mm, 3mm, 4mm, 5mm, and 6mm sizes; a folding set is a good investment. (You may need to take along an 8mm on a long tour, too, if your crank bolts are that size.)

- 8mm and 10 mm **open-end wrenches** for pre-1980s bikes. These are often included on multi-tools, eliminating the need to bring separate wrenches.

- Properly sized **spoke wrench.**

- Small clip-on **taillight.**

- **Warm outerwear.** Arm warmers, knee warmers, nylon vest, and a cap for any ride in the mountains or on any day that is not just plain hot. In the mountains and in questionable weather, thin gloves and shoe covers are also a good idea.

- **Identification.**

- **Cash** for food, phone calls, and to boot sidewall cuts in tires.

- A **cell phone** is not a bad idea. You can get a cell-phone case to fit in a water-bottle cage or keep the phone in a plastic bag in your back pocket.

b. For long or multiday trips

Bring the items in Fig. 1.6, as well as all of the items in Fig. 1.5.

- **Spare folding clincher tire** and a **second spare inner tube** or, if you ride tubulars, bring two spares.

- **Rain gear.**

- **Combination wrench and chain tool** in case you break your chain. Chain tools (or "chain breakers") are often included in compact multitools, eliminating the need to bring a separate chain tool (as well as separate screwdrivers, hex keys, and even box-end or open-end wrenches). Try the chain tool in the multitool at home to make sure that you can repair the chain 100% of the time. This testing is important insurance on long solo rides that include extended stretches without civilization or cell phone coverage.

- Spare **chain links** from your chain. If you are using a Shimano eight-speed or nine-speed

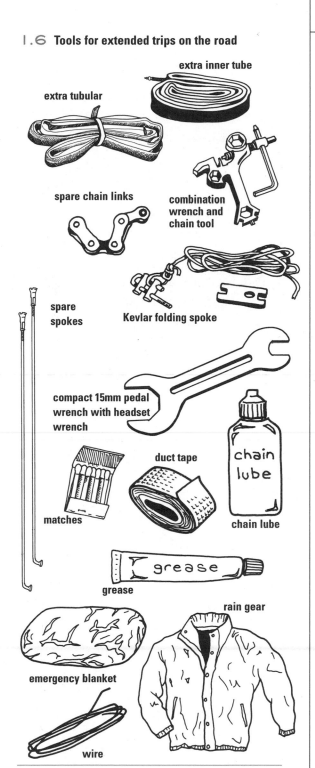

1.6 Tools for extended trips on the road

extra inner tube
extra tubular
spare chain links
combination wrench and chain tool
spare spokes
Kevlar folding spoke
compact 15mm pedal wrench with headset wrench
duct tape
chain lube
chain lube
matches
grease
grease
emergency blanket
rain gear
wire

chain, bring at least two "subpin" rivets. For ten-speed chains, either for Shimano or Campagnolo, you will have to replace the chain with a new one when you get home, so don't worry about bringing assembly pins, because the chain would still be shot, even if you were to use them. More on this subject comes up in Chapter 4.

- **Spare spokes.** Innovations in Cycling sells a really cool **folding spoke** made from Kevlar. It's worth getting one or two for emergency repairs on a long ride.
- Small plastic bottle of **chain lube.**
- Small tube of **grease.**
- Small amount of **duct tape.**
- Small amount of **wire.**
- Compact 15mm **pedal wrench.** Be sure to get one with a headset wrench on the other end.

- **Headlight.** This can be a lightweight unit to clip onto the handlebar or a headlamp with a strap that will fit over your helmet.
- **Matches.**
- A lightweight aluminized folding emergency **blanket.**

NOTE: *Read Chapter 3 on emergency repairs before embarking on a lengthy trip. And, if you are planning a bike-centered vacation, be sure to take along a Level 1 Tool Kit in your car, some headset wrenches (if your bike has a threaded headset), and incidentals like duct tape and sandpaper.*

**TOOLS
TO CARRY
WITH YOU**

CHAPTER 2

BASIC STUFF

Preride inspection, wheel removal, general cleaning, and mechanical methods guide

Basic research is what I am doing when I don't know what I am doing.
—Werner von Braun

It is a good idea to get in the habit of checking your bike before heading out on a ride. Performing this inspection regularly can help you avoid getting stranded far from home because of parts failure. You should also know how to properly remove and reinstall a wheel, so that you can deal with minor annoyances like flat tires or jammed chains. And even if you do absolutely nothing else to your bike, keeping its chain clean and properly lubricated, as outlined in this chapter, will make every ride smoother and quieter.

ii–1 PRERIDE INSPECTION

1. Check to be sure that the quick-release levers or axle nuts (the ones that secure the hub axle to the dropouts) are tight.

2. Check the brake pads for excessive or uneven wear.

3. Grab and twist the brake pads and brake arms to make sure that the bolts are tight.

4. Squeeze the brake levers. A good squeeze should bring the pads flat against the rims (or slightly toed in) without hitting the tires. Make certain that you cannot squeeze the levers all of the way to the handlebar. For details, see Chapter 7 on brake adjustment.

5. Spin the wheels. Check for wobbles while eyeing the rims, not the tires. Make sure that the rims do not rub on the brake pads.

6. Spin the wheels again, checking for wobbles while eyeing the tires this time. If a tire wobbles excessively on a straight rim, it may not be fully seated in the rim. There is usually a mold line or an edge of a tape strip on the tire that should be parallel to the rim edge all of the way around. Look for areas where the tire is bulged larger

and/or the mold line or tape edge is higher above the rim or deeper into the rim than the rest of the way around the tire. To fix an improperly seated tire, you need to completely deflate the tire and carefully seat it uniformly all of the way around before reinflating.

7. Check the tire pressure. On most road bike tires, the proper pressure is between 80 and 120 pounds per square inch (psi). Look to see that there are no foreign objects sticking in the tire. If there are, you may have to pull the tube out and repair or replace it. If you have an aversion to fixing flats, turn to the section on tire sealants (i.e., goop inside the tube that fills small holes) in Chapter 6.

8. Check the tires for excessive wear, cracking, or gashes.

9. Be certain that the handlebar and stem are tight and that the stem is lined up with the front tire.

10. Check that the gears shift smoothly and the chain does not skip or shift by itself. Ensure that each indexed ("click") shift moves the chain one cog, starting with the first click. Make sure that the chain does not overshift the smallest or biggest rear cog or the inner or outer front chainring.

11. Check the chain for rust, dirt, stiff links, or noticeable signs of wear. It should be clean and lubricated (although you need to be aware that overlubricated, gooey chains pick up lots of dirt). The chain should be replaced on a road bike about every 1,500 to 2,500 miles of paved riding—see §iv-6 to accurately evaluate chain wear.

12. Apply the front brake and push the bike forward and back. The headset should be tight and not

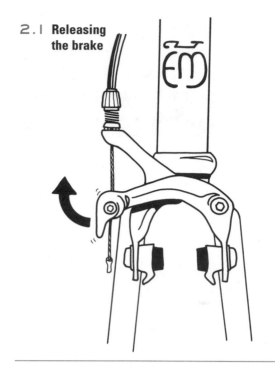

2.1 Releasing the brake

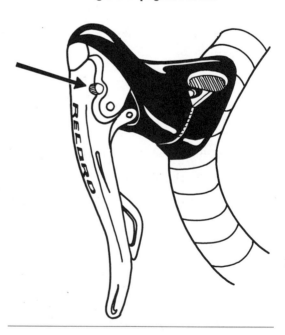

2.2 Releasing a Campagnolo brake

make "clunking" noises or allow the fork any fore-and-aft play.

13. Grasp one crankarm and push and pull it laterally, toward and away from the frame, to ensure that the crank bearings are not loose.

14. Grasp each wheel and push and pull it laterally, perpendicular to the plane of the wheel, to

ensure that the hub bearings are not loose.

15. If all this checks out, go ride your bike! If not, check the table of contents, go to the appropriate chapter, and fix the problems before you go out and ride.

ii-2 REMOVING THE FRONT WHEEL

You can't fix a flat if you can't remove the wheel. Front-wheel removal is also generally required for placing a bike on a roof rack or for putting a bike in a car. As outlined in the following sections, wheel removal involves releasing the brake (in most cases) and opening the hub quick release or bolt-on skewer or the axle nuts on inexpensive bicycles.

ii-3 RELEASING THE BRAKE

Most brakes have a quick-release (QR) mechanism to open the brake arms so that they spring away from the rim, allowing the tire to pass between the pads. Most road bike sidepull brakes have a lever on the brake caliper that is flipped up to open the brake (Fig. 2.1). Alternatively, Campagnolo Ergo Power systems have a pin near the top of the brake lever that is pushed outward to allow the lever (and consequently the caliper) to open wider (Fig. 2.2). Cheap sidepull brakes on cheap bikes—as well as early sidepull brakes on fine, classic racing bikes from the late 1960s and early 1970s—don't have a quick release for the brake. The same is often true with time-trial bikes and triathlon bikes, for instance, as well as those with Campagnolo brakes (with no QR) coupled with little aerodynamic brake levers on the ends of bullhorn bars (see Fig. i.2), (instead of with Campagnolo Ergo Power levers, which have an integrated QR).

If your brake has no quick release and your wheel does not have a skinny enough tire to fit between the brake pads, you will want to deflate the tire first to avoid damaging the tire and perhaps even dislodging the brake pads from their proper positions.

Center-pull brakes (rare now, but common on pre-1975 bikes) have a cable-hanger yoke that must be pulled down to release from the straddle cable while the pads are held against the rim.

Cyclo-cross bikes and some touring bikes have cantilever-type brakes (Figs. 7.16–7.25) that mount on pivots that are attached to fork legs or seatstays. Most standard cantilever brakes are released by pulling the enlarged head of the straddle cable out of a notch in the top of the brake arm while holding the pads against the rim with the other hand. Really old cantilever brakes are released like the center-pull brakes mentioned in the previous paragraph.

Another type of cantilever, less common on road bikes because of incompatibility with the brake levers on drop bars, is commonly called a "V-brake" (Fig. 7.34), after the Shimano design that popularized them. A V-brake is released by pulling the end of the curved cable-guide tube (a.k.a. "the noodle") out of the horizontal link atop one of the brake arms while squeezing the pads against the rim with the other hand.

ii-4 DETACHING A FRONT WHEEL WITH A QUICK-RELEASE SKEWER

You don't need a tool for this task.

1. Pull the lever outward to open it (Fig. 2.3).
2. After opening the hub quick-release lever, the wheel is ready to fall out on most bikes with forks older than 2003 or so. If it will not fall out, you most likely have wheel-retention tabs on the fork ends, which are designed to keep the wheel in place even if the quick release inadvertently

REMOVING THE
FRONT WHEEL
—
RELEASING
THE BRAKE
—
DETACHING
WHEELS

opens (or, more likely, is left open by mistake). In this case, unscrew the nut on the opposite end of the quick-release skewer's shaft until it clears the fork's wheel-retention tabs.

3. Lift the bike so the wheel falls out.

ii-5 DETACHING A WHEEL WITH AXLE NUTS

NOTE: *Some bikes—usually only those of light-weight fanatics, however—have bolt-on skewers (Fig. 2.4), often made of titanium to save weight. The wheel is removed by unscrewing the skewer with a 5mm Allen wrench.*

1. Unscrew the nuts on the axle ends (usually with a 15mm wrench) until they allow the wheel to fall out (Fig. 2.5). Really old road bikes may have wing nuts for finger-tightening instead.

2. Your bike may have some type of wheel-retention system consisting of nubs or bent tabs on the fork ends or an axle washer with a bent tooth hooked into a hole in the fork end. These systems prevent the wheel from falling out if the axle nuts loosen. Loosen the nuts enough to clear the retention tabs on the fork ends. Note that it's not usually necessary to remove the nuts completely from the axle.

3. Pull the wheel out.

ii-6 INSTALLING THE FRONT WHEEL

Leaving the brake open (or the tire deflated, if you have no brake quick release and the tire won't fit through the brake while inflated), lower the fork

DETACHING

WHEELS

—

INSTALLING

THE FRONT

WHEEL

—

TIGHTENING

THE QUICK-

RELEASE

SKEWER

2.3 Opening quick-release skewer

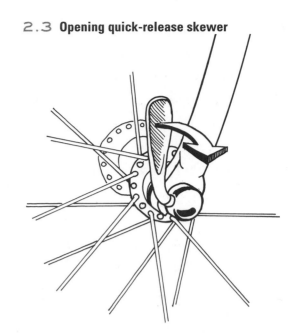

onto the wheel so that the bike's weight pushes the top of the dropout slots down onto the hub axle. This action will seat the axle fully into the fork and center the rim between the brake pads. If the fork or wheel is misaligned, you will need to hold the rim centered between the brake pads when securing the hub (and true the untrue wheel—see §vi-12—or get the bent fork fixed or replaced soon). To secure your wheel, continue with the steps given in the section that is appropriate for your bike's configuration (§ii-7, §ii-8, or §ii-9).

ii-7 TIGHTENING THE QUICK-RELEASE SKEWER

The quick-release skewer is not a glorified wing nut and should not be treated as such.

1. Hold the quick-release lever in the "open" position.

2.4 Bolt-on skewer

2.5 Loosening axle nut

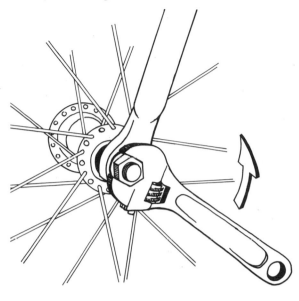

2. Tighten the opposite end nut until it snugs up against the face of the dropout. (If you have no wheel-retention tabs on the fork, and you did not unscrew the skewer nut, this step is unnecessary, because the skewer will still be in adjustment.)

3. Push the lever over (Fig. 2.6) to the "closed" position (it should now be at a 90-degree angle to the axle). It should take a good amount of hand pressure to close the quick-release lever properly; the lever should leave its imprint on your palm for a few seconds.

4. If the quick-release lever does not close tightly, open the lever again, tighten the end nut a quarter turn, and close the lever again. Repeat until tight.

5. If, on the other hand, the lever cannot be pushed down flat, then the nut is too tight. Open the quick-release lever, unscrew the end nut a quarter turn or so, and try closing the lever again. Repeat this procedure until the quick-release lever is fully closed and snug. The lever should leave an imprint on the palm of your hand for a few seconds. When you are done, it is important to have the lever pointing straight up or toward the back of the bike so that it cannot hook on obstacles and be accidentally opened.

6. Hit the top of the tire with your open palm to check that the wheel is not loose and you cannot bang it out.

2.6 Tightening the quick release

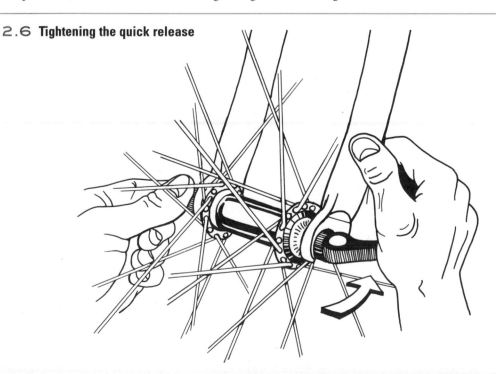

TIGHTENING
THE QUICK-
RELEASE
SKEWER

ii–8 TIGHTENING BOLT-ON SKEWERS

Hold the end nut with one hand and tighten the bolt-on skewer (Fig. 2.4) with a 5mm hex key. Control Tech recommends 65 inch-pounds (in-lbs) of tightening torque for steel bolt-on skewers and 85 in-lbs for titanium ones. You can approximate the accurate tightening torque by using a short hex key and tightening as tightly as you can with your fingers. These skewers can be overtightened; avoid that problem by being conscious of how much pressure a quick-release skewer applies and do not go higher than that, but make sure it is tight enough to securely hold the wheel and not loosen up.

ii–9 TIGHTENING AXLE NUTS

Snug up the nuts clockwise (opposite direction of Fig. 2.5) with a wrench (usually 15mm) a little from each side until they are quite tight. In the case of wing nuts, the procedure is the same; the tools are your fingers.

ii–10 CLOSING THE BRAKES

The steps required to close the brakes are always the reverse of what you did to release them.

1. With most road bikes, closing the brake caliper is simply a matter of flipping closed the quick-release lever on the sidepull brake caliper (Fig. 2.1 in reverse). With Campagnolo Ergo Power, you pull the brake lever and push the pin inward into its original position to engage the shallower notch in the lever body (Fig. 2.2).

2. With many a cantilever brake (cyclo-cross and some touring bikes, Figs. 7.16–7.25), hold the brake pads against the rim with one hand and hook the enlarged end of the straddle cable back into the end of the brake arm with your other

hand. On antique bikes with center-pull brakes, as well as with some cantilevers, hook the straddle cable yoke under the straddle cable. With V-brakes (Fig. 7.34), pop the end of the curved cable-guide tube (a.k.a. "the noodle") back into the horizontal link atop one of the brake arms while squeezing the pads against the rim with the other hand.

3. Check that the brake cables are connected securely by squeezing the levers. Lift the front end of the bike and spin the front wheel, gently applying the brakes several times. Check that the pads are not dragging. If they are, recenter the wheel (or adjust the brakes as described in Chapter 7). If everything is reconnected and centered properly, you're done. Go ride your bike.

ii–11 REMOVING THE REAR WHEEL

Removing the rear wheel is just like removing the front, with the added complication of the chain and cogs.

1. Open the brake (or deflate the tire), as outlined in §ii-3.

2. Shift the chain onto the smallest cog by lifting the rear wheel off the ground, turning the cranks, and shifting.

3. To release the wheel from the rear dropouts and the brakes, follow the same procedure as for the front wheel. When you push the wheel out, you will need to move the chain out of the way. This maneuver is usually a matter of grabbing the rear derailleur and pulling it back so that the jockey wheels (pulley wheels) move out of the way, while you push forward on the quick release or axle nuts with your thumbs and let the wheel fall as you hold the bike up (Fig. 2.7). If the bottom

TIGHTENING
BOLT-ON
SKEWERS
—
TIGHTENING
AXLE NUTS
—
CLOSING
THE BRAKES
—
REMOVING THE
REAR WHEEL

2.7 Removal and installation of rear wheel

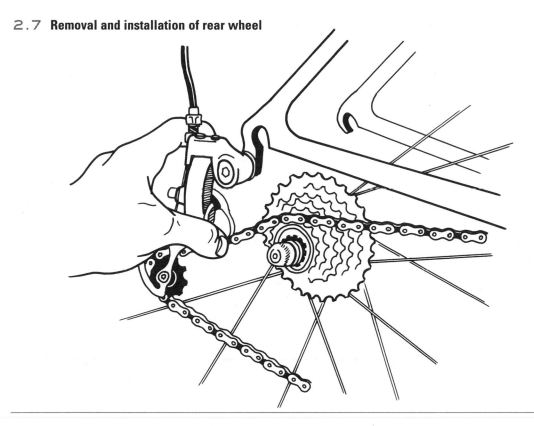

half of the chain catches the wheel as it falls, lift the wheel and jiggle it upward to free it.

ii-12 INSTALLING THE REAR WHEEL

1. Check to make sure that the rear derailleur is shifted to its outermost position (over the smallest cog).

2. Slip the wheel between the seatstays and between the brake pads. Maneuver the upper section of chain onto the smallest cog (Fig. 2.7).

3. Set the bike down on the rear wheel.

4. As you let the bike drop down, pull the rear derailleur back with your right hand and pull the axle ends back into the dropouts with your index fingers. Use your thumbs to push forward on the rear dropouts, which should now slide over the axle ends. (If the axle does not slip into the dropouts, you may need to spread the dropouts apart or squeeze them toward each other as you pull the wheel in.)

5. Check that the axle is fully seated in the dropouts, which should result in the wheel's being centered between the brake pads. If it is not, hold the rim in a centered position as you secure the axle. This procedure should not be necessary if your wheel and frame are both aligned and your brakes are centered.

6. Tighten the quick-release skewer, bolt-on skewer, or axle nuts the same way as explained for the front wheel.

7. Reconnect the rear brake the same way as you did on the front wheel. You're done. Go ride your bike.

ii-13 CLEANING YOUR BICYCLE

Most cleaning can be done with soap, water, and a brush. Soap and water are easier on you and the earth than stronger solvents, which are generally

2.8 Loop the chain over a dowel rod for cleaning

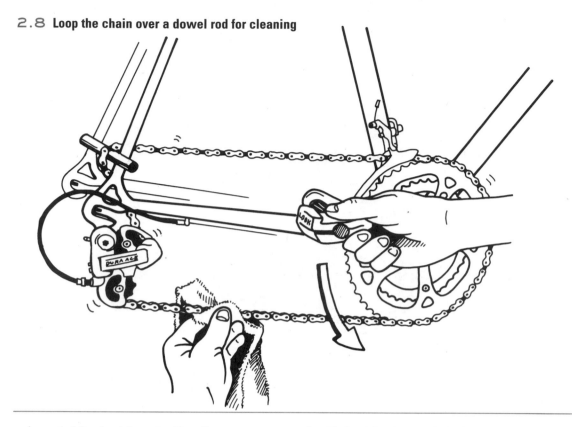

only needed for the drivetrain, if at all.

Avoid using high-pressure car washes to clean your bike. The soaps used are corrosive, and the high pressure forces them into bearings and frame tubes, causing extensive damage over time. If you do use a pressure washer, never point it toward the side of the bike, which can blow the bearing seals inward; instead, point it always in the plane of the bike.

The best way to set up your bike for cleaning is to put it in a bike stand. In the absence of a stand, you can hang the bike from a garage ceiling with rope. No good? Turn it upside down so it rests on the saddle and handlebar. Alternatively, you can remove the front wheel and stand the bike on the fork and handlebar, but you'll need to lean it against something, too, or it will pivot around its headset.

1. The wheels can be cleaned easily while they are on the bike. Remove the wheels to clean the frame, fork, and components.

2. If the bike has a chain hanger (a little nub attached to the inner side of the right seatstay, a few centimeters above the dropout), hook the chain over it. If not, pull the chain back over a dowel rod (Fig. 2.8) or an old rear hub secured in the dropouts.

3. Fill a bucket with hot water and dish soap. With a stiff nylon-bristle scrub brush, scrub the entire bike and wheels. Leave the chain, cogs, chainrings, and derailleurs for last.

4. Rinse the bike with water by hosing it off (low pressure!) or wiping it with a wet rag. Avoid getting water in the bearings of the bottom bracket, headset, pedals, or hubs. Note, too, that most frames and forks have tiny vent holes in the tubes; these were drilled at the factory to allow hot air to escape during welding. The holes are often open to the outside on the seatstays, fork legs, chainstays, and seatstay and chainstay

2.9 Cleaning jockey wheels

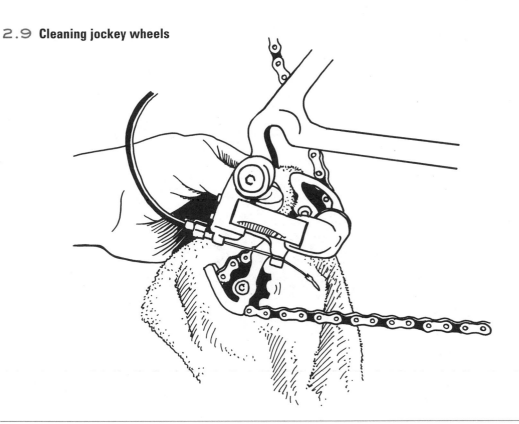

bridges. Avoid getting water in these holes. Taping over the vent holes is a good idea, and leaving them permanently taped to keep water out is even better.

ii-14 CLEANING THE DRIVETRAIN

The drivetrain consists of an oil-covered chain running over gears and through derailleurs. Sounds messy, doesn't it? Well, it is. In fact, because the whole affair is generally exposed to the elements, it inevitably picks up lots of dirt.

In glorious opposition to this tendency to dirtiness, the drivetrain is also what transfers your energy into the bike's forward motion, which means that it should be kept fastidiously clean so that it can move freely. Frequent cleaning and lubrication are required to keep it rolling well and to extend the life of your bike.

Fortunately, the drivetrain rarely needs to be completely disassembled for intensive cleaning. If you keep after it, regular maintenance can be confined to wiping down the chain, derailleur pulleys, and chainrings with a dry rag.

1. To wipe the chain, turn the cranks while holding a rag in your hand and grabbing the chain (Fig. 2.8).

2. Holding a rag, squeeze the teeth of the jockey wheels between your index finger and thumb as you turn the cranks (Fig. 2.9). This procedure will remove grease and dirt that has built up on the jockey wheels.

3. Slip a rag between each pair of rear cogs and work it back and forth until each cog is clean (Fig. 2.10).

4. Wipe down the derailleurs and the front chainrings with the rag.

Your chain will last much longer if you perform this sort of quick cleaning regularly, followed by

2.10 Cogset cleaning

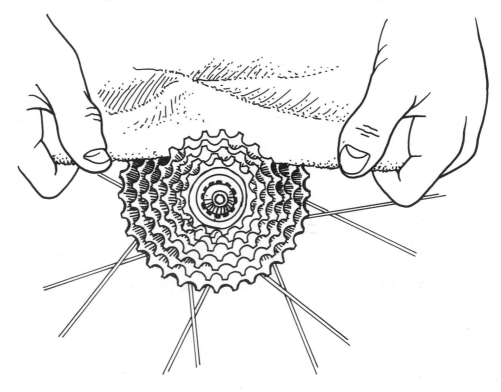

dripping chain lube on the chain and another light wipe down. You will also be able to skip the kind of heavy-duty solvent cleanings that become necessary when the chain and cogs get really grungy.

You can also remove packed-up road grit from derailleurs and cogs with the soapy water and scrub brush. Note, however, that the soap will not dissolve the dirty lubricant that is all over the drivetrain; rather the brush will smear it all over the bike if you're not careful. Use a different brush from the one you use for cleaning the frame. Follow the drivetrain cleanup with a cloth wipe down.

ii-15 CLEANING THE CHAIN WITH SOLVENT

When a chain gets really dirty, the only way to rescue it is with an immersion in solvent—a nasty task worth avoiding by performing the regular maintenance just described. In fact, if you are sparing with the chain lube—that is, if you only drip it on the

chain rollers where it is needed, rather than spraying it all over the chain—you can minimize, if not avoid, the need for solvent cleaning with its associated disposal and toxicity problems.

If you determine that using a solvent is unavoidable, work in a well-ventilated area, use as little solvent as necessary, and pick an environmentally friendly mixture. There are many citrus-based solvents on the market that will reduce the danger to your lungs and skin and be less of a major disposal problem. If you are using a lot of solvents, organic ones such as diesel fuel can be recycled, which may be a preferable solution to using citrus solvents, as long as you protect yourself from the fumes with a respirator. All solvents suck the oils from your skin, so be sure to wear rubber gloves, even with "green" solvents.

A self-contained chain cleaner with internal brushes and a solvent bath is a quick and convenient

2.11 Solvent cleaning of the chain

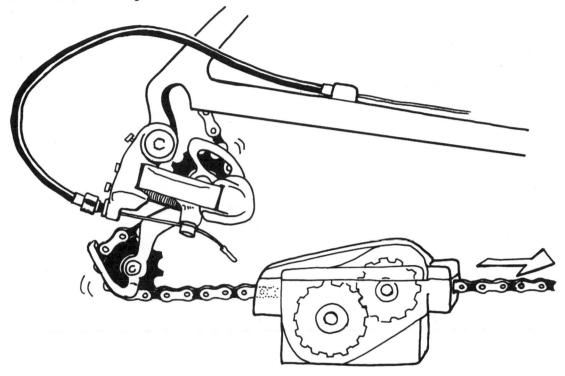

way to clean a chain (Fig. 2.11), but it may not clean well deep inside the rollers. A nylon brush or an old toothbrush dipped in solvent is good for cleaning cogs, pulleys, and chainrings, and it can be used for a quick cleanup of the chain as well. The way to clean the chain most thoroughly is to remove it and clean it in a solvent bath, but modern ten-speed, and, really, even nine-speed, chains don't allow this approach, because each chain rivet is so short that it can pop out of a hole enlarged by removal and rein-stallation of the rivet. That said, chains with master links, which are available all of the way up to super-narrow ten-speed models, can be removed for clean-ing without damaging them.

1. Follow the directions in Chapter 4 for removing the chain.

2. Put the chain in an old water bottle about one-quarter full of solvent.

3. Shake the bottle vigorously to clean the chain.

Hold the bottle close to the ground, in case it leaks.

4. Hang the chain to dry completely, especially inside the rollers.

5. Install the chain on the bike, following the direc-tions in Chapter 4.

6. Drip chain lubricant into each of the chain's links and rollers, one at a time (Fig. 2.12). Put a dot on your starting point with an indelible marker to make sure you hit each link.

7. Lightly wipe down the chain with a clean rag to

2.12 Drip oil only where it is needed

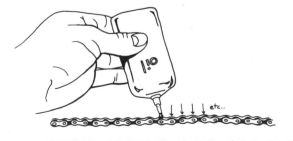

remove excess lubricant on the outside, where it is not needed.

8. After this sorry episode is concluded, wipe down the chain regularly and lubricate it as necessary (if you have the patience, use the one drop/one link method outlined in step 6) to avoid another visit to solvent city.

You can reuse much of the solvent by allowing it to stand in a clear container over a period of days or weeks. Decant and save the clear stuff and dispose of the settled sludge.

ii-16 A GENERAL GUIDE TO PERFORMING MECHANICAL WORK

a. Threaded parts

All threads must be prepped before tightening

Depending on the bolt in question (see descriptions in the following list), prep with lubricant, threadlock compound, or an antiseize compound. Clean off excess thread-prepping compound to minimize dirt attraction.

1. **Lubricated threads.** Most threads should be lubricated with grease or oil. If a bolt is already installed, you can back it out, drip a little chain lube on it, and tighten it back down. Bolts that appreciate lubrication include crank bolts, pedal axles, cleat bolts on shoes, derailleur- and brake-cable anchor bolts, and control-lever mounting bolts.

2. **Locked threads.** Some threads need to be locked in order to prevent them from vibrating loose; these are bolts that need to stay in place but are not tightened down fully for some reason or other, usually to avoid seizing a moving part, throwing a part out of adjustment, or stripping threads in a soft material. Examples

include derailleur limit screws, jockey-wheel center bolts, brake-mounting bolts, and spoke nipples. Use Loctite, Finish Line Threadlock, or the equivalent on bolts; use Wheelsmith Spoke-Prep or the equivalent on spokes.

3. **Antiseize threads.** Some threads have a tendency to bind up and gall, making full tightening as well as extraction problematic. They need antiseize compound on them to prevent galling. Any steel or aluminum bolt threaded into a titanium part (this statement includes any parts mounted to titanium frames, like bottom-bracket cups), and any titanium bolt threaded into a steel or aluminum part, must be coated with antiseize compound. Use Finish Line Ti-Prep or the equivalent.

CAUTIONARY NOTE: *Never thread a titanium bolt into a titanium part; even with the use of antiseize compound, these will almost certainly gall and rip apart when you try to remove them. If you must break this rule, use a liberal coating of antiseize compound on the threads, and every six months or so unscrew the bolt, clean it, and reapply the compound.*

Wrenches (see Fig. 2.13 for various types) must be fully engaged before tightening or loosening.

1. Hex keys and TORX wrenches must be fully inserted into the bolt head, or the wrench and/or bolt hole will round off. Shallow bolt heads, such as those used on shoe-cleat bolts, are especially susceptible, so be careful. And be sure to clean dirt and rocks out of bolt heads to get the hex key in all of the way.

2. Open-end, box-end, and socket wrenches must be properly seated around a hex bolt, or it will round off. Bicycles employ lots of soft aluminum nuts and bolts in the headset, brakes,

2.13 Types of wrenches

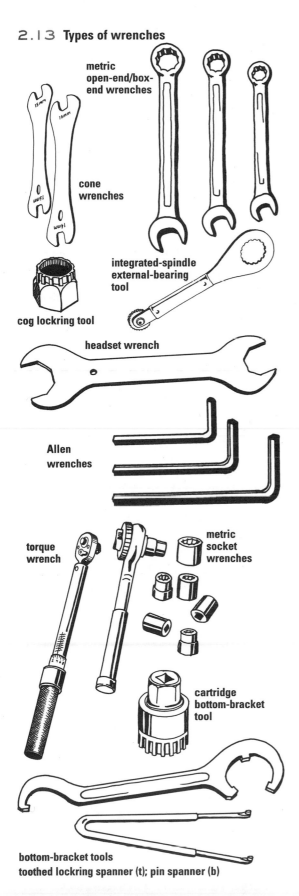

metric open-end/box-end wrenches

cone wrenches

integrated-spindle external-bearing tool

cog lockring tool

headset wrench

Allen wrenches

torque wrench

metric socket wrenches

cartridge bottom-bracket tool

bottom-bracket tools
toothed lockring spanner (t); pin spanner (b)

and cranks that are easily damaged by a bad wrench fit.

3. Splined wrenches must be fully engaged; if they are not, the splines will be damaged or the tool will snap. Be especially careful when removing a cassette lockring; if you strip the splines, you've got a real problem on your hands.

4. Toothed-lockring spanners need to stay lined up on the lockring, for example, on a bottom-bracket adjustable cup. If the teeth slide off, they will not only tear up the lockring, they will also damage the frame paint.

5. Pin spanners need to be fully seated in the holes to prevent slipping out and damaging the holes in the part. You'll find holes for a pin spanner in some bottom-bracket adjustable cups, hub-adjustment collars, and crank-bolt collars.

Tightening torque

A full list of specific tightening torques is in Appendix E. To best understand them it helps to know a little about metric bolt sizes, particularly as they are used on bikes.

The designation M in front of the bolt size number means millimeters and refers to the bolt shaft, not to the hex key that turns it; an M5 bolt is 5mm in diameter, an M6 is 6mm, and so on, but the M designation may not have any relationship to the wrench size. For instance, an M5 bolt usually takes a 4mm hex key (or in the case of a hex-head style, an 8mm box-end or socket wrench). However, M5 bolts on bicycles often accept different wrench sizes than are normally used on M5 bolts. Bolts that attach bottle cages to the frame are M5, and although some accept the normal 4mm hex key, many have a rounded "cap" head and take a 3mm hex key. The bolts that clamp a front derailleur around the seat tube or that anchor the cable on a front or rear derailleur are also M5, but they take a hex key size that is bigger than standard, namely a 5mm. And when you get to the big single-pinch bolts found on old stems, you find lots of different bolt sizes (M6, M7, and even M8), but usually only one wrench size (6mm hex key).

Generally, tightness can be classified in three levels:

1. Snug (10–30 in-lbs, or 1–3 N·m [newton-meters in SI units]): Small setscrews (such as computer-magnet mounting screws), bearing preload bolts (such as on Aheadset top cap), and screws going into plastic parts need to be snug.

2. Firmly tightened (30–80 in-lbs, or 3–9 N·m): Small bolts, often M5 size, such as shoe-cleat bolts, cable anchor bolts on brakes and derailleurs, small (M5) stem bolts, and brake-lever-clamp bolts need to be firmly tightened.

3. Tight (80–240 in-lbs, or 9–27 N·m): Wheel axles, old-style single-bolt stem bolts (M6, M7, or M8)

and stem-quill wedge bolts, brake-caliper mounting bolts, seatpost binder bolts, and seatpost saddle-rail clamp bolts need to be tight.

4. Really tight (300–600 in-lbs, or 31–68 N·m): Crankarm bolts, cassette lockring bolts, and bottom-bracket cups need to be really tight.

b. Cleanliness

1. Do not expect parts to work by just squirting or slathering lubricant on them (meanwhile patting yourself on the back for maintaining your bike). The lube will pick up lots of dirt and get very gunky.

2. Do not expect parts to work by washing them and not lubricating them. They will get dry and squeaky.

c. Test riding

Always ride the bike—slowly at first, and then harder—after adjusting in the bike stand. Parts behave differently under load.

take-along tool kit shown in Figure 1.5—and Figure 1.6, too, for longer tours

CHAPTER 3

EMERGENCY REPAIRS

*Eat a live toad the first thing in the morning and
nothing worse will happen to you the rest of the day.*
—Anonymous

f you ride your bike a fair distance from home, sooner or later you are likely to encounter a situation that has the potential to turn into an emergency. The best way to avoid an unpleasant surprise is to plan ahead and be prepared before it happens, which is what this chapter is all about. Proper planning involves steps as simple as bringing along a few tools, spare tubes, food, and extra clothes. And, of course, a little knowledge.

This chapter will acquaint you with ways to deal with most "emergencies," whether you have all the tools you need or not. Generally, any problem you're likely to encounter will involve only one component on the bike—a flat tire, a broken derailleur cable, or something similar—and in most cases it is pretty easy to find a workaround that will get you home. True, you always have the option of walking, but this chapter is designed to help you avoid that miserable fate.

Incidentally, a cell phone (or at least some change for a pay phone) is worth carrying on long solo rides, just in case something does break in a big way. Bottle-shaped cell-phone cases are available to keep your phone in one of your water-bottle cages.

On the other hand, you may find yourself with a perfectly functioning bicycle and a fully charged phone and still be in dire straits because you're either lost, cold, dehydrated, bonking (i.e., your body has run out of fuel), or injured. Carefully read the final part of this chapter for pointers on how to avoid these things and what to do if the worst does happen.

iii-1 RECOMMENDED TOOLS

The take-along tool kit for your seat bag is described in §i-6. If you're going to be a long way from civilization, take along the extra tools recommended for longer trips.

iii-2 FLAT TIRE PREVENTION

The best way to avoid flats is to always have good tires on your bike. Check them regularly for wear, cracking, and tread cuts. Steer clear of potholes, broken glass, and nails (Ha! As if!), and you'll rarely have a problem.

Flat tires can be minimized with the use of tire sealants; I use the product name Slime synonymously for all sealants. Tire sealants usually consist of a viscous liquid full of chopped fibers that plug holes in the tube as they occur (use of Slime is covered in §vi-11). Sealant can be injected into an existing tube that has a Schrader valve. Schrader valves have removable cores, and a core-remover tool comes with the bottle of sealant. Most Presta valves, on the other hand, do not have removable cores, and so you cannot inject sealant. Even on Presta valves with removable cores (you take the core out with an adjustable wrench), you cannot inject sealant, because the valve stem is so thin that the sealant clogs it up. You can purchase new Presta-valve tubes with sealant already inside. Note, however, that sealant adds detectable weight to your wheels and is unnecessary if you ride on good roads and keep your tires properly inflated.

In a pinch, you can use evaporated milk in any Presta-valve tube or tubular tire as a sealant. Just pour some canned evaporated milk into a pump you no longer care about, and pump it right into the tube or tubular tire. It actually works quite well to seal small leaks (it can be a lifesaver with a tubular tire with a slow leak), but if you ever get a blowout, boy, does it ever stink!

If you do have Slime or another tire sealant in your tube and your tire gets low owing to a puncture (this is most likely to happen when you put your bike away for a few weeks), put more air in and spin the wheel, or ride the bike for a couple of miles to get the sealant to flow out to the hole. Note that sealant will not fill a puncture if the hole in the tube is on the rim side, because the liquid will be thrown to the outside when the wheel turns.

Sealants cannot fill large punctures and blowouts, although amazingly big holes can be plugged sufficiently to get you home if you locate where the sealant is squirting out through the tire. Rotate the wheel so that spot is at the bottom and wait. The sealant may pool up enough there to plug the hole. Add more air and continue.

Plastic tire liners that fit between the tire and tube are often brandished to ward off flats, but I don't recommend them. Most are so stiff that they decrease traction and cornering ability, and they can slip sideways and cut into the tube.

iii-3 FIXING FLAT TIRES

a. If you have a spare or a patch kit

Simple flat tires are easy to deal with. The first flat you get on a ride is most easily fixed by installing your spare tube (§vi-1 through §vi-5). Make sure you remove whatever caused the flat (you'll probably see it sticking up from the tread), and feel around the inside of the tire for any other sharp objects.

If you can't find a thorn, nail, piece of glass, or the like in the tire or tube, check the rim to see whether the flat was caused by a protruding spoke or nipple, a metal shard from the rim, or the edge of a spoke hole protruding through a worn rim strip. The rim strip is the piece of plastic or rubber that covers the spoke holes in the well of the rim. Many rim strips are totally inadequate, being either too narrow or prone to cracking or tearing. Also, metal hunks left from the drilling of rims during manufacture can work their way out into the tube.

In fact, these flats are so common that on a new bike I recommend removing the tires and tubes before the first ride and checking the rims. Shake out any metal fragments that may be present. If the rim strips consist of limp, narrow strips of soft rubber or cloth, replace them with high-quality plastic or adhesive cotton rim strips, or apply a couple of layers of reinforced packing tape (the kind that has lengthwise fibers inside) to cover the spoke holes in place of the rim strips.

After you run out of spare tubes, additional flats must be patched (also covered in §vi-2 through §vi-4).

b. Torn sidewall

Rocks and glass can cut tire sidewalls. The likelihood of sidewall problems is reduced if you do not ride with tires so old that the cords are rotten and weak. If your tire's sidewall is torn or cut, the tube will stick out. Just patching or replacing the tube isn't going to solve the problem. Without reinforcement, your tube will blow out again very soon.

First, you have to look for something to reinforce the tire sidewall (Fig. 3.1). Dollar bills work surprisingly well as tire boots. The paper is pretty tough and should hold for the rest of the ride if you are careful. (I told you that cash will get you out of bad situations. Credit cards are not acceptable for this purpose.) Business cards are a bit small but work better than nothing. You might even try an energy bar wrapper or a piece of a plastic soda bottle. A small piece of lawn-chair webbing cut in an oval might be a good addition to your patch kit for this purpose. You get the idea.

1. Lay the cash or whatever inside the tire over the gash, or wrap it around the tube at that spot. Place several layers between the tire and tube to support the tube and prevent it from bulging out through the hole in the sidewall.

3.1 Fixing torn tire casing (temporarily)

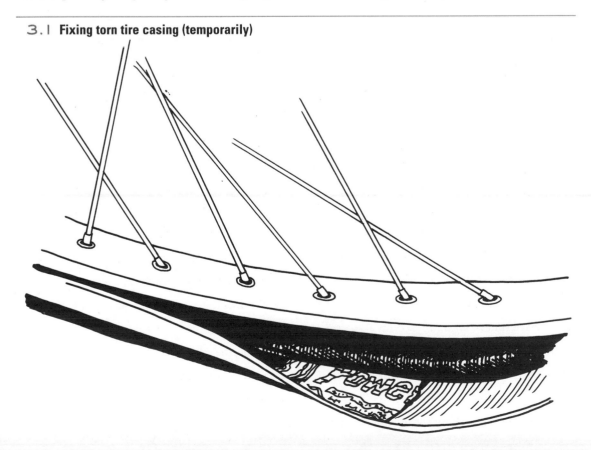

3.2 Freeing jammed chain

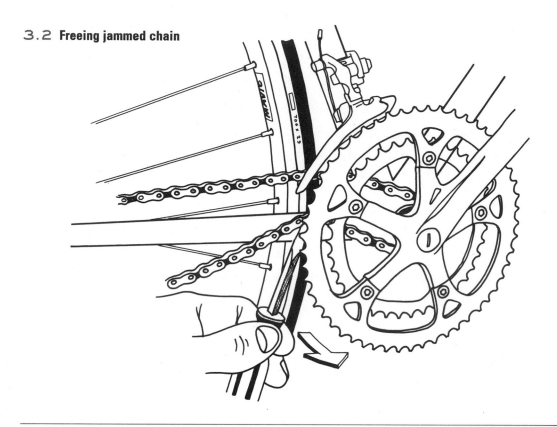

2. Put a little air in the tube to hold the makeshift reinforcement in place.

3. Mount the tire bead on the rim. You may need to let a little air out of the tube to do so.

4. After making sure that the tire is seated and the boot is still in place, inflate the tube to about 75 psi, if you are good at estimating without a gauge. Pressures lower than this will allow the boot to move around and may also lead to a pinch flat if you cross a train track.

Check the boot periodically on the ride home to make certain that the tube is not bulging out again.

c. **No more spare tubes or patches**

Now comes the frustrating part: You have run out of spare tubes and have used up all of your patches (or your CO_2 cartridge is empty, and you don't have a pump), and still you have a flat tire. The situation is obvious: You are going to have to ride home without air in your tire.

Riding a flat for a long way will destroy the tire, and it will probably damage the rim, too. You can minimize that damage, though, by filling the space in the tire with grass, leaves, or similar materials. Pack the stuff in tightly and then remount the tire on the rim. This "fix" should make the ride a little less dangerous by minimizing the flat tire's tendency to roll out from under the bike during a turn.

iii-4 JAMMED CHAIN

When the chain gets jammed between the chainrings and the chainstay, it can be surprisingly difficult to extract. You may find that you tug and tug on the chain, and it won't come out. Well, chainrings are flexible, and if you apply some mechanical advantage, the chain will come free quite easily.

Insert a screwdriver or similar thin lever between the chainring and the chainstay, and pry the space open while pulling the chain out (Fig. 3.2). You will

3.3 Fixing broken chain

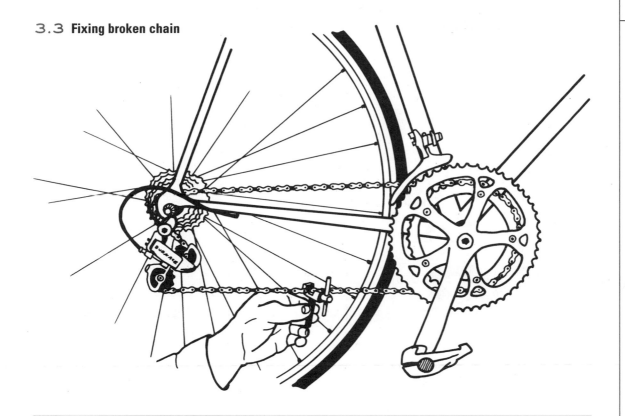

probably be amazed at how easy this operation is, especially in light of how hard tugging would not free the chain.

If you still cannot free the chain, however, disassemble the chain with a chain tool (§iv-7), pull it out, and put it back together (§iv-9 through §iv-11).

iii–5 BROKEN CHAIN

Chains seldom break on road bikes, but this problem is becoming more common with super-narrow ten-speed chains. Any chain weakness is also compounded by a bad cogset that causes the chain to skip. The chain "breaks" when a chain plate pops off the end of a rivet. As the chain rips apart, it can cause collateral damage as well. The open chain plate can snag the front-derailleur cage, bending it or tearing it off, or it can jam into the rear dropout.

When a chain breaks, the end link is certainly shot, and some others in the area may be as well. A broken ten-speed chain is irreparable for further long-term use, but you can often repair it well enough to ride home very carefully, pedaling gingerly.

1. Remove the damaged links with the chain tool. (You or your riding partner did remember to bring a chain tool, right?) Again, the procedures for removing the damaged links and reinstalling the chain are covered in Chapter 4, §iv-7 through §iv-11.

2. If you have brought along extra chain links, replace the same number you remove. If not, you'll need to use the chain in its shortened state; it will still work, but you probably won't be able to use the largest cogs when the chain is on the big chainring.

3. Join the ends and connect the chain (Fig. 3.3); the procedure is in Chapter 4, §iv-9, and §iv-10. Some lightweight chain tools and multitools are more difficult to use than a shop chain tool.

3.4 Tightening and loosening

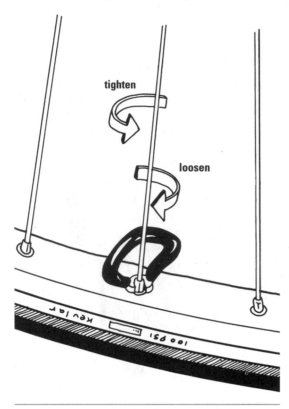

tighten

loosen

Some flex so badly that it is hard to keep the push rod lined up with the rivet. Others pinch the plates so tightly that the chain link binds up. It's a good idea to find these things out before you need the tool on the road.

iii-6 BENT WHEEL

If the rim is banging against the brake pads—or worse yet, the frame or fork—pedaling becomes very difficult. If you haven't hit a pothole or something similar that has bent the rim, the cause is probably a loose or broken spoke. Another culprit could be a broken rim—fairly rare, even with ultra-lightweight tubular wheels.

iii-7 LOOSE SPOKES

If you have a loose spoke or two, the rim will wobble all over the place.

BENT WHEEL

—

LOOSE OR

BROKEN

SPOKES

1. Find the loose spoke (or spokes) by feeling all of them. The really loose ones, which would cause a wobble of large magnitude, will be obvious. If you find a broken spoke, skip to the next section (§iii-8). If you have no loose or broken spokes, skip ahead to §iii-10.

2. Get out the spoke wrench that you carry for such an eventuality. If you don't have one, skip to §iii-9.

3. Mark the loose spokes, if necessary, by tying blades of grass, sandwich bag twist-ties, tape, or the like around them.

4. Tighten the loose spokes (Fig. 3.4) and true the wheel, following the procedures in §vi-12.

iii-8 BROKEN SPOKES

If you broke a spoke, the wheel will wobble wildly.

1. Locate the broken spoke.

2. Remove the remainders of the spoke, both the piece going through the hub, and the piece threaded into the nipple. If the broken spoke is on the freewheel side of the rear wheel, you may not be able to remove it from the hub, because it will be behind the cogs. If so, skip to step 6 after wrapping it around neighboring spokes to prevent it from slapping around (Fig. 3.5).

3. Get out your spoke wrench. If you have no spoke wrench, skip to §iii-9.

4. If you brought along a spare spoke of the right length or the Kevlar replacement spoke mentioned in §i-6b, you're in business. If not, skip to step 6. Put the new spoke through the hub hole, weave it through the other spokes the same way the old one was, and thread it into the spoke nipple that is still sticking out of the rim. Mark it with a pen or a blade of grass tied around it.

3.5 Wrapping a broken spoke

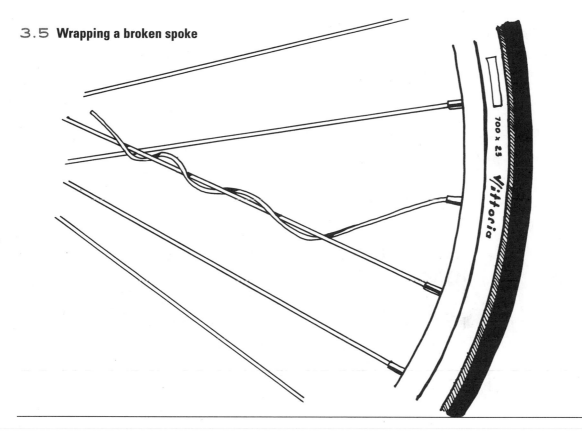

With the Kevlar spoke, thread the Kevlar string through the hub hole, attach the ends to the enclosed stub of spoke, adjust the ends to length, tie them off, and tighten the spoke nipple.

5. Tighten the nipple on the new spoke with a spoke wrench (Fig. 3.4), checking the rim clearance with the brake pad as you go. Stop when the rim is reasonably straight, and finish your ride.

6. If you can't replace the spoke and you do have a spoke wrench, bring the wheel into rideable trueness by loosening the spoke on either side of the broken one. These two spokes come from the opposite side of the hub and will let the rim move toward the side with the broken spoke as they are loosened. A spoke nipple loosens counterclockwise when viewed from its top (i.e., from the tire side—see Fig. 3.4). Ride home, conservatively, as this wheel will rapidly get worse.

7. Once at home, replace the spoke, following the procedure in §vi-13, or take it to a bike shop for repair. If you break a spoke more than once on a wheel, relace the wheel with new spokes (Chapter 13). The rim may need replacement as well.

iii-9 NO SPOKE WRENCH

If the rim is banging the brake pads, but the tire is not hitting the chainstays or fork blades, simply open the brake so that you can get home, as detailed here. If the tire is hitting the frame or fork, you may need more extreme measures to temporarily straighten it; see the next section.

1. Open the brake-caliper quick-release lever as far as is necessary for the pads to clear the rim. If the pads still rub, loosen the brake-cable tension by screwing in (clockwise) the barrel adjuster on the caliper (Fig. 3.6). Remember that braking effectiveness on that wheel will be greatly reduced or nonexistent, so ride slowly and carefully.

3.6 Loosening the brake cable

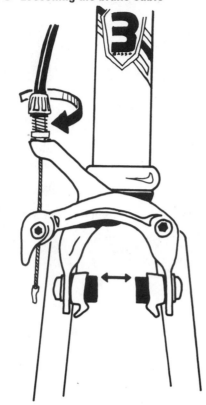

2. If the rim is still banging the brakes, and you have a wrench to loosen the brake cable (usually 5mm Allen), do so, and then clamp it back down. You now have no brake on this wheel; ride carefully.

3. If this still does not cut it, you can disconnect the cable and remove the brake caliper from the fork or brake bridge, put it in your pocket, and pedal home slowly. You will usually need a 5mm Allen wrench for this task.

iii-10 BENT RIM

If the rim is only mildly out of true, and you brought your spoke wrench, you can fix it. The procedure for truing a wheel is explained in §vi-12.

If the wheel is really whacked out, spoke truing won't do much. To get the wheel to clear the brakes so

3.7 Fixing a bent rim

KLONK

that you can pedal home, follow the steps in §iii-9.

If the wheel is bent to the point that it won't turn, even when the brake is removed, you can beat it straight as long as the rim is not broken.

1. Find the area that is bent outward the most and mark it.

2. Leaving the tire on and inflated, hold the wheel by its sides with the bent-outward part at the top facing away from you.

3. Smack the bent-outward section of the rim against flat ground (Fig. 3.7).

4. Put the wheel back in the frame or fork, and see if anything has changed.

5. Repeat the process until the wheel is rideable. You may be surprised how straight you can get a wheel this way.

iii-11 DAMAGED FRONT DERAILLEUR

If the front derailleur is mildly bent, straighten it with your hands or leave it until you get home.

If the front derailleur has simply rotated around the seat tube or twisted in the braze-on (see Fig. 3.8; the chain, your foot, or a pants leg can catch it and turn it), reposition it so that the cage is just above, and parallel to, the chainrings. Tighten the derailleur in place (usually with a 5mm Allen wrench).

If the derailleur is broken or so bent that you can't ride, or if the braze-on is bent, you will need to remove the derailleur or route the chain around it as described next. (If the braze-on is bent, trying to straighten it will either dent or crack the seat tube or cause a crack to form in the near future. You will need to have a frame builder remove the braze-on and put a new one on.)

3.8 Opening front-derailleur cage

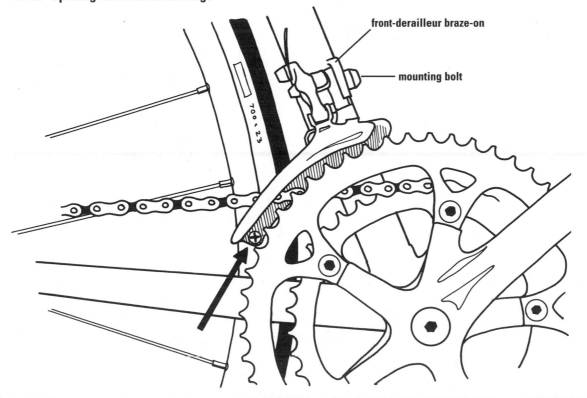

front-derailleur braze-on

mounting bolt

700 1 23

3.9 Bypassing a damaged rear derailleur

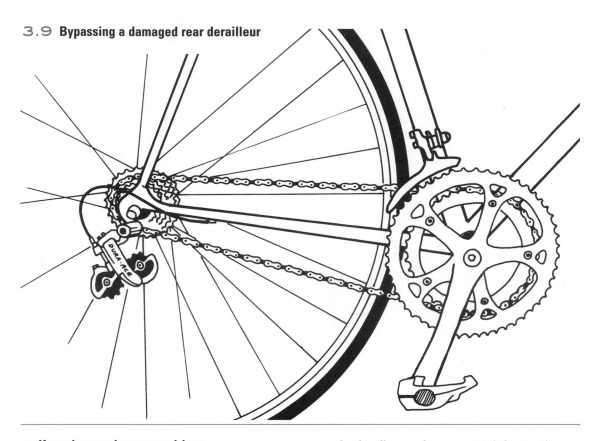

a. If you have only a screwdriver

1. Get the chain out of the derailleur cage. To do this, open the derailleur cage by removing the screw at its tail (Fig. 3.8). If, for some reason, the derailleur cage can't be opened this way, you'll have to open the chain with a chain tool (see the next section).

2. Bypass the derailleur by putting the chain on a chainring that does not interfere with it (either shift the derailleur to the inside and put the chain on the big chainring, or vice versa).

b. If you have Allen wrenches and a screw-driver (or a chain tool)

1. Remove the derailleur from the seat tube, usually with a 5mm Allen wrench.

2. Remove the screw at the tail of the derailleur cage with a screwdriver, if it has one.

3. Pry open the cage and separate it from the chain. You can also disassemble the chain, pull it out of

the derailleur, and reconnect it (Chapter 4).

4. Manually put the chain on whichever chainring is most appropriate for the ride home. If in doubt, put it on the inner one (or middle one, if you have a triple).

5. Tie the cable up so that it won't catch in your wheel.

6. Stuff the derailleur in your pocket and ride home.

iii-12 DAMAGED REAR DERAILLEUR

If the upper jockey wheel gets lost, put the lower one on top and thread a wire or zip-tie through three threaded Presta-valve collar nuts (off your inner-tube valves) as a lower wheel. If one of the jockey-wheel bolts gets lost, and you found the jockey wheel, try replacing the bolt with one of the water-bottle-cage bolts. If the return spring on the rear-derailleur cage breaks, the chain will

3.10 Tightening high-end limit screw

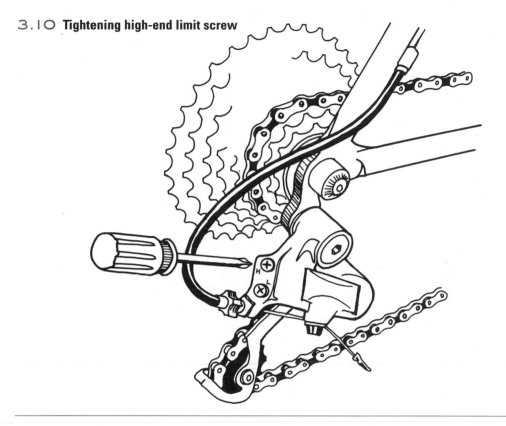

hang loosely. If you have a bungee cord, hook it to the lower cage, around the skewer (put the lever on the drive side), and up to the seat-tube bottle cage.

If the rear derailleur gets bent just a bit, you can probably straighten it enough to get home. If it gets really bent or broken or one of the jockey wheels falls off, you will need to bypass the derailleur, effectively turning your bike into a single-speed for the remainder of your ride (Fig. 3.9).

1. Open the chain with a chain tool (§iv-7) and pull it out of the derailleur.

2. Pick a gear combination in which you think you can make it home most effectively, and set the front derailleur over the chainring you have picked. Be aware that the chain will tend to fall off of the chainrings, or move down to smaller cogs, unless it is really tight.

3. Wrap the chain over the chainring and the rear

cog you have chosen, bypassing the rear derailleur entirely.

4. Remove any overlapping chain, making the chain as short as you can while still being able to connect the ends together.

5. Connect the chain with the chain tool as described in §iv-9.

6. Ride home.

iii–13 BROKEN FRONT-DERAILLEUR CABLE

The chain will be on the inner chainring, and you will still be able to use all of your rear cogs. Leave it on the inner ring and ride home.

iii–14 BROKEN REAR-DERAILLEUR CABLE

The chain will be on the smallest rear cog, and you will still be able to use both (or all three) front chainrings. You have three options:

1. Leave it on the small cog and ride home. Or . . . .

BROKEN

FRONT–

AND

REAR–

DERAILLEUR

CABLE

3.11 **After breaking the cable, wedge the rear derailleur into an easier gear**

2. Move the chain to a larger cog, push inward on the derailleur with your hand, and tighten the high-end limit screw on the rear derailleur (usually the upper one of the two screws) until it lines up with a larger cog (see Fig. 3.10). Move the chain to that cog and ride home. You may have to fine-tune the adjustment of the derailleur stop screw to get it to run quietly without skipping. Or . . . .

3. If you do not have a screwdriver, you can push inward on the rear derailleur while turning the crank with the rear wheel off the ground to shift to a larger cog. Jam a stick between the derailleur-cage plates to prevent the chain from moving back down to the small cog (Fig. 3.11).

iii–15 BROKEN BRAKE CABLE

Ride home slowly and carefully. Very slowly. Very carefully.

iii–16 BROKEN SEAT RAILS OR SEATPOST CLAMP

If you can't tape or tie the saddle back on, try wrapping your gloves or some clothing over the top of the seat post to pad it. Otherwise, remove the seat post and ride home standing up.

iii–17 BROKEN SEATPOST SHAFT

Ride home standing up.

iii–18 BROKEN HANDLEBAR

It's probably best to walk home (or phone home for a ride). You could splint it by jamming a stick inside and ride home very carefully, but the stick could easily break, leaving you with no way to control the bike. A sudden impact of your face with the road would follow.

If you decide to splint the handlebar, hold the pieces together with duct tape. If the break is adjacent the stem, slide the stem over the break so that both pieces are clamped.

iii–19 FROZEN PARTS

Riding in snow or freezing rain can freeze shift cables where they pass under the bottom bracket or can freeze the derailleurs themselves and fill the cogs you are not using with ice. You will just have to stay in the gear you are frozen in. But if the freehub mechanism freezes, you won't be able to coast for even a second. You may be able to free it by applying any hot liquid available (even urine!) and hitting the freehub with a stick until it rotates counterclockwise again.

iii–20 PREPARE FOR EVERY RIDE

1. Always take plenty of water.

2. Tell someone where you are going and when

BROKEN BRAKE
CABLE
—
BROKEN SEAT
RAILS/SEAT-
POST CLAMP
—
BROKEN
SEATPOST
SHAFT
—
BROKEN
HANDLEBAR
—
FROZEN PARTS
—
PREPARE FOR
EVERY RIDE

you expect to return. If you know of someone who is missing, call the police or sheriff, or see to it that someone goes out looking for that person in a car.

3. Take extra food for any ride over an hour.

4. Take a road map if you don't know the area. Be willing to ask for directions.

5. Take a cell phone and/or bring change for a pay phone.

6. Take matches, extra clothing and food, and perhaps a flashlight and an aluminized emergency blanket, in case you have to spend some time huddled under a tree.

7. Ride carefully and attentively on wet roads, gravel-covered turns, and areas with lots of traffic, especially traffic turning into and out of side roads.

8. Wear a helmet. It's hard to ride home with a cracked skull.

9. Don't ride beyond your limits if you are a long way from home or civilization. Take a break. Get out of the hot sun. Avoid dehydration and bonking by drinking and eating enough.

10. Have your bike in good working order before you leave.

In short, make appropriate decisions when taking long rides. Prepare well. Just because you have a $4,000 bike and are riding on paved roads, you are not immune to mechanical problems or getting exhausted, cold, bonked, injured, lost, or caught out in the dark.

EMERGENCY REPAIRS

PREPARE FOR
EVERY RIDE

CHAPTER 4

THE CHAIN

Take care of the luxuries and the necessities will take care of themselves.
—Dorothy Parker

TOOLS

chain lubricant
12-inch ruler
chain tool
lots of rags
rubber gloves

OPTIONAL

**solvent
  (citrus-based)**
chain-cleaning tool
old water bottle
caliper
pliers
solvent tank
**chain-elongation
  gauge**
**Rohloff cog-wear
  indicator**

The bicycle chain is one of those wondrous technological breakthroughs that we take for granted, but without which a bike would be a clumsy and inefficient contraption. The chain is nothing more than a simple series of links connected by rivets (also called pins). Rollers surround each rivet between the link plates and engage the teeth of the cogs and chainrings. Nothing to it, and yet it is an extremely efficient method of transmitting mechanical energy from the pedals to the rear wheel. In terms of weight, cost, and efficiency, the bicycle chain has no equal—and believe me, people have tried endlessly to improve upon it.

Perhaps because it is so simple and familiar, the chain is often ignored. To keep your bike running smoothly, though, you do have to pay at least some attention to it. It needs to be kept clean and well-lubricated in order to utilize your energy most efficiently, shift smoothly, and operate noiselessly. And because its length increases as it wears, thus contact-

ing gear teeth differently than intended, it needs to be replaced regularly to prolong the working life of other, more expensive, drivetrain components.

iv-1 LUBRICATION

For best results, use a lubricant intended for bicycle chains. Most lubes sold for this purpose work reasonably well at the basic task of keeping the chain protected and happy. However, I recommend against wax-based lubricants as they don't lubricate under load. Chain life with them is very short (1,000 to 1,500 miles).

If you want to get fancy about it, you can assess the type of conditions in which you ride and choose a lubricant intended for those conditions. Some lubricants are "dry," which means that they are formulated to pick up less dirt in dry conditions. Other lubes are "sticky" and therefore less prone to wash off in wet conditions. Still others claim to be "metal conditioners" that actually

4.1 Dripping oil only where it is needed

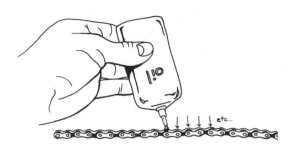

4.2 Wiping chain

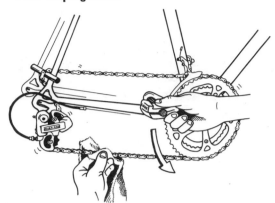

penetrate and alter the surface of the metal, and one of these, Pro Gold, gives me longer chain life in all riding conditions, with daily use, than anything else I have tried.

Lubricant companies usually advise against switching among types, and there is probably something to this from the standpoint of maintaining particular properties. That is, once you start using a "dry" lube, for example, it's best to stick with it if most of your riding calls for that type of stuff (remember— don't use wax-based lubes!). But the main thing is to take care of the chain regularly. If that means using a different brand of oil from time to time, because of travel or changing weather, so be it.

Chain lubes are generally sold in spray cans and in bottles. Sprays should be avoided for regular maintenance chores, because they tend to spew too much oil over everything. The chain only needs a reservoir of oil inside each link; on the outside, the thinnest film is sufficient to keep corrosion at bay. More oil on the outside than that will only attract dirt and gunk; it does nothing to improve the function of the chain.

1. Drip a small amount of lubricant across each roller from the inside out (Fig. 4.1), periodically moving the chain to give easy access to the links

you are working on. If you are in a hurry, you can turn the crank slowly while dripping lubricant onto the chain as it goes by, but this method will cause you to apply too much lubricant, which will pick up more dirt. Most of us do tend to be in a hurry and don't have the patience to just lubricate each roller on a daily basis, so don't sweat it. Overlubricating is far preferable to not lubricating.

2. Wipe the chain off lightly with a clean rag to remove excess oil.

3. If you want to do a champion job, perform this task at night, before putting the bike to bed, and then wipe the chain clean again the next morning or before the next ride. That way, you'll remove additional oil that has seeped onto the outside of the links, where it isn't needed.

If you're riding in wet conditions, you'll need to apply lubricant frequently (after every ride, or even several times during a long, rainy ride). The lubricant for wet conditions needs to adhere well to the chain and not be easily washed off; this usually means a thick and sticky lubricant—even a grease. For dry conditions, a smaller amount of a lubricant that does not pick up dirt is preferable.

4.3 Chain cleaning on the bike

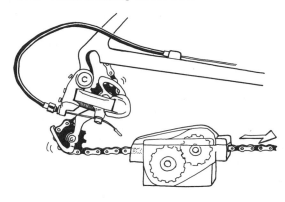

iv-2 CLEANING BY FREQUENT WIPING AND LUBRICATION

The simplest way to maintain a chain is to wipe it down frequently and then lubricate it. If you follow this scheme prior to every ride, you will never need to clean your chain with a solvent. The lubricant softens the old sludge buildup, which is driven out of the chain when you ride.

The problem, you're undoubtedly eager to point out, is that the fresh lubricant also picks up new dirt and grime. True, but if this gunk is wiped off before it is driven deep into the chain, and the chain is relubricated frequently, it will stay relatively clean as well as supple. Chain cleaning can be performed with the bike standing on the ground or in a bike stand.

1. With a rag in your hand, grasp the lower length of the chain (between the bottom of the chainring and the lower jockey wheel of the rear derailleur).

2. Turn the crank backward a number of revolutions, pulling the chain through the rag (Fig. 4.2). Periodically rotate the rag to present a clean section of it to the chain.

3. Lubricate each chain roller carefully as in Figure 4.1, or take the faster method of running the chain past the dripping bottle tip.

To simplify this procedure, I recommend leaving a pair of rubber gloves, a rag, and some chain lube next to your bike. Then whenever you return from a ride, put on the gloves, wipe and lube the chain, and put your bike away. It takes maybe a minute, your hands stay clean, and your bike is ready for the next ride. Wipe the chainrings, cogs, front derailleur, and jockey wheels while you're at it, and your entire drivetrain will always work ideally.

iv-3 USING CHAIN-CLEANING UNITS

Several companies make chain-cleaning gizmos that scrub the chain with solvent without removing the chain from the bike. These types of chain cleaners are generally made of clear plastic and have two or three rotating brushes that scrub the chain as it moves through the solvent bath (Fig. 4.3). These units offer the advantage of letting you clean your chain without removing it from the bike, because regularly removing your chain is a pain, and it shortens chain life.

Most chain cleaners are supplied with a nontoxic, citrus-based solvent. For your safety and other environmental reasons, I strongly recommend that you purchase nontoxic citrus solvents for your chain cleaner, even if the unit came with a petroleum-based solvent. If you recycle used diesel fuel, then go ahead and use it. In either case, wear gloves and glasses when using any sort of solvent, citrus- or petroleum-based.

Citrus-based chain solvents often contain some lubricants as well, so that they won't dry the chain out. The lubricant carried with the solvent is one reason diesel fuel used to have such a following as a chain cleaner. A really strong solvent without lubricant (acetone, for example) will displace the oil from

THE CHAIN

CLEANING BY
FREQUENT
WIPING AND
LUBRICATION
—
USING CHAIN-
CLEANING
UNITS

inside the rollers. It will later evaporate, leaving a dry, squeaking chain that is hard to rehabilitate. The same thing can happen with a citrus-based solvent without an included lubricant, especially if the chain is not allowed to dry sufficiently before it is relubricated.

Here's the procedure for cleaning the chain with a chain-cleaning unit:

1. Remove the top of the chain-cleaner case and pour in solvent up to the fill line.
2. Place the unit against the bottom of the chain, and reinstall the top of the unit so that the chain runs through it (Fig. 4.3).
3. Turn the bike's crank backward.
4. Remove the unit, wipe off the chain with a clean cloth, and let it dry.
5. Lubricate the chain as described in §iv-1.

iv-4 REMOVAL AND CLEANING

You can also clean the chain by removing it from the bicycle and cleaning it in a solvent. I recommend against this approach unless your chain has a master link, because repeated disassembly by pushing rivets in and out weakens the chain.

Chain disassembly and reassembly also expands the size of the rivet hole where you put it together, allowing the rivet to pop out more easily. Two special "subpins" that are meant to prevent this problem are supplied by Shimano for reassembly of its chains. Campagnolo supplies only one, making removal and reinstallation impossible. A hand-opened "master link" can avoid the chain weakening caused by pushing pins out. Master links are standard on Wippermann and Taya chains, many KMC chains, and on Sachs and SRAM chains of 1998 and beyond; the aftermarket "Super Link" or any of the

brand-name master links can also be installed into any chain, as long as you make sure that the master link you use is of the right width.

If you do disassemble the chain (see §iv-7 for instructions), you can clean it well, even without a solvent tank. Just drop the chain into an old jar or water bottle half filled with solvent and agitate. Using an old water bottle or jar allows you to clean the chain without touching or breathing the solvent—something to be avoided even with citrus solvents.

Here's the procedure for cleaning the chain if you don't want to use a chain-cleaning unit:

1. Remove the chain from the bike (§iv-7).
2. Drop it in a water bottle or jar.
3. Pour in enough solvent to cover the chain.
4. Shake the bottle vigorously (low to the ground, in case the top pops off).
5. Hang the chain to air dry.
6. Reassemble it on the bike (see §iv-8 to §iv-11).
7. Lubricate it as described in §iv-1.

Allow the solvent in the bottle to stand for a few days so that you can decant the clear stuff and use it again. I'll say it again: it is important to use a citrus-based solvent. It is not only safer for the environment, it is gentler on your skin and less harmful to breathe. Wear rubber gloves when working with any solvent, and use a respirator meant for volatile organic compounds if you are not using a citrus-based solvent. There is no sense in fixing your bike so that it goes faster if you end up becoming a slower, sickly bike rider.

iv-5 CHAIN REPLACEMENT

As the rollers, pins, and plates wear out, the chain will grow in length. That, in turn, will hasten wear and tear on the other parts of the drivetrain. An

4.4 Checking chain wear

elongated chain (see §iv-6) will concentrate the load on each individual gear tooth, rather than distributing it over all of the teeth that the chain contacts. The concentrated load will cause the gear teeth to become hook-shaped and the tooth valleys to become wider.

If such wear has already occurred, a new chain will not solve the problem. A new chain will not mesh with deformed teeth, and it is likely to skip whenever you pedal hard. The only cure is to replace the chain, the chainrings, and the rear cogset. So before all of that extra wear and tear takes place, get in the habit of checking the chain on a regular basis (§iv-6) and replacing it as needed.

Chain life varies depending on chain type, maintenance, riding conditions, and strength and weight of the rider. As a ballpark number, figure on replacing the chain every 1,000–1,500 miles if the bike is ridden in dirty conditions or with infrequent lubrication (or with wax-based lubricants) by a heavy rider. Lighter riders riding mostly on clean, dry roads can extend the replacement time to 2,000–3,000 miles with poor maintenance and up to 5,000 miles with daily lubrication with a good lube.

iv-6 CHECKING FOR CHAIN ELONGATION

The most reliable way to see whether the chain is worn out is to employ a chain-elongation gauge,

4.5 One complete chain link

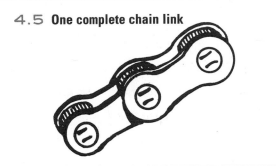

such as the model made by Rohloff (Fig. 4.4). The indicator's curved tooth falls completely into the chain if the chain is shot. If the chain is still in good shape, the tooth will not go all of the way in. Use the tooth marked "S" for steel cogs and the tooth marked "A" for aluminum and titanium cogs. Park, Wippermann, Bicicletta, and others offer similar chain-elongation gauges as well.

Another way to measure for elongation is with an accurate ruler. Bicycle chains are on an inch standard, and they measure a half-inch between adjacent rivets. There should be exactly 12 links in one foot, where each complete link consists of an inner and outer pair of plates (Fig. 4.5).

1. Set one end of the ruler on a rivet edge, and measure to the rivet edge at the other end of the ruler.

2. The distance between these rivets should be 12 inches exactly. If it is 12⅛ inches or greater, replace the chain; if it is 12 1⁄16 inches or more, it is a good idea to replace it (and a necessity to do

4.6 Pushing out the pin (link rivet)

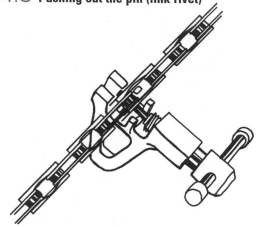

4.7 Proper chain length with a double

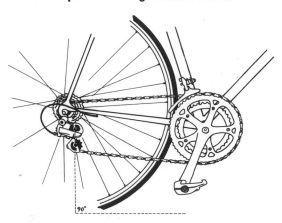

so if you have any titanium or aluminum cogs or an eleven-tooth small cog).

Chain manufacturer Sachs (now SRAM) recommends replacement if elongation is 1 percent, or ½ inch in 100 links (50 inches). If the chain is off of the bike, you can hang it next to a new chain; if it is more than a half-link longer for the same number of links, replace it.

If you always replace your chain as soon as it becomes elongated beyond spec, as indicated by a chain-elongation gauge, you will replace three to four chains before needing to change your cogs.

iv-7 CHAIN OPENING

The following procedure applies to all derailleur chains when new and when shortening them to length. It also applies to removing a chain from a bike, except for those chains with a "master link" hand openable with a chain tool (Figs. 4.21–4.23). Master-link equipped chains include all Wippermann, Taya, SRAM, and late "Power Link"-equipped Sachs chains, and chains with the "Super Link"; all of these chains snap open by hand at the master link (see §iv-12), although they can also be opened at any other link with a chain tool, as

described next. Old Campagnolo ten-speed chains have a master link that cannot be opened, so open those chains like any other chain, at a different link, but they can't be used again (see §iv-11).

1. Place any link over the back teeth on a chain tool (Fig. 4.6).

2. For most road bikes, tighten the chain-tool handle clockwise to push the pin almost all the way out. Be careful to leave a millimeter or so of pin protruding inward from the chain plate to hook the chain back together when reassembling. However, if you have a chain with a master link or a Shimano or Campagnolo chain and a new connecting pin for it, go ahead and drive the pin all the way out.

3. Separate the chain by flexing it away from the pushed-out pin if you left the stub in. If you pushed the pin all of the way out, the two ends will just pull apart.

Incidentally, removing the chain from the bike creates an ideal opportunity to check the rear-derailleur limit-screw adjustment. The derailleur limit screws are the marshals that keep the derailleur from moving too far at the travel extremes—keep it, in other words, from shifting into the spokes or

4.8 Determining chain length with a triple

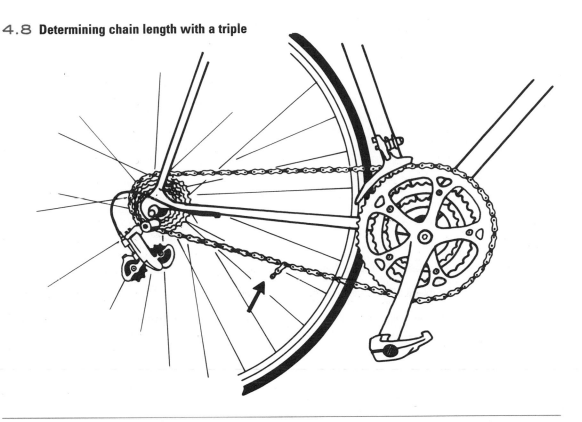

throwing the chain into the dropout. See the next chapter, and Figure 5.2, for a look at the limit screws.

To check the limit adjustments with the chain out of the way, shift the derailleur to high gear and, while looking at the derailleur from the rear, see whether the jockey wheel in the cage is aligned with the smallest cog. Then push the derailleur inward until it contacts the inner adjustment screw and look to see whether the jockey wheel is aligned below the largest cog. If either adjustment is off, adjust the limit screw by using the procedure in §v-2.

iv-8 DETERMINING CHAIN LENGTH AND ROUTING

a. Methods for determining the chain length

If you are putting on a new chain for double cranks (including compact doubles), determine how many links you will need in one of the following four ways. Methods 2 and 3 are approximately equivalent, and

both work for standard double-chainring setups as well as for compact-drive (smaller) double chainrings. If you have a triple crankset (three chainrings up front) and a long-cage rear derailleur on your bike, however, you should take the third approach.

1. Under the assumption that your old chain was the correct length, compare the new with the old chain and use the same number of links.

2. With a standard double-chainring setup, route the chain through the derailleurs and over the large chainring and smallest cog. The jockey wheels in the rear derailleur should then align vertically (Fig. 4.7).

3. Wrap the chain around the big chainring and the biggest cog without going through either derailleur. Bring the two ends together until the ends overlap; one full link (Fig. 4.5) should be the amount of overlap (Fig. 4.8). This method also works with a standard double and is a must

4.9 Installing the chain pin (link rivet)

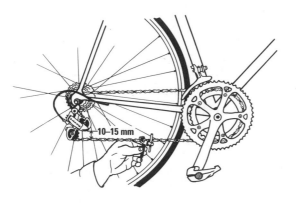

10–15 mm

4.10 Pushing in the pin (link rivet)

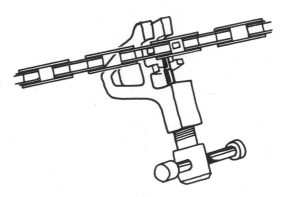

if you are using a double with a big mountain-bike cogset (like an 11-32 or 11-34) and a long-cage rear derailleur.

4. Campagnolo suggests a different method with a double crank, namely, routing the chain over the inner chainring and the smallest cog, as shown in Figure 4.9. You need to make sure that the lower jockey wheel does not lift the chain to the point that the chain going around the bottom of the upper jockey wheel hits the section of chain coming from the bottom of the chainring. Campagnolo further suggests checking for about 10–15mm of clearance between the upper jockey wheel and the chain (see Fig. 4.9).

5. Remove the remaining links (§iv-7, Fig. 4.6), and save them in your spare-tire bag so that you have spares in case of chain breakage on the road.

b. Route the chain properly

Shift the derailleurs so that the chain will rest on the smallest cog in the rear and on the smallest chainring up front. Starting with the rear-derailleur pulley that is farthest from the derailleur body (this will be the bottom pulley once the chain is taut), guide the chain up through the rear derailleur, going around the two jockey pulleys. Make sure the chain passes inside of the prongs on the rear-derailleur

cage. Guide the chain over the smallest rear cog and through the front-derailleur cage. Wrap the chain around the smallest front chainring and bring the chain ends together so that they meet (Fig. 4.9).

iv-9 CONNECTING A STANDARD CHAIN (WITHOUT A MASTER LINK OR A SPECIAL CONNECTING PIN)

NOTE: *If you have a Shimano or Campagnolo chain, or one with a master link, go to the appropriate section; don't connect it the way described in this section by using the original rivet. Not heeding this warning could result in injury if the chain breaks.*

FURTHER NOTE: *This section only applies to wider chains, such as five-, six-, seven-, or perhaps even eight-speed chains. Never use the same pin (except in an emergency on a ride) on a nine- or ten-speed chain or on any Shimano or Campagnolo chain.* Connecting a chain that has no special connecting pin or link is much easier if the link rivet (pin) that was partially removed when the chain was taken apart is facing outward (toward you). Positioning the link rivet this way allows you to use the chain tool (Fig. 4.9) in a much more comfortable manner (driving the rivet toward the bike, instead of back at you). Be sure that the chain length allows about

4.11 **A stiff link**

4.12 **Freeing a stiff link**

10–15mm of clearance between the upper jockey wheel and the lower length of chain.

1. Push the ends together, snapping the end link over the little stub of pin you left sticking out to the inside between the opposite end plates. You will need to flex the plates open as you push the link in to get the pin to snap into the hole.

2. Push the pin through with the chain tool (Fig. 4.10) until the same amount protrudes on either end. If you have a nine-speed system, you really shouldn't be using the original rivet in the first place. But if you are, and your chain tool prongs seem to be getting bent as you push the rivet, see the note in §iv-10, step 5.

3. If there is a stiff link (Fig. 4.11), free it either by flexing it back and forth with your fingers (Fig. 4.12) or, better, by using the chain tool's second set of teeth, as illustrated in Figure 4.13. Push the pin a fraction of a turn to spread the plates apart.

iv–10 CONNECTING A SHIMANO CHAIN (NON-TEN-SPEED)

1. Make sure you have the appropriate Shimano "subpin" connecting pin, which looks like a segmented rivet with one segment ending in a pointed tip. It has a breakage groove at the middle

4.13 **Loosening a stiff link**

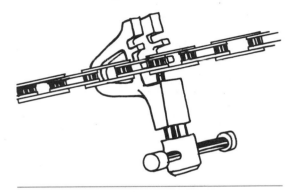

of its length. Two subpins come with a new Shimano chain. If you are reinstalling an old Shimano chain, use a new subpin, and make sure it is the right length for the chain (ten-speed subpins are shorter than nine-speed subpins, which are shorter than seven- or eight-speed subpins; see §iv-11). If you don't have a subpin and are going to connect a seven- or eight-speed chain anyway, follow the procedure in §iv-9, but be aware that the chain is now more likely to break than if it had been assembled with the proper subpin. With a nine-speed chain, this is an extremely dangerous approach; don't do it. With a ten-speed chain, it is a complete no-no to connect the chain without a new connector pin; the chain will break immediately. And a broken chain is no fun; it can wreck

4.14 Pushing a connector pin into a Campagnolo (or Shimano) chain with a chain tool

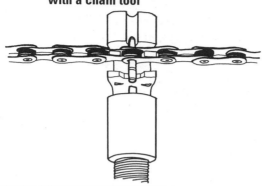

4.15 Breaking off Shimano subpin

CONNECTING
TEN-SPEED
CHAINS

other parts, and you can get injured. Before assembling a ten-speed chain, read §iv-11.

2. Remove any extra links, pushing the appropriate rivet completely out (§iv-7, Fig. 4.6).

3. Line up the chain ends.

4. Drip some oil on the subpin and push it in with your fingers, pointed end first. It will go in about halfway.

5. With the chain tool (Fig. 4.14), push the subpin through until there is only as much left protruding at the tail end as the other rivets in the chain. It will feel hard, then easy, and then very hard to tighten the tool as you move the pin past its various high points and valleys. Stop when it gets very hard and check for binding. Go by feel more than by sight to determine when the pin is seated correctly.

6. Break off the leading half of the subpin with the hole in the end of a Shimano chain tool or with a pair of pliers (Fig. 4.15).

7. The individual links should move freely when the pin is correctly seated. If not, push the link rivet in a little deeper (Fig. 4.10), or push it back a hair from the other side with the chain on the teeth closer to the screw (Fig. 4.13). As a (poor) last resort (and never with nine- or ten-speed

chains), flex the chain back and forth with your thumbs at the stiff rivet (Fig. 4.12).

NOTE: *If you have a nine-speed chain and an older chain tool, you may find that the prongs in the tool to hold the chain are too far from the backing plate of the tool and will get bent. Shimano tools TL-CN23 (Fig. 4.16) and TL-CN32 (Fig. 4.17) work on all Shimano chains. Many other brands also work.*

iv-11 CONNECTING TEN-SPEED CHAINS

Campagnolo was the first to introduce ten-speed rear drivetrains and consequently more complex chain-assembly methods. Because of the tighter spacing between the ten cogs required to fit them

4.18 Pedro's chain tool. Note the flange with an extra chain-retaining tooth extending out to either side of the tool.

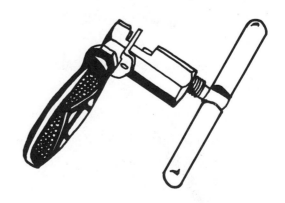

4.16 **Shimano TL-CN23, TL-CN22, or TL-CN21 chain tool (for ten-, nine-, seven-, or eight-speed chains, respectively)**

4.17 **Shimano TL-CN32, TL-CN31, or TL-CN30 professional chain tool (for ten-, nine-, seven-, or eight-speed chains, respectively). Has an extra pair of chain-retaining teeth extending out to either side of the tool.**

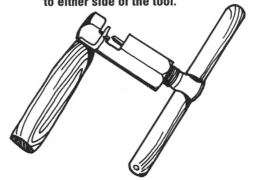

onto a hub the same width as an eight- or a nine-speed hub, ten-speed chains are narrow. Because the cog and chainring teeth themselves did not get significantly narrower, neither did the inner spacing of the chains. On the other hand, their outer chain width has come down substantially, from 7.3mm, to 7.1mm, to 6.6mm, to 6.1mm and 6.05mm, and even to 5.9mm for 2006 Campagnolo chains, in going from five-speed, then six-, seven-, eight-, nine-, to ten-speed cogsets. New problems come with a chain whose outer width is narrower; because the spacing

between the inner plates has remained fixed, there is very little protrusion of the chain rivets and hence less security of the chain against breakage under high side loads. It is so critical to install the connecting pin on a ten-speed chain properly that you need a really good chain tool that is intended for use on ten-speed chains (see Figs. 4.16 to 4.20 and the Pro Tip on chain tools). The only exception is that some ten-speed chains have hand-openable master links (Figs. 4.21 to 4.23) that allow opening the chain without using a chain tool. If yours has a master link, skip to §iv-12.

4.19 **Rohloff Revolver chain tool. The large-diameter knurled knob can be turned to select different backing-plate shapes. The smaller-diameter knurled knob tightens the backing plate against the chain.**

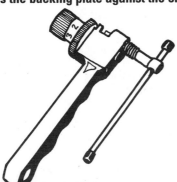

4.20 **Park CT-3 chain tool has front and back pairs of teeth.**

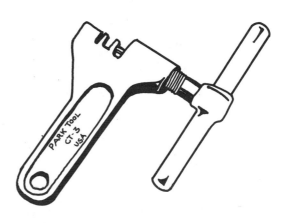

Campagnolo original ten-speed chain rivets protrude very little (only 0.1mm), and Shimano as well as 2006 Campagnolo ten-speed chain rivets protrude not at all. Less rivet protrusion means that the margin of safety of a rivet popping out of a chain plate is reduced, and new steps must be taken to prevent chain plates from peeling off the end of rivets.

If a chain breaks, it is usually under high load while shifting. Shifting creates the lateral stress because, when the rear derailleur shifts with a modern cogset, the chain is simultaneously engaged on two cogs, and when the front derailleur pushes the

PRO TIP

PROPER CHAIN TOOLS

If you ride a lot, you will change your chain frequently, and it then becomes worthwhile to have a good chain tool (i.e., chain-breaker tool). If you currently just have a cheap little chain tool, you will be glad you made the investment to upgrade.

If you're strictly a Campagnolo ten-speed rider and don't ride mountain bikes, you might as well get the Campy C10 HD-L ten-speed tool. Campagnolo is pretty proud of that tool—it retails for $150 or so. It looks similar to the tool in Figure 4.17, except that it has no wing with extra teeth extending out to either side and it has a wire loop that you push in once the chain is in place to hold the links down.

According to Shimano, you should only use its $35 TL-CN23 or its $120 TL-CN32 tool on its ten-speed chains; in addition, both of these tools work on all seven-, eight-, nine-speed Shimano chains. The Shimano TL-CN23 is a small tool (Fig. 4.16), and the TL-CN32 (as well as its predecessors, the TL-CN31 and TL-CN30) is a professional tool with wooden handles (Fig. 4.17) that even has spare driver pins hidden in the base. The most important feature of the TL-CN32 (and the TL-CN31 and TL-CN30) is that it has four locating teeth in a row to hold the chain, rather than just two, as most chain tools have. These extra two teeth, one extending out on either side of the tool,

really hold the chain well and do much of what Campagnolo's tool accomplishes with its wires to hold the chain down. Pedro's $45 Pro Chain Tool (Fig. 4.18) also has these extra two locating teeth extending out on either side.

Holding the chain in place is nothing new. Before the invention of special connecting pins, we really needed to hold the chain lined up properly, because we did not have a leading tip on a connecting pin that we could slip in by hand and hold the chain together (§iv-9). The $200 Rohloff Revolver tool (Fig. 4.19), which has been around for well over a decade, has a thumbscrew that tightens down against the chain and really holds it in place. The tool also has a revolving plate with different patterns on it to repeen the end of the rivet in whatever style you choose. Park's $35 CT-3 (Fig. 4.20) is a standard shop chain tool, with both a front set of teeth and a back set of teeth, for prying a link apart a bit to free a stiff link, as shown in Figure 4.13.

I have used a Shimano TL-CN31 (nine-speed tool) for years on every kind of chain from Shimano, Campagnolo, Wippermann, and SRAM, for seven, eight, nine, and ten speeds. As the chains became narrower on the outside, the supporting center section on newer Shimano chain tools was moved closer

CONNECTING
TEN-SPEED
CHAINS

chain from one chainring to another, it obviously flexes the links sideways. Easing off on the pedals when you shift will greatly decrease the possibility of a broken chain. However, a chain can break under any high load if a cage plate is just barely hanging onto the end of a rivet. Breaking a chain is danger-

to the chain-locating teeth, to fully support the rear outer link plate while driving the pin in. If you use an older-generation chain tool (for wider chains) with a one-generation newer (narrower) chain, eventually you will damage the tool as it puts too much lateral load on the chain-locating teeth. A two-generation-older chain tool will not seat the chain connector pins, so don't use it. Ideally, to do the best job with the latest chains, get the latest tool, and it will also be compatible with all of the older (wider) chains.

If you are careful, I think that you only need one good tool that is at most one generation back (i.e., it is meant for at least nine-speed chains) and that can be used on any chain. By "careful," I mean that you must make sure that the connecting pin and the holes are all lined up perfectly (which the Campy, Rohloff, Shimano, and Pedro's pro tools definitely help guarantee). Furthermore, by "careful," I mean that you must make sure that you stop at the right point and do not go too far or not far enough. You must have a feel for the loose-tight-loose-tight pressure changes as you push a Shimano or Campagnolo connecting pin into place, as well as an eye for when the pin is protruding (or recessed) the same amount on both faces of the chain.

ous, because when the tension on the chain is suddenly removed, your weight drops straight down, as there is no longer anything supporting the pushing foot. You can easily fall hard. Very hard.

So, pay attention to the extra steps required with a ten-speed chain to ensure its security. To reuse a Campagnolo ten-speed chain, you must have a new section of chain with a "virgin" outer link at either end and two new connector pins. Shimano's new ten-speed connector pin (on the 7801, 6600, and 5600 chains) can be installed in an old chain. This new connector pin is not compatible with CN-7800 first-generation Dura-Ace ten-speed chains.

a. Connecting a Campagnolo ten-speed chain

Original Campagnolo ten-speed chains, when introduced in 1999, came with a separate closing link with two pins, called a PermaLink, and it required a special installation tool. Fortunately, Campagnolo abandoned that closing method and replaced it with a system similar to Shimano's.

Now Campagnolo has a connecting pin, except that it is a two-piece unit that slides together, rather than a one-piece pin with a breakoff end like Shimano's. Remember, you get only one connecting pin with each Campagnolo chain (as opposed to the two you get with a Shimano chain), so don't lose it! Replacing one ain't cheap!

Campagnolo, like Shimano, has a special chain tool and highly recommends that you buy it. Its major difference is that it has a wire retainer that you slide into the tool through some holes to hold the chain down. The Campy tool also has a locator stop for the drive pin specific for its chains. I, too, recommend that you get this tool if you have a Campy ten-speed bike. However, although Campagnolo will not guarantee the results with anybody else's tool, I find

THE CHAIN

CONNECTING
TEN–SPEED
CHAINS

that, if you are careful to hold the chain down well on a Shimano ten-speed chain tool and make sure that you push the pin in so that exactly the same amount protrudes at either end, it works fine.

1. Cut excess length from the chain (§iv-8) only from the end that terminates in an inner link. That way, the holes in the plates of the outer link you will be connecting will never have had a rivet through them and consequently will not have been enlarged and distorted by the insertion and removal of a rivet, ensuring the strongest possible connection. Campagnolo calls these the "virgin holes," and it ships its chains with a zip-tie through this pair of holes at the end of the final outer link so that you will make sure to close the chain by using these virgin holes.

2. Remove the zip-tie from the virgin holes, and install the connecting pin as in §iv-10, being careful to insert the connecting pin from the bike side of the chain outward. If you don't have the Campy chain tool, hold the chain down in the chain tool so that the tool's drive pin lines up exactly with the connecting pin. Note that the Campy connecting pin is in two pieces, and you can just insert the leading "guide pin" segment by hand, with or without the other half of the pin on it. The segment that you press into the chain has two hole sizes in it, so that only one end will fit on the guide pin, thus ensuring proper orientation. Make sure the same amount of pin is sticking out of both ends (it will only be about 0.1mm) and that you have no stiff link.

b. Connecting a Shimano ten-speed chain

The assembly is the same as in §iv-10, except for a couple of important differences.

1. Cut excess length from the chain (§iv-8) only from the end that terminates in an inner link. That way, the holes in the plates of the outer link you will be connecting will have never had a rivet through them and consequently will not have been enlarged and distorted by the insertion and removal of a rivet, ensuring the strongest possible connection.

2. You want the connecting pin you insert to be the leading pin, as the outer link it is on comes over the top of the chainring and—most critically—leads when shifting onto the next larger rear cog. Accomplish this link orientation by making sure that, if you are connecting the chain at the bottom as in Figure 4.9, the inner link on one end is to the left (toward the rear derailleur) of the outer link on the other end you are connecting it to. (This approach will ensure that, at the top of the chainring or cog, the inner link is to the right of the outer link, and thus the connecting pin will be to the right of the other rivet in the same outer plate, i.e., leading it.)

3. Obviously, make sure that you are using a Shimano ten-speed connecting pin. Two connecting pins come with the chain.

4. Otherwise, follow the instructions in §iv-10, except that, rather than having both ends of the connecting pins protruding a bit from their plates (as they are for seven-, eight-, and nine-speed chains), you want the ten-speed connector pin to be slightly recessed, below flush. Go by feel rather than by how much pin you see exposed. Keep tightening beyond where you would normally stop with a nine-speed chain because it feels hard. It will feel easy and then very hard while you continue to push. At this

4.21 SRAM Power Link (also Sachs Power Link and Lickton's Super Link)

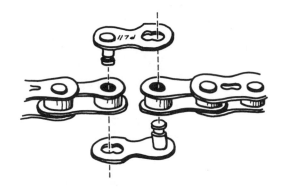

4.22 Wipperman ConneX link—note its orientation with the link's high bump away from the chainring

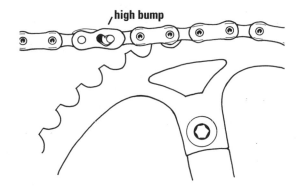

high bump

point, stop to check for binding. The chain will be connected perfectly when there is no binding at the connector pin link, without the need for you to flex it sideways to free it. Back off on the chain-tool screw, check the link for freedom of movement, and retighten the tool if you feel any binding. According to Shimano, if the link is still binding, there is a 99 percent chance that the pin isn't pushed in far enough to be fully seated. As usual, finish by breaking off the tip of the connecting pin, as shown in Figure 4.15, or by slipping the hole at the end of the Shimano chain tool over the end of the pin and using that to snap it off.

iv-12 CONNECTING AND DISCONNECTING A MASTER LINK

a. The Super Link and SRAM (Sachs) Power Link

These links are the same; SRAM (who purchased Sachs) licensed the Lickton's Super Link design (Fig. 4.21). The master link is made up of two symmetrical link halves, each of which has a single pin sticking out of it. There is a round hole in the center of each plate that tapers into a slot on the end opposite the pin.

4.23 Taya Master Link

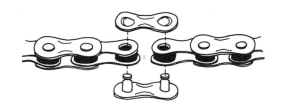

Connecting

1. Put the pin of each half of the link through the hole in each end of the chain; one pin will go down and one up (Fig. 4.21).
2. Pull the links close together so that the each pin goes through the keyhole in the opposite plate.
3. Pull the chain ends apart so that the groove at the top of each pin slides to the end of the slot in each plate.

Disconnecting

1. While squeezing the master-link plates together to free the pins, push the chain ends toward each other so that the pins come to the center hole in each plate.
2. Pull the two halves of the master link apart.

NOTE: *In practice, this is often hard to do with an old chain. Try squeezing the link plates toward each other with a clothespin or a pair of Visegrip pliers set on very* *low pressure to disengage the link plates from the pin grooves while you push the ends toward each other. In desperation, you may have to just open the chain somewhere else, reassembling it as in §iv-9 or using a second master link.*

b. Wippermann ConneX link

The Wippermann link works much the same way as the SRAM Power Link just discussed, but unlike other master links, the edges of the link plates are not symmetrical. This asymmetry means that there is a definite orientation for the link, and you want to make sure you don't install it upside down.

Orient the chain so that the convex edge is away from the chainring or cog (Fig. 4.22). The link plate is bowl-shaped, and if you have the convex bottom of the bowl toward the cog or chainring, then when it is on an eleven-, or twelve-, maybe even a thirteen-tooth cog, the convex edge will ride up on the spacer between cogs, lifting the rollers out of the tooth valleys and causing the chain to skip under load.

So, remove and install the ConneX link the same way as the SRAM Power Link in §iv-12a, but make sure the convex link edge is facing outward from the chain loop (Fig. 4.22), so that the concave edge can run over the cog spacers on the smallest cogs without lifting the chain.

c. Taya Master Link

Connecting

1. Connect the two ends of the chain together with the master link that has two rivets sticking out of it (Fig. 4.23).
2. Snap the outer master-link plate over the rivets and into their grooves. To facilitate hooking each keyhole-shaped hole over its corresponding rivet, flex the plate with the protruding rivets so that the ends of the rivets are closer together.

Disconnecting

1. Flex the master link so that the pins come closer together.
2. Pull the plate with the oval holes off the rivets.

TROUBLESHOOTING CHAIN PROBLEMS

iv-13 CHAIN SUCK

"Chain suck" is the horribly appropriate name for a condition that occurs when the chain does not release from the bottom of the chainring. Instead, it sticks to the ring and gets "sucked" up until it hits the chainstay. Sometimes the chain becomes wedged between the chainstay and the chainring.

Chain suck is rare on a double-chainring setup on a road bike, but it does happen. It is more likely with a triple crank, but fortunately is still rare.

A number of things can cause chain suck. To eliminate it, try the simplest methods first.

1. Clean and lube the chain and see if it improves; a dry, rusty chain will hold the curved shape of the chainring too long.
2. Check for tight links by watching the chain move through the derailleur jockey wheels as you slowly turn the crank backward. Loosen tight links by flexing them side to side with your thumbs (Fig. 4.12).
3. If chain suck persists, check that there are no bent or torn teeth on the chainring. Try straightening any broken or torn teeth you find with pliers.
4. If the chain still sucks, try another chain with wider spacing between link plates (if it is too narrow, it can pinch the chainring). You can use a caliper (Fig. 1.4) to compare link spacing of various chains.

5. Another approach is to replace the inner (and perhaps middle) chainring. The new, unworn rings will release the chain more easily, and some chainrings are thinner than others.

6. If the problem still persists, an "anti-chain suck" device that attaches under the chainstays may help. Ask at your bike shop about what is available.

iv-14 SQUEAKING CHAIN

Squeaking is caused by dry or rusted surfaces inside the chain rubbing on each other.

1. Lubricate and wipe down the chain (Figs. 4.1 and 4.2), and then lubricate it again. Remember not to use a wax-based lubricant; using one might have even brought on the chain chirp in the first place.

2. If the squeak does not go away after a single ride with fresh lubricant, replace the chain. (If the initial remedy does not work, the chain is too dry inside and probably rusted as well. Chains seldom heal from this condition. Life is too short and bike riding is too joyful to put up with the sound of a squeaking chain.)

iv-15 SKIPPING CHAIN

There can be a number of causes for a chain to skip and jump as you pedal.

a. Stiff links

1. Turn the crank backward slowly to see whether a stiff chain link (Fig. 4.11) exists; a stiff link will be visible because it will be unable to bend properly as it goes through the rear-derailleur jockey wheels. It will jump and move the jockey wheels as it passes through.

2. Loosen stiff links by flexing them side to side

between the index finger and thumb of both hands (Fig. 4.12) or by using the second set of teeth on a chain tool (Fig. 4.13). Set the stiff link over the teeth closest to the screw handle, and push the pin a fraction of a turn to spread the link.

3. Wipe down and lubricate the chain (Figs. 4.1 and 4.2).

b. Rusted chain

A rusted chain will squeak. If you watch it move through the rear derailleur, it will look like many links are tight; the links will not bend easily and will cause the jockey wheels to jump back and forth.

1. Lubricate the chain (Fig. 4.1).

2. If this does not fix the problem after a few miles of riding, replace the chain.

c. Worn-out chain

If the chain is worn out, it will be elongated and will skip because it does not mesh well with the cogs. A new chain will fix the problem if the condition has not persisted long enough to ruin some cogs.

1. Check for chain elongation as described in §iv-6.

2. If the chain is elongated beyond the specifications in §iv-6, replace it.

3. If replacing the chain does not help or actually makes matters worse, see the next section.

d. Worn cogs

If you just replaced the chain and it is now skipping, probably at least one of the cogs is worn out. If this is the case, the chain will probably skip on the cogs you use most frequently and not on others. However, if it only skips on the smallest cog or two and you have a Wippermann chain, check that you have not installed the ConneX Link upside down—see §iv-12b.

1. Check each cog visually for wear. If its teeth

are hook-shaped, the cog is shot and should be replaced. Rohloff makes a simple "HG-Check" tool that checks for cog wear by putting tension on a length of chain wrapped around the cog (see Chapter 6). If the last chain link on the tool can be flipped in and out of the tooth pocket while the tool is under tension, the cog is worn out.

2 . Replace the offending cogs or the entire cassette or freewheel. See cog installation in §vi-20.

3 . Replace the chain as well, if you have not just done so. An old chain will wear out new cogs rapidly.

e. Maladjusted rear derailleur

If the rear derailleur is poorly adjusted or bent, it can cause the chain to skip by lining up the chain between gears.

1 . Check that the rear derailleur shifts equally well in both directions and that the chain can be pedaled backward without catching.

2 . Adjust the rear derailleur by following the procedure described in §v-2.

f. Sticky shift cable

If the shift cable does not move freely enough to let the derailleur spring over to be lined up under the cog, the chain will jump off under load. Frayed, rough, dirty, rusted, or worn cables or housings will cause the problem, as will kinked or sharply bent housings. Replacing the shift cables and housings (Chapter 5, §v-6 to §v-14) should eliminate the problem.

g. Loose rear-derailleur jockey wheel(s)

A loose jockey wheel on the rear derailleur can cause the chain to skip by letting it move too far laterally.

1 . Check that the bolts holding the jockey wheel to the cage are tight, by using an appropriately sized wrench (usually 3mm Allen).

2 . Tighten the jockey-wheel bolts if necessary;

hold the Allen wrench close to the bend so that you don't have enough leverage to over-tighten them. If the jockey-wheel bolts loosen regularly, put Loctite or another threadlock compound on them.

h. Bent rear derailleur or rear-derailleur hanger

If the derailleur or derailleur hanger is bent, adjustments won't work. You will probably know when it happened, too. It was either when you shifted your derailleur into your spokes, when you crashed onto the derailleur, or when you pedaled a plastic bag or a tumbleweed through the derailleur.

1 . Unless you have a derailleur-hanger-alignment tool and know how to use it (Chapter 15, Fig. 15.3), take the bike to a shop and have it checked for correct dropout-hanger alignment. Some bikes, especially those made out of aluminum or carbon, have a replaceable (bolt-on) right-rear dropout and derailleur hanger, which you can purchase and install yourself.

2 . If a straight derailleur hanger does not correct the misalignment, the rear derailleur is bent. This is generally cause for replacement of the entire derailleur (see §v-1). With some derailleurs, you can replace the jockey-wheel cage, which is usually what is bent. If you know what you are doing and are careful, you can sometimes bend a bent derailleur cage back with your hands. It seldom works well, but it's worth a try if your only other alternative is to replace the entire rear derailleur. Just make sure you don't bend the derailleur hanger in the process.

i. Worn derailleur pivots

If the derailleur pivots are worn, the derailleur will be loose and will move around under the cogs, causing the chain to skip. Replacing the derailleur is the solution.

j. Bent rear-derailleur mounting bolt

If the mounting bolt is bent, the derailleur will not line up straight. To fix it, get a new bolt and install it following the "upper-pivot overhaul" in §v-26. Observe how the spring-loaded assembly goes together during disassembly to ease reassembly.

k. Missing chain rollers

You can have a chain that passes the elongation tests mentioned in §iv-6 yet will skip because every here and there, one of the cylindrical rollers has broken and fallen off its rivet or is so worn that it is spool-shaped. If you don't happen to check that particular link with the chain-elongation gauge, you'll likely miss broken rollers. The width of the gauge is the same as between the inner plates, so that it won't catch spool-shaped rollers either, because it will ride up on the edges of the rollers and not fall down into the center of the narrower waist of the worn roller. You might never know the chain is shot without inspecting every link, so do that.

l. Inverted ConneX link

If you have a Wippermann chain and have the ConneX master link upside down (described in §iv-12b), the taller link edge will ride up on the spacers between the smallest cogs, lift the rollers off the cog, and cause the chain to skip. Remove, invert, and reinstall the ConneX master link as described in §iv-12b.

CHAPTER 5

THE SHIFTING SYSTEM

Never mistake motion for action.
—Ernest Hemingway

Riding a bike is much more enjoyable when the derailleurs are working well. It is so sweet to feel the chain respond quickly and positively to shifting commands. On the other hand, it can really ruin a ride to have the chain shift unexpectedly or skip when you pedal hard.

Derailleurs, fortunately, are simple beasts. When they act up, a few turns of some screws or a cable-tension adjustment will usually get them working again. However, on most current road bikes, the brake levers have the shift levers integrated into them, and so these parts do have considerable complexity. Master this chapter, and you will be able to fix most shifting problems on your bike in seconds, even when you are on the road.

This chapter is organized with all cable-operated systems at the beginning and electronic systems at the end.

THE REAR DERAILLEUR

The rear derailleur (Figs. 5.1 and 5.2) moves the chain from one rear cog to another, and it also takes up chain slack (such as when the front derailleur is shifted or the bike bounces over a bump). The rear derailleur bolts to a hanger on the frame's rear dropout about which the derailleur can pivot (Fig. 5.3).

Two jockey wheels (pulley wheels) that live in a guide assembly called a chain cage hold the chain tight and help guide the chain as the derailleur shifts. Depending on the model, a rear derailleur has either one or two springs that pull the jockey wheels tight against the chain, creating a desirable amount of chain tension.

Increasing the tension on the rear shift cable (as when you shift to a lower gear) moves the derailleur inward toward the larger cogs. When cable tension is released (that is, when you shift to a higher gear), a

5.1 Rear derailleur exploded

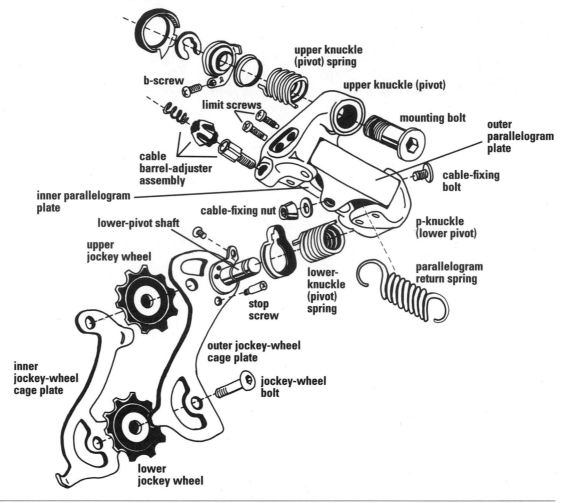

b-screw

limit screws

upper knuckle (pivot) spring

upper knuckle (pivot)

mounting bolt

outer parallelogram plate

cable-fixing bolt

cable barrel-adjuster assembly

inner parallelogram plate

cable-fixing nut

p-knuckle (lower pivot)

lower-pivot shaft

upper jockey wheel

lower-knuckle (pivot) spring

parallelogram return spring

stop screw

outer jockey-wheel cage plate

inner jockey-wheel cage plate

jockey-wheel bolt

lower jockey wheel

spring between the derailleur's two parallelogram plates pulls the chain back toward the smallest cogs. The two limit screws on the rear derailleur (Fig. 5.2) prevent the derailleur from moving the chain too far to the inside (into the spokes) or to the outside (into the dropout).

In addition to limit screws, most rear derailleurs have a barrel adjuster located at the back of the derailleur, where the cable enters it (Fig. 5.2). The barrel adjuster increases cable tension when it is unscrewed (and reduces cable tension when it is screwed in). The barrel adjuster is thus used to fine-tune the shifting mechanism to land the chain precisely on each cog with each cor-

responding click of the shifter.

Rear derailleurs also often have a screw underneath and to the rear (visible in Fig. 5.3). This screw, conventionally called the "b-tension" screw, presses against the dropout or a tab attached to the dropout and is largely responsible for controlling the space between the bottom of the cogs and the upper jockey wheel (Figs. 5.4 and 5.5) The other factor affecting the size of this space is chain length.

The chain length, the balance between the springs in the upper and lower pivots, and the b-screw (Fig. 5.3) adjustment determine how closely the derailleur tracks to the cogs during its lateral movement and keeps the chain from

5.2 Limit screws and barrel adjuster

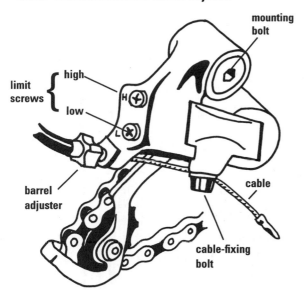

5.3 Right rear dropout

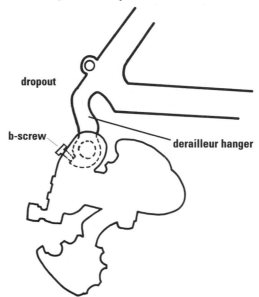

bouncing off the front chainrings when the bike hits bumps.

v-1 REAR-DERAILLEUR INSTALLATION

1. Apply a small amount of grease to the derailleur's mounting bolt and then thread the bolt a few turns into the large hole on the right-rear dropout.

2. Pull the derailleur back so that the b-screw or tab on the derailleur ends up behind the tab on the dropout (Fig. 5.3).

3. Tighten the mounting bolt until the derailleur fits snugly against the hanger.

4. Route the chain through the jockey wheels and connect it. (See Chapter 4, §iv-9 to §iv-12).

5. Install the cables and housings (see §v-6 to §v-13).

6. Pull the cable tight with a pair of pliers, and tighten the cable-fixing bolt (Fig. 5.20).

7. Follow the adjustment procedure described in the next section.

v-2 ADJUSTMENT OF REAR DERAILLEUR AND RIGHT-HAND SHIFTER

Perform all of the following derailleur adjustments with the bike in a bike stand or hung from the ceiling. That way, you can turn the crank and shift gears while you put the derailleur through its paces. After adjusting it off the ground, test the shifting while riding. Derailleurs often perform differently under load than in a bike stand.

Before starting, lubricate or replace the chain (Chapter 4) so that the whole drivetrain runs smoothly.

a. Limit-screw adjustments

The first and most important rear-derailleur adjustment is of the limit screws. Properly set, these screws (Fig. 5.2) should make certain that you will not ruin your frame, wheel, or derailleur by shifting into the spokes or by jamming the chain between the dropout and the smallest cog. It is never pleasant to see your expensive equipment turned into shredded metal. Adjustment requires nothing but a small screwdriver; remember, it's lefty loosey, righty tighty for the limit screws.

REAR-
DERAILLEUR
INSTALLATION
—
ADJUSTMENT
OF REAR
DERAILLEUR
AND
RIGHT-HAND
SHIFTER

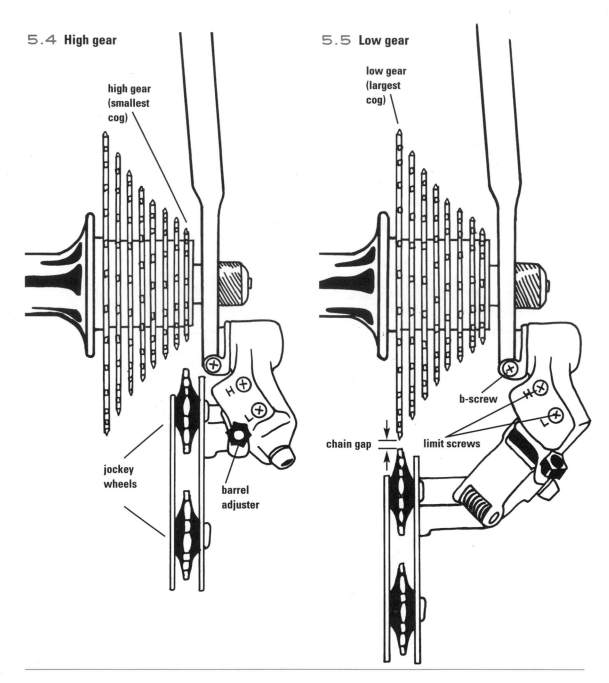

5.4 High gear

high gear
(smallest
cog)

jockey
wheels

barrel
adjuster

5.5 Low gear

low gear
(largest
cog)

b-screw

chain gap

limit screws

ADJUSTMENT

OF REAR

DERAILLEUR

AND

RIGHT-HAND

SHIFTER

b. High-gear limit-screw adjustment

This screw limits the outward movement of the rear derailleur. You tighten or loosen this screw until the derailleur shifts the chain to the smallest cog quickly but does not overshift.

How do you determine which limit screw works on the high gear? Often, it will be labeled with an "H," and it is usually the upper of the two screws (Fig. 5.2). If you're not certain, try both

screws. Whichever one moves the derailleur when the cable tension is released (and the chain is on the smallest cog) is the one you're looking for. On most derailleurs, you can also see which screw to adjust by looking between the derailleur's parallelogram side plates. You will see one tab on the back end of each plate. Each is designed to hit a limit screw at one end of the movement. Shift to the smallest cog, and notice which screw is touching one of the tabs; that is the high-gear limit screw.

All of these adjustments require knowing how to work your shift levers. If you want a refresher on shifting Shimano STI or Campagnolo Ergopower, skip to §v-16.

1. Shift the chain to the large front chainring.

2. While slowly turning the crank, shift the rear derailleur to the smallest rear cog (highest gear) (Fig. 5.4).

3. If there is hesitation in the chain's shifting movement, loosen the cable a little to see if it is stopping the derailleur from moving out far enough. You loosen the cable either by (a) turning the barrel adjuster on the derailleur or down-tube barrel adjuster clockwise or (b) loosening the cable-fixing bolt.

4. If the chain still won't drop smoothly and without hesitation to the smallest cog, loosen the high-gear limit screw one-quarter turn at a time, continuously repeating the shift, until the chain repeatedly drops quickly and easily.

5. If the derailleur throws the chain into the dropout, or it tries to go past the smallest cog, tighten the cable by turning the barrel adjuster counterclockwise (or tighten the high-gear limit screw one-quarter turn) and redo the shift. Repeat until the derailleur shifts the chain quickly and easily into the highest gear without throwing the chain into the dropout.

NOTE: *Make sure that the washer under the cable-fixing bolt on your rear derailleur is rotated into the right position, or it may hit on the derailleur cage and stop the rear derailleur from getting to the smallest cog. Some derailleurs have a tooth or two on the washer to dovetail into corresponding notches in the derailleur, and a number of positions may seem to fit. Look at the cable groove scored in the washer for a locating hint.*

c. Low-gear limit-screw adjustment

This screw stops the inward movement of the rear derailleur, preventing it from going into the spokes. This screw is often labeled "L," and it is usually the bottom screw (Fig. 5.2). You can check which one it is by shifting to the largest cog, and while maintaining pressure on the shifter, turn the screw to see if it changes the position of the derailleur.

1. Shift the chain to the inner chainring on the front. Shift the rear derailleur to the lowest gear (largest cog, Fig. 5.5). Do it gently, in case the limit screw does not stop the derailleur from moving into the spokes.

2. If the derailleur touches the spokes or pushes the chain over the largest cog, tighten the low-gear limit screw until the derailleur does not.

3. If the derailleur cannot bring the chain onto the largest cog, loosen the screw one-quarter turn. Repeat this step until the chain shifts easily up to the largest cog but does not touch the spokes or push the chain over the top of the cog.

d. Cable-tension adjustment on indexed rear shifters

With an indexed shifting system (one that "clicks" into each gear), it is the cable tension that determines whether the derailleur moves to the proper gear with each click.

1. With the chain on the large chainring in the front, shift the rear derailleur to the smallest cog. Keep clicking the shifter until you are sure it will not let out any more cable.

2. Shift back one click; this should move the chain smoothly to the second cog.

3. If the chain does not climb to the second cog, or

THE SHIFTING SYSTEM

ADJUSTMENT
OF REAR
DERAILLEUR
AND
RIGHT-HAND
SHIFTER

if it does so slowly, increase the tension in the cable by unscrewing (counterclockwise) either the cable-tensioning barrel adjuster on the derailleur (Fig. 5.2) or the barrel adjuster on the frame-mounted cable stop (Fig. 5.6)—or the notched lever adjuster on the frame for Shimano STI. (If you have down-tube shifters, the only barrel adjuster is at the rear derailleur.) If you run out of barrel-adjustment range, retighten both adjusters, loosen the cable-fixing bolt on the derailleur, and pull some of the slack out of the cable. Tighten the cable-fixing bolt and repeat the adjustment.

4. If the chain overshifts the second cog or comes close to overshifting, decrease the cable tension by turning one of the barrel adjusters clockwise (that is, screw it in). If both barrel adjusters are already screwed in, you will need to loosen the cable at the cable-fixing bolt.

5. Keep adjusting the cable tension in small increments while shifting back and forth between the two smallest cogs until the chain moves easily in both directions.

6. Shift the rear derailleur back and forth among the smallest five cogs, again checking for precise and quick movement of the chain from cog to cog. Fine-tune the shifting by making small corrections with to the cable-tensioning barrel adjuster.

7. Shift to the inner ring in the front and to the largest cog in the rear. Shift up and down one click in the rear, again checking for symmetry and precision of chain movement in either direction between the two largest cogs. Fine-tune the barrel adjusters until you get the shifting just right.

8. Go back through the gears. With the chain on the big chainring, the rear derailleur should shift easily on all but perhaps the largest one or two cogs in the rear. With the chain on the inner chainring, the rear derailleur should shift easily on all but perhaps the two smallest cogs. Fine-tune while riding.

NOTE: *If you can't get the tension to work properly on all cogs, there is likely something incompatible between your cogs and shifter or something wrong with your cogset. See §v-35b and §v-35e regarding compatibility between shifters and cogsets. If the cogs and shifters are supposed to work with each other, then it may be that there is some spacing off within the cogset. If, for instance, it shifts fine in mid-size cogs but acts like the cable tension is too high in the large cogs and too low in the small cogs (and your shift cables and housings are new or in good working order—see the next Pro Tip), you need some more spacing somewhere within the cogset. Try cutting a circular shim from a beer can that just fits over the freehub body, and slip the shim between a spacer and a cog somewhere in the middle of the cogset. If it improves things, you can play with the number and position of the shims to get it perfect.*

e. Cable-tension adjustment on frictional rear shifters

If you do not have indexed shifting, adjustment is complete after you remove the slack in the cable. With proper cable tension, when the chain is on the smallest cog, the derailleur should move as soon as the shift lever does. If there is free play in the lever, tighten the cable by turning the barrel adjuster on the derailleur counterclockwise. If your rear derailleur has no barrel adjuster, loosen the cable-fixing bolt, pull tension on the cable with pliers, and retighten the bolt.

ADJUSTMENT
OF REAR
DERAILLEUR
AND
RIGHT-HAND
SHIFTER

f. Final details of rear-derailleur adjustment: b-screw adjustment

You can get a bit more precision by adjusting the small screw (b-screw) that changes the derailleur's position against the derailleur hanger tab on the right-rear dropout (Fig. 5.3).

NOTE: *This does not apply to Campagnolo 10-speed rear derailleurs, since they do not have a b-screw. You adjust the jockey-wheel-to-cog spacing by changing the spring tension in the lower pivot. See §v-27.*

View the bike from behind with the chain on the inner chainring and largest cog (Fig. 5.5), and adjust the screw so that the upper jockey wheel is close to the cog, but not pinching the chain against the cog. Repeat on the smallest cog (Fig. 5.4). You'll know that you've moved the jockey wheel in too closely when it starts making noise when you turn the crank.

NOTE: *If, despite your best efforts, you cannot get the rear derailleur to shift well and not make noise, refer to the chain-line discussion under "Troubleshooting" at the end of this chapter.*

THE FRONT DERAILLEUR

The front derailleur moves the chain between the chainrings. The working parts consist of a cage, a linkage mechanism, and an arm attached to the shift cable. The front derailleur is attached to the frame, often by a bolt passing through a front-derailleur boss attached to the frame's seat tube (Fig. 5.7). In an alternative arrangement, a braze-on-type front derailleur may bolt into a separate wraparound clamp that has an integral front-derailleur boss shaped like an ear. A derailleur may also be a "band type" that has an integral band clamp surrounding the seat tube (Fig. 5.8).

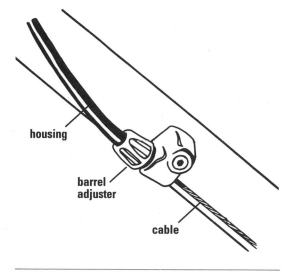

5.6 Barrel adjuster on down-tube shifter boss

housing

barrel adjuster

cable

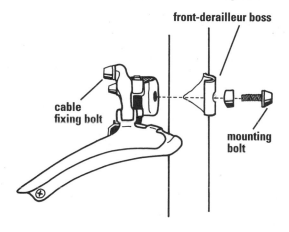

5.7 Front-derailleur boss on seat tube with front derailleur and mounting bolt

front-derailleur boss

cable fixing bolt

mounting bolt

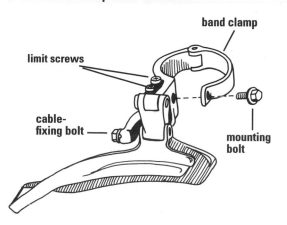

5.8 Band-clamp front derailleur

band clamp

limit screws

cable-fixing bolt

mounting bolt

5.9 Proper front-derailleur vertical clearance

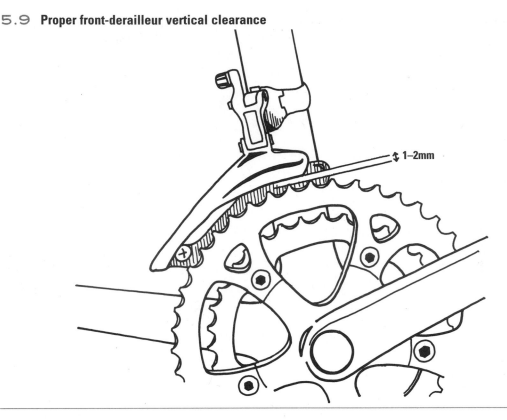

↕ 1–2mm

FRONT-

DERAILLEUR

INSTALLATION

—

ADJUSTMENT

OF FRONT

DERAILLEUR

AND

LEFT-HAND

SHIFTER

v-3 FRONT-DERAILLEUR INSTALLATION

1. Clamp the front derailleur to the frame boss or around the seat tube.

2. Adjust the height and rotation as described in §v-4a.

3. Tighten the clamp bolt (Fig. 5.7 or 5.8).

v-4 ADJUSTMENT OF FRONT DERAILLEUR AND LEFT-HAND SHIFTER

a. Position adjustments

A 5mm hex key is all you need to adjust the position of a front derailleur attached to a welded-on front-derailleur boss (Fig. 5.8). With a band-type front derailleur (Fig. 5.8), the position is adjusted with a 5mm Allen (or 8mm box) wrench on the band-clamp bolt.

1. Position the height of the front derailleur so that the outer cage passes about 1–2mm (1/16 to 1/8 inch) above the highest point of the outer chainring (Fig. 5.9).

2. Position the outer plate of the derailleur cage parallel to the chainrings or to the chain in the lowest and highest gears when viewed from above. When on the inner (smallest) chainring and largest cog, the inner cage plate should parallel with the chainring or the chain (Fig. 5.10). Similarly, check this by shifting to the big chainring and smallest cog and sighting from the top (Fig. 5.11).

b. Limit-screw adjustments

The front derailleur has two limit screws that stop the derailleur from throwing the chain to the inside or outside of the chainrings. These are sometimes labeled "L" for low gear (small chainring) and "H" for high gear (large chainring) (Fig. 5.12). On most derailleurs, the low-gear screw is closer to the frame.

If in doubt, you can determine which limit screw controls which function by the same trial-and-error method outlined in §v-2b for the rear derailleur. Shift the chain to the inner ring, and then tighten

ADJUSTMENT

OF FRONT

DERAILLEUR

AND

LEFT-HAND

SHIFTER

5.10 Proper rotational alignment of front derailleur on smallest chainring

5.11 Proper rotational alignment of front derailleur on largest chainring

5.12 Front-derailleur limit screws

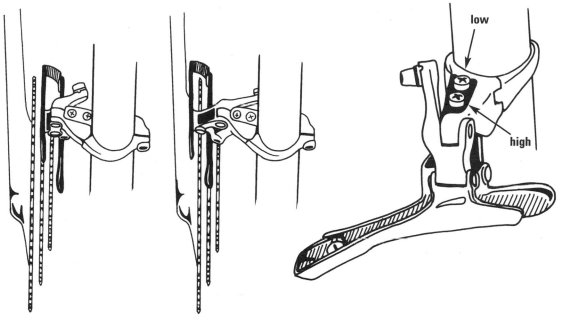

one of the limit screws. If turning that screw moves the front derailleur outward, then it is the low-gear limit screw. If turning that screw does not move the front derailleur, then the other screw is the low-gear limit screw.

c. Low-gear limit-screw adjustment

1. Shift back and forth between chainrings.

2. If the chain drops off the inner ring to the inside, tighten the low-gear limit screw (clockwise) one-quarter turn, and try shifting again.

3. If the chain does not shift easily onto the inner chainring, loosen the low-gear limit screw one-quarter turn and repeat the shift.

d. High-gear limit-screw adjustment

1. Shift the chain back and forth between chainrings.

2. If the chain jumps over the big chainring, tighten the high-gear limit screw one-quarter turn and repeat the shift.

3. If the chain is sluggish going up to the big chainring or does not go up at all, loosen the high-gear limit screw one-quarter turn and try the shift again.

e. Cable-tension adjustment

1. With the chain on the inner chainring, remove any excess cable slack by turning the barrel adjuster on the cable stop (Fig. 5.6) counterclockwise (or loosen the cable-fixing bolt, pull the cable tight with pliers, and tighten the bolt).

2. Check that the cable is loose enough to allow the chain to shift smoothly and repeatedly from the outer (or middle on a triple) to the inner chainring.

3. Check that the cable is tight enough that the derailleur starts to move as soon as you move the shifter. Fine-tune while riding.

NOTE: *This method of tension adjustment should work for indexed as well as friction shifters. With indexed* *front shifting, you may want to fine-tune the cable tension to avoid noise from the chain dragging on the derailleur in some cross gears or to get more precise shifting.*

ANOTHER NOTE: *Some front derailleurs have a cam screw at the end of the return spring to adjust the spring tension. For quicker shifting to the smaller rings, increase the spring tension by turning the screw clockwise one-quarter or one-half turn.*

NOTE ON SHIFTING TROUBLE: *If you cannot get the front derailleur to shift well, not rub in cross gears, or not throw the chain off, refer to the chain-line discussion under "Troubleshooting" at the end of this chapter.*

CHAIN WATCHER: *And if you just can't stop the chain from falling off to the inside, install a Third Eye Chain Watcher (see Fig. 5.31), Deda Dog Fang, or N'Gear Jump Stop, an inner-stop gizmo clamped to the seat tube that nudges the chain back up onto the inner ring whenever it tries to drop off.*

v-5 FRONT-DERAILLEUR FEATHERING ADJUSTMENT

"Feathering" is adjusting the front derailleur slightly to not rub the chain in cross-gears.

a. Shimano STI shifters

To stop the chain from rubbing the front-derailleur cage while on a small rear cog and the inner chainring of a double crank, you push the brake lever blade inward about half as far as you would to shift to the big chainring and let go. You will feel a soft click, and the front derailleur will stay a few millimeters out from its farthest-in position.

If the chain is rubbing in a cross-gear while on the big chainring, move the derailleur inward a couple of millimeters by pushing the chain-dump lever (the small lever behind the brake lever) inward lightly a few degrees. When you feel a soft click, let go.

With most road bikes, if the derailleurs are adjusted properly, the frame is in alignment, and the chain and chain line are to Shimano specification, these feathering positions will eliminate chain rub in all of the cross-gears except perhaps a small-small or big-big combination.

NOTE: *You lose the feathering adjustment of an STI lever if you are using it with a triple crank.*

b. Campagnolo Ergopower shifters

With Campagnolo Ergopower, the front shift lever has a number of closely spaced click stops; it does not have two definitive "indexed" positions. This setup means that you can move the derailleur in small increments by a single click in either direction. Feathering is simple and obvious, and you can generally avoid chain rub in any gear. The front shifter's incremental movements are small enough to find a rub-free position as long as the outer chainring is not bent and the frame is aligned properly. As you ride, you may want to play with the left barrel adjuster a bit to get the chain tension just right for noise-free operation in cross-gears.

REPLACING AND LUBRICATING SHIFT CABLES AND HOUSINGS

To function properly, derailleurs need to have clean, smooth-running cables (also called "inner wires"). As with replacing a chain, replacing cables is a maintenance operation, not a repair operation. Do not wait until cables break to replace them. Replace any cables that have broken strands, kinks, or fraying between the shifter and the derailleur. You should also replace housings (also called "outer wires") if they are bent, mashed, or just plain gritty or the color clashes with your bike (this is really important!).

FRONT-
DERAILLEUR
FEATHERING
ADJUSTMENT
—
REPLACING
AND
LUBRICATING
CABLES AND
HOUSINGS

PRO TIP

REPLACING YOUR CABLES AND HOUSINGS BEFORE YOU THINK THEY NEED IT

Perhaps the best thing you can do for your bike is not to buy any expensive new parts but rather to replace your cables and housings. Increased drag on shift cables caused by contamination will prevent accurate and consistent shifts.

v-6 BUYING CABLES

1. Buy new cables and housing that are at least as long as the ones you are replacing.

2. Make sure that the cables and housing are for indexed systems. These cables will stretch minimally, and the housings will not compress in length. Under its external plastic sheath, indexed housing is not made of steel coil like brake housings; it is made of parallel (coaxial) steel strands of thin wire. If you look at the end (Fig. 5.13), you will see numerous wire ends sticking out surrounding a central Teflon tube (make sure the housing you buy has this liner!).

3. Buy two cable-end crimp caps (Fig. 5.13) to prevent fraying and a tubular cable-housing end (ferrule) for each end of every housing section. These ferrules will prevent kinking at the cable-entry points, cable stops, shifters, and derailleurs.

4. It is a good idea to buy extra cables, cable caps, and ferrules (Fig. 5.13) to keep on hand in your work area. They're inexpensive, and if you have a small supply, you will be able to change cables when you need to without mak-

5.13 Cable-housing types and end caps

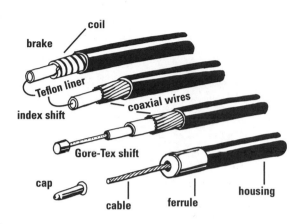

ing a special trip to the bike shop to get a little cable-end cap.

v-7 CUTTING HOUSING TO LENGTH

1. Use a special cutter made for the purpose; Park, Shimano, and Wrench Force make good ones (see Chapter 1 tools). Standard wire cutters (i.e., "side cutters") will not cleanly cut index-shift housing.

2. Cut the housing to the same lengths as the pieces you are replacing. If you have no old housings for comparison, cut the new pieces so that they curve smoothly. When you turn the handlebar, the housing should not pull or kink. Allow enough length for the rear derailleur to swing backward (Fig. 5.14) and forward (Fig. 5.15) freely.

3. With a nail or toothpick, open each Teflon sleeve-end that has been smashed shut by the cutter.

4. Place a ferrule over each housing end (Fig. 5.13). After the cable has been threaded into the housing (see next sections for details), clip the cable 1–2cm past the bolt and crimp on a cap to prevent fraying (Fig. 5.16).

5.14 **Rear derailleur swinging back to check housing length**

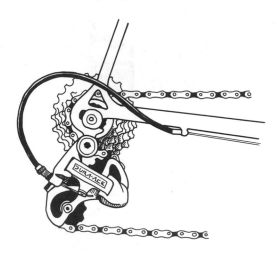

5.15 **Rear derailleur swinging forward to check housing length**

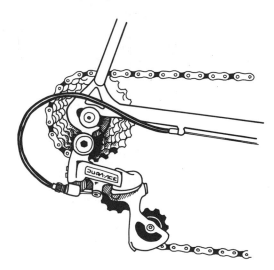

5.16 **Crimping the cable-end cap**

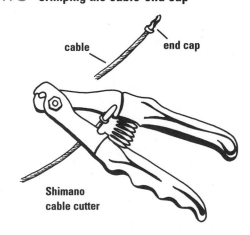

cable

end cap

Shimano
cable cutter

v–8 REPLACING SHIFT CABLE IN SHIMANO STI SHIFT/BRAKE LEVER

1. Disconnect the cable at the derailleur and snip off the cable-end cap (if installed).

2. Shift the inner chain-dump lever to the gear setting that lets the most cable out. This setting will be the highest-gear position for the rear shift lever (small cog) and the lowest for the front (small chainring).

3. Pull the brake lever to reveal the access hole for the shift cable; the hole is on the outboard side of the lever. On Dura-Ace levers, you must first remove a thin, black plastic cover with a small Phillips screwdriver to get at the access hole. Push the cable until the cable head emerges from the hole far enough to grab it. Pull out the old cable and recycle it.

4. The recessed hole into which the cable head seats should be visible through the access hole. Thread the new cable through the hole and out through the inboard side of the lever (Fig. 5.17).

5. Guide the cable through each housing segment (making sure each segment has a ferrule on the end; see Fig. 5.13) and cable stop and reconnect it at the cable-fixing bolt on the derailleur.

6. Clip the cable 1–2cm past the bolt and crimp on a cap to prevent fraying (Fig. 5.16).

v–9 REPLACING SHIFT CABLE IN CAMPAGNOLO ERGOPOWER LEVER

1. Disconnect the cable at the derailleur and snip off the cable-end cap (if installed).

2. Push the cable until the cable head emerges from the cable hole in the slot near the bottom of the lever (it's toward the outboard side—just outboard of the little gear teeth; Fig. 5.18). Push

the cable head out far enough to grab it. Pull out the old cable and recycle it.

3. Click the thumb lever until it will click no more.

4. Push the new cable in through the hole and up through the lever body until the cable emerges from the housing-entry hole at the upper base of the lever body on the outboard side.

5. Guide the cable through each housing segment (making sure each segment has a ferrule on the end; see Fig. 5.13) and cable stop and reconnect it at the cable-fixing bolt on the derailleur.

6. Clip the cable 1–2cm past the bolt and crimp on a cap to prevent fraying (Fig. 5.16).

NOTE: *The Ergopower cable hook (i.e., the enlarged, countersunk hole into which the cable head seats) is too small to fit a Shimano cable head—just another of those maddening parts' incompatibilities. You can file a Shimano cable head down enough to fit in, but expect to need to push hard with pliers to get the cable back out next time. It's simplest to just buy a new Campagnolo shift cable.*

v-10 REPLACING CABLE IN A DOWN-TUBE SHIFT LEVER, BAR-END LEVER, OR SHIFT LEVER ON AN AERO HANDLEBAR

1. Disconnect the cable at the derailleur and snip off the cable-end cap.

2. Flip the lever forward to the gear setting that lets the most cable out. This setting will be the highest gear position for the rear shift lever (small cog) and the lowest for the front (small chainring).

3. Push the cable until the cable head pops out of the hole in the shift lever. Pull out the old cable and recycle it.

4. Thread the new cable through the hole and out

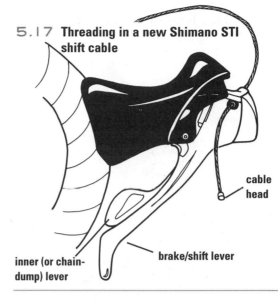

5.17 Threading in a new Shimano STI shift cable

cable head

inner (or chain-dump) lever

brake/shift lever

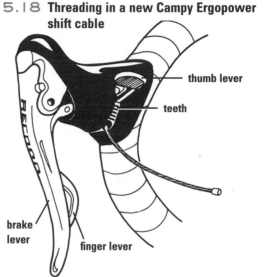

5.18 Threading in a new Campy Ergopower shift cable

thumb lever

teeth

brake lever

finger lever

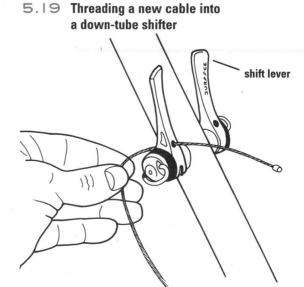

5.19 Threading a new cable into a down-tube shifter

shift lever

5.20 **Attaching rear-derailleur cable**

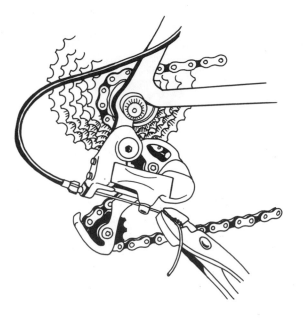

5.21 **Attaching front-derailleur cable**

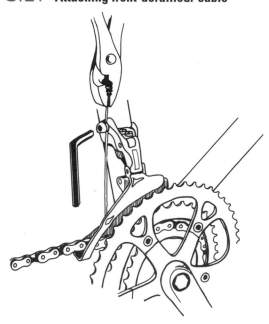

ATTACH

CABLE TO

REAR/FRONT

DERAILLEUR

—

FINAL CABLE

TOUCHES

through the other side of the lever (Fig. 5.19).

5. Guide the cable through each cable stop and housing segment (making sure each segment has a ferrule on the end; see Fig. 5.13) and reconnect it at the cable-fixing bolt on the derailleur.

6. Clip the cable 1–2cm past the bolt and crimp on a cap to prevent fraying (Fig. 5.16).

v–11 ATTACH CABLE TO REAR DERAILLEUR

1. Put the chain on the smallest cog so that the rear derailleur moves to the outside.

2. Run the cable through the barrel adjuster, and route it through each of the housing segments until you reach the cable-fixing bolt on the derailleur. Make sure that the rear shifter is on the highest-gear setting so that the maximum amount of cable is available to the derailleur.

3. Pull the cable taut and into its groove under the cable-fixing bolt (Fig. 5.20).

4. Tighten the bolt. On most derailleurs this step takes a 5mm Allen wrench.

5. Clip the cable 1–2cm past the bolt and crimp on a cap to prevent fraying (Fig. 5.16).

v–12 ATTACH CABLE TO FRONT DERAILLEUR

1. Shift the chain to the inner ring so that the derailleur moves farthest to the inside. This ensures that the maximum amount of cable is available to the derailleur.

2. With a 5mm hex key, tighten the cable to the cable anchor on the derailleur while pulling the cable taut with pliers. Be sure that the cable lies in the groove beneath the cable-fixing bolt (Fig. 5.21).

3. Clip the cable 1–2cm past the bolt and crimp on a cap to prevent fraying (Fig. 5.16).

v–13 FINAL CABLE TOUCHES

A high-quality cable assembly includes the cable-housing end ferrules (Fig. 5.13) throughout, and crimped cable caps (Fig. 5.16); cables are clipped about 1–2cm past the cable-clamp bolts.

v-14 CABLE LUBRICATION

New cables and housings with Teflon liners do not need to be lubricated. Old cables can be lubricated with chain lubricant. Standard bike grease can slow their movement, but some manufacturers recommend (and supply) their own molybdenum disulfide grease for cables.

1. Disconnect the cable at the derailleur, and clip off the cable-crimp end. Be aware that if the cable frays at all when clipped, you may not be able to slide it back in through the housings and may have to replace both the cable and its housings.

2. Coat with chain lubricant the areas of the cable that will be inside of the cable-housing segments. Squirt lubricant into each housing section.

NOTE: *If you have any trouble reinstalling the cable because of fraying, or the housings are dirty and rusty, you might as well replace both the cable and the housings.*

ANOTHER NOTE: *On bikes with a slotted chainstay cable stop, pull the housing out of the stop, slide it up the cable, and lubricate that section of cable without disconnecting it from the derailleur.*

v-15 REDUCE CABLE FRICTION

In addition to replacing your cables and housings with good-quality cables and lined housings, the following specific steps can improve shifting efficiency:

1. The most important friction-reducing steps are to route the cable so that it makes smooth bends and to make sure that it is just long enough that turning the handlebar does not increase the tension on the shift cables.

2. Choose cables that offer especially low friction. "Die-drawn" cables, which have been mechanically pulled through a die (a small hole in a piece of hard steel), move with lower friction than standard cables. Die-drawing flattens the outer strands, smoothing the cable surface. Thinner cables and Teflon-lined housings with a large inside diameter also reduce friction.

THE SHIFTERS

v-16 OPERATING INTEGRATED SHIFT/BRAKE LEVERS

a. Rear Shimano STI—right-hand lever

To shift to a larger cog (lower gear), push the brake/shift lever (the larger lever in Fig. 5.17) to the left (inward) with your fingers. The most you can move the chain is three cogs with a single push.

To shift to a smaller cog (higher gear), push the smaller lever to the left (inward) with your second finger. It will click only one gear at a time.

b. Front Shimano STI—left-hand lever

To shift to a larger chainring (higher gear), push the brake/shift lever (the larger lever) to the right (inward) with your fingers. It takes a firm push. If it moves a small click, but the chain does not climb up the outer ring, give another push. If you have a triple, you can shift only one chainring at a time.

To shift to a smaller chainring (lower gear), push the smaller lever to the right (inward) with your second finger. If you have a triple, you can shift only one chainring at a time.

You can feather the front derailleur so that it does not rub on the chain in a cross-gear (see §v-5 for more on this). When the chain is on the inner chainring, give the brake/shift lever a gentle inward push until you hear a soft click. When the chain is on the outer chainring, give the inner lever a gentle push until you feel the soft click. Feathering may take

THE SHIFTING SYSTEM

CABLE LUBRICATION
—
REDUCE CABLE FRICTION
—
OPERATING INTEGRATED SHIFT/BRAKE LEVERS

REPLACING
AND
INSTALLING
INTEGRATED
BRAKE/SHIFT
LEVERS
—
REHABILITATING
OR REPLACING
SHIFTER UNIT

some practice, as you can easily overdo it, dropping the chain onto the inner ring.

c. Rear Campagnolo Ergopower—right-hand lever

To shift to a larger cog (lower gear), push the finger lever (behind the brake lever; see Fig. 5.18) to the left (inward) with your fingers. Depending on model and year, you can move the chain as much as three cogs with a single push.

To shift to a smaller cog (higher gear), push the thumb lever down (yes, with your thumb). Depending on model and year, you can move the chain across three to ten cogs with a single push.

d. Front Campagnolo Ergopower—left-hand lever

To shift to a larger chainring (higher gear), push the finger lever (behind the brake lever) to the left (inward) with your fingers. If the chain does not climb up the outer ring, give another push. If you have a triple, you can shift only one chainring at a time.

To shift to a smaller chainring (lower gear), push the thumb lever down.

You can feather the front derailleur so that it does not rub on the chain in a cross-gear (see §v-5 for more on this). When the chain is on the inner chainring, give the finger lever a gentle inward push to move one click at a time. When the chain is on the outer chainring, give the thumb lever a single-click push at a time.

v-17 REPLACING AND INSTALLING INTEGRATED BRAKE/SHIFT LEVERS

Shifters can be replaced as an entire unit and sometimes as separate parts. Brake/shift levers are generally labeled right and left, but if you're in doubt, you can tell which is which because the levers should flip

to the inside. Here are the steps for you to replace the entire brake/shift lever unit:

1. Remove the handlebar tape and bar plugs.
2. Remove the old brake/shift lever by loosening its mounting bolt with a 5mm Allen wrench and sliding the lever assembly off. The position of the bolt varies. On current dual-control levers, it is on the outboard side of the lever under the lever hood. Slip the hex key down from the top between the lever body and the hood rather than trying to roll back the hood far enough to get at it from outside of the hood (Chapter 7, Fig. 7.11). On Campagnolo Ergopower, the bolt is on the outboard side toward the top; on Shimano STI it is on the middle of the outboard side.
3. Slide the new lever on the bar to where you like it. A good rule of thumb is to put a straightedge against the bottom of the bar and slide the lever down until its end touches the straightedge. The lever can sit a little higher than this, but generally not any lower. Put a long straightedge across the top of both levers to make sure that they are level with each other.
4. Tighten the mounting bolt.
5. Install the barrel-adjuster cable stops on the shifter bosses, if not already in place.
6. Install the cables (see §v-6 to §v-15 and Chapter 7, §vii-4).
7. Wrap the handlebar with tape (see Chapter 11, §xi-10).

v-18 REHABILITATING OR REPLACING SHIFTER UNIT ON STI INTEGRAL BRAKE/SHIFT LEVER

If you have a jammed Shimano STI shifter, you cannot really go into the mechanism like a watch-

5.22 Exploded nine-speed Dura-Ace STI lever

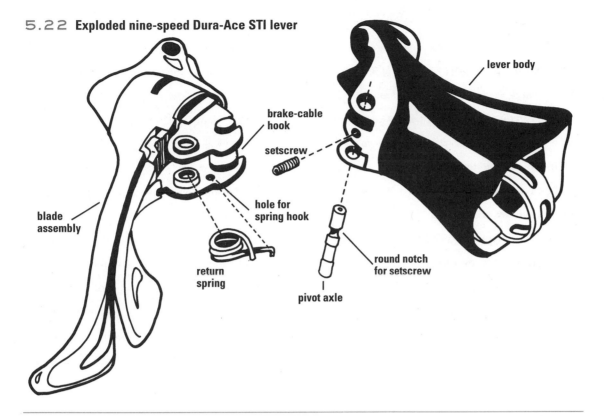

lever body

brake-cable hook

setscrew

blade assembly

hole for spring hook

return spring

pivot axle

round notch for setscrew

maker and replace parts. Shimano doesn't sell the internal parts separately, and opening the mechanism voids the warranty. But, with a little lube, you can often rehabilitate a sticky mechanism or an STI lever that does not always engage when you try to shift. Use the thin tube attachment on an aerosol chain lube to flush the guts of the lever from the side by sticking the aerosol tube into the little hole visible when you pull the brake; the hole is above the rounded upper section of the main lever on the noncable side. Many riders have used this technique to get years of extra life out of levers that otherwise looked destined for replacement. Don't do this over your carpet.

If that does not work, you can replace the entire shifter unit of two blades with the internal ratchet. Note that this approach may be false economy; you save the lever base, rubber hood, and band clamp but pay over half of the cost of a pair of levers for a single blade assembly. For a Dura-Ace ten-speed, you pay the same for an entire lever as for the blade assembly; for a Dura-Ace nine-speed, you pay about $15 more for an entire lever than for the blade assembly; and for a Dura-Ace eight-speed, you pay around $80 less for an entire lever than for the blade assembly! But if you find a bargain somewhere, here's the procedure:

1. Remove the shift and brake cables and the brake-cable hook from its notches.

2. With a 2mm hex key, remove the setscrew holding the pivot axle in place under the lever. Expect it to make noise unscrewing and be hard to remove. There is a lot of threadlock compound on it to keep it from vibrating loose.

3. Push out the axle with a blunt nail struck by a hammer, and catch the spring.

4. Pull off the old blade assembly (Fig. 5.22) and insert the new blade assembly.

NOTE: *If you have a lever that is FlightDeck-computer compatible, you will need to unscrew the cover on the inboard side of the lever under the gum hood and push the end of the wiring harness up through the lever as you pull off the blade. Fish the wires of the new blade back in the same way, and replace the cover to hold the little rubber part and the four terminals in place.*

5. Replace the return spring and axle. The return-spring hook goes in the hole adjacent to the cable-hook notches, and its other end must sit on the shelf adjacent the setscrew, not down in the wide notch in the lever body. Line up the rounded groove in the axle with the setscrew.

6. Replace the setscrew, putting some threadlock compound on it first.

7. Replace the cable hook into its notches.

v-19 OVERHAULING CAMPAGNOLO ERGOPOWER LEVERS

LEVEL 3

This is an extremely satisfying maintenance task. As with any mechanism that has lots of precision internal parts, it can be great fun, if you are in the right state of mind, to take an Ergopower lever all apart, clean it up, put it back together, and feel it work more smoothly afterward. You can also increase the number of speeds in your lever; see the Pro Tip sidebar on Increasing (or Decreasing) the Number of Speeds in Your Lever.

Ride enough hours with your levers, especially in rain and muck, and they will get dirty inside and will work so much better if you clean 'em up and regrease 'em. Also, every Ergopower lever has two little G-shaped springs (Figs. 5.23A and 5.23B) that click into teeth in a ratchet, giving you the indexing steps. These springs can get worn, flattened, or bro-

ken, and shifting performance will drop off or cease to exist. These G-springs are the same for every model and year, so get a couple, if you think you need them, and follow along. Your levers will be good as new again!

As is typical with Campagnolo components, every little Ergopower part is replaceable. Refer to the exploded diagrams, Figure 5.23A (eight-speed right-hand lever) and Figure 5.23B (nine- or ten-speed right-hand lever). You can also magnify all those parts and find their part numbers for your particular year and model of lever on Campagnolo's Web site, www.campagnolo.com.

The following instructions cover overhaul and lubrication, as well as replacing broken or damaged index springs and other parts. They also cover replacing ratchets to change the number of speeds. When I mention eight-speed levers, I am referring to 1992–1997 Ergopower levers (Fig. 5.23A), both right and left. The lever body and the rubber hood come to a point on top of these (and the lever body allows a brake cable to be installed "old-style" straight into the top of the lever, as well as "aero-style" under the handlebar tape). The reference to nine- and ten-speed levers applies to 1999 and later levers (both sides) whose lever body and rubber hood are rounded on top (Fig. 5.23B) and only allow the brake cable to be routed under the tape to the base of the lever.

NOTE: *The internals of 1998 nine-speed levers are similar to those of an eight-speed lever. On the outside, 1998 levers look like the lever in Figure 5.23B, but a 1998 lever will not have a bump on the inboard side of the rubber cover for the button to control an ErgoBrain computer. Also, a Record 1998 lever will be aluminum, whereas from 1999 on, the lever will be carbon fiber.*

5.23A Exploded Campagnolo Ergopower lever—eight-speed

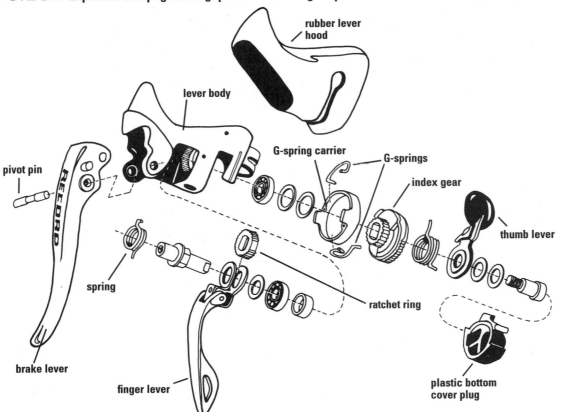

rubber lever hood

lever body

G-spring carrier

G-springs

index gear

pivot pin

RECORD

spring

thumb lever

ratchet ring

brake lever

finger lever

plastic bottom cover plug

5.23B Exploded Campagnolo Ergopower lever—nine-speed
(ten-speed has a different bottom bushing
and washer, but is otherwise the same)

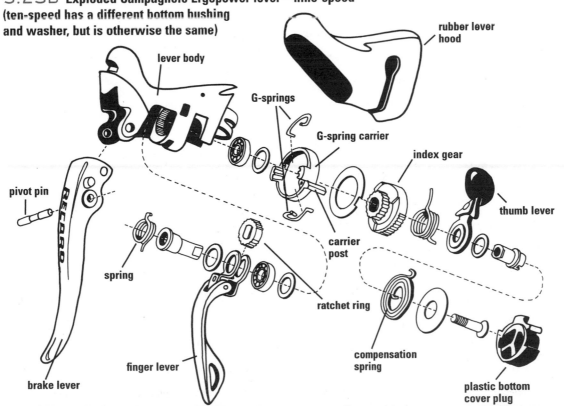

rubber lever hood

lever body

G-springs

G-spring carrier

index gear

pivot pin

RECORD

spring

thumb lever

carrier post

ratchet ring

finger lever

compensation spring

brake lever

plastic bottom cover plug

OVERHAULING

ERGOPOWER

LEVERS

1. Remove the rubber hood—it's easier to pull it off the base of the lever, but it will come off over the top as well. On composite lever bodies, pull off the plastic piece that covers the bottom of the shift mechanism; use pliers if necessary.

2. Push out the lever-pivot pin by tapping it out with a blunt nail and a hammer. Support the lever body near the pin so that the edge of the lever does not flex outward as you tap. Holding the lever body flat on a block of wood with a drilled hole that is lined up under the pin does the trick nicely. Pull off the brake lever.

3. Clamp the lever body onto the end of a handlebar held in a vise so that the bar-clamp strap is right at the edge of the bar and the lower part of the lever body is hanging off the end of the bar; you want to be able to get at the lever's mechanism from the bottom. Hold the bar in the vise so that the lever is upside down.

    (a) With a nine- or ten-speed lever, shift to the lowest-gear position with the finger lever to release tension on the flat coil spring at the bottom of the lever; you can see it stick out around the large flat washer when you get to the low-gear position.

    (b) With an eight-speed lever, you do the opposite; shift the thumb lever to the highest-gear position.

4. Hold the top nut with one hex key while you unscrew and remove the bottom bolt with another hex key. On a nine- or ten-speed lever, the top nut takes a 5mm hex key, and the lower bolt takes a 3mm (avoid using a 3mm ball-end hex key on this bolt, as you can snap it off—and you won't be able to get the ball out of the bolt, because Campagnolo's thread-locking com-

pound should have been used to hold the space shuttle's tiles on). On an eight-speed lever, the nut and bolt both accept 4mm hex keys, and the bolt may have a brass washer or two on it, so watch for them.

IMPORTANT NOTE: *The bolt on a right-hand eight-speed lever is left-hand threaded, so it unscrews in a clockwise direction! Also note that 1998 nine-speed levers are configured this way.*

5. With an eight-speed lever, skip to step 7. With a nine- or ten-speed lever, remove the bottom washer, pop the compensation spring (a flat coil) out with a thin screwdriver, and take out the thin, play-removing washer, if installed.

6. Hold the (nine- or ten-speed) assembly together with your thumb while shifting to the high-gear position with the thumb lever. Hold the thumb lever in place and, with needle-nose pliers, pull out the next part: the bushing in the center of the coil spring.

7. Pop out the thumb lever, the ratchet spring, the ratchet (also known as the index gear—see Figs. 5.23A and 5.23B), and, on a nine- and ten-speed right-hand lever, the notched washer. The two G-shaped index springs, which are the most common replacement item in Ergopower levers, are now visible. One or two washers that sit on top of the cartridge bearing underneath may come out with the ratchet. If not, you can pop the washer(s) out, if installed, after step 8 and clean, grease, and replace it/them at that time.

8. Pop the G-spring carrier and G-springs out. Clean and grease all parts.

9. With an eight-speed lever, unless you want to replace the top ratchet ring, skip to step 11. To

OVERHAULING
ERGOPOWER
LEVERS

upgrade from a nine- to a ten-speed, you need to install a new ratchet ring in the finger-lever assembly, which will come out as is now, with the pins and bearings intact. Flip the lever over so that it is clamped upright on the bar. It is hard to get the top spring out; grab it with thin needle-nose pliers and twist it upward with the other end still hooked into the loop atop the finger lever. Pull the finger-lever assembly out. Push the center pivot out. Now you can slip the ratchet ring out and replace it with a ten-speed one.

10. Orient the ratchet ring with the number (9 or 10) up (it will be pointed forward when the lever is installed on the bike). Push the pivot nut and washer through the ratchet ring (line up the flats). Hook the top spring's short hook onto the hook atop the finger lever. Push the assembly back in place, hooking the long spring end into the notch in the lever body with needle-nose pliers. Flip the lever back over to get at the bottom side again.

11. Put the new (or clean and regreased) G-springs on the underside of the G-spring carrier, and coat them with grease to hold them in place. Push the G-spring carrier back into place in the lever body.

12. On a right-hand nine- and ten-speed lever, replace the notched washer on top of the G-spring carrier with the washer's tab facing down. The notch fits around the vertical post on the G-spring carrier. This washer (and the vertical carrier post) do not exist in left-hand nine- and ten-speed levers or in eight-speed ones, so ignore this step.

13. Drop the (greased) indexing ratchet down onto the pivot post so that the flats in both parts interlock. Now is the time to put in a new ratchet if you are changing speeds (for instance, from eight to nine or from nine to ten) or if your ratchet is worn. Make sure that the cable-hook tab on the ratchet butts against the outboard side of the lever body. Slip the long end of the return spring down into the ratchet, out the ratchet's slot, and into the hole in the lever body, dropping the (greased) spring down into the ratchet with the short end of the spring sticking up.

14. Push the small hole in the thumb-lever ring onto the upward-pointing end of the return spring inside the ratchet; the convex side of the ring should face the spring. Push back on the thumb-lever ring to align it over the ratchet.

15. On nine- and ten-speed levers, while holding the thumb-lever ring down, push the central bushing down through the ring. Push down and turn the bushing (on a 1998 nine-speed lever, use a 5mm hex key; on later nine-speed and all ten-speed levers, use a large screwdriver in the larger set of slots) until the flats on the end of the bushing engage the flats on the end of the top bolt protruding into the ratchet. If there were washers on the bushing, make sure you have installed them.

(a) On 1999 and later nine-speed and on ten-speed levers, the bushing is larger in diameter and has flats that engage over the flats on the top bolt, rather than inserting into them. An unfortunate consequence of this larger diameter of the bushing is that it is harder to push the bushing into place without disengaging the return spring from the thumb lever. Keep at it until you get it.

OVERHAULING ERGOPOWER LEVERS

OVERHAULING
ERGOPOWER
LEVERS

PRO TIP

INCREASING (OR DECREASING) THE NUMBER OF SPEEDS IN YOUR LEVER

While you are verhauling your right-hand lever, you can make an eight-speed lever into a nine-speed one, or a nine-speed lever into a ten-speed one, and vice versa.

You cannot change an eight-speed lever into a ten-speed one (sorry), as the indexing ratchet gear is a different size; compare the index gear in the lever in Figure 5.23A to the one in Figure 5.23B. Also, you cannot upgrade a 1998 nine-speed Ergopower lever (the first year they were made). On the outside, 1998 levers look like the lever in Figure 5.23B, but the internals are different. A 1998 lever will not have a bump on the inboard side of the rubber cover for the button to control an ErgoBrain computer. Also, a Record 1998 lever will be aluminum, whereas from 1999 on, the lever will be carbon fiber.

To upgrade an eight-speed lever, you need only buy a nine-speed index gear (ratchet) for that lever type. To upgrade a nine-speed lever, you will want to buy both a ten-speed index gear and a ten-speed ratchet ring. Your shifter will work with the old nine-speed ratchet ring, but not as well, and as long as you are going to all of this trouble . . . .

(b)　On eight-speed levers, insert the bolt, with any washers it had on it, down through the thumb-lever ring until it engages the nut. While holding the nut with a 4mm hex key inserted into the top of the lever, tighten the bolt with another 4mm hex key. Remember that the bolt is reverse-threaded on a right-hand eight-speed lever! Skip to step 18 now.

16. Steps 16–19 only apply to nine- and ten-speed levers. While holding the bushing in place (it will turn), shift the finger lever all the way to the lowest-gear position.

17. Lay the flat compensation spring on top of the thumb-lever ring. The inner end of the spring hooks into a notch in the end of the bushing, and the outer spring end hooks around either the post on the spring carrier (right-hand lever) or the outboard edge of the lever body (left-hand lever).

18. Holding the flat spring down, tip the bushing back and forth until you feel the flats in the end of the bushing disengage from the flats on the top bolt (use the 5mm hex key on a 1998 nine-speed lever and the large screwdriver on 1999 and later nine-speed and ten-speed levers). Still holding the spring down, turn the bushing about a quarter to a half turn to wind the spring (counterclockwise on the right lever; clockwise on the left lever), and jiggle the bushing back and forth with the 5mm hex key or large screwdriver until its flats reengage the top bolt.

NOTE: *Campagnolo suggests an alternative method for steps 17 and 18, which I find to be more of a hassle, but which you may prefer: When laying the flat spring in place, hook the inner spring end into a more advanced bushing slot; the outer end of the spring will be squished up against the back wall of the lever body. While holding the bushing with the 5mm hex key or large screwdriver, pull the outer spring end with a*

5.24 Exploded Campagnolo Nuovo Record frictional lever

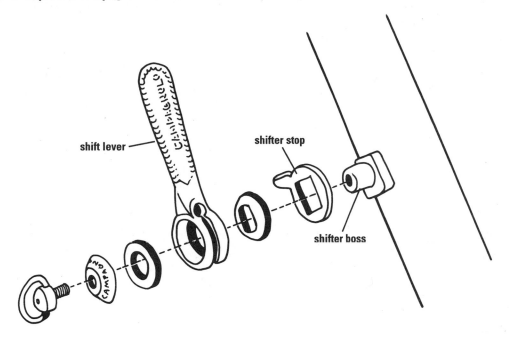

shift lever

shifter stop

shifter boss

hooked awl or small crochet hook, and pull it to the post (right-hand lever) or to the notch in the lever-body's outboard wall (left-hand lever).

19. Holding the flat spring down with your finger, slide the large washer under your finger and on top of the flat spring so that it snaps over the end of the bushing. The 1999 and later nine-speed or ten-speed washer has two notches to fit the larger slots in the bushing. Start the 3mm Allen bolt while holding the other end of the pivot shaft with a 5mm hex key. Snug the bolt down.

20. Check the mechanism. If it works smoothly, reinstall the brake lever, the bottom cap, and the rubber hood (engaging all of the hood's nubs into holes, slots, and protrusions in the lever body). It's easier to pull the hood on over the levers from the front than from the base of the lever body.

Congratulations! You are done!

v-20 OVERHAUL OR REPLACE DOWN-TUBE SHIFTERS

Much of this instruction will also apply to shifters attached to bosses on the end of aero bars as well as bar-end shifters.

1. Remove the screw holding the shifter to the frame's shifter boss, and pull the shifter off.

2. If you have a frictional shifter (Fig. 5.24), all of its pieces come apart. To get the shifter working smoothly, simply clean the parts, grease them, and put them back together. If you have an indexed Shimano shifter, the mechanism cannot be serviced. Buy a new lever if the mechanism has failed.

3. Replace the stop piece that fits over the square base of the shifter boss. With old frictional shifters, the shifter stop boss is simply a washer with a square hole and a bent tab (Fig. 5.24). With more recent shifters, the stop is a cast piece that has a square stop on it that is to be lined up along the down tube projecting forward.

4. Put on the brass or plastic washer, slip the shifter on, and install the top washer(s) and the screw. Some Shimano left-hand shifters have a return spring in them and must be installed with the lever flipped down in order to fit properly over the stop on the base. It is not until the screw is tightened down that one of these spring-loaded levers will stay in place when rotated counterclockwise to its starting position, pointed forward, parallel with the down tube.

5. Install the cable and tighten it at the derailleur.

DERAILLEUR MAINTENANCE

v-21 JOCKEY-WHEEL MAINTENANCE

With proper attention, the jockey wheels on the rear derailleur will last a long time. They should be wiped off every time you wipe down and lubricate the chain (daily is a good idea). The only other maintenance involved is a light overhaul every 1,000–2,000 miles in dirty conditions; otherwise an overhaul every time you replace your chain should be frequent enough.

The mounting bolts on jockey wheels also should be checked regularly. If a loose jockey-wheel bolt falls off while you are riding, you'll need to follow the procedure for a "broken rear derailleur on the road" in Chapter 3, §iii-12.

Standard jockey wheels turn on a bushing made of steel or ceramic. Some high-end models have cartridge bearings. A washer with an inwardly bent rim is usually installed on both sides of a standard jockey wheel. Some jockey wheels also have rubber seals around the edges of these washers.

v-22 OVERHAULING STANDARD JOCKEY WHEELS

1. Remove the jockey wheels by undoing the bolts

JOCKEY-WHEEL MAINTENANCE

—

OVERHAULING STANDARD JOCKEY WHEELS

—

OVERHAULING CARTRIDGE-BEARING JOCKEY WHEELS

5.25A Exploded derailleur

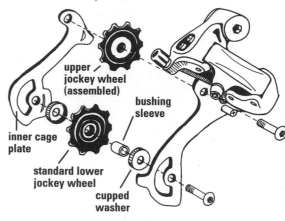

upper jockey wheel (assembled)

inner cage plate

bushing sleeve

standard lower jockey wheel

cupped washer

5.25B Exploded jockey wheel with cartridge bearing

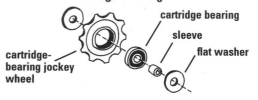

cartridge bearing

sleeve

flat washer

cartridge-bearing jockey wheel

that hold them to the derailleur (Fig. 5.25A). This usually takes a 3mm Allen wrench.

2. Wipe all parts clean with a rag. Solvent is usually not necessary but can be used.

3. If the teeth on the jockey wheels are broken or badly worn, replace the wheels.

4. Smear grease over each bolt and bushing and inside each jockey wheel.

5. Reassemble the jockey wheels onto the derailleur. Be sure to orient the inner cage plate properly (the larger part of the inner cage plate should be at the bottom jockey wheel).

v-23 OVERHAULING CARTRIDGE-BEARING JOCKEY WHEELS

LEVEL 2

If the cartridge bearings in high-end jockey wheels (Fig. 5.25B) do not turn freely, they can usually be overhauled.

5.26 Rear-derailleur pivots

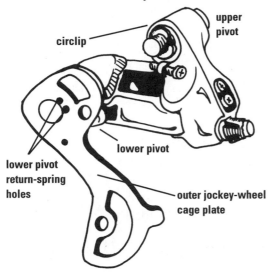

upper pivot

circlip

lower pivot

lower pivot return-spring holes

outer jockey-wheel cage plate

1. With a single-edge razor blade, pry the plastic cover (bearing seal) off one side or—preferably—both sides of the bearing (Fig. 6.29). (Steel covers on bearings cannot be removed. If such a bearing is not turning freely, the entire bearing needs to be replaced.)

2. With a toothbrush and solvent, clean the bearings. Use citrus-based solvent, and wear gloves and glasses to protect skin and eyes.

3. Blow the solvent out with compressed air or your tire pump, and allow the parts to dry.

4. Squeeze new grease into the bearings and replace the covers.

v-24 REAR-DERAILLEUR OVERHAUL

Except for the jockey wheels and pivots, most rear derailleurs are not designed to be disassembled. If the pivot springs seem to be operating effectively, all you need to do is overhaul the jockey wheels (see previous section), and clean and lubricate the parallelogram and spring as described next.

v-25 MINOR REAR-DERAILLEUR WIPE AND LUBE

1. Clean the derailleur as well as you can with a rag, including between the parallelogram plates.

2. Drip chain lube on both ends of every pivot pin.

3. If you have the clothespin-type spring between the plates of the parallelogram (as opposed to the full coil spring running diagonally from one corner of the parallelogram to the other), put a dab of grease where the spring end slides along the underside of the outer parallelogram plate.

v-26 REAR-DERAILLEUR UPPER-PIVOT OVERHAUL

LEVEL 3

These steps apply to Shimano derailleurs.

CAUTION: *Don't do this job unless you absolutely have to in order to rehabilitate a poorly functioning rear derailleur. The strong spring resists your best intentions at reassembly, and you may not be able to get the derailleur back together properly, even with a second set of hands.*

1. Remove the rear derailleur; it usually takes a 5mm Allen wrench to unscrew it from the frame and to disconnect the cable.

2. With a screwdriver, pry the circlip (Fig. 5.26) off the threaded end of the mounting bolt. Don't lose it; it will tend to fly when it comes off.

3. Pull the mounting bolt and the upper pivot spring out of the derailleur (Fig. 5.1).

4. Clean and dry the parts with or without the use of a solvent.

5. Grease liberally, and replace the parts.

6. Each end of the spring has a hole that it needs to go into. If there are several holes, and you don't

THE SHIFTING SYSTEM

REAR-
DERAILLEUR
OVERHAUL
—
MINOR REAR-
DERAILLEUR
WIPE AND LUBE
—
REAR-
DERAILLEUR
UPPER–PIVOT
OVERHAUL

5.27 **Removing and installing lower-pivot setscrew from a modern Shimano rear derailleur**

5.28 **Removing and replacing the cage-stop screw from an older Shimano rear derailleur**

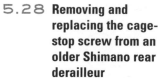

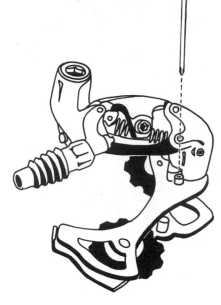

know which one it was in before, try the middle one. (If the derailleur does not keep tension on the chain well enough, you can later try another hole that increases the spring tension.)

7. Push it all together and replace the circlip with pliers.

v–27 REAR-DERAILLEUR LOWER-PIVOT OVERHAUL AND SPRING TENSION ADJUSTMENT

LEVEL 3

On its 10-speed rear derailleurs, Campagnolo has eliminated the b-screw, the traditional means of adjusting the spacing between the upper jockey wheel and the cogs (see §v-2f). Instead, an external screw engaging a number of external teeth around the base of the rear derailleur's lower pivot performs the adjustment.

If shifting is sluggish, simply tighten the lower-pivot spring by turning the adjusting screw clock-wise until the upper jockey wheel is close to the cog but not pinching the chain against it. Perform this adjustment when the chain is on the inner chainring and on the largest cog.

Similarly, if the drivetrain is making noise or running roughly in low gears (because the chain is bumping along or being pinched between the cog and the upper jockey wheel), turn the adjusting screw counter-clockwise to loosen the lower-pivot spring. This drops the upper jockey wheel down away from the cogs.

On a Shimano rear derailleur, fine-tuning the lower-pivot spring tension is a secondary adjustment to turning the b-screw, and the derailleur must first be disassembled to perform the lower-pivot spring tension adjustment.

1. Remove the derailleur from the bike.

2. Shimano derailleurs can be divided into two types: those that have a setscrew on the side of the lower pivot, and older ones that do not.

5.29 **Removing and replacing the lower-pivot center bolt from an older Shamano rear derailleur**

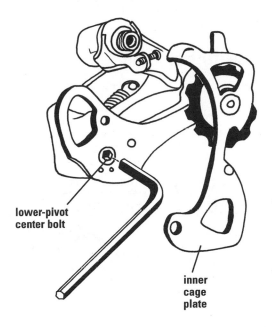

lower-pivot
center bolt

inner
cage
plate

5.30 **Removing and replacing the lower-pivot return spring in one of the two holes in the jockey-wheel inner cage plate**

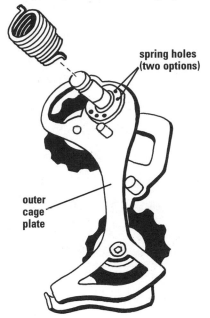

spring holes
(two options)

outer
cage
plate

(a) If yours has a setscrew (Fig. 5.27), remove it using a 2mm hex key and pull the jockey cage away from the derailleur.

(b) If your derailleur has no setscrew, find and unscrew the tall cage-stop screw on the derailleur cage (Fig. 5.28); it is located near the upper jockey wheel. It is designed to maintain tension on the lower pivot spring and prevent the cage from springing all the way around. Once the stop screw is removed, slowly guide the cage around until the spring tension is relieved. Remove the upper jockey wheel and unscrew the pivot bolt from the back with a 5mm (sometimes 6mm) hex key (Fig. 5.29). Be sure to hold the jockey-wheel cage to keep it from twisting.

3. Determine in which hole the spring end has been placed, and then remove the spring.

4. Clean and dry the bolt and the spring with a rag.

A solvent may be used if necessary.

5. Grease all parts liberally.

6. Replace the spring ends in their holes in the derailleur body and jockey-wheel cage (Fig. 5.30). Put the spring in the adjacent hole in the jockey-wheel cage plate if you want to increase its tension. Increasing the lower-pivot spring tension pulls the chain tighter; if you have problems with the chain drooping or falling off, increasing the spring tension is worth a try.

7. Replace the derailleur.

(a) If your derailleur has a setscrew, push the assembly together, wind the spring, and replace the setscrew (Fig. 5.27).

(b) If your derailleur does not take a setscrew, wind the jockey-wheel cage back around, screw it all back together with the pivot bolt (Fig. 5.27), and replace the stop screw (Fig. 5.28).

REAR-
DERAILLEUR
LOWER-PIVOT
OVERHAUL

v-28 REAR-DERAILLEUR PARALLELOGRAM OVERHAUL

Very few derailleurs can be completely disassembled. Those that can (Mavic cable-actuated derailleurs) have removable pins holding them together. The pins have circlips on the ends that can be popped off with a screwdriver to remove the pins. If you have such a derailleur, disassemble it in a box so that the circlips do not fly away, and make note of where each part belongs so that you can get it back together again. Clean all parts, grease them, and reassemble.

v-29 REPLACING STOCK REAR-DERAILLEUR BOLTS WITH LIGHTWEIGHT VERSIONS

Lightweight aluminum and titanium derailleur bolts are available as replacement items for many derailleurs. Removing and replacing jockey-wheel bolts is simple, as long as you keep all of the jockey-wheel parts together (Fig. 5.25) and put the inner cage plate back on the way it was. Upper and lower pivot bolts (Fig. 5.1) are replaced following the instructions outlined earlier in this chapter for overhauling the pivots (§v-26 and §v-27).

TROUBLESHOOTING DERAILLEUR AND SHIFTER PROBLEMS

Once you have made the adjustments outlined previously in this chapter, the drivetrain should operate quietly and shift smoothly. The drivetrain should stay in gear, even if you turn the crank backward. If you cannot fine-tune the adjustment so that each click with the right shifter results in a clean, quick shift, you need to check some of the following possibilities. For skipping- and jumping-chain problems, see also the Troubleshooting section at the end of Chapter 4.

v-30 SHIFTER COMPATIBILITY

Make certain that the shifter and derailleur are made by the same company, are compatible models, and are made for the cogset you have (brand, model, and number of cogs). If the brands are different, make sure that they are designed to work together. For instance, Modolo makes an integral brake/shift lever that can be set up to work either Campagnolo or Shimano derailleurs. If the shifter and derailleur are incompatible, you will need to change one of them (probably whichever item is less costly). For more on compatibility, see §v-35.

v-31 STICKY CABLES

Check to see whether the derailleur cables run smoothly through the housing. Sticky cable movement will cause sluggish shifting. Lubricate the cable by smearing it with chain lube or a specific lubricant that came with your shifters (§v-14). If lubricating the cable does not help, replace the cable and housing (see §v-6 to §v-13).

v-32 BENT REAR-DERAILLEUR HANGER

A bent hanger will hold the derailleur crooked and bedevil shifting. Instructions for straightening the hanger are in Chapter 15, §xv-4.

v-33 BENT REAR-DERAILLEUR CAGE

A bent derailleur cage will align the jockey wheels at an angle. Mild bending can be straightened by hand; eyeball the crankset for a vertical reference.

REAR-DERAILLEUR PARALLELOGRAM OVERHAUL
—
REPLACING STOCK REAR-DERAILLEUR BOLTS
—
SHIFTER COMPATABILITY
—
STICKY CABLES
—
BENT REAR-DERAILLEUR HANGER/CAGE

v–34 LOOSE OR WORN-OUT REAR DERAILLEUR

Grab the derailleur and twist it with your fingers to feel for excessive play. Loose pivots, a symptom of a worn-out rear derailleur, will cause the rear derailleur to be loose and floppy. Replace it if it has this problem.

A loose mounting bolt will also mess up shifting by allowing the derailleur to flop around. Tighten the bolt.

v–35 COMPATIBILITY ISSUES BETWEEN BRANDS, MODELS, AND FIVE-, SIX-, SEVEN-, EIGHT-, NINE-, AND TEN-SPEEDS

The number of rear cogs on a road bike keeps going up every few years. But does any of the old stuff work with any of the new stuff? And can you mix Shimano and Campagnolo parts?

Well, if you have resolutely stuck with your old frictional down-tube shifters, you can let Campagnolo and Shimano throw however many cogs they want at you, and you will still be able to shift. That old Campagnolo Nuovo Record shifter and derailleur worked on five cogs, six cogs, seven cogs, eight cogs, nine cogs, and it will probably work on ten cogs! Modern indexed systems shift more precisely, but they don't offer that kind of flexibility.

Compatibility problems occur because the chain required gets narrower as the number of cogs goes up. The spacing also narrows between chainrings, between rear-derailleur jockey-wheel plates, between front-derailleur cage plates, and between the right-rear hub flange and the largest cog. Also, the rear hub axles have gotten longer. The spacing between rear dropouts (and hence the rear-axle "overlock" dimension) was at 120mm during five-speed days, 126mm during the six-

and seven-speed era, and it is now 130mm for eight, nine, and ten speeds.

a. Threaded freewheels

The five-, six-, and seven-speed era marked the beginning of the transition from freewheels that threaded onto the rear hub to cassette freehubs built into the hub onto which separate cogs could be installed. With some minor exceptions, freewheels were completely compatible with every hub, because nearly all shared the same threading. Spacers sometimes had to be moved around from one end of the axle to the other to prevent the chain from dragging on the frame in the smallest cog. And, of course, you had to get a longer axle and redish the wheel when frames went from 120mm to 126mm rear spacing. But that was about it.

Freewheels did appear with eight speeds so that you could still space your old hub one more time with a new axle to 130mm. But freewheel makers threw in the towel when we hit nine speeds.

Five-speed freewheel cogs were spaced farther apart than current cogs, and there was no consistency of cog spacing between brands or even between different pairs of cogs on the same freewheel. There did not have to be, because the rider was manually lining up the derailleur with each cog. You were also lucky to have a thirteen-tooth first cog, rather than the fourteen-tooth first cog that the previous generation saw as a high gear.

The first Suntour six-speed freewheels were called "Ultra-6" and had narrower spacing between cogs (and a narrower chain) so that they would fit on a 120mm rear hub. Not everyone embraced narrowness, but many riders wanted twelve-tooth cogs. Splitting the difference, many frames at the end of the 1970s (especially Italian ones) were built with

126mm rear spacing and equipped with six-speed freewheels with cogs set at the old wide spacing.

Suntour answered with "Ultra-7" narrow-spaced freewheels and chains. Sedis started making narrow chains as well, and narrow spacing became the standard, carrying on into eight-speed bikes.

b. Cassette freehubs

Shimano's spacing between cogs has gone from 3.70mm for five- and six-speed, to 3.10mm for seven-speed, 3.00mm for eight-speed, 2.56mm for nine-speed, and 2.35mm for ten-speed bikes. The original Shimano freehubs appeared around 1980 and accepted six speeds widely spaced on a 126mm hub. The first five cogs were splined to fit on the splined freehub body, and the last cog threaded on. Shimano chains, called "Uniglide," were wide and had the bent-plate configuration of present-day Shimano chains. Shimano began making its first indexed shifting systems in the mid-1980s as well.

When Suntour came out with narrow Ultra-7 freewheels in the early 1980s, Shimano countered with wider freehub bodies that fit seven widely spaced cogs and the wide Shimano chain. These hubs had unique flanges with all of the spokes emerging on the outside to reduce wheel-dish problems brought on by the wide cassette on a 126mm hub. The wheels still fell apart under the loads of big riders, though. The smallest cog still threaded on, and all of the spline grooves were the same width, but the width caused the first freehub incompatibility with previous models.

In the second half of the 1980s, Shimano succumbed to the rising popularity of narrow chains, and it made narrow bent-plate (Uniglide) chains. Its new freehub body was the old six-speed length, and it fit seven narrowly spaced cogs. But the new cogs

would not fit on the old freehub bodies for two reasons. The new freehubs were splined end-to-end and had internal threads at the outboard end to fit a lockring holding the cogs on instead of a threaded small cog. And one spline groove was wider than the others, because the new cogs had shifting ramps that had to be oriented a particular way relative to the adjacent cog in order to shift properly. You could have weathered the short-lived, wide, seven-speed freehubs, but now you really had to throw out all of your old wheels and cogs.

The 1990s began with the introduction of eight speeds. Shimano had dictated that frames now had to have 130mm rear ends to accommodate new hubs with wider freehub bodies. The one-wide-spline arrangement and threaded lockrings continued, but you could not fit eight cogs on a seven-speed body.

The advance to eight speeds set the stage for nine speeds, which had narrower spacing, a narrower chain, and fit on eight-speed freehubs at first. But the desire for an eleven-tooth cog forced the reduction of the freehub diameter by removing the outboard 2–3mm of spline ridges, so that you had to get new hubs again (unless you were handy enough with a file or a grinder to knock off the last couple of millimeters of the spline ridges to be flush with the freehub outer diameter). This Shimano freehub configuration carries on into the current millennium.

With the advent of ten-speed cogs, the freehub body changed again, utilizing deeper spline valleys so that aluminum freehub bodies would not get so torn up by the cogs. The outer diameter of the bottom of the spline valleys in the freehub body remains unchanged; therefore ten-speed cogs will fit on nine-speed freehub bodies. But nine-speed Shimano cogs will not fit on Shimano ten-speed freehub bodies.

But what about Suntour, Mavic, and Campagnolo? Well, all of them began making freehub bodies and cogs with their own spline configurations, and only Campagnolo's systems survived the shakeout. Suntour disappeared completely from the road bike market, while Mavic went with the flow, making Shimano- and Campagnolo-compatible hubs, wheels, and even cogs. Campagnolo, the great, reliable, and unchanging bastion of compatibility and small-parts availability in the 1970s and early 1980s, changed its eight-speed freehub body when it came out with nine speeds. Campagnolo nine-speed freehub bodies have much deeper splines that do not fit Campy eight-speed cogs, but fortunately its ten-speed cogsets fit on the same Campy nine-speed freehub bodies. The ultranarrow, 6.1mm-wide, ten-speed chain allows ten cogs to fit in the same space that used to only accept nine with the wider nine-speed chain and cogset. The tooth-to-tooth distance on a Campagnolo nine-speed is 4.55mm; it is 4.15mm on ten-speed.

c. Chainrings

The spacing between chainrings keeps getting narrower with more speeds, as does the width and index-spacing of the front derailleur. If you have upgraded piecemeal, you may find your nine- or ten-speed chain falling between the two chainrings held over from an earlier seven- or eight-speed system. The narrow chain will generally slip uselessly as you pedal, but it can jam between the rings as well, causing all sorts of expensive havoc.

Chainring teeth are made to fit more closely together, either by reducing the thickness of the chainring-mounting flats on the crank spider arms or by offsetting the teeth to one side of the chainring. Shimano seven-, eight-, nine-, and ten-speed spider-arm mounting tabs are all the same thickness, but the teeth on Shimano nine- and ten-speed chainrings are offset toward each other.

Campagnolo's spider arms got thinner when going from seven- and eight-speeds to nine-speed, but the chainring teeth got offset going to ten-speed, and the spider arms stayed the same as nine-speed. You can upgrade a Campagnolo nine-speed crank to a ten-speed system by changing the chain rings.

In general, I have encountered no problems when using nine-speed cranks and chainrings with ten-speed drivetrains from either Campagnolo or Shimano.

Compact-drive double cranks have smaller chainrings, with 34 and 48, 34 and 50, or 36 and 50 teeth on the chainrings of each pair—designated 34-38-, 34-50-, and 36-50 tooth chainrings, respectively. These cranks have a 110mm bolt-circle diameter, rather than the 130mm of Shimano or the 135mm or (old) 144mm bolt-circle diameters of Campagnolo. With the smaller curvature to the chainrings, double front derailleurs do not work great, although they do work. Campagnolo's CT system works well; it has a dedicated compact crank with a dedicated compact front derailleur. An IRD or FSA compact front derailleur often works better with FSA and other brands of compact cranks than with a standard Shimano or standard or compact Campagnolo front derailleur.

d. Shifting compatibility of models within brands

All Campagnolo shifting-system components can be interchanged within models. In other words, you can use Athena nine-speed Ergopower shifters with a Veloce rear derailleur, Mirage front derailleur, Record cogs, Chorus crank, and Centaur hub. The same holds true if all components are eight-speed.

THE SHIFTING SYSTEM

COMPATABILITY

ISSUES

Shimano components have more interchangeability exceptions. Until nine-speed bikes came out, the stroke length for Dura-Ace derailleurs was different from all other Shimano derailleurs, mountain or road. Put another way, you could use any Shimano shifter you wanted with any Shimano derailleur except that Dura-Ace was only compatible with Dura-Ace.

With the advent of nine speeds, all Shimano rear derailleurs and shifters work together. But the same is not true with front derailleurs. If you try to use a road STI, brake/shift lever with a top-swing (low-mount), top-pull mountain bike front derailleur (you might try this for a triple on a hybrid bike, for instance), it won't work. You can, however, use a nine-speed Shimano front or rear derailleur with Shimano ten-speed shifters, chain, and cogs. You can use any Shimano top-mount, top-pull front derailleur with road STI, though. And all current Shimano cassettes fit on any Shimano freehub model designed for the same number of speeds.

e. Shifting compatibility between brands

Until the advent of nine-speed bikes, a Campagnolo cogset did not shift acceptably on a Shimano indexed drivetrain or vice versa. But the limited amount of space available for nine speeds brought Shimano's and Campagnolo's cog spacing close enough that rear wheels could be switched back and forth between the two with workable shifting performance—certainly not as good as you would pay the big bucks for, but acceptable for wheel changes during races. Neutral-support vehicles only had to stock one variety of nine-speed wheels to cover every rider in the peloton.

Of course, ten-speed systems have changed all of that again. For instance, in a Shimano ten-speed drivetrain, a Campy ten-speed cogset shifts accept-

ably in maybe eight of the ten gears, the ninth cog just barely, and the tenth cog not at all.

As for front derailleurs and cranksets, mixing parts seems to cause few problems as long as you use parts designed for the same number of speeds. Campagnolo and Shimano road front derailleurs and cranksets work fine with each other's road bike shifters.

All nine-speed chains work with all nine-speed systems. And any eight-speed chain works on any seven-speed or eight-speed system. For ten speeds, you'd better stick with a ten-speed chain meant for that system. It is worth experimenting, though, because you may find a different chain, for instance, that will improve the shifting on your system. The seven- and eight-speed chains are 7–7.2mm wide; nine-speed chains are 6.5–6.7mm wide; and Shimano's and Campagnolo's ten-speed chains are 6.1mm wide.

v–36 CHAIN SUCK

Though relatively rare on road bikes, chain suck (where the chain sticks to the chainring and is dragged around until it jams between the chainring and the chainstay) can still occur. See Troubleshooting at the end of Chapter 4, §iv-13.

v–37 CHAIN FALLS ONTO THE GRANNY RING ON A TRIPLE

This problem will tend to happen spontaneously when the chain is on the middle chainring and the largest rear cog, and it is very common on bikes with a chainring-tooth combination of 30-39-53. The extra four-tooth difference of the 39-53 outer pair (often found on Shimano Dura-Ace triples) over a 42-52 pair (found on Ultegra, which almost always works great) is more than the system can handle. The

COMPATABILITY
ISSUES
—
CHAIN SUCK
—
CHAIN FALLS
ONTO
GRANNY RING

derailleur on a 30-39-53 triple is placed so much higher relative to the middle chainring than on a 30-42-52 that it would have difficulty derailing the chain down to the smallest chainring. Shimano addressed this problem by changing the tooth profile to derail more easily, but then it often derailed too easily. Shimano redesigned the middle chainring again, but the problem often persists because of the inherent geometry problems of the higher front derailleur. Replacing the outer rings with 42-52 chainrings usually fixes the problem. If you don't want to do that, adjust the front derailleur so that its inner cage plate is very close to the chain when it is on the middle ring.

Also, when shifting from a bigger ring to a smaller one, the derailleur may overshift and throw the chain to the granny ring or completely off to the inside. This is more of a problem with stiffer shift levers, because it derails the chain so suddenly that it can jump. My recommendation is to always install an inner stop like a Third Eye Chain Watcher (Fig. 5.31), Deda Dog Fang, or N'Gear Jump Stop along with any triple crankset.

If you don't want to shell out ten bucks or so for an inner stop, you can minimize the possibility of a dropped chain with a simple adjustment of your front derailleur. Turn the derailleur cage's tail slightly more inboard than its leading tip. This tweak decreases the downshift force that the derailleur applies. More importantly, you can then tighten the inner limit screw further without rubbing the small gear. Then the inside plate of the front-derailleur cage acts similarly to an anti-chain-drop device.

v-38 CHAIN LINE

The chain line is the relative alignment of the front chainrings with the rear cogs; it is the imag-

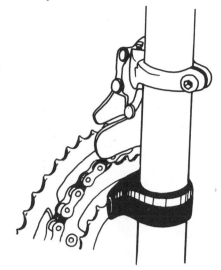

inary line connecting the center of the middle chainring with the middle of the cogset (Fig. 5.32). This line should in theory be straight and parallel with the vertical plane of the bicycle. Even owners of new bikes may discover poor chain lines on their bikes, owing to mismatched cranks and bottom brackets.

If the frame is aligned properly (if it is not, see Chapter 15, §xv-5), the chain line is adjusted by moving or replacing the bottom bracket to move the cranks left or right. You can roughly check the chain line by placing a long straightedge between the two chainrings (or, in the case of a triple, against the middle chainring) and back to the rear cogs; it should come out in the center of the rear cogs. (If that's not good enough for your purposes, a more precise method is outlined in the next section.)

If your chain falls off to the inside no matter how much you adjust the derailleur's low-gear limit screw, cable tension, and derailleur position, or you have chain rub, noise, or auto-shift problems in mild cross-gears that are not corrected with derailleur adjustments, a likely culprit is a poor chain line.

5.32 Measuring chain line

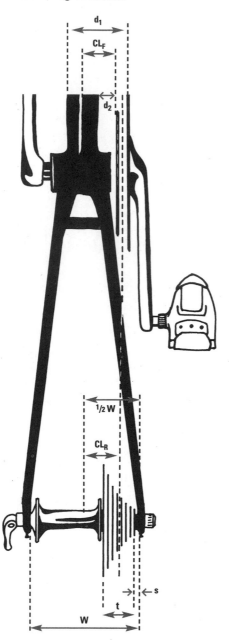

v-39 PRECISE CHAIN-LINE MEASUREMENT

You will need a caliper with a vernier (or digital) scale. If you have a triple, you may want to consult the chain-line discussion in Chapter 5 of *Zinn & the Art of Mountain Bike Maintenance*.

The position of the plane centered between the two chainrings—as measured from the center of the down tube to the centerline between the chain-rings—is often called the chain line, although this position is only the front endpoint of the line.

1. Find the centerline between the chainrings, or the front endpoint of the chain line (CL_F in Fig. 5.32).

   (a) Measure from the left side of the down tube to the outside of the large chainring (d_1 in Fig. 5.32). (Do not measure from the seat tube, as this tube is often pinched into an oval cross section at the bottom.)

   (b) Measure the distance from the right side of the down tube to the inside of the inner chainring (d_2 in Fig. 5.32).

   (c) To find CL_F (the front chain line), add these two measurements, and divide the sum by two.

$$CLF = (d_1 + d_2) \div 2$$

2. Find the position of the centerline of the rear cogs, or the rear endpoint of the chain line (CL_R in Fig. 5.32).

   (a) Measure the thickness of the cog stack, end to end (t in Fig. 5.32).

   (b) Measure the space between the face of the smallest cog and the inside face of the dropout (s in Fig. 5.32).

   (c) Measure the length of the axle from dropout to dropout (W in Fig. 5.32); this length is also called the "axle overlock dimension," referring to the distance from locknut face to locknut face on either end. Generally, on any road bike built since the late 1980s, this will be 130mm.

   (d) To find CL_R, subtract one-half of the thickness of the cog stack and the distance from the inside face of the right-rear dropout from one-half of the rear-axle length.

$$CLR = w/2 - t/2 - s$$

3. If $CL_F = CL_R$, the chain line is perfect. Perfection may not be possible to attain, however, because of considerations of chainstay clearance and prevention of chain rub on large chainrings in cross-gears. Shimano specifies a "chain line" (meaning CL_F, the front endpoint of the chain line) of 43.5mm for a double and 45.0mm for a triple on road bikes. CL_R, the rear endpoint of the chain line, on the other hand, usually comes out around 42.6mm for a Shimano nine-speed, 41.8mm for a Campagnolo nine-speed, and 41.7mm for a Campagnolo eight-speed. Your bike will shift best and run quietest if you get the CL_F to be around 42mm, to best line up with CL_R. However, this ideal may cause problems on your particular bike for the following reasons:

   (a) The inner chainring might rub the chain-stay.

   (b) The front derailleur may bottom out on the seat tube before moving inward enough to shift to the inner chainring (this is particularly a problem with bikes with triples and oversized seat tubes).

   (c) When crossing to the smallest cog from the inner chainring, the chain may rub on the next larger ring (this problem will go away if you simply avoid those cross-gears).

4. To improve the chain line, move the chainrings, because there is little or nothing you can do with the cogset position. My general recommendation is to have the chainrings in toward the frame as far as possible without rubbing the frame or bottoming out the front derailleur before it shifts cleanly to the inner chainring.

The chainrings are moved by using a different bottom bracket, by exchanging bottom-bracket spindles with a longer one, or by moving the bottom bracket right or left (bottom-bracket installation is covered in Chapter 8).

NOTE: *Some brand-new bikes have terrible chain lines that can only be corrected by buying a new bottom bracket. This predicament usually has to do with a conceptually impaired, bean-counting product manager's selecting the parts for a given bike model. Product managers know that customers often pay attention to the quality and brand of the cranks on the bike but pay little heed to the quality of the bottom bracket—an unseen part. A cheap bottom bracket that does not match the cranks is often specified to save the manufacturer some money. The cranks will sit too far out, and the chain line will stink. You will end up having to replace the long bottom bracket with a shorter one if you want the bike to shift decently. Good shops will replace the bottom bracket before selling the bike to you.*

ANOTHER NOTE: *The chain line can also be off if the frame is out of alignment (see Chapter 15, §xv-5). If that's the case, it is probably something you cannot fix yourself.*

If improving the chain line does not fix your problem, or if you don't want to mess with the chain line, buy and install an anti-chain-drop device like a Third Eye Chain Watcher (Fig. 5.31), Deda Dog Fang, or N'Gear Jump Stop. These are inexpensive gizmos that clamp around the seat tube next to the inner chainring. Adjust the device's position so that it nudges the chain back on when the chain tries to fall off to the inside.

THE SHIFTING SYSTEM

PRECISE
CHAIN-LINE
MEASUREMENT

CHAPTER 6

WHEELS AND TIRES

All you need in this life is ignorance and confidence,
and then success is sure.
—Mark Twain

TOOLS

tire levers

pump

patch kit

spoke wrench

grease

5mm hex keys

13mm, 14mm, and
   15mm cone
   wrenches

metric open-end
   wrenches or
   adjustable
   wrenches

OPTIONAL

tubular rim cement

teflon tape

pliers

miter clamp

sewing needle for
   leather

braided high-test
   fishing line

thimble

barge cement (or
   other strong con-
   tact cement)

truing stand

tire sealant

freehub cassette-
   lockring remover

freewheel remover

citrus solvent

soft hammer

Rohloff cog-wear
   indicator

Freehub Buddy

fine-tip grease gun

Most road bike wheels are strung together with spokes connecting the hub to the rim. The rim, which serves as both support for the tire and as the surface on which the brakes are applied, is supported and aligned by the tension on the spokes. Bearings in the hub, when clean and properly adjusted, allow the wheel to turn freely around the axle.

Composite wheels, be they disc wheels or three-, four-, or five-spoke wheels, generally use rigid members to hold the wheel up. An exception is the Spinergy Rev-X, which relies on tension on eight flat carbon spokes to support the wheel. Composite wheels generally cannot be trued, although the rim is replaceable on some models.

Wheels intended for aerodynamic efficiency either have solid sides (disc wheels) or have aerodynamically shaped rims and few spokes, which are often themselves aerodynamic in shape. The spokes can be steel, titanium, or composite (often carbon fiber).

A cassette freehub or freewheel with cogs attached allows the rear wheel to spin while you are coasting, and it engages when force is applied to the pedals (Fig. 6.1). The tires provide suspension as well as grip and traction for propulsion and steering. The air pressure in the tire is the primary suspension system on a road bike.

Two types of road bike tires are available. "Clinchers" (Fig. 6.2), which are C-shaped in cross section, are held into a C-shaped rim by a steel or Kevlar bead on each edge of the tire. A separate inner tube inside of the clincher holds the air. "Tubulars" (Fig. 6.3), which are circular in cross section, have a casing that is wrapped around an inner tube and stitched or glued together. The tire is glued onto a box-section rim that has no vertical rim walls like a clincher rim.

6.1   The whole thing

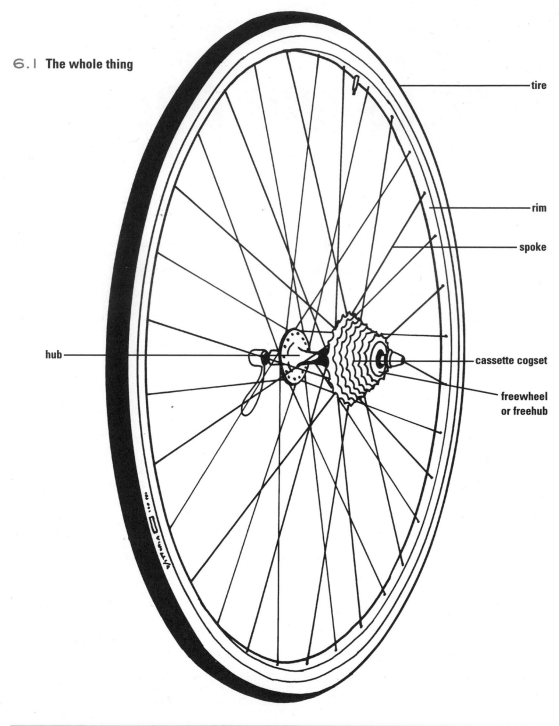

tire

rim

spoke

hub

cassette cogset

freewheel
or freehub

WHEELS

AND TIRES

6.2 Clincher tire   **6.3 Tubular tire**

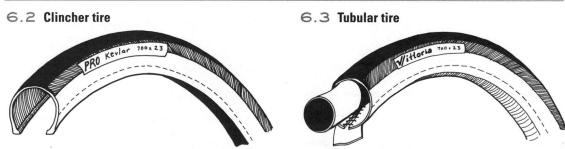

6.4 Presta valve

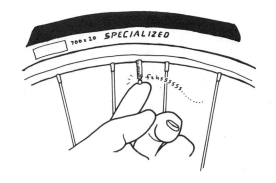

6.5 Schrader valve

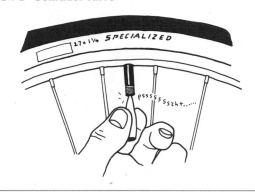

This chapter addresses how to fix a flat or replace a tire or tube, true a wheel, fix a broken spoke or bent rim, overhaul hubs, change rear cogs, and lubricate cassettes and freewheels. Have at it.

CLINCHER TIRES

vi-1 REMOVING THE TIRE

1. Remove the wheel (See Chapter 2, §ii-2 and §ii-11).

2. If your tire is not already flat, deflate it. First remove the valve cap (if installed) to get to the valve. Most road bike tires have "Presta," or "French" valves. These valves are thinner than "Schrader" valves (the kind found on cars) and have a small threaded rod with a tiny nut on the end. To let air out, unscrew the little nut a few turns, and push down on the thin rod (Fig. 6.4). To seal, tighten the little nut down again (with your fingers only!); leave it tightened down for riding. To deflate a Schrader valve, push down on the valve pin with something thin enough to fit in that won't break off, like a pen cap or a paper clip (Fig. 6.5).

NOTE: *If you have deep-section rims (i.e., Mavic Cosmic, Campagnolo Shamal, Vento, Bora, Hed, Rolf, Spinergy, Zipp, or any of a myriad of others), the wheels will likely have "valve extenders"—thin threaded tubes that screw onto the Presta valve stems.*

To deflate tires that have valve extenders installed, you need to insert a thin rod (a spoke is perfect) down into the valve extender to release the air.

To install valve extenders so that they seal properly and allow easy inflation, you need to unscrew the little nut on the Presta valve until it is against the mashed threads at the top of the valve shaft (they are mashed to keep the nut from unscrewing completely off). Back the nut firmly into these mashed threads with a pair of pliers so that it stays unscrewed and does not tighten back down against the valve stem from the vibration of riding and prevent air from going in when you pump it. Some valve extenders (like Spinergy) also extend the valve nut and thus do not require this procedure; they actually allow you to tighten or loosen the valve nut with the extender in place.

You also should wrap a turn or two of Teflon pipe thread tape around the top threads on the valve stem before screwing on the valve extender to seal it; if you do not, air will leak out when pumping, and your pressure gauge on your pump will not give an accurate reading of the pressure in the tire. Tighten the valve extender onto the valve stem with a pair of pliers.

Some inner tubes now come with extra-long Presta valves for deep-section wheels. These are operated just like standard Presta valves.

REMOVING

THE TIRE

6.6 Removing clincher tire with levers

6.7 Pulling out bead with third lever

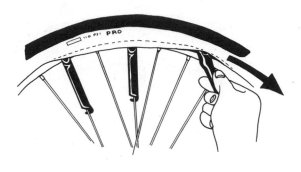

3. If you can push the tire bead off the rim with your thumbs without using tire levers, by all means do so, because there is less chance of damaging either the tube or the tire if you avoid the use of levers or other tools. It's easiest if you start just to one side or the other of the valve, after squeezing the tire beds into the center of the rim all of the way around (see Pro Tip).

PRO TIP

TIRE REMOVAL AND REPLACEMENT HINT

Removal of the tire is most easily accomplished by starting near the valve stem. That way, the beads of the deflated tire can fall into the dropped center of the rim on the opposite side of the wheel, making it effectively a smaller-circumference rim off of which you are pushing the tire bead. If you instead try to push the tire bead off of (or onto) the rim on the side opposite the valve stem, the circumference on which the bead is resting is larger, because the valve stem is forcing the beads to stay up on their seating ledges opposite where you are working.

4. If you can't get the tire off with your hands alone, insert a tire lever (with its scoop toward you) between the rim sidewall and the tire until you catch the edge of the tire bead. Make sure you do not pinch the tube between the lever and the tire. Again, start near the valve. This approach allows the beads on the side opposite the valve to drop into the center of the rim, effectively reducing the diameter about which the tire is stretched.

5. Pry down on the lever until the tire bead is pulled out over the rim (Fig. 6.6). If the lever has a hook on the other end, hook it onto the nearest spoke. Otherwise, keep holding it down.

6. Place the next lever a few inches away, and do the same thing with it (Fig. 6.6).

7. If needed, place a third lever a few inches farther on, pry it out, and continue sliding this lever around the tire, pulling the bead out as you go (Fig. 6.7). Some people slide their fingers around under the tire bead, but beware of cutting your fingers on a sharp bead.

NOTE: *There are a few quick-change tire levers on the market that work differently and more quickly than the separate standard tire levers. If the tire bead is very tight on the rim, though, using separate tire levers may be the only method that works effectively.*

6.8 Removing the inner tube

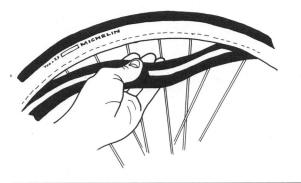

6.9 Checking for puncture

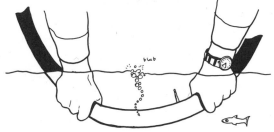

8. Once the bead is off the rim on one side, pull the tube out (Fig. 6.8).

9. If you are patching or replacing the tube, you do not need to remove the other side of the tire from the rim. If you are replacing the tire, the other bead should come off easily with your fingers. If it does not, use the tire levers as just outlined.

vi-2 PATCHING AN INNER TUBE

1. If the leak location is not obvious, put some air in the tube to inflate it until it is two to three times larger than its deflated size. Be careful. You can explode it if you put too much air in, especially with lightweight latex or urethane tubes.

2. Listen and feel for air coming out, and mark the leak(s).

3. If you cannot find the leak by listening, submerge the tube in water. Look for air bubbling out (Fig. 6.9), and mark the spot(s).

NOTE: *Keep in mind that you can only patch small holes. If the hole is bigger than the eraser end of a pencil, a round patch is not likely to work. A slit as much as an inch long or so can be repaired with an oval patch.*

vi-3 STANDARD PATCHES

Use a patch designed for bicycle tires; it will generally have a thin, usually orange, gummy edge surrounding a slightly thicker patch of black rubber. Rema and Delta are common brands.

1. Dry the tube thoroughly near the puncture and mark the location of the hole with a pen.

2. To provide a suitable surface for the patch, clean and then rough up the tube surface within about a 1-inch radius around the hole with a small piece of sandpaper (usually supplied with the patch kit). Do not touch the sanded area. If the patch kit you are using came with a little metal "cheese grater" for the purpose, discard it and replace it with sandpaper. The grater-style rougheners tend to do to your tube what they do to cheese.

3. Apply glue (patch cement) in a thin, smooth layer all over an area centered on the hole (Fig. 6.10). Use the end of the glue container or a brush, rather than your finger, to spread the glue around. Cover an area that is bigger than the size of the patch. By the way, the glue is similar to rubber cement, so if the tube in your patch kit has dried out, you can use any rubber cement sold in office supply and hardware stores for the purpose. If you do this, and use

6.10 Applying glue

6.11 Removing cellophane

the brush attached to the top of the bottle cap, wipe the brush almost dry before spreading the cement on the tube. You only need a thin layer for the patch.

4. Let the glue dry 10 minutes or so until there are no more shiny, wet spots.

5. Peel the patch from its foil backing (but do not remove the cellophane top cover yet).

6. Stick the patch over the hole, and push it down in place, making sure that all of the gummy edges are stuck down. With the tube sitting on a hard surface, burnish the patch with the plastic handle of a screwdriver to stick the edges down securely.

7. Optional: Remove the cellophane top covering, being careful not to peel up the edges of the patch (Fig. 6.11). Often, the cellophane top patch is scored. If you fold the patch, the cellophane will split at the scored cuts, allowing you to peel outward and avoid pulling the newly adhered patch up off the tube. If you can't get the cellophane off without peeling up the patch, just leave it alone. It won't do any harm in the tire.

vi-4 GLUELESS PATCHES

There are a number of adhesive-backed patches on the market that do not require cement to stick them

on. Most often, you simply need to clean the area around the hole with the little alcohol pad supplied with the patch. Let the alcohol dry, peel the backing, and stick on the patch.

The advantages of glueless patches are that they are very fast to use and take little room in a seat bag; also, you never open your patch kit to discover that your glue tube is dried up. On the downside, I have not found any glueless patches that stick nearly as well as the standard type. With a standard patch installed, you can inflate the tube to look for more leaks without having it in the tire. If you do that with a glueless patch, the patch usually lifts enough to start leaking. You must install the tube in the tire and on the rim before putting air in it after glueless patching. And it is probably not a permanent fix, such as a Rema-type patch would be.

vi-5 INSTALLING PATCHED OR NEW TUBE

If you've just fixed a flat, feel around the inside of the tire to see if there is still anything sticking through that can puncture the tube again. Sliding a rag all the way around the inside of the tire works well. The rag will catch on anything sharp and will save your fingers from being cut by whatever is stuck in the tire.

1. Replace any tire that has damaged areas (inside

6.12 Installing tire by hand

6.13 Finishing at the valve

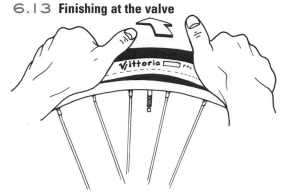

or out) where the casing fibers appear to be cut or frayed.

2. Examine the rim to be certain that the rim tape is in place and that there are no spokes or anything else sticking up that can puncture the tube. Replace the rim tape if necessary. Two layers of fiberglass strapping tape work great.

3. By hand, push one bead of the tire onto the rim.

4. (Optional) Smear talcum powder around the inside of the tire and on the outside of the tube, so the two do not adhere to each other. Don't inhale this stuff, by the way.

5. Put just enough air in the tube to give it shape. Close the valve, if Presta.

NOTE: *If you have a deep-section rim and a standard-length Presta valve, you will need to install a valve extender so that you can get air into the tire once it is on the rim. To install valve extenders so that they seal properly and allow easy inflation, unscrew the little nut on the Presta valve against the mashed threads at the top of the valve shaft (they are mashed to keep the nut from unscrewing completely). Back the nut firmly into these mashed threads with a pair of pliers so that the nut stays unscrewed and does not tighten back down against the valve stem and prevent air from going in when you pump it. You also should wrap a turn or two of Teflon pipe thread tape around the top threads on the*

valve stem before screwing on the valve extender to seal it. If you do not, air will leak out when pumping, and the pressure gauge on your pump will not give an accurate reading of the pressure in the tire. Tighten the valve extender onto the valve stem with pliers.

6. Push the valve through the valve hole in the rim.

7. Push the tube up inside the tire all of the way around.

8. Starting at the side opposite the valve stem, push the tire bead onto the rim with your thumbs. Be sure that the tube doesn't get pinched between the tire bead and the rim.

9. Work around the rim in both directions with your thumbs, pushing the tire onto the rim (Fig. 6.12). Finish from both sides at the valve (Fig. 6.13), deflating the tube when it gets hard to push more of the tire onto the rim. (See Pro Tip on Tire Removal and Replacement.) You can often install a tire without tools. If you cannot, use tire levers, but make sure you don't catch any of the tube under the edge of the bead. Finish the same way, at the valve.

10. Reseat the valve stem by pushing up on the valve after you have pushed the last bit of bead onto the rim (Fig. 6.14). You may have to manipulate the tire so that all the tube is tucked under the tire bead.

6.14 Seating the tube

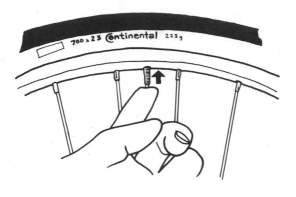

11. Go around the rim and inspect for any part of the tube that might be protruding from under the edge of the tire bead. If you have a fold of the tube under the edge of the bead, it can blow the tire off the rim when you inflate it or while you are riding. It will sound like a gun went off next to you and will leave you with an unpatchable tube.

12. Pump the tire up. Generally, 85–100 psi is correct for a good-quality road bike tire. Much more, and you are pushing the limits of some tires. Much less, and you run the risk of a pinch flat or "snake bite."

vi-6 PATCHING TIRE CASING (SIDEWALL)

Unless it is an emergency, don't do it! If the tire casing is cut, get a new tire. Patching the tire casing is dangerous. No matter what you use as a patch, the tube will find a way to bulge out of the patched hole, and when it does, your tire will go flat immediately. Imagine coming down a steep hill and suddenly your front tire goes completely flat . . . you get the picture.

In an emergency, you can put layers of non-stretchable material between the tube and tire (see Chapter 3, §iii-3b, Fig. 3.1). Candidates for this duty

---

PRO TIP

TIRE PRESSURE AND ROLLING RESISTANCE

Using overly high pressure is a common mistake road bike riders are prone to. The danger of blowing the tire off the rim and really hurting yourself is high, and it does not accomplish what high-pressure devotees set out to accomplish, namely, to reduce rolling resistance. If the tire cannot absorb small bumps into its surface because it is pumped up too high, the bike will roll slower, even though it may feel very fast because it is so stiff and bouncy and lively. Every little bump lifts the bike and rider and also provides a backward force on impact. Overcoming this backward force costs energy compared to absorb-

ing the bump into the tire while the bike and rider continue to roll along smoothly without up-down motion.

Pressures of 140 psi and higher are only fast on a very smooth surface, which you find nowhere other than a smooth velodrome (banked track). On any road surface, anything higher than 120 psi is costing you speed. A handmade tire with thinner, more tightly packed threads forming the tire casing will always roll faster than one with a casing made of fewer, thicker, stiffer threads. So, if you want to roll fast, choose a tire with a high thread count that feels supple when you fold it in your hand, and forget the bomber tire pressures that also endanger your life!

include a dollar bill, an empty energy bar wrapper (or two), or even a short section of the exploded tube (double thickness is better).

TUBULAR TIRES

Tubular tires, or sew-ups, are expensive, hard to install (they must be glued to the rim), hard to repair, and these days can even be hard to find. So why bother with them?

For one thing, tubular wheelsets (front/rear wheel pairs) are generally lighter than clincher wheelsets, because tubular rims do not require flanges for the tire bead. Tubular tires by themselves are usually lighter than clinchers, too, although the difference these days is often quite small. Tubulars are enjoying a renaissance now with the advent of superlight carbon-fiber tubular rims for racing.

Another reason for the continuing popularity of these quirky throwbacks is that a lot of people say that they ride and corner better than clinchers. And being sewn together, they can be made to hold extremely high pressures.

But perhaps the main reason to consider tubulars is their inherent safety. In the event of a blowout, they stay on the rim. Clincher tires, when flat, fall into the rim well, and you may find yourself trying to ride on the slippery metal rim, rather than on a piece of rubber.

Tubulars usually deflate more slowly when punctured than clinchers, too, because the air can only escape through the puncture hole. Clinchers can let air escape all the way around the rim.

If these advantages appeal to you—and the disadvantages listed here don't put you off—tubulars are a worthwhile alternative to the standard clincher setup.

vi-7 REMOVING A TUBULAR

1. Remove the wheel (see Chapter 2, §ii-2 and §ii-11).

2. If the tire is not already flat, deflate it. Tubular tires have "Presta," or "French" valves. To let air out, unscrew the little nut atop the valve stem a few turns, and push down on the thin rod (Fig. 6.4). To seal, tighten the little nut down again (with your fingers only!); leave it tightened for riding.

N O T E : *If you have deep-section rims (i.e., Mavic Cosmic, Campagnolo Shamal, Vento, Bora, Hed, Rolf, Spinergy, Zipp, or any of a myriad of others), the wheels will likely have "valve extenders"—thin threaded tubes that screw onto the valve stems. To deflate the tire, you may need to insert a thin rod (a spoke is perfect) into the valve extender to release the air.*

Some tubulars now come with extra-long Presta valves for deep-section wheels. These are operated just like standard Presta valves.

3. Push the tire off the rim in one section with your thumbs pushing up against one side. Avoid using tools. If you use a tool to pry the tire away from the glue, you will tear the base tape at the least and more likely tear casing cords as well. The tire will always be lumpy in that area after such damage.

4. Peel the tire off the rim by hand.

vi-8 GLUING TUBULAR TIRES

LEVEL 2

Gluing tubular tires to the rims properly is critical to continuing the attachment you have with your epidermis. I can say from experience and from watching many riders roll improperly glued tires off rims that you do not want it to happen to you. Follow these steps and your tire will really be secure! Pay particular attention to the second step, because all the rim cement in the world will not keep your tire on if the cement is not adhered to the tire.

NOTE: *For tires without a latex coating on the base tape (or after scraping —see step 2), Tufo sells easy-to-use, single-hand double-sided tape to attach a tubular to a rim without using rim cement. Tufo standard, or cyclo-cross tape, has backing on one side only. To use, peel the backing off, stick it on the rim, and cut open the valve hole to then install, center, and inflate the tire. Tufo Extreme tape has backing on both sides. Remove the rim-side backing (it will be labeled) first, and stick the tape onto the rim. Peel back the corners of the topside backing at each end so that the corners stick out from the sides of the rim. Cut open the valve hole and then install, inflate, and center the tire. Centering is easy with the help of the slick backing. Pull the backing out from under the entire tire before inflating it to 130 psi. Ride on the tire for five minutes. Tufo tapes are ready to ride immediately after completing the inflation and five minutes of riding on the tire.*

1. Before gluing a new tubular, stretch it first over the rim (Fig. 6.15). To do this, install the tire without any glue on it by using the method described in step 6.

2. Scrape the base tape of the tubular with a serrated knife edge or metal file edge to produce a good gluing surface. The base tape on most tires is cotton and has a coating of latex over it, to which the rim cement will not bond well. The tire can roll off even a thick layer of cement on the rim if the base tape has not been properly prepared. This step does not apply to most

6.15 Stretch the tubular tire over the rim

Continental tubulars, which usually have no latex over the base tape.

3. Start by pumping the tire (not on the rim) until it turns inside out and the base tape faces outward. By using the serrations of a table knife or the rough side of a metal file, scrape the base tape back and forth (Fig. 6.16) until the latex coating on the tape balls up into little sticky hunks. I have also heard of people brushing rubbing alcohol on the base tape to make the surface tacky. I generally discourage the use of solvents on the base tape for fear of solvent penetrating the tape and dissolving the glue holding the tape onto the tire. I have seen many a tire roll right off the base tape, even though the tape is well-adhered to the rim.

4. Prepare the rim for glue. With a new rim, clean off any oil with alcohol or acetone (while wear-

6.16 Scrape the base tape before gluing

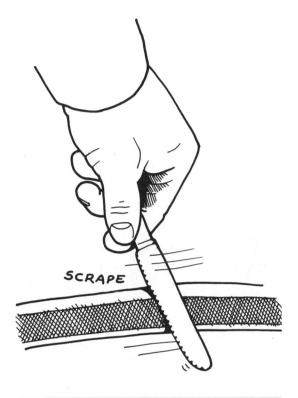

SCRAPE

rim thinly and uniformly, or, better yet, brushing it on with an acid brush. Let it dry overnight. Repeat.

NOTE: *Except for carbon rims (see Pro Tip on Gluing a Tubular onto a Carbon Rim), I recommend using clear tubular rim cement, ideally either Continental rim cement or Vittoria Mastik'One, rather than red glues. Red glues harden up; if you leave them on for years, they get so dried out that the tire is not held well and needs to be reglued, but primarily, they will not be working as a contact cement and continually regluing the tire the way they ought to wherever it may peel up a bit.*

7. After the second layer of glue on the rim and tire has dried overnight as well, smear another thin layer of glue on the rim. Let this layer set overnight again.

8. After the glue on the rim and tire has dried overnight again, smear or brush another thin layer of glue on the rim. Let this layer set for 15 minutes.

9. Deflate and mount the tire as follows:

    (a) Stand the wheel up with the valve hole facing up.

    (b) Put the valve stem through the hole, and, leaning over the wheel, grab the tire and stretch outward as you push the base tape into the top of the rim. Keep stretching down on the tire with both hands, using your body weight, as you push the tire down around the rim (Fig. 6.15). I like to lean hard enough on the tire that my feet lift repeatedly off the ground. The farther you can stretch the tire at this point, the easier it will be to get the last bit of tire onto the rim.

    (c) Lifting the rim up to horizontal with the valve side against your belly, roll the last bit

ing rubber gloves and a respirator) and sandpaper. Roughing up the gluing surface with sandpaper does not help the tire stick to the rim better, but solvent will not remove everything (Teflon, for instance), and sandpaper can remove some invisible contaminants that would prevent the glue from sticking to the rim.

5. With a rim that has been glued before, you can just apply a uniform layer of glue, unless there is a really thick, lumpy layer of old glue on the rim. In this case, scrape the big lumps off, and get the surface as uniform as you can, or strip the entire rim with acetone.

6. Put a thin layer of glue on the rim, edge-to-edge, and edge-to-edge on the base tape of the tire, as well. I recommend squeezing a bead out of the tube and then putting a plastic bag over your finger and spreading the glue on the tire and

of the tire onto the opposite side of the rim. If you can't get the tire to pop over the rim, peel the tire back and start over, pushing down again from the valve stem. You want to avoid the temptation of prying a stubborn tire onto the rim with screwdrivers or other tools, as you will likely tear cords in the base tape and tire casing, leading to a bulge in the tire in this area.

10. By pulling the tire this way and that, get the edge of the base tape aligned with the rim. You want to see the same amount sticking out from the rim all the way around on both sides around the wheel.

11. Pump the tire to 100 psi and spin the wheel, looking for wobbles in the tire. If you find that the tread snakes back and forth as you spin the wheel, deflate the tire and push it over where required. Reinflate and check again, repeating the process until the tire is as straight as you are willing to get it. The final process will depend somewhat on how accurately the tubular was made; you'll find that some brands and models glue on straighter than others.

12. Pump the tire up to 120–130 psi and leave it overnight to bond firmly.

You can get an even better bond by using a woodworker's band (miter) clamp around the entire inflated tire. The miter clamp (see Fig. 1.2 in Chapter 1) is a piece of nylon webbing with a cam-lock buckle on it. Depress the tab on the buckle to let out enough strap to surround the inflated tire and wheel. Pull the end of the strap to tighten the loop around the tire. Use a wrench to tighten the clamp and put extra pressure down on the tire to conform its bottom surface to the rim and bond it tightly. Tomorrow you can release the miter clamp

PRO TIP

GLUING A TUBULAR ONTO A CARBON RIM

Carbon rims are notoriously hard to glue to. In this case, the thick, gloppy red glue of yesteryear, namely, Clément rim cement, seems to adhere to the rim best, but it is no longer available unless you know somebody with a stash. Otherwise, Vittoria Mastik'One seems to be the best available glue choice, according to research done at the University of Kansas; see www.engr.ku.edu/~ktl.

Tires tend to snap off of carbon rims, rather than peel off, meaning that it may take as much force to get tires started off the rim as it would with an aluminum rim, but then they can roll right off, rather than requiring pulling and peeling to continue to get them off. The best thing you can do is follow the multiple-layer gluing procedure in §vi-8 with clean rims and scraped base tape. It is worth pulling your tire off after you have it all glued on to see how you did. Then reglue it the same way again, especially if all the glue pulled off the rim in the process.

(by using the release [thumb] tab) and go ride or race on this wheel.

vi-9 CHANGING A TUBULAR TIRE ON THE ROAD

If you get a puncture out on the road with a tubular tire, you will find that it is easier to deal with than a flat clincher. You want to make sure that you are carrying a spare tubular that already has glue on the base tape. For your spare, bring along an old tubular that has been glued to a rim in the past, or, with a new tire as a spare, follow steps 1–4 in §vi-8.

Remove the wheel and pull the flat tire off the rim. If you did a good gluing job, this may take some doing. (On the other hand, if the tubular is easy to peel off, you need to improve your gluing technique.) Stretch the spare tire onto the rim as in steps 6 and 7 in §vi-8. Pump it up hard (over 100 psi) to get it to stay on the rim for the rest of the ride. Corner carefully going home, as the glue bond is marginal. When you get home, glue a tire securely on the rim before riding that wheel again.

vi–10 PATCHING TUBULAR TIRES

LEVEL 2

In the early 1980s, my racing buddies and I spent countless hours patching tubular tires, often while sitting in the car on the way to distant races. Now that everyone trains on clinchers, nobody seems to patch tubulars any more. Tubulars are arguably still the best tires for racing, being lighter, requiring lighter rims, and being able to hold tremendous pressures because of being sewn together (the high air pressure reduces the rolling resistance of the tire on the road). However, even though tubulars are expensive, it makes no sense to patch a racing tire, because you invest too much time, energy, and money competing in races to run the risk of getting a puncture because of a weakened tire.

If for some reason you still wish to patch a tubular, here are the steps involved:

1. Remove the tire from the rim.

2. Pump up the tire to 70 psi, or as high as you can, and find the leak by submerging the inflated tire in a bucket of water. If you're lucky, air will come out through a hole in the tread. In the case of a pinched tube, though, the air may seep out through the casing randomly at the stitches, and be hard to localize. See the next step for help.

3. In the region 2 inches on either side of the puncture, peel away the base tape covering the stitching. If you were unable to precisely locate the hole, try submerging the inflated tire now to watch the bubbles coming out through the stitching. Peel more base tape back if necessary until you are sure that you have exposed the stitching at the hole.

4. Deflate the tire and carefully cut the outer layer of stitching threads for an inch or so on either side of the hole. Pull the casing open in that spot, and pull enough of the tube out through the hole to find and access the hole(s) in it.

5. Patch the tube in the same manner as outlined in §vi-2. Use the same type of recommended patches.

6. Push the tube back in place, and sew the opening in the stitching closed by hand. I recommend using a needle for leather with a triangular cross-section tip and braided high-test fishing line. Stitch one way across the opening, turn the tire around, and double back over the stitches again. For obvious reasons, be careful not to poke the tube. You may need a thimble to push the needle in and a pair of pliers to pull it out on each stitch.

7. Inflate the tire to 70 psi or so to make sure all of the leaks have been patched.

8. Deflate the tire and coat the peeled-back section of base tape and the exposed stitching area with contact cement. Barge glue for shoes works great. Wait 15 minutes or so for the glue to set, and carefully stick the base tape back down over the stitching. (If the tape stretched when you pulled it loose, it's permissible to cut it and overlap the ends.)

9. Coat the rim and the tire base tape with a thin layer of rim cement. Let it sit 15 minutes to an hour. Because this is an old tire, there should already be a good layer of rim cement on the tire and the rim.

10. Glue the tire onto the rim (see §vi-8).

vi–11 TIRE SEALANTS

Tire sealants can virtually eliminate flat tires caused by tread punctures; they do not fix sidewall cuts, pinch flats, or rim-side punctures. The most popular tire sealant, Slime, is a green goo full of chopped fibers; when poured into an inner tube, it flows to punctures and seals them. There are other brands and colors of tire sealants as well; these instructions generally apply to them all.

Only use Slime in a clincher tube without cuts in it. The tube must also have a Schrader valve in good condition (Figs. 1.1B and 6.5); you cannot insert Slime into a Presta valve, because it will block the valve. By the way, you can put sealant in a tube that already has a slow leak; simply inject it as detailed in the next section, pump it up, and spin the wheel for about five minutes.

NOTE: *If you have Presta valves (Figs. 1.1B and 6.4), and you want to use tire sealant, you can purchase tubes with sealant already inside. If you have a slow leak in a tubular, or you want to have some puncture resistance in a Presta tube, you can pour a can of evaporated milk into a pump you don't care about and pump it into the tire via the Presta valve. It works quite well for tiny leaks, but if you get a blowout, boy, does it ever stink!*

a. Slime installation into a tube that's already installed in a tire

1. Shake the Slime bottle.

2. Remove the Schrader valve core by using the valve-cap core remover packaged with the Slime.

3. Rotate the wheel so that the valve stem is at the four o'clock position.

4. Cut off the bottle spout, and connect the bottle spout and valve stem with the supplied tubing.

5. Squeeze the bottle slowly to inject the Slime.

6. Stop squeezing after injecting 4 ounces; wait several minutes to clear the stem.

7. Remove the tube.

8. Screw the valve core firmly back into the valve stem in a clockwise direction.

9. Inflate the tube.

10. If the tube has a leak, spin the wheel for five minutes to spread the Slime around in the tube.

b. Maintaining tire-sealant–filled tubes

Inflating

Always have the stem at four o'clock and wait a minute for the sealant to drain away; if you don't, sealant will leak out, eventually clogging the valve.

Sealing punctures

1. If you find the tire has gone flat, pump it up and ride it a bit to see if it seals.

2. If you get numerous punctures, you may need to pump repeatedly and ride before the tube seals up.

3. Pinch flats, caused by pinching the tube between the tire and rim, are hard to seal because the two "snake-bite" holes are on the side. Try laying the bike on the same side as the holes.

4. Imbedded nails and other foreign objects can be removed; spin the wheel to seal the hole.

5. Punctures on the rim side of the tube will not seal, because the sealant is thrown to the outside by centrifugal force.

6. Sidewall gashes need to be patched, and the tire needs to be replaced.

6.17 Lateral truing if rim scrapes on left

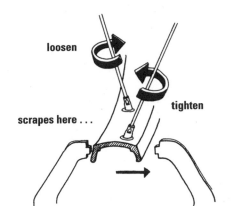

loosen

tighten

scrapes here . . .

6.18 Lateral truing if rim scrapes on right

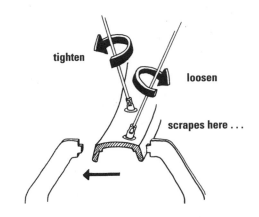

tighten

loosen

scrapes here . . .

RIMS AND SPOKES

vi-12 TRUING A WHEEL

LEVEL 2

For more information on truing wheels, see Chapter 13 on wheel building, §xiii-4.

If the wheel has a mild wobble in it, you can fix it by adjusting the tension on the spokes. An extreme bend in the rim cannot be fixed by spoke truing alone, because the spoke tension on the two sides of the wheel will be so uneven that the wheel will rapidly fall apart.

1. Check that there are no broken spokes in the wheel, or any spokes that are so loose that they flop around. If there is a broken spoke, follow the replacement procedure in the following section, §vi-13. If there is a single loose spoke, check to see that the rim is not dented or cracked in that area. I recommend replacing the rim if it is. If the rim looks okay, mark the loose spoke with a piece of tape and tighten it up with the spoke wrench until it feels the same tension as adjacent spokes on the same side of the wheel (pluck the spoke and listen to the tone). Then follow the truing procedure in step 2.

2. Grab the rim while the wheel is on the bike, and flex it side to side to check the hub-bearing adjustment. If the bearings are loose, the wheel will clunk side to side. The play in the bearings will have to be eliminated before you true the wheel or the rim will wobble erratically because of the loose hub. Follow the hub-adjustment procedure, §vi-16d, steps 28–31.

3. Put the wheel in a truing stand, if you have one. Otherwise, leave it on the bike and suspend the bike in a bike stand or from the ceiling, or turn it upside down on the handlebar and saddle.

4. Adjust the truing stand feeler, or hold one of your brake pads so that it scrapes the rim at the biggest wobble.

5. Where the rim scrapes, tighten the spoke (or spokes) that come(s) to the rim from the opposite side of the hub, and loosen the spoke(s) that come(s) from the same side of the hub (Figs. 6.17 and 6.18). This process will pull the rim away from the feeler or brake pad.

NOTE: *When correcting a wheel that is laterally out of true (wobbles side-to-side), always adjust spokes in pairs: one spoke coming from one side of the wheel, the other coming from the opposite side. Tightening spokes is like opening a jar upside down. With the jar right-*

6.19 Tightening and loosening spokes

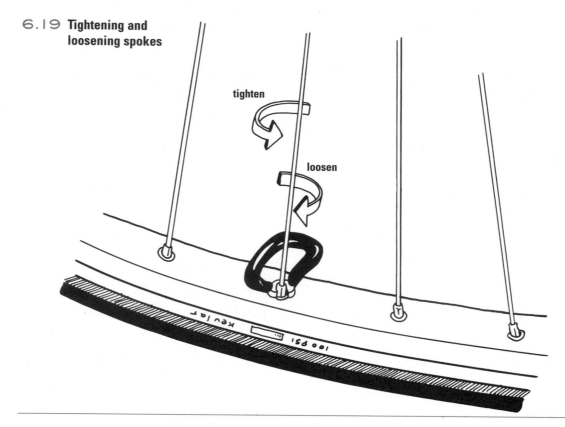

tighten

loosen

side up, turning the lid to the left (counterclockwise) opens the jar, but this direction apparently reverses when you turn the jar upside down (try it and see). Spoke nipples are just like the lid on that upside-down jar: When the nipples are at the bottom of the rim, counterclockwise tightens, and clockwise loosens (Fig. 6.19). The opposite is true when the nipples to be turned are at the top. It may take you a few attempts before you catch on, but you will eventually get it. If you temporarily make the wheel worse, simply undo what you have done and start over.

It is best to tighten and loosen by small amounts (about a quarter-turn at a time), decreasing the amount you turn the spoke nipples as you move away from the spot where the rim scrapes the hardest. If the wobble gets worse, then you are turning the spokes in the wrong direction.

ANOTHER NOTE: Shimano's prebuilt wheels have their spoke nipples at the hub, not at the rim. Before

you turn them, think carefully about which way tightens and which way loosens.

6. As the rim moves into proper alignment, readjust the truing-stand feeler or the brake pad so that it again finds the most out-of-true spot on the wheel.

7. Check the wobble first on one side of the wheel and then the other, adjusting spokes accordingly, so that you don't end up pulling the whole wheel off center by chasing wobbles only on one side. As the wheel gets closer to true, you will need to decrease the amount you turn the spokes; otherwise, you will overcorrect.

8. Accept a certain amount of wobble, especially if you are truing the wheel in a bike; the method is not very accurate and is not at all suited for making a wheel absolutely true. If you have access to a wheel-dishing tool, check to make sure that the wheel is centered (Chapter 13, §xiii-5).

6.20 Weaving a new spoke

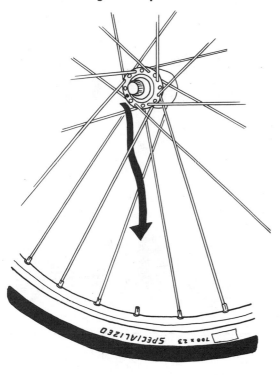

vi-13 REPLACING A BROKEN SPOKE

Go to the bike store and get a new spoke of the same length. Remember: the spokes on the front wheel are usually not the same length as the spokes on the rear wheel. Also, the spokes on the drive (right) side of the rear wheel are almost always shorter than those on the nondrive (left) side.

1. Make sure you are using a replacement spoke of the proper thickness and length.

2. Thread the spoke through the spoke hole in the hub flange. If the broken spoke is on the drive side of the rear wheel, you will need to remove the cassette cogs or the freewheel to get at the hub flange (§vi-20 and §vi-21).

3. Weave the new spoke in with the other spokes just as it was before (Fig. 6.20). It may take some bending to get it in place.

4. Thread it into the same nipple, if the nipple is in good shape. Otherwise, use a new nipple; you'll need to remove the tire, tube, and rim strip (or the tubular tire) to install the nipple.

5. Mark the new spoke with a piece of tape, and tighten it up about as snugly as the neighboring spokes on that side of the wheel.

6. Follow the steps for truing a wheel as outlined in §vi-12.

HUBS

vi-14 OVERHAULING HUBS

Hubs should turn smoothly and noiselessly. If you maintain them regularly, you can expect them to still be running smoothly when you are ready to give up on the rest of your bike.

All hubs have a "hub shell" that contains the axle and bearings and is connected to the rim with spokes or, in the case of disc wheels, by sheets of composite material. Beyond that, they diverge into two types: the standard "cup-and-cone" type (Fig. 6.21), and the "sealed-bearing" (or "cartridge-bearing") type (Fig. 6.22).

Standard cup-and-cone hubs have loose ball bearings that roll along very smooth bearing surfaces called "races" or "cups"; an axle runs through the center of the hub. Conical nuts, called "cones" (Fig. 6.21), thread onto the axle. The cones create an inner race for the bearings. In high-quality hubs, the cup-and-cone surfaces that contact the bearings are precisely machined to minimize friction. The operation of the hub depends on the smoothness and lubrication of the cones, ball bearings, and bearing cups. The cones are held in place on the axle by one or more spacers (washers) followed by threaded locknuts that tighten down against the

6.21 **Cup-and-cone front hub with standard ball bearings**

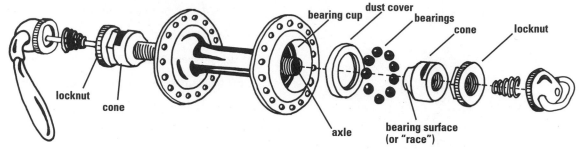

6.22 **Front hub with cartridge bearing**

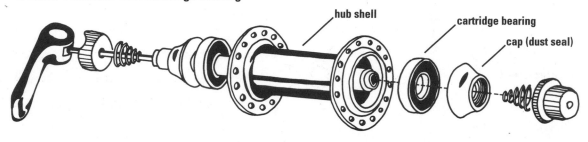

ALL HUBS,

PRELIMINARY

—

OVERHAUL

STANDARD

CUP–AND–

CONE HUB

cones and spacers to keep the hub in proper adjustment. The rear hub will have more spacers on both sides, especially on the drive side (Fig. 6.31).

The term "sealed-bearing" hub is a bit of a misnomer, because many cup-and-cone hubs offer better protection against dirt and water than some sealed-bearing hubs. The phrase "cartridge-bearing hub" is more accurate, because the distinguishing feature of these hubs is that the bearings, races, and cones are assembled, at the bearing factory, as a complete unit—the cartridge—that is then plugged into a hub shell machined to accept the premade cartridge. Cartridge-bearing front hubs have two bearings, one on each end of the hub shell (Fig. 6.22). Rear hubs (Fig. 6.30) may have a cartridge bearing on the left side only and may employ a stock Shimano freehub with loose hub bearings as well as loose freehub bearings on the drive side. Some manufacturers make their own freehubs and have cartridge bearings on both sides of the hub as well as internal to the freehub.

Cartridge-bearing hubs can have any number of axle-assembly types. Some have a threaded axle with

locknuts quite similar to a cup-and-cone hub. More common in the more expensive setups are aluminum axles, often very fat with correspondingly large bearings. Their end caps usually snap on or are held on with setscrews or circlips. The end caps may also thread into the axle and accept a 5mm hex key in the end of each cap.

vi-15 ALL HUBS, PRELIMINARY

1. Remove the wheel from the bike (Chapter 2, §ii-2 and §ii-11).

2. Remove the quick-release skewer or the nuts and washers holding the wheel onto the bike. (This step is unnecessary for hubs that have solid axles held on with nuts or wing nuts, rather than having skewers that pass through hollow axles.)

vi-16 OVERHAUL STANDARD CUP-AND-CONE HUB (FRONT OR REAR)

To isolate problems, take some time to evaluate the hub's condition before disassembling it. Spin the

6.23 Loosening and tightening locknut

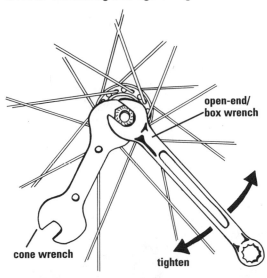

open-end/box wrench

cone wrench

tighten

hub while holding the axle, and turn the axle while holding the hub. Does it turn roughly? Is the axle bent or broken? Wobble the axle side to side. Is the bearing adjustment loose?

a. Disassembly

1. Set the wheel flat on a table or workbench. Slip a cone wrench of the appropriate size (usually 13mm, 14mm, or 15mm) onto the wrench flats on one of the cones. On a rear wheel, work on the left (noncog) side.

NOTE: *On current Campagnolo and Fulcrum high-end hubs, you unscrew the axle into two pieces with 5mm hex keys inserted into either end of the axle. Loosen the setscrew on the large, aluminum, split lock-nut with a 2.5mm hex key (loosen the setscrew three turns). Unscrew and remove the locknut with your fingers or with a 22mm (or adjustable) wrench. Push the axle end toward the hub to free the slide-on cone. Follow steps 7 to 26, and then assemble in the reverse order. For a rear hub, see §vi-22d for hints on rein-stalling the freehub pawls into the hub shell. Adjust the hub by turning the locknut by hand or with a 22mm (or adjustable) wrench until the bearing end play is*

removed, and tighten the setscrew with a 2.5mm hex key. This adjustment can even be performed while the wheel is installed in the frame or fork to get it extremely precise—free-running with no end play.

2. Put an appropriately sized wrench or adjustable wrench on the locknut on the same side.

3. While holding the cone with the cone wrench, loosen the locknut (Fig. 6.23). This may take considerable force, because the parts are usually tightened against each other very securely to maintain the hub's adjustment. Make sure that you are unscrewing the locknut counterclock-wise ("lefty loosey, righty tighty").

4. As soon as the locknut loosens, move the cone wrench from the cone on top to the cone on the opposite end of the axle, in order to hold the axle in place as you unscrew the locknut. On a rear hub, put another open-end wrench on the opposite locknut. Unscrew the loose locknut with your fingers; use a wrench if necessary.

5. Slide any spacers off, keeping track of where they came from. If they will not slide off, the cone will push them off when you unscrew it. Note that some spacers have a small tooth or "key" that corresponds to a lengthwise groove along the axle. Keep these lined up to facilitate removal.

6. Unscrew the cone from the axle. Again, you may need to hold the opposite cone with a wrench. An easy way to keep track of the various nuts, spacers, and cones is to lay them on your work bench in the order they were removed. If that seems too casual, you can slide a twist-tie through all the parts in the correct order and orientation. Either method serves as an easy guide when reassembling the hub.

7. To catch any bearings that might fall out, put your hand over the end of the hub from which you removed the nuts and spacers and flip the wheel over. Have a rag underneath the wheel to catch stray bearings.

8. Pull the axle up and out, being careful not to lose any bearings that might fall out of the hub or might stick briefly to the axle. Leave the cone, spacers, and locknut all tightened together on the opposite end of the axle from the one you disassembled. If you are replacing a bent or broken axle, measure the amount of axle sticking out beyond the locknut. Put the cone, spacers, and locknut on the new axle identically.

9. Remove all of the ball bearings from both sides of the hub. They may stick to a screwdriver with a coating of grease on the tip, or you can push them down through the center of the hub and out the other side with the screwdriver. Tweezers or a magnetic screwdriver might also be useful for removing bearings. Put the bearings in a cup, a jar lid, or the like. Count the bearings, and make sure you have the same number from each side.

10. With a screwdriver, gently pop off the seals (i.e., the dust caps) that are pressed into either end of the hub shell (Fig. 6.24). Be careful not to deform them; leave them in if you can't pop them out without damage. If they are not removed, it is tedious, but not impossible, to clean the dirty grease out of their concave interior with a rag and a thin screwdriver.

b. Cleaning

11. Wipe out the hub shell with a rag. Remove all dirt and grease from the bearing surfaces. With a screwdriver, push a rag through the hub shell and

6.24 Removing dust cap

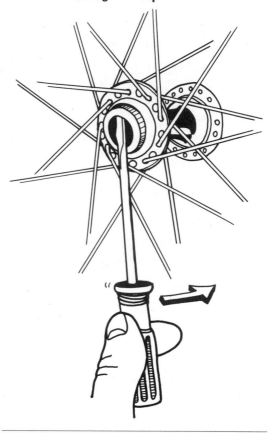

spin it to clean out the hub-shell axle hole. Wipe off the outer faces of the shell. Finish with a very clean rag on the bearing surfaces, which should be shiny and completely free of dirt or grease. If the hub has been neglected, the grease may have solidified and glazed over so completely that you will need a solvent to remove it. Use gloves with the solvent. If you are working on a rear cassette hub, take this opportunity to lubricate the cassette. (See §vi-22 on lubricating cassettes and freewheels.)

12. Wipe down the axle, nuts, and cones with a rag. Clean the cones well with a clean rag; strive for spotless. Again, solvent may be required if the grease has solidified. Get any dirt out of the threads on the disassembled axle end to prevent the cone from pushing the dirt into the hub upon reassembly.

13. Wipe the grease and dirt off the seals. A rag over the end of a screwdriver is sometimes useful to get inside. Again, glaze-hard grease may have to be removed with a solvent. Keep solvent out of the freehub body.

14. Wipe off the bearings by rubbing all of them together between two rags. This may be sufficient to clean them completely, but small specks of dirt can still adhere to them, so I advise the next step as well.

15. If you are overhauling low-quality hubs, skip to step 16. Otherwise, polish the bearings. I prefer to wash them in a plugged sink with an abrasive soap like Lava, rubbing them between my hands as if I were washing my palms. This really gets them shining, unless they are caked with glaze-hard grease. Make sure you have plugged the sink drain! This method has the added advantage of getting my hands clean for the assembly step. It is silly to contaminate your super-clean parts with dirty hands. If there is hardened glaze on the bearings, soak them in solvent. If that does not remove it, buy new bearings at the bike shop. Take a few of the old bearings along so that you get the right size.

16. Dry all bearings and any other wet parts. Inspect the bearings and bearing surfaces carefully. If any of the bearings have pits or gouges in them, replace all of them. Same goes for the cones. A patina or lack of sheen on balls and cones indicates wear and is cause for replacement. Most bike shops stock replacement cones. If the bearing races (or cups) in the hub shell are pitted, the only thing you can do is buy new hubs. Regular maintenance and proper adjustment can prevent pitted bearing races.

NOTE: *Using new ball bearings when overhauling standard cup-and-cone hubs assures round, smooth bearings; however, do not avoid performing an overhaul just because you don't have any new ball bearings. Inspect the bearings carefully. If there is even the slightest hint of uneven wear or pitting on the balls, cups, or cones, throw the bearings out and complete the overhaul with new bearings. Err on the side of caution.*

c. Assembly and lubrication

17. Press the seals or dust covers in on both ends of the hub shell.

18. Smear grease with your clean finger into the bearing race on one end of the hub shell. I like using light-colored or clear grease so that I can see if it gets dirty, but any bike grease will do. Grease not only lubricates the bearings, it also forms a barrier to dirt and water, so use enough grease to cover the balls halfway. Too much grease will slow the hub by packing around the axle.

19. Stick half of the ball bearings into the grease, making sure you put in the same number of bearings that came out. Distribute them uniformly around in the bearing race.

20. Smear grease on the cone that is still attached to the axle, and slide the axle into the hub shell. Lift the wheel up a bit (30-degree angle), so that you can push the axle in until the cone slides into position, keeping all the bearings in place. On rear hubs, it is important to replace the axle and cone assembly into the same side of the hub from which it was removed to preserve drive-side cog spacing.

21. Holding the axle pushed inward with one hand to secure the bearings, turn the wheel over (Fig. 6.25).

22. Smear grease into the bearing race that is now

WHEELS AND TIRES

OVERHAUL
STANDARD
CUP-AND-
CONE HUB

facing up. Lift the wheel and allow the axle to slide down just enough that it is not sticking up past the bearing race. Make sure no bearings fall out of the bottom. If the race and bearings are properly greased and the axle remains in the hub shell, they are not likely to fall out.

23. While the top end of the axle is still below the bearing race, place the remaining bearings uniformly around in the grease. Make sure you have inserted the correct number of bearings.

24. Slide the axle back up into place by setting the wheel down on the table, so that the wheel rests on the lower axle end, seating the cone into the bearings (Fig. 6.26).

25. Cover the top cone with a film of grease and then, with your fingers, screw it into place, seating it snugly onto the bearings.

26. In correct order, slide on the washer and any spacers. Properly align any washers that have a little tooth or "key" that fits into a lengthwise groove in the axle.

27. Use your finger to screw on the locknut. Note that the two sides of the locknut are not the same. If you are unsure about which way the locknut goes back on, check the orientation of the locknut that is on the opposite end of the axle (this locknut was not removed during this overhaul and is assumed to be in the correct orientation). As a general rule, the rough surface of the locknut faces out so that it can get a better purchase on the dropout.

d. Hub adjustment

28. Thread the cone onto the axle until it lightly contacts the bearings. The axle should turn smoothly without any roughness or grinding, and there should be a small amount of lateral

6.25 Push inward on the axle and flip the wheel over

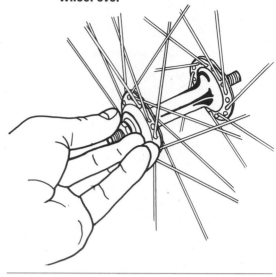

play. Thread the locknut down until it is snug against the cone.

29. Place the cone wrench into the flats of the hub cone. While holding the cone steady, tighten the locknut with another wrench (Fig. 6.27). Tighten it about as snugly as you can against the cone and spacers, in order to hold the adjustment. Be sure that you are tightening the locknut and not the cone; you can ruin the hub if you tighten the cone hard against the bearings.

30. If there is too much play in the axle when you are done, or if the bearings are tight, loosen the locknut while holding the cone with the cone wrench. If the hub is too tight, unscrew the cone a bit. If the hub is too loose, screw the cone in a bit. You may need to put a wrench on the opposite-side cone to effectively tighten or loosen the cone you are adjusting.

31. Repeat steps 28–30 until the hub adjustment feels right. There should be a slight amount of axle-end play so that the pressure of the quick-release skewer will compress it to perfect adjustment. (A hub held on with a nut—no quick release—

6.26 **Seat the bottom cone in the bearings**

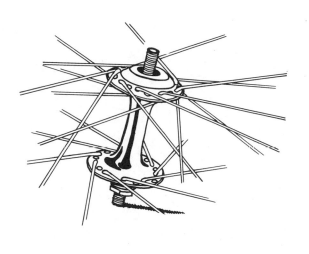

6.27 **Loosening and tightening locknut**

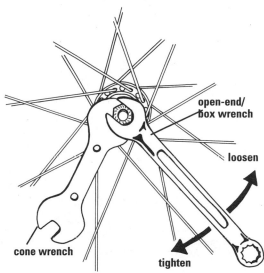

open-end/box wrench

loosen

tighten

cone wrench

should be adjusted with no bearing play.) Tighten the locknut firmly against the cone to hold the adjustment.

NOTE: *You may find that tightening the locknut against the cone suddenly turns your "Mona Lisa" perfect hub adjustment into something slightly less beautiful. If it is too tight, back off both cones (with a cone wrench on either side of the hub, each on one cone) a fraction of a turn. If too loose, tighten both locknuts a bit. If still off, you might have to loosen one side and go back to step 29. It's rare that I get a hub adjustment perfectly dialed-in on the first try, so don't be dismayed if you have to tinker with the adjustment a bit before it's right. You have to have the wheel tightened into the bike to assess the hub adjustment.*

32. Put the skewer back into the hub. Make sure that the conical springs have their narrow ends toward the inside (Fig. 6.21).

33. Install the wheel in the bike and tighten the skewer. Check that the wheel spins well without any side play at the rim. If it needs readjustment, go back to step 31.

34. Congratulate yourself on a job well done! Hub

overhaul is a delicate job, and it makes a difference in the longevity and performance of your bike.

vi–17 OVERHAUL CARTRIDGE-BEARING HUB

LEVEL 2

Cartridge-bearing hubs generally do not need much maintenance. If you ride through water above the hubs, however, you can expect water and dirt to get through any kind of seal. If the ball bearings inside the cartridges get wet, they should be overhauled or replaced.

There are many types of cartridge-bearing hubs, and it is outside the scope of this book to explain how to disassemble every one of them, but it is usually not too hard to figure out how to take apart any hub by looking at it. Some types have externally threaded axles with locknuts on them that you simply unscrew. After that, they may still require insertion of hex keys in the ends to unscrew parts from internal axle threads. On those devoid of external locknuts, though, there will generally be end caps that can be removed by one of the following approaches (overhauling Mavic hubs is explained in §vi-22d):

OVERHAUL
CARTRIDGE-
BEARING HUB

6.28 Tapping out cartridge bearing

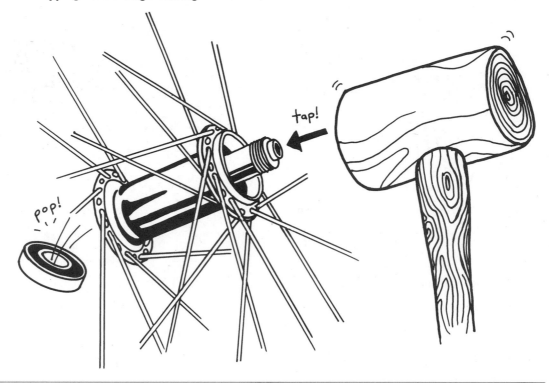

- pulling or prying them off,
- sliding them off after loosening a setscrew on each cap,
- unscrewing the caps with a 5mm Allen wrench inserted into the 5mm hex flats in the through-hole in either axle end,
- on Mavic, unscrewing the axle with a 5mm hex key while holding the other end with either a pin tool in the adjuster ring or a 5mm or 10mm hex key in the bore of the axle, often after pulling off the end cap on the adjuster end, or
- yanking the rear cassette cogset straight off the hub by hand.

Once the end cap is removed, you can often smack the end of the axle with a soft hammer or on a table to remove the axle and perhaps even to dislodge the opposite bearing (Fig. 6.28). Pop the other bearing out the same way. The axle sometimes has a shoulder on each side, internal to the bearings, that can force the bearings out when tapping on the end of the axle.

If the axle has no shoulder to push out the bearing (i.e., Mavic), you need to tap the bearings out with another tool. If you have a bearing puller for your hub, then great. Otherwise, you can often tap on a large screwdriver placed through the bore of the hub against the bearing. Move the tip of the screwdriver around against different points around the inner bearing ring.

Cartridge bearings are vulnerable to lateral stress; if you have damaged them by pounding them out, they will need to be replaced. Be careful when tapping them back in; hold one of the old bearings against each new bearing, and tap the old bearing with the hammer to drive the new one into place.

Once the cartridge bearings are out, you can sometimes overhaul them (otherwise you'll need to buy new ones):

1. Gently pop the bearing covers (i.e., bearing seals) off with a single-edge razor blade (Fig. 6.29). If the bearing seals are steel, you cannot remove them; buy new bearings.

2. Squirt citrus-based solvent into the bearing under pressure (wear rubber gloves and protective glasses) to wash out the grease, water, and dirt. Scrub with a clean toothbrush.

3. Dry the bearing with compressed air.

4. Pack the bearing with grease and snap the bearing covers back on. Replace the bearing if it doesn't turn smoothly.

5. Reassemble the hub the opposite way it came apart. Sometimes the bearings will be out of alignment slightly after installation, making the hub noticeably hard to turn. A light tap on either end of the axle with a soft hammer will often free them.

On Mavic, you adjust the bearing with a pin tool on the adjuster ring, once the hub is tightened into the frame or fork with the quick-release skewer. A little threadlock on the adjuster's threads is a good idea.

NOTE: *Reinstalling the bearings in most of today's cartridge-bearing hubs is relatively easy: simply press the bearings with your hand, or use the shoulder on the axle as a punch to press the bearings into place. In most cases, even a soft hammer is not necessary. However, with some cartridge-bearing hubs (Suntour, Sanshin, Specialized, Mavic, and others), it isn't so easy. The tolerance between the hub cups and the outer surface of the bearing is so tight that these bearings must be pressed in or pounded in with a hammer. A direct blow from a hammer would ruin the bearing, so with these types of hubs, it is best to place the old cartridge bearing you just removed against the new bearing and tap against the old bearing with a hammer.*

6.29 Removing bearing seal

vi-18 GREASE GUARD HUBS

Wilderness Trail Bikes, Suntour, Campagnolo, and others make high-end hubs, some labeled Grease Guard, equipped with grease ports that accept a small-tipped grease gun. Injecting grease into the ports forces lubricant through the bearings from the inside and flushes the old grease out. Also, look for these grease ports on the freehub body under the cogs. Grease injection systems do not eliminate the need for overhauling your hubs, but they extend the amount of time between overhauls. While convenient, these systems are only as good as you are about using them.

FREEHUBS, FREEWHEELS, AND COGS

Freehubs and freewheels allow the rear wheel to turn freely, independent of the chain. Most rely on a series of spring-loaded pawls that engage when pressure is applied to the pedals and disengage when the rider is coasting.

A freehub is an integral part of the rear hub. The cogs slide onto the longitudinal splines of the freehub body (Fig. 6.30). Changing gear combinations is accomplished by removing the cogs from the freehub body and putting on different ones. A freehub can usually be lubricated without removing it from the hub.

6.30 Rear freehub with cartridge bearings and cassette cogs

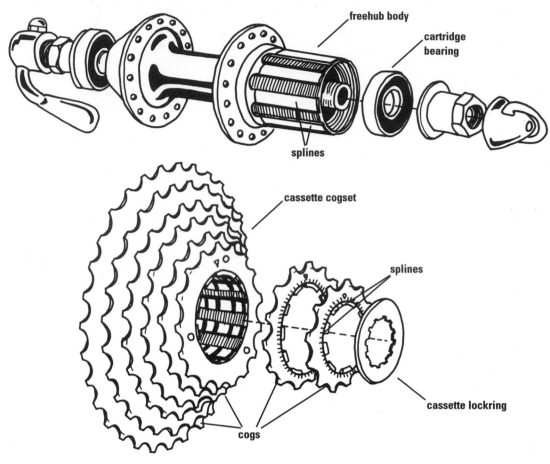

freehub body

cartridge
bearing

splines

cassette cogset

splines

cassette lockring

cogs

A freewheel is a separate unit with the cogs attached to it. The entire freewheel threads onto the drive side of the rear hub (Fig. 6.31). Thread-on freewheels have fallen out of fashion relative to freehubs; changing cogs on freewheels is difficult, and freewheels do not support the drive side of the hub axle. Freewheels can only be removed with a freewheel tool that matches the pattern of the freewheel. Entire freewheels with different gear combinations can be interchanged in this way.

Fixed-gear cogs, as used on track bikes or some winter-training setups on the road, do not freewheel; the cog drives the chain forward. There are two kinds of fixed gears: a standard ³⁄₃₂-inch width for a standard road bike chain and a ⅛-inch width for a

track chain. Neither can be used with a derailleur, and the frame needs to have long horizontal dropouts in order to pull the wheel back enough to tension the chain.

When put on a standard threaded wheel for a road bike, a fixed-gear cog can unscrew when pedaled backward, but the cog is meant to be removed with a chain whip. On a track wheel, there is a second set of threads outboard of the standard hub threads. These threads are smaller in diameter and are left-hand threaded. A left-hand-threaded lockring holds the cog on and is tightened whenever the rider pushes backward on the pedals. The cog is removed by unscrewing the lockring in a clockwise direction with a lockring spanner of the appropriate

6.31 Threaded rear hub with standard ball bearings and freewheel

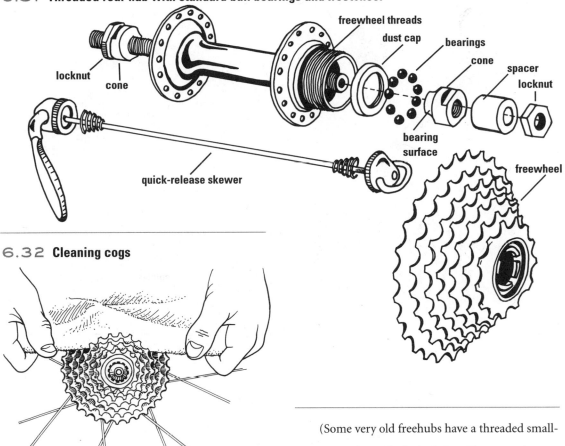

6.32 Cleaning cogs

size, and then unscrewing the lockring in a counter-clockwise direction with a chain whip.

vi-19 CLEANING REAR COGS

The quickest, albeit perfunctory, way to clean the rear cogs is to slide a rag back and forth between each pair of cogs while they are on the hub (Fig. 6.32). The other way—usually unnecessary unless the bike has been neglected—is to remove them (see §vi-20) and wipe them off with a rag or immerse them in solvent.

vi-20 CHANGING CASSETTE COGS

1. Get out a chain whip, a cassette-lockring remover, a wrench (adjustable or open) to fit the remover, and the cog(s) you want to install.

(Some very old freehubs have a threaded small-est cog instead of a lockring. These require two chain whips and no lockring remover.)

2. Remove the skewer.

3. Wrap the chain whip around a cog at least two up from the smallest cog. Wrap in the drive direction (clockwise) so that the cassette is held in place.

4. Insert the splined lockring remover into the lockring; it's the internally splined ring that holds the smallest cog in place. Unscrew it in a counterclockwise direction while using the chain whip to keep the cassette from turning (Fig. 6.33). If the lockring is so tight that the tool pops out without loosening it, install and tighten the skewer, sans springs, through the hub and lockring tool. Loosen the lockring a fraction of a turn, remove the skewer, and unscrew the lockring the rest of the way.

CLEANING
REAR COGS
—
CHANGING
CASSETTE
COGS

6.33 Removing a cassette lockring

chain whip

adjustable
wrench

loosen

6.34 Spline vs. spleen

large spline

large spleen
(not to scale)

**CHANGING
CASSETTE
COGS**

5. Pull the cogs straight off. Some cassette cogsets
   are composed of single cogs separated by loose
   spacers, some cogsets are bolted together, and
   some cogsets are a combination of both.

6. Clean the cogs with a rag or a toothbrush; use solvent if necessary, observing the usual precautions.

7. Inspect the cogs for wear. If the teeth are
   hooked, they may be ripe for replacement.
   Rohloff makes a cog-wear indicator tool; if you
   have access to one, use it according to its supplied instructions.

8. Replace the cogs.

   (a) If you are replacing the entire cogset, just
       slide the new set on. Usually, you'll find
       that one spline is wider than the others
       (Fig. 6.34), so line them up accordingly.

   (b) If you are installing a ten- or nine-speed
       cassette, see the note under step 9.

   (c) If you are replacing some individual cogs
       within your cogset, be certain that they are
       of the same type and model. For example,
       not all 16-tooth Shimano cogs are alike.
       Most cogs have shifting ramps, differen-
       tially shaped teeth, and other asymmetries.
       They differ with model as well as with sizes
       of the adjacent cogs, so you need to buy
       one for the exact location and model.
       Install cogs in decreasing numerical
       sequence with the numbers facing out.

NOTE: *Some bolt-together cogsets can be disassembled for cleaning and then reinstalled onto the freehub
as separate cogs to facilitate future cog changes and
cleaning (the bolts are there for the manufacturer's
convenience, not yours). Note that there are two kinds
of bolt-together cogsets: (1) those with three long, thin
bolts holding the stack of cogs and spacers together*

(Fig. 6.30) and (2) those with cogs bolted or riveted to an aluminum spider that has internal splines to fit on the cassette body. For the type with the three bolts, just unscrew the bolts, take it apart, and put in the replacement cogs. The other type is not to be disassembled from the aluminum spider, and the individual cogs are not to be replaced; you replace each carrier with attached cogs as a complete assembly.

9. First, ensure that the lockring you are using is the right one for both the freehub and the particular cogset. The diameter of the lockring depends on the size of the first cog. With everything back in place, tighten the lockring with the lockring remover and wrench. (If you have the old-type six- or seven-speed freehub with the thread-on first cog, tighten that with a chain whip instead.) Make sure that all of the cogs are seated and can't wobble from side to side, which would indicate that the first or second cog is sitting against the ends of the splines. If the cogs are loose after tightening the lockring, loosen the lockring, line up the first and second cogs to make sure they are in place, and tighten the lockring again.

NOTE ON COMPATIBILITY: *These instructions for removing and replacing cogs apply for ten-, nine-, eight-, seven-, and six-speed cogsets. But the freehub body is usually different for each, so make sure you only use a seven-speed cogset on a seven-speed freehub body, etc.*

NOTE ON 11-TOOTH COGS: *Although all Shimano eight-speed freehubs are wide enough for a ten- or nine-speed cogset, some eight- or nine-speed freehub bodies will not accept 11-tooth cogs (for instance, 1992–1994 Shimano eight-speed freehub bodies will not accept 11-tooth cogs). To accept the small, 11-tooth cog, the splines of current freehub bod-ies stop about 2mm before the outer end of the freehub body. You can file the last 2mm of splines off an old-style eight-speed freehub so that it will accept an 11-tooth cog. The steel is very hard on high-end freehubs, so a grinder may be needed for this job.*

vi-21 CHANGING FREEWHEELS

If you have a freewheel (Fig. 6.31) and want to switch it with another one, follow this procedure. Replacing individual cogs on an existing freewheel is beyond the scope of this book and is rarely done these days owing to unavailability of spare parts.

1. Obtain the appropriate freewheel remover for your freewheel, and round up a big adjustable wrench to fit it.

2. Remove the quick-release skewer and take the springs off it.

3. Slide the skewer back in from the left side, place the freewheel remover into the end of the freewheel so that the notches or splines engage, and thread the skewer nut back on, tightening it against the freewheel remover to keep it from popping out of its notches.

4. Put the big adjustable wrench onto the flats of the freewheel remover and loosen it (counterclockwise). It may take considerable force to free it, and you may even need to put a large pipe on the end of the wrench for more leverage. Set the tire on the ground for traction as you do it. As soon as the freewheel pops loose, loosen the skewer nut before continuing; otherwise, you may snap the skewer in two.

5. Loosen the skewer nut a bit, unscrew the freewheel a bit more, etc., until it spins off freely and there is no longer any danger of having the freewheel remover pop out of the notches.

6. Remove the skewer and spin off the freewheel.

7. Grease the threads on the hub and the inside of the new freewheel.

8. Thread on the new freewheel by hand. You can snug it down with the freewheel remover and a wrench if you like, but it will tighten itself into place with the first few pedal strokes anyway.

9. Replace the skewer with the narrow ends of its conical springs facing inward (Fig. 6.31).

vi-22 LUBRICATING FREEHUBS

a. Simple, minor freehub lubrication

LEVEL 2

Freehubs and freewheels can usually be lubricated for the short term simply by dripping chain lube into them.

Some high-end freehubs have grease-injection holes on the freehub body. Add lightweight grease (frequently) to avoid thickening of the grease inside. Remove the cogs to get at the hole, and meticulously clean any dirt out of the hole before injecting the grease. To be thorough, also before injecting the grease, inject diesel fuel or biodegradable chain cleaner into the hole from a squeeze bottle with a thin tip pressed into the hole. Keep adding solvent until the hub spins without any crunching noises. With a fine-tip grease gun (Fig. 1.3 in Chapter 1), inject the grease.

If the freehub has teeth on the faces of the hub shell and freehub (DT-Hügi or old Mavic freehubs have these radial teeth), just drip oil into the crease between the freehub and the hub shell as you turn the freehub counterclockwise.

For most freehubs, here is the general procedure. The details for lubricating the major types of freehubs follow in separate sections.

1. Disassemble the hub-axle assembly (see §vi-14).

2. Wipe clean the inside of the drive-side bearing surface.

3. With the wheel lying flat and the freehub pointed up toward you, flow chain lube between the bearing surface and the freehub body as you spin the freehub counterclockwise. You will hear the clicking noise of the freehub pawls smooth out as lubricant reaches them. Keep it flowing until old black oil finishes flowing out of the other end of the freehub.

4. Wipe off the excess lube, and continue with the hub overhaul (§vi-16 and §vi-17).

b. Thorough Shimano freehub lubrication

LEVEL 3

By far the best way to lubricate a Shimano freehub is to inject lubricant under pressure into it by using a Morningstar Freehub Buddy tool (Fig. 6.35). Once the hub is apart, most of the work is done. This tool is easy to use, but first you may want to order a reusable dust cap from Morningstar (see the note after step 4).

1. To use this tool, you must first disassemble the hub-axle assembly as described in §vi-16.

2. Pry out the freehub dust cover—ideally with the Morningstar J-tool (Fig. 6.36)—to expose the hub bearing race. On newer, deeper freehubs for ten- or nine-speeds, you can only start moving the dust cap by prying against the freehub-fixing bolt. Then you drop a 6mm bolt down into the 10mm-hex-key hole of the freehub-fixing bolt deep down inside and use its head as a fulcrum for the J-tool to pry against to remove the dust cover the rest of the way.

3. Once the dust cover is off, push the Freehub Buddy into the bearing race (Fig. 6.37).

4. If the freehub has a crunchy feel to it when you

6.35 **Morningstar Freehub Buddy tool**   6.36 **Prying out freehub dust cover with a J-tool**

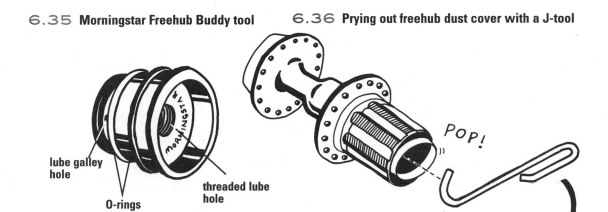

lube galley
hole

O-rings

threaded lube
hole

POP!

spin it, first inject a cleaning solvent such as diesel fuel or bio-degreaser followed by a lubricant into the threaded hole (or the smaller tapered section below the threads) in the center of the Freehub Buddy; it will exit through the lube galley hole in the side of the tool between the two rubber O-rings (Fig. 6.35). The smaller O-ring at the closed end of the Freehub Buddy seals off the center of the hub to prevent lubricant from going in there, and the larger O-ring prevents lube from squirting back out the front of the freehub.

I recommend force-threading the tip of a turkey baster filled with bio-degreaser or diesel fuel into the threaded hole in the center of the Freehub Buddy and squirting it in as you slowly turn the freehub. Tilt the wheel with a bucket below to catch the dirty solvent. Then force-thread the tip of a tube of outboard-motor gear oil or Morningstar's Freehub Soup syringe into the Freehub Buddy's threaded hole and squeeze the gear oil in. Outboard-motor gear oil works great—it's the perfect weight for a freehub, and it comes in a huge toothpaste-type tube whose end fits nicely into the center hole of the tool. Morningstar also sells a "Freehub Soup" lubricant mixture that comes

6.37 **Freehub Buddy installed in the end of a Shimano freehub**

in a syringe that fits in the Freehub Buddy. You can also force-thread a tube of grease, or, better yet, the tip of a glue syringe or turkey baster filled with oil or your own custom mixture of compatible (i.e., synthetic with synthetic or petroleum with petroleum) oil and grease into the Freehub Buddy. Aerosol chain lube can also be squirted into the Freehub Buddy via an included plastic adapter that screws into the threaded hole and accepts the long, thin tube that comes with the spray lube.

Whatever lubricant you use, squeeze it into the Freehub Buddy until all the solvent with the old, dirty lubricant squeezes through the freehub and out the back end of it. Keep going until clean lube oozes out.

Other than by disassembling the entire free-hub, the Freehub Buddy is the only way you can get a lubricant thicker than thin chain lube into your freehub, and a thicker lubricant protects better. Be certain that it's not too thick, how-ever. Filling a freehub with thick grease in cold weather may cause the pawls to stick and not spring back into the freehub teeth to lock it up when you want to pedal forward. You could end up freewheeling in both directions! Always spin the freehub by hand, and, if it does not engage well, purge again with lighter oil that is com-patible with the grease you put inside.

NOTE: *Many freehub dust caps will be ruined upon removal; they are usually made of stamped sheet metal. Shimano does not sell them separately, which complicates freehub service considerably. Morningstar sells machined, removable dust caps with an O-ring seal as well as freehub tools and lubricants. Contact Morningstar Tooling at P.O. Box 213, Bodfish, CA 93205-0213; e-mail: sales@morningstartools.com.*

5. Once the freehub is finished, overhaul the hub and replace the axle assembly.

c. Alternative method of thorough Shimano freehub lubrication without completely disassembling it

1. Disassemble the hub-axle assem-bly as described in §vi-16.
2. Remove the freehub body with a 10mm hex wrench inserted into the freehub-fixing bolt.
3. Completely flush out the freehub. With a rubber stopper from a hardware store, close off the bottom of the freehub body. Pour solvent into the outer opening, spinning the mechanism, letting contaminants run out. If there is a rub-

ber seal, remove it. Repeat until clean.

4. Squirt in a quantity of outboard gear lube, then park the body on paper towels and let the excess drain off. With this method, you do not need to remove the freehub body dust seal.

NOTE: *You can also disassemble a Shimano freehub by unscrewing (clockwise—it's left-hand threaded) the hub bearing cup (that the hub bearings roll in). Morningstar sells a tool that fits into the bearing cup's two notches. I won't go into the details here, but I do illustrate it photographically in my Mountain Bike Performance Handbook.*

d. Mavic freehub lubrication

1. Remove the axle. Depending on model, this step usually involves first pulling the non-drive-side dust cap straight off or unscrew-ing external locknuts from external threads on a steel axle.
2. Depending on the model, using two hex keys (two 5mm hex keys or one 10mm and one 5mm), one in either end, loosen the axle coun-terclockwise, unscrew, and remove.
3. Turn the wheel on its side, freehub up, on a clear surface where you can catch—or at least see—any pawls or pawl springs that might fly away.
4. Rotate the freehub body slowly counterclockwise as you pull up on it, and remove it (Fig. 6.38).
5. Clean the pawls, springs, and hub shell.
6. Replace the springs and pawls, and put 10–20 drops of light oil (Mavic has a mineral oil, M40122, for this) into the freehub (on the plas-tic bushing and the ratchet teeth).
7. Reinstall the freehub body, turning it counter-clockwise while holding the pawls down with your fingers.

6.38 **Removing a Mavic Ksyrium axle and freehub in order to lubricate the freehub and pawls**

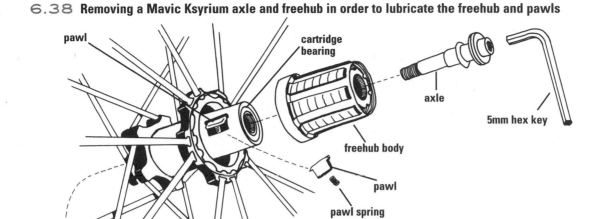

8. Replace the axle. Simple.

NOTE: *This is the same method you use to interchange Mavic freehub bodies from, say, a Shimano-compatible type to a freehub body that accepts Campagnolo cogs.*

e. Campagnolo freehub lubrication

1. On recent high-end Campagnolo or Fulcrum rear hubs, begin by removing the skewer.

2. Insert a 5mm hex key into the drive-side axle end, and put a 17mm open-end or box wrench on the drive-side locknut. While holding the 5mm hex key, unscrew the locknut clockwise (in other words, it's left-hand threaded, and you need to unscrew it the opposite direction from what you would expect). Older Campagnolo models instead have a little setscrew on the 17mm locknut that you loosen with a 2mm hex key in order to unscrew the locknut.

3. Now pull the freehub straight off. Older Campagnolo models have individual little coil springs under each of the three pawls. These can go flying, and they are hard to clean and to insert back into the hub shell. Newer Campagnolo and Fulcrum models have a single, circular, wire spring wrapped around all three pawls (it fits in a groove in the freehub body as well as one cut across the flanks of each pawl). With the new style, you can pull the freehub off with abandon, and nothing will go flying. When removing the freehub body, older models require wrapping a twist-tie around the three pawls as they expose themselves from the hub shell as you pull; if you don't do this, the three pawls and the three springs will fly away.

4. Clean and grease the three pawls and the radial teeth inside the hub shell.

5. Slide the freehub back in while slowly turning it backward. Push inward on each pawl with a pencil tip as you do this, until all three are engaged and the freehub body drops into place. Again, older Campagnolo models require using a twist-tie to hold the pawls in place as you push the freehub in. Pull the twist-tie off after the pawls are inside the hub shell and before the freehub is pushed all the way in.

6. While holding the drive-side end of the axle with a 5mm hex key inside its bore, tighten the locknut on, counterclockwise—remember, it's left-hand threaded!—with a 17mm hex key. Elegant, eh?

NOTE: *This is the same method you use to interchange Campagnolo or Fulcrum freehub bodies from, say, a Campagnolo-compatible type to a freehub body that accepts Shimano cogs.*

f. Lubrication of recent high-end DT Swiss and DT-Hügi freehubs

1. Lay the wheel on its side, cogs up.

2. Grasp the cogset and pull straight up; it will pull the hub end cap off, and the freehub will come off.

3. Clean and grease the spring, both star-shaped ratchets, and the teeth they engage.

4. Push the freehub and dust cap back on.

vi-23 LUBRICATING FREEWHEELS

LEVEL 2

1. Wipe dirt off the face of the fixed part of the freewheel surrounding the axle.

2. With the wheel lying flat and the cogs facing up, drip lubricant into the crease between the fixed and moving parts of the freewheel or cassette as you spin the cogs in a counterclockwise direction. You will hear the clicking noise inside get smoother as the lubricant seeps in. Keep the flow of lubricant going until old, dirty oil finishes flowing out the back side around the hub flange.

3. Wipe off the excess oil.

CHAPTER 7

BRAKES

What do I say to complaints that my brakes are no good?
I'll tell you this: Anyone can stop. But it takes a genius to go fast.
—Enzo Ferrari

TOOLS

2mm, 3mm, 4mm,
5mm, and 6mm
hex keys

cable cutter

wet chain lube

grease

pliers

OPTIONAL

8mm socket
wrench

8mm and 10mm
open-end
wrenches

13mm and 14mm
cone wrenches

adjustable wrench

By far the most common brake for road bikes is the dual-pivot sidepull brake (Fig. 7.1). The predecessor of the road bike dual-pivot brake is the center-pivot sidepull brake (Fig. 7.2), which is also a very powerful and lightweight brake. And going way back to the 1970s, dual-pivot center-pull brakes (Fig. 7.3) were the standard. A couple of other dual-pivot center-pull brakes that did not require a cable hanger (a.k.a. cable stop) or a straddle cable (notably Shimano AX, Campagnolo C-Record, and Croce d'Aune Delta brakes) had brief popularity in the 1980s.

Center-pull cantilever brakes (Fig. 7.4) and sidepull cantilever brakes (i.e., V-brakes, Fig. 7.5) are found on cyclo-cross bikes and many touring bikes and tandems. Both types are light and simple and offer good clearance for mud and big tires. V-brakes and cantilevers pivot on bosses attached to the frame and fork; V-brakes offer the advantage of not requiring a cable hanger fixed to the frame or fork, because the cable routes directly to the brake arm. But a road bike brake lever does not pull enough cable to operate a V-brake without some sort of adapter installed to increase cable pull—hence the continuing popularity of center-pull cantilevers.

And there has long been a tiny contingent using hydraulic brakes that drive the pads straight toward the rim by hydraulic pressure. Road bike models mount in the same bolt hole as standard road bike brakes, but mountain bike versions that mount on the cantilever bosses can be used on cyclo-cross bikes and touring bikes with cantilever studs. Hydraulic brakes are beyond the scope of this book; please consult Chapter 7 of *Zinn & the Art of Mountain Bike Maintenance* for details on these brakes.

7.1 Shimano dual-pivot sidepull brake caliper

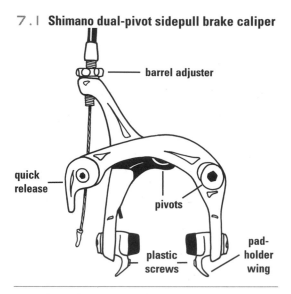

barrel adjuster

quick
release

pivots

plastic
screws

pad-
holder
wing

7.2 Center-pivot sidepull brake caliper

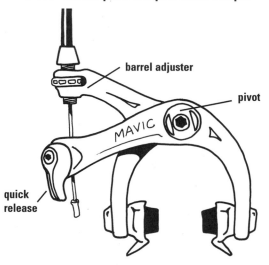

barrel adjuster

pivot

MAVIC

quick
release

7.3 Dual-pivot center-pull brake caliper

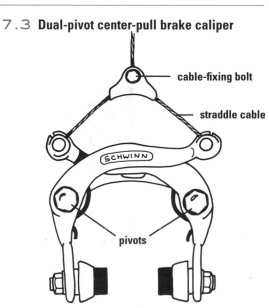

cable-fixing bolt

straddle cable

SCHWINN

pivots

vii-1 RELEASING BRAKES TO REMOVE A WHEEL

Road bike tires are often narrow enough to slip past the brake pads without opening the brakes. With a wide tire or with a brake adjusted for very little clearance between the rim and the pads, the brake will need to be opened a bit. The following instructions describe how to open the vast majority of road bike brakes out there, both old and new. When you put your wheel back in, remember to follow these instructions in reverse so that your brakes will work when you need them.

1. Opening dual-pivot sidepull brakes: For Shimano (Fig. 7.1) and other dual-pivot sidepull brakes besides Campagnolo and Mavic, flip open the quick-release lever on the brake arm. Campagnolo and Mavic dual-pivot sidepull brakes and Campagnolo dual-pivot center-pull brakes do not have a quick-release mechanism on the brake caliper. Instead, there is a cable-release button on the brake/shift lever. On a Campagnolo Ergopower lever (Fig. 7.6), push the button inward so that it clears the edge of the lever housing and allows the lever to flip open wider.

2. Opening center-pivot sidepull brakes: Flip open the lever on the brake arm (Fig. 7.2), the same as on a Shimano dual-pivot sidepull brake. Although older Campagnolo brakes open this way (after the mid-1980s), modern Campagnolo center-pivot sidepull brakes have the quick release on the brake/shift lever (as in Fig. 7.6) and not on the caliper.

3. Opening cantilevers and ancient dual-pivot center-pull brakes: For cantilevers (Fig. 7.4) and older dual-pivot center-pull brakes (Fig. 7.3),

hold the pads against the rim and pull the head of the straddle cable out of the hook at the end of one brake arm.

4. Opening V-brakes: For V-brakes (Fig. 7.5), hold the pads against the rim and pull the cable noodle back and up to release it from the brake-arm link.

5. Opening Shimano AX dual-pivot center-pull brakes: Pull the cable-tensioning barrel adjuster up and out.

CABLES AND HOUSINGS

Given that cables transfer braking force from the levers to the brakes, their proper installation and maintenance are critical to good brake performance. If there is excess friction in the cable system, the brakes will not work properly, no matter how well the brakes, calipers, and levers are adjusted. Cables with broken strands should be replaced immediately.

vii-2 CABLE TENSIONING

As brake pads wear and cables stretch, the cable needs to be tightened. The barrel adjuster on the brake arm of any road bike sidepull brake (Fig. 7.7) and on top of Shimano AX and Campagnolo Delta center-pull brakes serves exactly this purpose.

Center-pull brakes, cantilever brakes, and V-brakes (Figs. 7.3, 7.4, and 7.5) have no barrel adjuster on the brake lever (or brake/shift lever). Therefore, cable tensioning requires either turning a barrel adjuster on a cable hanger on the frame or fork (Fig. 7.8), or loosening the cable-fixing bolt at the brake caliper (Figs. 7.3, 7.4, and 7.5), pulling the cable taut, and tightening the bolt again.

The cable should be tight enough that the lever cannot be pulled to the bar, yet loose enough that

7.4 Center-pull cantilever brake caliper

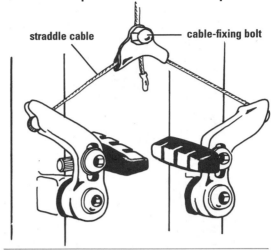

straddle cable — cable-fixing bolt

7.5 Sidepull cantilever brake (V-brake) caliper

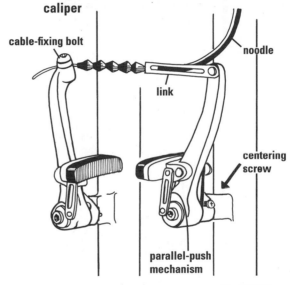

cable-fixing bolt — noodle

link

centering screw

parallel-push mechanism

7.6 Cable-release button on a Campagnolo Ergopower lever

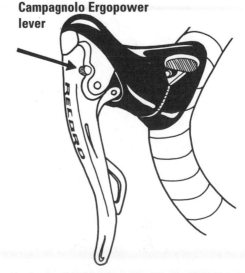

CABLE

TENSIONING

7.7 **Turning the barrel adjuster on the brake arm of sidepull brake caliper**

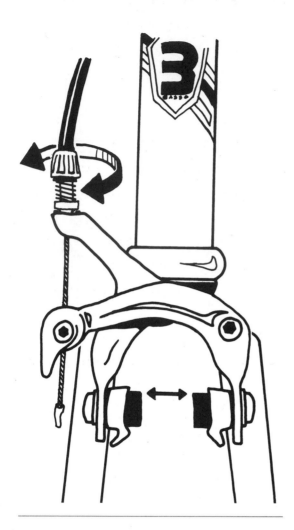

7.8 **Headset cable hanger**

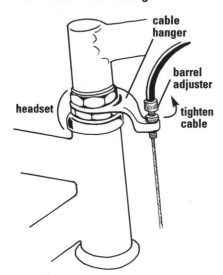

the brakes—assuming they are centered and the wheels are true—are not dragging on the rims.

a. Increasing cable tension

1. For brakes with the barrel adjuster on the caliper (Figs. 7.1, 7.2, and 7.7), back out the barrel adjuster by turning its collar nut clockwise (when viewed from above [at least for most brakes]). For cantilever brakes, recall that the barrel adjuster is on a cable stop (Fig. 7.8). The underside of the adjuster nut usually has bumps that drop in and out of notches in the top of the brake arm or cable hanger to hold its adjustment, so you may wish to hold the pads against the rim with your thumb and fingers to make turning the nut easier.

2. Increase the tension sufficiently that the brake lever (or brake/shift lever) does not hit the handlebar when the brake is applied fully, yet do not make the tension so tight that the brake rubs or comes on with very little movement of

7.9 **Pull the brake cable taut and tighten the cable-fixing bolt**

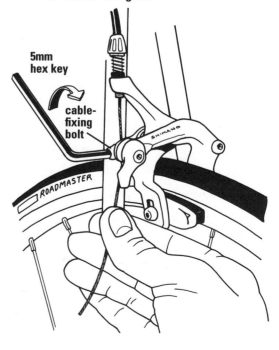

the lever. Lock in the adjustment with the notches in the top of the caliper arm engaging the adjuster nut.

3. You may find that the barrel adjuster cannot take up enough cable slack alone to get the brakes as tight as you want. If so, you need to tighten the cable at the brake. First, screw the barrel adjuster back in most of the way; this step leaves some adjustment in the system for brake setup and cable stretch over time. Loosen the cable-fixing bolt clamping the cable at the brake (Figs. 7.3, 7.4, 7.5, 7.9, and 7.29). Check the cable for wear. If it's badly frayed, replace it. (See Cable Replacement and Installation, §vii-4.) Otherwise, pull the cable tight, and retighten the clamping bolt. Tension the cable as needed with the barrel adjuster.

b. Reducing cable tension

1. Turn the barrel adjuster (Figs. 7.1, 7.2, 7.7, and 7.8) counterclockwise (when viewed from the top) until your brake pads are properly spaced from the rim. You want some movement of the lever before the pads contact the rim, but not so much that the lever comes back to the handlebar under hard braking. Within that range it is up to your personal preference.

2. Let the notches and bumps in the barrel adjuster and brake arm engage to lock in the adjustment.

3. Double-check that the cable is tight enough that the lever cannot be squeezed all the way to the handlebar.

vii-3 CABLE MAINTENANCE

1. If the cable is frayed or kinked or has any broken strands, replace it (see §vii-4).

2. If the cable is not sliding well, lubricate it. Use an oil-based chain lubricant (not a chain wax or other dry lube) or molybdenum disulfide grease, if possible. Lithium-based greases and chain waxes can eventually gum up cables and restrict movement.

3. To lubricate, open the brake (via the cable quick release as when you remove a wheel; see §vii-1).

4. If you have slotted cable stops, pull the ends of the rear brake-cable-housing segments out of each stop. On the front brake—and on the rear brake if your bike does not have slotted cable stops—you will have to disconnect the cable at the brake, clip off the cable end, and pull out the entire cable.

5. Slide the housing up the cable, wipe the cable clean with a rag, rub chain lubricant on the cable section that was inside the housing, and slide the housing back into place. If you have pulled the housing completely off the cable, squirt chain lube through the housing as well.

6. If the cable still sticks, replace the cable and housing.

vii-4 CABLE REPLACEMENT AND INSTALLATION

1. Disconnect the cable at the brake caliper, clip off the cable-end cap, and pull out the old cable from the lever. You will need to pull the lever and then let it back a bit to free the head of the cable from the cable hook in the lever.

NOTE: *When installing a new cable, it is a good idea to replace the housings as well, even if they seem okay. Daily riding in particularly dirty conditions may require cables and housings to be replaced every few months. As with chains and derailleur cables, brake-cable* *replacement is a maintenance operation, not a repair operation; don't wait until a cable breaks or seizes up to replace it.*

2. Purchase good-quality cables and lined housings. For cables, try using "die-drawn" cables; the exterior strands have been flattened by being pulled through a constricting die. They will move with less friction. For housing, you'll find that most brake-cable housing is spiral-wrapped to prevent splitting under braking pressure (see Chapter 5, Fig. 5.13). Plastic-lined housing (i.e., Teflon) reduces friction and is a must.

3. Cut the housing sections long enough to reach the brakes, and route them so that they do not make any sharp bends. If you are replacing existing housing, look at the bends before removing the old housings (after unwrapping the handlebar tape to get at them). If the housing bends are smooth and do not bind when the front wheel is swung through its arc, cut the new housings to the same lengths. Otherwise, cut each new segment longer than you think necessary and keep trimming it back until it gives the smoothest path possible for the cable, without the cable tension's being affected by steering. Use a cutter specifically designed for cutting housings, or a sharp side-cutter.

4. After cutting, make sure the end faces are flat. If not, square them off with a file or a clipper.

5. If the end of the Teflon liner is mashed shut after cutting, open it up with a sharp object like a nail or a toothpick.

6. Slip a ferrule (cylindrical cap) over each housing end for support (see Chapter 5, Figure 5.13). Some brake-arm barrel adjusters function as a ferrule and are too narrow for a ferrule to fit in; they are designed to accept only bare cable housing.

7. Decide which hand you want to control which brake (the standard is that the right hand controls the rear brake, but if you're the only one riding the bike, you can switch it around to match the setup on your motorcycle, for example). Install the housings into each housing stop, brake lever (or brake/shift lever), and brake caliper.

8. Tighten the adjusting barrel on the brake caliper or cable hanger to within one turn of being screwed all of the way in (Figs. 7.7 or 7.8).

9. Insert the cable into the lever, through the cable hook, and out the cable exit hole (Fig. 7.10). On current brakes, the cable exits the inboard side of the lever under the edge of the lever hood so that it can be wrapped under the handlebar tape. Many brake levers prior to 1988 or so, and almost all of them prior to 1980, had the cable coming out the top of the lever.

10. Slide the cable through the housings and to the brake, making sure there is a ferrule on the end of the housing, if one will fit into the barrel adjuster.

NOTE: *With new cables and lined housing, it is usually best not to use a lubricant on the cable. It is not necessary, so why run the risk of it gumming up inside the housing and attracting dirt? (Down the road, when the cable starts to stick, you may need to lubricate it; see §vii-3.)*

11. Attach the cable to the brake. (See the section titled Brake Calipers for the details on your type of brake caliper.) Pull it taut and tighten the cable-fixing bolt (Figs. 7.3, 7.4, 7.5, or 7.9). Pull

CABLE
REPLACEMENT
AND
INSTALLATION

7.10 **Insert the cable into the lever, through the cable hook, and out the exit hole**

7.11 **Tightening a Shimano STI brake/shift lever to the bar with a 5mm hex key**

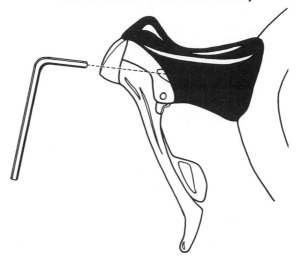

the lever as hard as you can and hold it for 60 seconds to stretch the new cable.

12. Adjust cable tension with the caliper barrel adjuster (as in §vii-2).

13. Cut off the cable about an inch past the cable-fixing bolt. Crimp an end cap on the exposed cable end to prevent fraying (Fig. 5.16 in Chapter 5). Wrap the handlebar tape (see §xi-10 in Chapter 11).

NOTE: *Once the cable has been properly installed, the lever should snap back quickly when released. If it does not, recheck the cable and housing for free movement and sharp bends. Release the cable quick release and hold the pads to the rim with your hand while checking the lever for free movement. With the cable still loose, check that the brake pads do not drag on the tire as they return to the neutral position; make sure the brake arms rotate freely on their pivots, and check that the brake-arm return springs snap the pads away from the rims. If the lever and caliper move freely and spring back strongly, and if there are no obvious binds in the system, check for frayed strands within the housing sections, and then try lubricating the cable as in §vii-5).*

BRAKE LEVERS (OR BRAKE/SHIFT LEVERS)

The levers must operate smoothly and be set up so that you can reach them easily while riding.

vii-5 LUBRICATION AND SERVICE

1. Lubricate all pivot points in the lever with grease or oil.

2. Check return-spring function on the lever (note, though, that not all levers have springs in them).

3. Make sure that the lever or lever body is not bent in a way that hinders movement.

4. Check for stress cracks. If you find any, replace the lever.

5. Replace torn or cracked lever hoods.

vii-6 REMOVAL, INSTALLATION, AND POSITIONING

Most current brake levers integrate the brake lever and the shifter in a single unit (Figs. 7.6 and 7.11). To work on the brake/shift (or "dual control") levers, follow these steps:

LUBRICATION
AND SERVICE
—
REMOVAL,
INSTALLATION,
AND
POSITIONING

1. Remove the handlebar tape.

2. Loosen the brake/shift lever's (or the brake lever's) mounting bolt with a 5mm Allen wrench and slide the lever off. The position of the bolt varies. On current dual-control levers, it is on the outboard side of the lever under the lever hood. Slip the hex key down from the top between the lever body and the hood rather than trying to roll back the hood far enough to get at it from outside (Fig. 7.11). On Campagnolo Ergopower (Fig. 7.6), the bolt is on the outside toward the top; on Shimano STI (Fig. 7.11), it is on the middle of the outer side. Old-style brake levers have the mounting bolt in the center of the lever body, and it is reached by pulling the lever and sticking the hex key straight in. Campagnolo and other European levers from the early 1980s and before used a hex nut (accessed with an 8mm socket wrench) rather than an Allen bolt.

3. Slide the new lever on the bar to where you like it. A good rule of thumb is to put a straightedge against the bottom of the bar and slide the lever down until its end touches the straightedge. The lever can sit a little higher than this if you like (and the post–Lance Armstrong style is to have the levers quite high on the handlebar), but generally not any lower. Put a straightedge across the top of both levers to make sure they are level.

4. Tighten the mounting bolts.

5. Install the cables (see §v-6 to §v-15 in Chapter 5 and §vii-4).

6. Wrap the handlebar tape (see §xi-10 in Chapter 11).

vii-7 REACH

There is no reach-adjustment screw on a road bike brake lever or brake/shift lever. If you have small hands and have difficulty reaching the levers, there are a few things you can try.

First, you can try different positions on the bar for the lever. This may bring the lever closer to the bar.

Another option is to buy a bar with a different bend that puts the palm of the hand closer to the lever. There are some bars specifically made to accomplish this feat.

Finally, you can try to buy a smaller lever. This used to be relatively simple when brake levers were just brake levers. But now, with dual-control levers that incorporate the shifters, you cannot swap a shorter lever from another manufacturer, and the levers made by derailleur manufacturers do not come in different reaches, with one mid-range exception from Shimano. You can buy a whole new brake and derailleur system to get one with a reach you prefer, if necessary, but I recommend investigating a different handlebar first.

BRAKE CALIPERS

The caliper of a brake is the mechanism that pinches the pads inward against the wheel rim. In most cases, a road bike caliper is a sidepull device that bolts on through a hole in the brake bridge or fork crown (Figs. 7.1, 7.2, 7.12, and 7.13). But the word "caliper" has other uses, including the name of a type of measuring tool (see Fig. 1.4). The word can also refer to the pair of arms of a cantilever or V-brake that attach to pivot posts welded onto the frame and fork (Figs. 7.4 and 7.5). And then there are those old center-pull calipers (Fig. 7.3) from 1970s Raleighs and Peugeots . . . .

7.12 **Tightening a caliper to the brake bridge with a 5mm hex key**

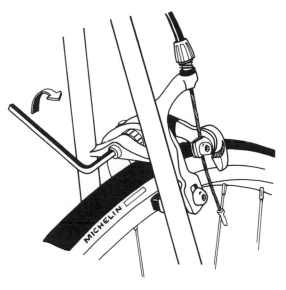

7.13 **Turning setscrew with a 3mm hex key to center a Shimano dual-pivot brake caliper**

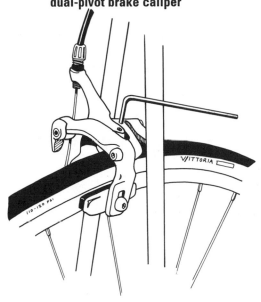

vii–8 DUAL-PIVOT SIDEPULL BRAKES

Dual-pivot sidepull brakes (Figs. 7.1 and 7.13) have become the industry standard. They are powerful and easy to keep in adjustment.

Campagnolo and Mavic dual-pivot brakes have some features distinct from Shimano brakes in this category. Shimano brakes generally share features with Asian copies.

a. Installation

Stick the center bolt through the hole in the brake bridge or fork crown and tighten it in place with a 5mm hex key inserted into the recessed nut (Fig. 7.12). Hold it roughly centered over the wheel as you tighten the nut.

b. Cable hook-up

Have the quick release on the caliper (or on the lever on Campagnolo) open as you do the cable hook-up. Route the cable housing into the barrel adjuster on the upper brake arm. On the end of the housing, install a ferrule if one will fit into the barrel adjuster (see §vii-4). Push the cable through the housing and

the barrel adjuster and under the cable-fixing-bolt washer on the lower brake arm. Pull the cable taut, and tighten the bolt with a 5mm hex key (Fig. 7.9). Close the quick release after the cable is connected.

c. Centering

You are trying to achieve an equal amount of space between the pad and the rim on each side. The simplest and quickest way to center these brakes requires no tools. Just grab the brake and twist the entire thing into position (don't mess with the mounting bolt; leave it tight). Or just pull outward on the pad that is closer to the rim. But do make sure before riding that the recessed nut on the back of the brake bridge or fork is tight (Fig. 7.12).

The centering method built in by Campagnolo and Shimano consists of a setscrew, while Mavic brakes involve the mounting bolt.

Campagnolo has a 2mm hex setscrew on the side opposite the cable, just above the pad on the arm. As you tighten the screw, the pad on that side moves away from the rim. Loosen the screw, and the other pad (the

7.14 Line the pad up with the rim

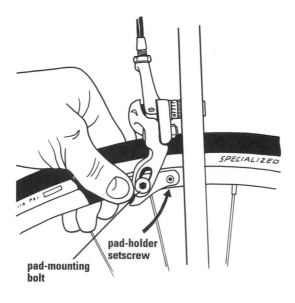

pad-holder setscrew

pad-mounting bolt

one on the cable side) moves away from the rim.

Shimano's setscrew is on the upper end of the opposite brake arm. It takes a 3mm hex key (Fig. 7.13), and tightening it moves the pad on that side away from the rim. Loosen it, and the other pad (the one on the cable side) moves away from the rim.

Mavic dual-pivot sidepull brakes require working a 5mm hex key in the recessed mounting nut along with a 14mm cone wrench on the nut behind the brake caliper (similar to center-pivot centering—see Fig. 7.15).

d. Pad adjustment

Loosen the pad-mounting bolt with a hex key (generally 4mm or 5mm). Slide the pad up and down along the groove in the arm to get the pad even with the height of the rim's braking surface. Twist the pad in the vertical plane to have the top edge of the pad follow the curve of the top edge of the rim (Fig. 7.14). While squeezing the brake lever to hold the pad against the rim, tighten the pad-mounting bolt. Make sure the pad does not twist as you tighten (if it

does, you will have to hold it with your fingers as you cinch the bolt).

Current Campagnolo brakes also have an orbital adjustment of the pads to align the face of the pad flat against the rim and to allow a toe-in adjustment of the pad by means of a concave washer that nests against the convex face of the pad holder. If you have brake squeal or want to reduce grabbiness, toe the pads in a bit so that the forward end of the pad is a little bit closer to the rim than the rearward end. A 1mm toe-in is sufficient to eliminate squeal and grabbiness.

NOTE: *Users of Shimano pre-built wheels with Dura-Ace or Ultegra brakes will want to remove the little plastic screw in the pad-holder wing (below the pad—see Fig. 7.1). Otherwise, as soon as the pad gets a bit worn, that screw will thump-thump-thump against the bend in the spoke where it exits the side of the rim.*

e. Spring-tension adjustment

Campagnolo dual-pivot brakes have a setscrew that pushes on the end of the return spring. It is located on the side of the arm above the cable-side pad. If you tighten this screw (with a 2mm hex key), you tighten the spring, thus making the brake both harder to pull and quicker to snap back. There is no tension adjustment on Shimano brake springs or on the leaf spring in new Mavic brakes. Some springs can be bent with pliers to increase tension.

f. Cable-tension adjustment

Follow the instructions in §vii-2.

g. Pad replacement

When the pads get so worn that the grooves cut into the pads are almost gone, you ought to replace them. Most pads these days are molded in one piece with the mounting nut insert or stud, so you just unscrew the old pad and bolt the new one in place.

DUAL-PIVOT SIDEPULL BRAKES

High-end Shimano, Campagnolo, and Mavic dual-pivot brakes surround the pad with an aluminum holder that is bolted to the brake arm. The pad can be replaced separately by sliding it from the holder. Some Shimano and Mavic pad holders have a setscrew (Fig. 7.14) that must first be backed out to free the pad. Buy the correct pad for your year and model of brake.

It is not easy to slide any pad in or out of the holder. You may have to yank out the old pad with pliers and slide in the new pad with the aid of a vise, or hold the post in a vise while you push on the pad grooves with a screwdriver.

Make sure that you put the proper pad in the proper holder; look at the old one for guidance. Campagnolo pads say DX (right) or SX (left) on the back side. Shimano pads often say R or L on the back side and indicate the forward direction. Be prepared for some work pushing the new pads into the holders, at least with Campagnolo; use a vise and keep cutting off the burrs of pad material that may get peeled back by the edges of the pad holder.

When you reinstall the pad to the brake arm, make sure that the closed end of the pad holder faces forward. Otherwise, the first time you brake hard, you may see two pieces of rubber fly ahead of you and feel two more hit the backs of your legs. You may not remember anything after that.

vii-9 CENTER-PIVOT SIDEPULL BRAKES

Center-pivot sidepull brakes (Fig. 7.2) are found on lots of bikes, because they were the standard from the late 1970s to the early 1990s, and current high-end Campagnolo brake sets use them on the rear to save weight. They, too, work great and are easy to set up and adjust. Many adjustments are the same as those on dual-pivot brakes.

PRO TIP

BRAKE PAD SELECTION FOR CARBON RIMS

Although not all brake pads are created equal, and braking improvements can be had by upgrading the pads used with aluminum rims, it is absolutely critical to get the right pad if you are using all-carbon rims. The pad compound appropriate for all-carbon rims is quite different, because normal high-rubber brake pads cannot take the heat of braking on carbon rims and can actually melt. This is because carbon is an insulator and does not transmit heat easily and evenly away from where it is being generated. Aluminum, on the other hand, is a conductor that allows the heat to spread and dissipate throughout the rim. Add to that the fact that carbon rims are generally lighter and hence have less thermal mass to absorb heat, and you are talking some hot brake pads.

Carbon rims often come with pads made for them, and approaches vary in their manufacture. Cork pads are also often used for carbon rims owing to cork's high coefficient of friction and its resistance to heat.

Even with specific carbon-rim pads, wear rates are very high on most carbon braking surfaces. After descending a few kilometers of switchbacks, you will notice a buildup of melted pad material sticking out the front of your pads. Make sure that you check your pads frequently and replace them before they get too worn. You would not be the first to have brake failure on a carbon rim.

7.15 **Centering a center-pivot sidepull brake with a cone wrench**

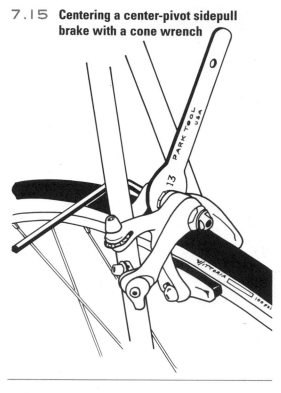

a. Installation

Stick the center bolt through the hole in the brake bridge or fork crown and tighten it in place with a 5mm hex key inserted into the recessed nut (Fig. 7.12). Hold it roughly centered over the wheel as you tighten the nut.

Some older bikes do not have a countersunk hole in the back of the brake bridge and fork crown. With these, you need a brake with a longer center bolt and a standard nut, which you tighten with a 10mm box wrench.

b. Cable hook-up

Have the quick release on the caliper (or on the lever on some current Campagnolo levers) open as you make this hook-up. Route the cable housing into the barrel adjuster on the upper brake arm. If one will fit into the barrel adjuster, install a ferrule on the end of the housing (see §vii-4). Push the cable through the housing and the barrel adjuster and under the cable-fixing bolt washer on the lower brake arm. Pull the

cable tight and tighten the bolt with a 5mm hex key (same as with a dual-pivot brake, Fig. 7.9) or an 8mm box wrench.

c. Centering

You want an equal amount of space between the pad and the rim on each side. Turn the brake the direction you need with a cone wrench (usually 13mm or 14mm) slipped onto the flats of the center bolt between the brake and the frame (Fig. 7.15). Hold the brake-mounting nut at the same time, making sure that it is tight when you are finished.

d. Pad adjustment

Loosen the pad-mounting bolt with a hex key or box wrench. Slide the pad up and down along the groove in the arm to get the pad even with the height of the rim's braking surface. Twist the pad in the vertical plane to make the top edge of the pad follow the curve of the top edge of the rim (the same as with a dual-pivot brake, Fig. 7.14). While squeezing the brake lever to hold the pad against the rim, tighten the bolt. Make sure the pad does not twist as you tighten (if it does, you will have to hold it with your fingers as you cinch down on the bolt).

e. Spring-tension adjustment

Some center-pivot sidepull brakes have a spring-tension adjusting screw. And on some Shimano center-pivot brakes, the piece of plastic at each end of the spring can be reversed to tighten or loosen the spring. The hole through which the end of the spring slides is offset in the wafer-shaped plastic piece. Push inward on the end of the spring to free the plastic wafer from the brake-arm tab, flip the wafer over, and push it back in place under the tab. If the hole is to the outside, the spring is looser; if the wafer is flipped so that the hole is toward the inside, the spring is as tight as it is going to get.

7.16 Cantilever brake assembly

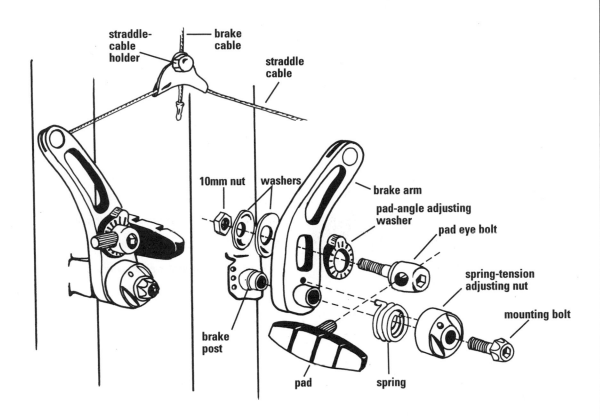

straddle-cable holder — brake cable

straddle cable

10mm nut — washers

brake arm

pad-angle adjusting washer

pad eye bolt

spring-tension adjusting nut

mounting bolt

brake post

pad

spring

f. Cable-tension adjustment

Follow the instructions in §vii-2.

g. Pad replacement

When the pads are worn down to the point that the grooves cut into the pads are almost gone, you ought to replace them.

Most pads are molded in one piece with the mounting nut insert or mounting stud, so you just unscrew the pad and bolt the new one in place.

High-end Shimano, Campagnolo, Mavic, and Modolo brake pads are held inside a holder that is bolted to the brake arm. You slide the rubber pad to remove it from the holder, but often it is not easy. You may have to yank out the old pad with pliers and slide in the new pad with the aid of a vise; see §vii-8g for more on this.

When you reinstall the pad to the brake arm, make sure that the closed end of the pad holder faces forward. Otherwise, the first time you brake hard, you may see two pieces of rubber fly ahead of you and feel two more hit the backs of your legs. You may not remember anything after that.

vii-10 CANTILEVER BRAKES

Found on cyclo-cross bikes as well as some touring bikes and tandems, cantilever brakes offer greater clearance over the tire for mud to pass through or for fenders, or large tires, to fit. They mount onto brake posts integral to the frame and fork and have two separate arms that are pulled toward each other when the brake cable pulls up on a link wire connecting the two arms (Fig. 7.4).

Short-arm cantilever brakes work acceptably with road bike levers, but long-arm ones require more cable pull than road bike levers are able to muster.

In order to mount cantilevers, a cable stop is required on the frame's seatstays or hanging off the seat binder bolt, and another one is required attached to the fork steering tube, below the stem (Fig. 7.8). Whether it is on the front or rear, a barrel adjuster, as on the cable hanger in Figure 7.8, makes brake setup far easier, because there is not a barrel adjuster on a road bike brake/shift lever, as there is on a mountain bike lever.

a. Installation

1. Grease the outside of the brake posts (Fig. 7.16). Avoid getting grease inside the brake post threads; brake-mounting bolts are treated with threadlock goop to prevent them from vibrating loose.

2. If you have the installation directions that came with your brakes, follow them. If not, follow the general installation instructions here.

3. Make sure you install the brakes with all of the parts in the order in which they were originally in the package (or on a previous bike). In particular, the springs will often be of different colors and are not interchangeable from left to right.

4. If the brake has a separate inner sleeve bushing to fit over the cantilever boss, install that first. Slip the brake arm and return spring over it.

5. Determine what sort of return system your brakes use:

   (a) If the brake arms have no spring-tension adjustment, or a setscrew on the side of one of the arms for adjusting spring tension, go to step 6; such brakes use the

hole in the cantilever boss to anchor the bottom end of the spring.

   (b) If the brake arms have a large nut surrounding the mounting bolt for adjusting spring tension behind the brake arm or in front of it (Fig. 7.16), skip to step 8; these brakes do not use the hole in the cantilever boss as a spring anchor.

6. Slip the brake arm onto the boss, inserting the lower end of the spring into the hole in the cantilever boss (if the boss has three holes, try the center hole first; use a higher hole to make the brake response snappier, a necessity with lower-quality or old brakes). You want to make sure that the top end of the spring is inserted into the corresponding hole in the brake arm as well.

7. Install and tighten the mounting bolt into the cantilever boss. Skip steps 8–10.

8. If step 5b brings you here, slip the brake arm (with any included bushings) onto the cantilever boss.

9. Install the spring so that one end inserts into the hole in the brake arm and the other inserts into the hole in the adjusting nut.

10. Install and tighten the mounting bolt while holding the adjusting nut with the appropriate open-end wrench (usually 15mm) so that the pad is touching the rim to facilitate pad adjustment later.

b. Pad replacement and installation

1. Remove the old pad, if applicable.

2. Install the new pad. Most cantilevers rely on an eye bolt with an enlarged head and a hole through it to accept the pad post (Fig. 7.16). Some cantilevers (Avid and Onza, for example), have a slotted clamp with a hole for the pad

7.17 Cantilever brake with pad clamps on cylindrical brake arms

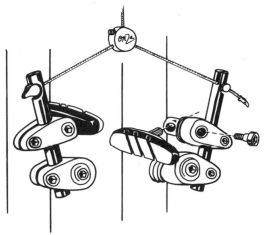

7.18 Threaded-post cantilever brake

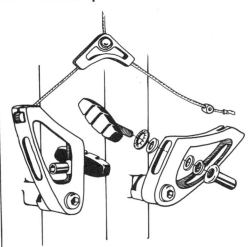

post (Fig. 7.17). A few types of cantilever brakes use a threaded pad post that passes through a slot in the brake arm (Fig. 7.18) like on a V-brake (Fig. 7.5).

3. If your brake spring can be adjusted so that it holds the pad against the rim, set it up that way now. It will make the pad adjustments much easier. If not, you will have to push each arm toward the rim as you adjust the pad.

c. Pad adjustment

Pad adjustments are quite easy with some brakes and a real pain in the rear with others. There are five separate adjustments (a through e in Figs. 7.19–7.21) that must be made for each pad:

- offset distance of the pad from the brake arm (extension of the pad post) (distance a in Fig. 7.19),
- vertical pad height (distance b in Fig. 7.20),
- pad swing in the vertical plane for mating with the rim's sidewall angle (angle c in Fig. 7.19),
- pad twist to align the length of the pad with the rim's curvature (angle d in Fig. 7.20), and
- pad swing in the horizontal plane to set toe-in (angle e in Fig. 7.21).

Cantilevers that feature a cylindrical brake arm are by far the easiest to adjust (Fig. 7.17). Pad adjustment is simple because the pad is held to the cylinder with a clamp that offers almost full range of motion. Avid, Onza, Gravity Research Pipe Dreams, and Dia-Compe VC900 all rely on this type of system. Other cantilevers employ a single eye bolt to hold all five pad adjustments (the eye bolt and washers are exploded in Fig. 7.16 and are seen from above in Fig. 7.21). A bit of manual dexterity is required to hold all five adjustments simultaneously while tightening the bolt. Here is the pad-adjustment procedure for all types of cantilevers:

1. Loosen the pad-clamping bolt, lubricate the pad-fixing threads, and set the pad offset (distance a in Fig. 7.19) by sliding the post in or out of the clamping hole. The farther the pad is extended away from the brake arm, the greater the angle of the brake arm will be from the plane of the wheel. A benefit of this geometry is that leverage is increased (see straddle-cable angle in Figs. 7.24 and 7.25). However, there are two drawbacks: (a) the brake feels less firm, because less force is required to pull the lever,

7.19 **Distance of pad to fixing bolt (a, pad offset) and angle against rim (c, pad swing in vertical plane)**

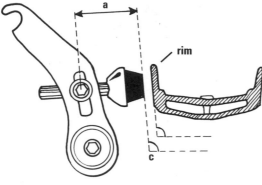

7.20 **Up and down (b, vertical pad height) and rotate (d, pad twist)**

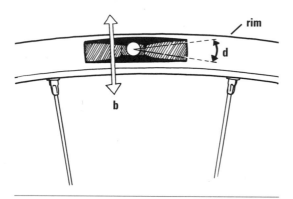

7.21 **Brake-pad toe-in (e, horizontal pad swing)**

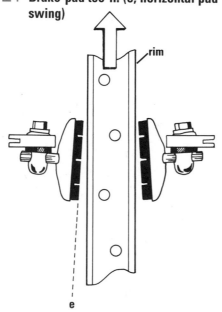

and (b) clearance between the rider's heel and the rear-brake arms is reduced, particularly for small frames. A good initial position is with the post clamped in the center of its length.

NOTE: *With threaded-post pads (Fig. 7.18), placing spacers between the brake arm and the pad sets pad offset. Lube the pad threads.*

2. Roughly adjust the vertical pad height (distance b in Fig. 7.20) by sliding the pad-clamping mechanism up and down in the brake-arm slot. For cantilever brakes with pad clamps on cylindrical brake arms (Fig. 7.17), loosen the bolt clamping the pad holder to the brake arm, and snug the bolt back up once the rough adjustment is reached. With all other types, leave the pad bolt just loose enough so that you can move the pad easily.

3. Adjust pad swing in the vertical plane (angle c in Fig. 7.19) so that the face of the pad meets the rim flat with its top edge 1–2mm below the top of the rim. Fine-tune this adjustment by simultaneously sliding the pad up or down while rotating it to meet the rim flat.

4. Adjust the pad twist (angle d in Fig. 7.20) so that the top edge of the pad is parallel to the top of the rim. Modern pads are quite long and require precision with this adjustment. For cantilever brakes with pad clamps on cylindrical brake arms (Fig. 7.17), the pad-securing bolt may now be tightened.

5. Finally, adjust the pad toe-in (angle e in Fig. 7.21). The pad should be adjusted either flat to the rim or toed-in so that, when the forward end (note the arrow in Fig. 7.21) of the pad touches the rim, the rear end of it is 1mm to 2mm away from the rim.

7.22 Curved-face cantilever brake (Ritchey)

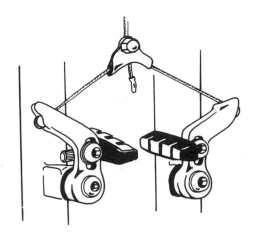

7.23 Ball-joint cantilever brake (Campagnolo)

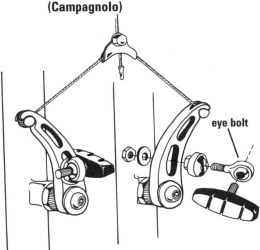

eye bolt

If the pad is toed-out, the heel of it will catch the rim and will tend to chatter, making an obnoxious squealing noise. If the brake arms are not stiff, or they fit loosely on the cantilever boss, the same thing will happen when the pad is flat; toe-in is a must with flimsy brake arms and will have to be adjusted frequently as the pads wear in order to keep them quiet.

On cylindrical-arm brakes with two fixing bolts (Fig. 7.17), the toe-in is adjusted by again loosening the bolt that holds the vertical-height adjustment of the pad. Because you have already tightened the other bolt that holds the pad in place, you simply loosen this second bolt and swing the pad horizontally until you arrive at your preferred toe-in setting. Tighten the bolt again, and you are done with pad adjustment.

With any brake using a single bolt to hold the pad as well as control its rotation, you now have a tricky task of holding all of the adjustments you have made and simultaneously tightening the nut. Most eye-bolt systems are tightened with a 10mm wrench on the nut on the back of the brake while the front is held with a 5mm Allen wrench. Help from someone else to either hold or tighten is use-

ful here. Probably the trickiest brake to adjust has a big toothed or notched washer between the head of the eye bolt and a flat brake arm (Fig. 7.16). The adjusting washer is thinner on one edge than the other, so rotating it (by means of the tooth or notch) toes the pad in or out. With this type, you must hold all of the pad adjustments as you turn this washer, and then keep it and the pad in place as you tighten the nut. It's not an easy job, and the adjustment changes as you tighten the bolt.

The other common type of brake has a convex or concave shape to the slotted brake arm (Shimano, most Dia-Compe, Ritchey [Fig. 7.22], Paul, etc.). Cupped washers separate the eye-bolt head and nut from the brake arm. The concave or convex surfaces allow the pad to swivel, and tightening the bolt secures everything. Again, you may not get it on the first try. Threaded posts also employ such washers.

NOTE: *Some of these curved-face brakes do not hold their toe-in adjustment well; you may need to sand the brake arm faces and washers to create more friction between them.*

Brakes with a cylindrical arm and a clamp secured only by the pad eye bolt (WTB, SRP, etc.) are

7.24 **Straddle-cable angle when open**

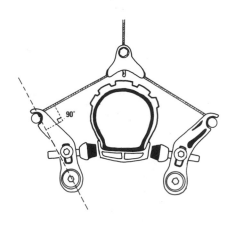

7.25 **Straddle-cable angle when closed**

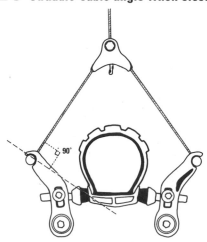

CANTILEVER

BRAKES

adjusted functionally the same as the curved-face ones with cupped washers.

A rare but simple-to-adjust type of brake has a ball joint at each pad's eye bolt (Campagnolo, Fig. 7.23).

d. Straddle-cable adjustment

The straddle cable should be set so that it pulls on the brake arms in such a way as to provide optimal braking. This is not always the adjustment that produces the highest leverage, for sometimes brake feel (i.e., stiffness when pulling the lever) is improved when leverage is reduced, because you are doing more of the work. In general, I recommend setting the straddle cable for high leverage and reducing it from there to improve lever feel.

With any lever arm, the mechanical advantage is highest when the force is applied at right angles to the lever arm. For general purposes, set the straddle cable so that it pulls as close to 90 degrees to the brake arm (i.e., the lever arm) as you can (Fig. 7.24). An esoteric and more precise argument is that, once the pad hits the rim, the actual lever arm is the line from the face of the pad to the cable attachment point on top of the arm (because the pad, not the brake post, now becomes the fulcrum). If you set the straddle cable at 90 degrees

from this line, the leverage is maximized (Fig. 7.25).

With low-profile brake arms (i.e., more vertical arms that don't stick out to the sides as much), however, a 90-degree straddle-cable angle results in a short straddle cable set very low and close to the tire. Make sure that you allow at least an inch of clearance over the tire to prevent mud or a bulge in the tire from engaging the brake.

The straddle cable (Figs. 7.26–7.28) usually has a metal blob on one end. On a standard straddle cable (Fig. 7.26), the other end is clamped to one brake arm by the cable-fixing bolt, as in Figure 7.31. The blob fits into the slotted brake arm and acts as a quick release for the brake.

With Shimano cantilevers built since 1988, the brake cable connects directly to the cable clamp on one brake arm, and a link wire hooks to the other arm. On post-1993 Shimano cantilevers, the cable passes through a link-wire holder carrying not only a link wire but also a fixed length of cable housing (Fig. 7.27). The brake cable passes directly through the link-wire holder and housing segment to the cable clamp on the brake arm. The mechanic has no choice of straddle-cable settings; it is predetermined.

7.26–7.28 Straddle cables

7.29 Tightening cantilever brake cable

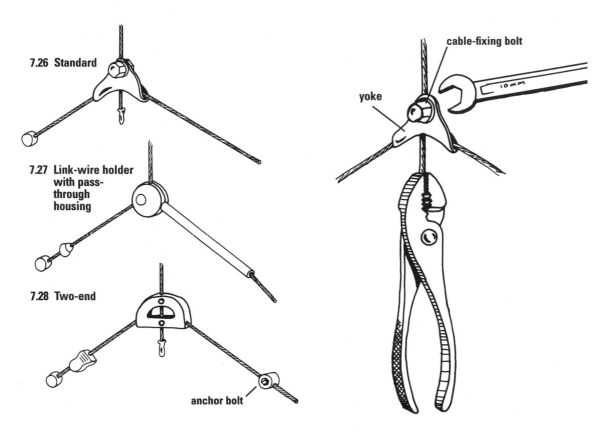

7.26 Standard

7.27 Link-wire holder with pass-through housing

7.28 Two-end

anchor bolt

cable-fixing bolt

yoke

IOmm

Between 1988 and 1993, Shimano brakes did not have the housing segment on the link-wire holder; the holder was instead clamped to the brake cable, and its position was set by a plastic gauge. If you have this type and no gauge, simply set the cable length from link-wire holder to brake arm the same on both sides.

Some brakes do not have a cable clamp on either brake arm; both arms are slotted to accept the blob on the end of a straddle cable or link wire. Figures 7.16, 7.17, 7.18, 7.23, 7.24, and 7.25 all illustrate this type of brake. In this case, a small, cylindrical clamp forms a second blob on the end of the straddle cable (Fig. 7.28), or a link-wire holder that holds two separate link wires is used.

With any straddle cable, after setting its length,

the straddle-cable holder position is set by loosening the bolt or setscrews that hold it onto the end of the brake cable and sliding it up on the brake cable. Tighten it in place (Fig. 7.29, or see Figs. 7.26–7.28 for other types). It is set properly when the brake engages quickly, and the lever cannot be pulled closer than a finger's width from the bar. The lateral position of the straddle-cable holder can be changed with setscrews as well. The holder should generally be centered on the straddle cable, but some brake cables pull asymmetrically as they come around the seat tube. In these cases, the straddle-cable holder may need to be offset for the brakes to work (Fig. 7.30).

e. Spring-tension adjustment

The spring-tension adjustment centers the brake pads

7.30 An offset straddle-cable stop requires an offset straddle hanger

7.31 Adjusting return-spring tension with a setscrew

cable-fixing bolt

spring-tension adjuster bolt

about the rim and also determines the return spring force. There is only one adjustment to make on brakes with a single setscrew on the side of one brake arm. Turn the screw until the brake arms are centered and the pads hit the rim simultaneously when applied (Fig. 7.31). Higher spring tensions can be achieved by moving the spring to a higher hole in the brake post.

Some brakes rely on a large spring-tension adjusting nut (Fig. 7.16) surrounding the mounting bolt and do not use the holes in the brake posts as anchors. On these, the tensioning nuts may be turned on both arms to get the combination of return force and centering you prefer. You must loosen the mounting bolt while holding the tensioning nut with a wrench. Turn the nut to the desired tension, and, while holding it in place with the wrench, tighten the mounting bolt again (Fig. 7.32).

On really old brakes without a tension adjustment, centering is accomplished by removing the brake arm and moving the spring to another hole on the boss. It is a rough adjustment at best, and some bosses do not have more than a single hole. When this adjustment fails, you can twist the arm on the boss to tighten or loosen the spring a bit. That, of course, is an even rougher adjustment.

NOTE: *If the brake arms do not rotate easily on the brake post, there is too much friction. Remove the brake and check that the post is not bent or split, in which case a new one needs to be screwed in or welded on. If not bent, the post is probably too fat to slide freely inside the brake arm, because of paint on it or bulging or mushrooming of the post due to overtightening of the brake-mounting bolt. In this case, if it's the replaceable type, screw a new post into the frame or*

7.32 Adjusting return-spring tension with tensioning nut

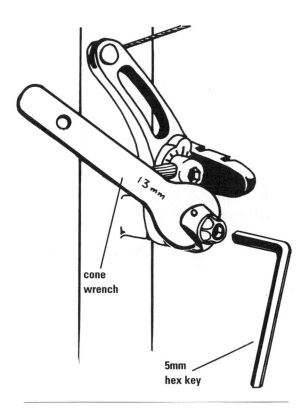

cone
wrench

13 mm

5mm
hex key

fork. Otherwise, file and sand the circumference of the post to reduce its diameter. File and sand uniformly, only a little at a time; avoid making it too thin.

f. Lubrication and service

The only lubrication necessary on cantilever brakes is on the cables, levers, and brake arms. Lubrication should be performed whenever braking feels sticky. Cable lubrication and replacement and lever lubrication are covered in §vii-3, §vii-4, and §vii-5. Cantilevers can be lubricated by removing them, cleaning and greasing the pivots, and replacing them (§vii-10a).

g. Top-mount brake levers

Top-mount or "cross-top" levers (Fig. 7.33) allow the brakes to be accessed from little levers mounted on the top, straight section of the handlebar as well as from the normal levers on the drops of the handle-

bar. The brake cable from the normal lever passes through the top-mount lever and can hence be pulled from either lever.

Top-mount levers are quite simple to set up, as long as you are using modern brake levers with the brake cable running under the tape along the front of the handlebar. For installation, follow these steps:

1. Clamp the top-mount lever onto the handlebar, with the lever tip facing outward, toward the brake lever it will be connected to, and lever logos up (in other words, the mounting bolt is usually underneath).

    (a) If you have a standard-diameter handlebar (i.e., with a 26.0mm-diameter clamping section at the stem), you will be mounting the levers just beyond the bulged stem-clamping section, on the 24mm-diameter part of the handlebar (Fig. 7.33).

    (b) If you have an oversized handlebar (i.e., with a 31.8mm stem clamp), you will need different, oversized, top-mount levers, because there probably will not be enough room for the top-mount lever between the point where the bar tapers down to 24mm and the bend. You can get top-mount levers with a 31.8mm clamp diameter, and you would mount these up on the bulged clamping section of the bar.

2. Orient the levers in a comfortable position for your hands.

3. Cut a section of brake-cable housing so that it runs from its insertion point on the brake lever, along the front of the bar, to the bottom of its insertion hole in the top-mount lever clamp. If your bike is already set up, you can just pull the brake cable out (or at least until the end is

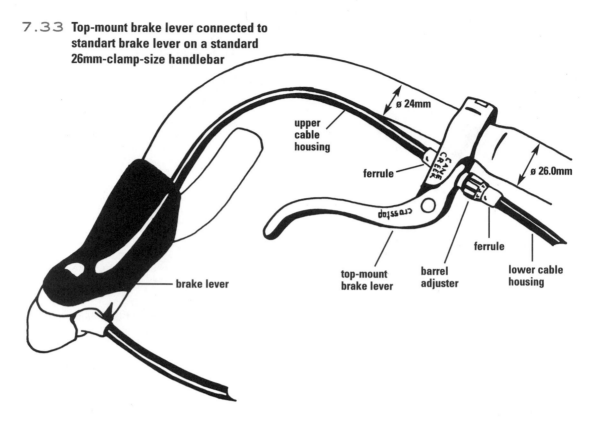

7.33 Top-mount brake lever connected to standart brake lever on a standard 26mm-clamp-size handlebar

upper cable housing

ø 24mm

ferrule

ø 26.0mm

crosstop

CANE CREEK

brake lever

top-mount brake lever

barrel adjuster

ferrule

lower cable housing

between the top-mount lever and the brake lever). Then you can cut the housing at about the centerline of the top-mount lever.

4. Install the housing from the brake lever to the insertion hole in the top-mount lever clamp (Fig. 7.33), ideally reinforcing each end of the housing with a ferrule (see Fig. 5.13).

5. Cut a piece of housing to run to the brake caliper (front) or frame cable stop (rear) from the other cable-insertion point on the top-mount lever. This cable-insertion point will be on the moving part of the lever and usually will have a barrel adjuster on it. If you are just cutting your brake housing of your preexisting setup, then you already cut this piece of housing (because it was leftover) when you made your cut in step 3.

6. Again, by using ferrules (Fig. 5.13) to reinforce the ends, run the housing section you just cut

from the top-mount lever's barrel adjuster to the brake or frame cable stop (Fig. 7.33).

7. Install the brake cable, running it right through the top-mount lever to pass from one housing section into the next. If you are using your old cable and it is frayed, it may not go through, so you may need to buy a new cable.

8. Hook up the brakes as normal. Turn the barrel adjuster to get the right cable tension so that the brakes apply properly. You're ready to ride and now have another position from which to brake!

vii–11 SIDEPULL-CANTILEVER (A.K.A. V-BRAKE) CALIPERS

Some cyclo-cross, touring, and tandem bikes have V-brakes, which, like cantilevers, mount on pivot studs attached to the frame and fork.

V-brakes (Figs. 7.5 and 7.34) have tall, cantilever-like arms, a horizontal cable-hook link on top of one arm, and a cable clamp on the top of the other. A curved aluminum guide pipe, or "noodle," hooks into the horizontal link and takes the cable from the end of the housing and out through the link and then directs the cable toward the cable-fixing bolt on the opposite arm. V-brakes usually have long, thin brake pads with threaded posts. Some V-brakes have "parallel-push" linkages (Fig. 7.5) that move the brake pads horizontally rather than in an arc around the brake post like a cantilever. Simple V-brake designs (Fig. 7.34) mount the pad directly to the arm so that the pads move in a cantilever-like arc.

V-brakes are extremely powerful, but they require more cable pull than road bike brakes and don't work with road bike levers unless you install a cam unit that increases the cable pull. This cam unit usually replaces the noodle and bolts onto the cable-fixing bolt. A cable stop is bolted onto the end of the cable and hooks into the brake link.

Because of this leverage problem and consequent need for a cable-pull multiplier, V-brakes are extremely rare on road bikes. If you have one of these setups, please consult Chapter 7 of *Zinn & the Art of Mountain Bike Maintenance* for details on adjusting these brakes.

vii-12 SHIMANO AX AND CAMPAGNOLO C-RECORD AND CROCE D'AUNE DELTA CENTER-PULL CALIPERS

Not many of these little items were produced, but they were coveted as high-end brakes, so there are still some around. They attach in the same manner as sidepull calipers, and the pad adjustment and cable-tension adjustment procedure is pretty much the same as well. The major differences have to do with cable connection and centering.

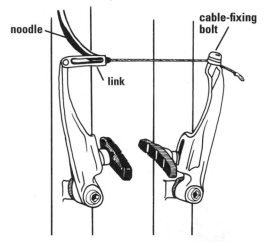

7.34 **Simple V-brake (a.k.a. sidepull cantilever brake)**

The cable housing stops at a barrel adjuster above the center of the brake. The cable goes straight down through a crosswise hole in the cable-fixing bolt. The Shimano fixing anchor is in a separate triangular piece that tends to turn as you tighten the bolt.

Centering either of these brakes could not be simpler. Just grab the part sticking straight up (with the cable entry on top) and twist it as needed. Make sure the mounting nut is tight behind the fork or brake bridge.

vii-13 TROUBLESHOOTING

1. Possible causes for squealing brakes include the following:
   - grease or oil on the rim and/or pad,
   - toe-out of the pads under hard braking so that the heel of the pad does the work,
   - brake arms that are too flimsy for the rider (and chatter or toe-out when the brakes are applied), and
   - ceramic-coated rims paired with pads not intended for ceramic braking surfaces.

   Solutions include the following:

   (a) In the case of dirty or oily rims, clean them

with solvent (rubbing alcohol may be sufficient), and wipe them clean. In the case of dirty pads, reveal a clean layer of the pad with sandpaper.

(b) If your pads toe-out while braking, you should toe them in. Some pads (recent high-end Shimano and Campagnolo) have an orbital adjustment on the pads that allows toe-in. Otherwise, the only way to toe road bike pads is to remove the pad, put an adjustable wrench on the end of the brake arm, and twist it. This will help eliminate squeal on a brake with flimsy arms, too. If the arms flex too much for you, get new brakes.

(c) High-end rims with ceramic braking surfaces can squeal if the pads are not specifically made for ceramic rims. Easy enough—get new pads.

2. Insufficient braking power is available. Possible causes include the following:
- flexing of brake arms or lever,
- stretching of cable,
- compression of brake housing,
- squishing of pads,
- insufficient coefficient of friction between the pads and rim,
- oil and grime on the rims and pads (or water, but that will dry off soon), or
- the pads may not work with your particular rim.

Try the following solutions:

(a) If the brake arms or levers are too flexible, you need new brakes, but you can try eliminating the other factors first and see if braking power comes up enough for you.

(b) If the cables and housings are old, frayed, thin, or cheap, chances are the cable is stretching more than a new one would, and the cable housing is compressing more than new housing would. Replace both.

(c) If the pads are too soft, they will squish rather than applying full pressure against the rim. Replace them with higher-quality ones.

(d) Insufficient friction is common with chromed steel rims (found only on cheap bikes). The only cure is to fit especially aggressive pads (or replace the rims—not a bad idea, because chromed steel rims do not provide much braking power when wet).

(e) Another cause of weak braking power can be oil and grime on the rims and pads (or water, but that will dry off soon). The pads might also be overly worn and need replacement.

(f) And finally, try different pads.

3. The levers come back all the way to the bar before the bike slows down enough.

(a) Check that the brake quick release is closed. If so, the cable needs to be tightened. See §vii-2.

(b) The causes and solutions in item 2 (insufficient braking power) may also apply.

4. Brake rubs on wheel because of off-center caliper, the brakes are too tight, or a wheel is untrue. Solutions:

(a) If one pad rubs all the way around the rim, see the sections regarding centering the caliper for your type of brakes.

(b) If both pads rub all the way around, loosen

the cable as in §vii-2.

(c) If the wheel wobbles back and forth against the pad(s), true the wheel; see Chapter 6, §vi-12, or Chapter 13, §xiii-4.

5. Pads do not meet flat to the rim.

(a) Other than on late-model high-end Shimano and Campagnolo brakes, if the pad will not mount so that it meets the rim flat or slightly toed-in, the only way to adjust it is to remove the pad and twist the end of the arm with an adjustable wrench. (Late-model high-end Shimano and Campy brakes have an orbital pad mount that allows freedom of adjustment in all planes, once the pad bolt is loosened.)

(b) If one pad toes in and one toes out, it is possible that either the brake center-bolt is bent or the brake hole in the frame or fork is drilled crooked.

6. Brake caliper returns slowly or not at all. Possible causes include the following:

• the caliper's center bolt or secondary pivot bolt is bent or the nuts on it are too tight where it passes through the brake arm,

• the end of the spring is not riding in its plastic friction piece or it needs lubrication, or

• the cable is sticking.

Solutions include the following:

(a) You can adjust the tightness of the pivot-bolt nuts and replace bent bolts.

(b) Replacing the end of the spring in its plastic friction-reducing piece is easy enough, and you can put a dab of grease between the spring and the spring tab on the arm for those springs without the friction-reducing piece.

(c) If the cable is sticking, replace or lubricate it (see §vii-3 and §vii-4).

7. Brake arms are loose or the front nut is missing from a center-pivot sidepull brake:

(a) The nut(s) holding the caliper together are missing. Replace any missing nuts.

(b) Tighten the nuts until there is no play in the caliper, yet it still moves freely. If the brake has two nuts, make sure they are both there (the end of the bolt should be observed by the front cap-nut). Hold the back one with one wrench while you tighten the front one against it with another wrench.

8. You just got new brakes for your old (pre-1980) racing bike or for a touring bike and (a) the pads will not slide down far enough to hit the rim, and/or (b) the hole on the back of the fork crown and/or brake bridge is too small for the recessed brake nut.

(a) You need to get a long-reach brake for the pads to hit the rim, and to fit the small, unrecessed brake hole, you need to get a brake with a long center bolt and a standard nut and washer. This either means you need to buy a new brake with these features, which will be a low-end brake, or you need to find a good, old brake. In the 1980s, Campagnolo and others made top-quality brakes with your choice of brake reach and center-bolt style.

(b) You can get drop-style center bolts for old Campagnolo single-pivot sidepull brakes to lower a short-reach brake so that the pads can reach the rim on a long-reach frame.

TOOLS

5mm, 6mm, 7mm, and 8mm hex keys

14mm socket wrench

crank puller

chainring-nut tool

pin spanner (or adjustable pin tool)

splined bottom-bracket wrench

adjustable wrench

toothed lockring spanner

grease

OPTIONAL

15mm and 16mm socket wrenches

dust-cap pin tool

⅜-inch drive socket-wrench handle

ISIS bottom-bracket installation tool

integrated-spindle bottom-bracket installation tool

left arm-cap installation tool for Shimano integrated bottom brackets

CHAPTER 8

CRANKS AND BOTTOM BRACKETS

When someone tells you something defies description,
you can be pretty sure he's going to have a go at it anyway.
—Clyde B. Aster

The crankset consists of the crankarms, bottom bracket, chainrings, chainring bolts, and crank bolt (Fig. 8.1). The forces applied through this system are large, so all parts need to be quite tight to prevent ruining expensive components by using them when loose. In addition, bottom-bracket bearings need to run smoothly under high loads in order not to sap your energy.

CRANKARMS AND CHAINRINGS

viii-1 CRANK REMOVAL AND INSTALLATION

To take off traditional crankarms, you will need, depending on the crankset, either a large hex key alone, or a crank puller along with a socket wrench or large hex key (Figs. 8.2 and 8.3).

Until 2003, most Shimano cranks and their clones were secured with a crank bolt accepting either an 8mm hex key or a 14mm socket wrench. Current Campagnolo cranks accept an 8mm hex key; older Campagnolo cranks take a 7mm hex key or a 15mm socket. Early-1980s Shimano Dura-Ace and 600 Dyna-Drive cranks are removed with a 6mm hex key, and you may still find pre-1980 French (TA, Stronglight) cranks with 16mm crank bolts.

Integrated-spindle cranks, which first appeared on road bikes in 2003, only require removing one of the crankarms, because the other arm is permanently fixed to the oversized bottom-bracket spindle. The spindle just slides in and out of the bearings, which are external to the bottom bracket, and to remove the arm, you may only need a 5mm or 8mm hex key. For Shimano, you also need a special splined tool for the left arm cap.

Really old bikes (pre-1980 and older) may actually

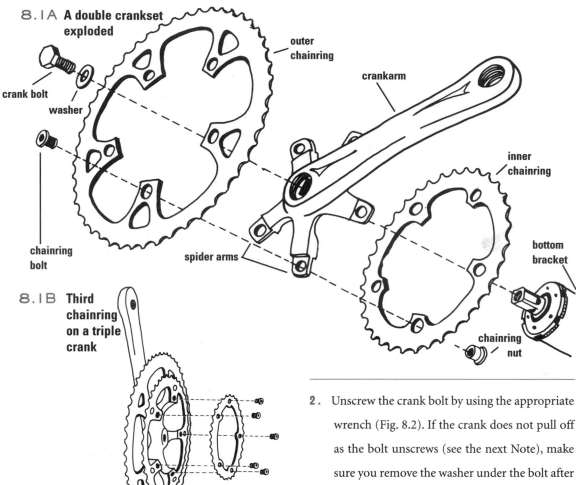

8.1A **A double crankset exploded**

crank bolt

washer

chainring bolt

outer chainring

crankarm

inner chainring

spider arms

bottom bracket

chainring nut

8.1B **Third chainring on a triple crank**

have steel, "cottered" cranks, requiring a wrench and a hammer to remove them.

NOTE: *"Right" in this chapter and generally throughout this book refers to the drive side of the bike, and "left" refers to the nondrive side.*

a. Removal

Traditional cranks (square-taper, Shimano Octalink, and ISIS)

1. Older cranksets (and some current inexpensive ones) have a dust cap covering the crank bolt. If it's there, remove it. Depending on the type, it may take a 5mm Allen wrench, a two-pin dust-cap tool, or a screwdriver.

2. Unscrew the crank bolt by using the appropriate wrench (Fig. 8.2). If the crank does not pull off as the bolt unscrews (see the next Note), make sure you remove the washer under the bolt after you remove the bolt (Fig. 8.1A). A washer left in will prevent the crank puller from pushing on the end of the axle. If the crank comes right off, read the note following this step, and skip steps that follow the note.

NOTE: *Most recent traditional road bike cranks, as well as old (1980s) Shimano Dyna-Drive cranks, are self-extracting; that is, they require no crank puller. A ring threaded into the crank holds down the crank bolt; as the bolt is unscrewed, its outer lip pushes on the ring and pushes the crank off. Sometimes the ring is not properly secured, and it unscrews. In this case, you need to hold the ring by its two holes with a pin tool while you unscrew the bolt with a hex key. If this approach fails, you can unscrew and remove the ring, remove the crank bolt, and use a crank puller (see step 3).*

8.2 Removing and installing crank bolt

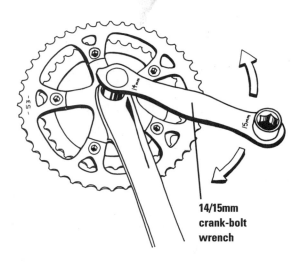

14/15mm crank-bolt wrench

8.3 Using crank puller

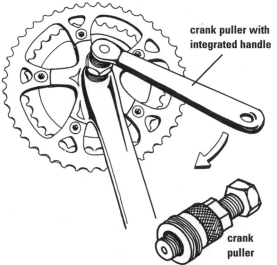

crank puller with integrated handle

crank puller

3. Holding the crank puller (Fig. 8.3) in your hand, unscrew its center push bolt so that the inner and outer threaded ends of the tool are flush. Crank pullers vary in size of the push rod. The standard type, pictured in Figure 8.3, has a 1.15cm-diameter push rod just small enough to pass through the square hole in the crankarm to push it off a square-taper bottom bracket (Figs. 8.10–8.12 and 8.16). However, if you need to use a puller to get a crank off a Shimano Octalink or splined ISIS pipe-spindle bottom bracket (Figs. 8.13 and 8.14), you need a crank puller with a larger (1.7cm-diameter) push rod.

4. Thread the outer part of the crank puller into the hole in the crankarm. Thread it in as far as it can go (preferably by hand; clean the threads if it won't thread in easily); otherwise, you will not engage sufficient crank threads when you tighten the push bolt, and the threads will be damaged. Future crank removal depends on those threads being in good condition.

5. Tighten the push bolt clockwise (Fig. 8.3), with

a wrench or a socket-wrench handle or a handle built into the tool, until the crankarm pulls off of the axle. Unscrew the puller from the crankarm.

Integrated-spindle cranks

1. On Shimano (Fig. 8.15) and FSA aluminum integrated-spindle cranks, unscrew and remove the cap on the end of the left arm (with the special splined tool for Shimano; with a hex key for FSA). With a 5mm hex key, loosen the two pinch bolts holding the arm onto the spindle, and pull off the left arm. On many other integrated-spindle cranks, unscrew the left arm with an 8mm hex key, in the same way as for a nonintegrated self-extracting crank; the arm will come right off.

2. Pull the right arm straight outward by hand, which brings the spindle out of the cups with it. On some FSA cranks, you will have a rubber O-ring to pull off each end of the spindle.

NOTE: *Race Face integrated-spindle cranks are the opposite; the left arm is fixed to the spindle, and the right, drive-side crank is removable.*

CRANK
REMOVAL AND
INSTALLATION

Old steel, cottered cranks

A steel, cottered crank is secured to the spindle by means of a tapered, wedge-shaped cotter bolt with a nut on the end. The cotter bolt runs transverse to the crankarm and wedges into a notch in the spindle. You remove these cranks by pounding each cotter bolt out with a hammer after removing the nut on the bolt's end.

b. Installation

Traditional cranks (square taper, ISIS, and Octalink)

1. Slide the crankarm onto the bottom-bracket axle. With square-taper spindles, clean off all grease from both parts. Greasing the axle may allow the soft aluminum crank to slide too far onto the hard steel or titanium axle and could deform the square hole in the crank. Apply grease to an ISIS or Shimano Octalink splined spindle. With ISIS and Octalink cranks, you must be careful to line up the crank splines with those on the spindle before tightening the crank bolt. You can wreck a crank this way, and no warranty covers improper installation.

2. Install the crank bolt. Apply grease or thread-lock compound on the threads, and tighten (Fig. 8.2). Apply titanium-specific antiseize compound for titanium spindles or crank bolts. If you have aluminum or titanium crank bolts, tighten the cranks on to the specified torque with a greased steel bolt first, then replace the steel bolt with the lightweight bolt and tighten that to spec.

   NOTE: *If you have a torque wrench, here is an excellent place to break it out and tighten the bolt to about 32–49 N·m (300–435 in-lbs) and as high as 59 N·m for steel oversized bolts for splined spindles (see the torque table, Appendix E). If you're not using a torque wrench, make sure that the bolt is quite snug, but don't muscle it until your veins pop.*

3. Replace the dust cover, if the crank has one.

4. Removing and reinstalling the right crankarm could position the crank farther inboard than it was previously, which will affect shifting, so check the front-derailleur adjustment. (See Chapter 5, §v-5.)

5. Recheck the bolt torque after the first few hours of riding. Retighten it to the proper torque spec if it has loosened up. Check it again after a few more hours of riding until you are assured that it no longer loosens up.

Integrated-spindle cranks

1. Push the bottom-bracket spindle (which is attached to the right crankarm—or, in the case of Race Face, to the left arm) in through the cups, whose oversized bearings are external to the bottom-bracket shell.

2. Slide the left arm onto the spindle protruding on that side from the cups; check that the crank is at 180 degrees from the right arm (Shimano IS spindles have two wider splines to ensure this).

3. Finish the installation according to the type of crank you have:

   (a) On Truvativ Giga X Pipe cranks and on FSA Mega Exo carbon-fiber cranks, tighten the left arm with an 8mm hex key, the same as for a normal crank. Put on your pedals and go riding.

   (b) On Shimano and FSA aluminum arms, tighten in the left-side dust cap (not very tightly [0.4–0.7 N·m], just enough to pull the right and left cranks over against the bottom-bracket cups) with the special splined cap tool for Shimano and a hex key for FSA. Shimano's tool is just a round disc meant to be turned by hand to prevent overtightening it; watch out with tools for this task that have a long handle.

(c) On Shimano and FSA aluminum arms, with a 5mm hex key, tighten the two opposing (greased) pinch bolts (to 10–15 N·m), by alternately tightening each one a quarter turn at a time.

4. Recheck the torque after one ride, as the crank may settle in and the bolts will need retightening. Periodically check the torque from then on.

Old steel, cottered cranks

To reinstall a steel, cottered crank, you need to buy a new pair of cotter bolts at a bike shop, because after removal, the old ones will be deformed and will not secure the crankarms anymore. Installation consists simply of inserting the new (greased) cotter once the crank is slid back into place on the spindle and tightening the nut to pull the cotter tightly into the notch in the spindle.

viii-2 CHAINRINGS

You should get into the habit of checking the chainrings regularly. They do wear out and need to be replaced. It's hard to say how often, so include chainrings as part of your regular maintenance checklist. Always check them for wear when you replace the chain.

The chainring teeth should be checked periodically for wear; the chainring bolts should be checked periodically for tightness; the chainrings themselves should be checked for trueness by watching them as they spin past the front derailleur.

1. Wipe the chainring down and inspect each

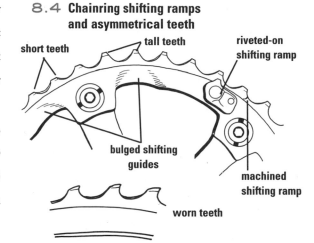

8.4 Chainring shifting ramps and asymmetrical teeth

short teeth
tall teeth
riveted-on shifting ramp
bulged shifting guides
machined shifting ramp
worn teeth

tooth. The teeth should be straight and uniform in size and shape. If the teeth are worn into a hook shape, the chainring needs to be replaced. The chain should be replaced as well (see §iv-5 in Chapter 4), because this tooth shape effectively changes the spacing between teeth and accelerates wear on the chain, and it indicates that the chain was already worn in order to cause the hook shape in the first place.

CAUTION: *Don't be deceived by the erratic tooth shapes (some tall, some short) on modern chainrings designed to facilitate shifting (Fig. 8.4); that's probably what they are supposed to look like if the odd shapes repeat regularly. Shifting ramps on the inboard side, meant to speed chain movement between the rings, often look like cracks on cheaper chainrings, where they are pressed into the ring rather than being a separate piece riveted on.*

NOTE: *Another wear evaluation method is to lift the chain from the top of the chainring; the greater the wear of either part, the farther the chain separates. If it lifts more than one tooth, the chain, and perhaps the chainring as well, needs to be replaced.*

2. Remove minor gouges in the chainrings with a file.

CHAINRINGS

8.5 Straightening warped chainrings

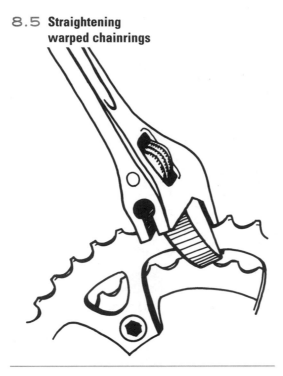

8.6 Removing and installing chainring bolts

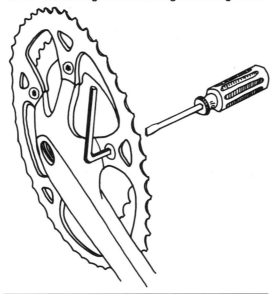

8.7 Outer and inner chainrings on a double crank

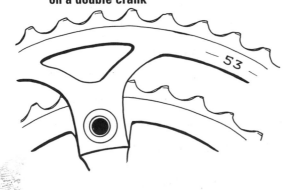

3. If an individual tooth is bent, try bending it back carefully with a pair of pliers or a Crescent wrench (Fig. 8.5). If it breaks off, take the message and buy a new chainring.

4. While turning the crank slowly, watch where the chain exits the bottom of the chainring. See if any of the teeth are reluctant to let go of the chain. If the chain gets pulled up a bit as it leaves the bottom of the chainring, it can get sucked up between the chainring and the chainstay. Locate any offending teeth and see if you can correct the problem. If the teeth are really chewed up or cannot be improved with pliers and a file, the chainring should be replaced.

NOTE: *Never rotate the chainring position relative to the spider arms of the crank, because the shifting ramps will not be in the proper places to function correctly in picking up the chain as you shift. The outer chainring will generally have a protruding pin to locate it behind the crankarm, and each of the other two rings will have a radially-inward-pointed tooth, also to line up behind the crankarm.*

viii-3 CHAINRING BOLTS

Check that the bolts are tight by turning them clockwise (usually with a 5mm Allen wrench, Fig. 8.6). As you try to tighten the bolt, its nut may turn; if so, hold the nut with a two-pronged chainring-nut tool (Fig. 1.2) designed especially for this purpose or with a screwdriver—but use a screwdriver with caution; it can slip off the chainring nut.

Some chainring bolts take a star-shaped TORX T30 tool instead of a 5mm hex key. Yet others take a 6mm hex key on the nut on the backside, rather than the pronged chainring-nut tool.

8.8 Removing and installing 1996–2002 Shimano XTR chainring spider

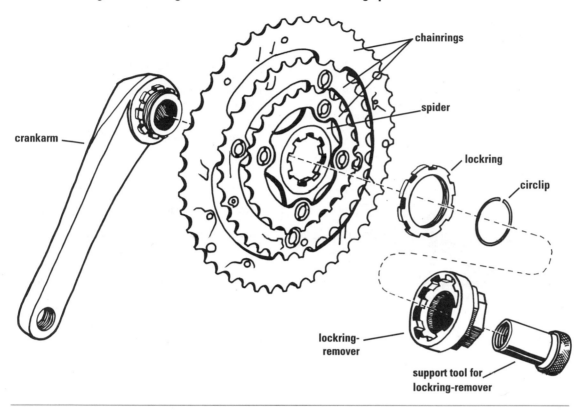

viii-4 WARPED CHAINRINGS

Looking down from above, turn the crank slowly and see whether the chainrings wobble back and forth relative to the plane of the front derailleur.

If they do, make sure there is no play in the bottom bracket by grabbing the crankarms and attempting to rock the bottom-bracket axle back and forth. If there is play, adjust the bottom bracket (step 15, §viii-8). It is normal to have a small amount of chainring wobble and flex when you pedal hard, but excessive wobbling will compromise shifting. Small, localized bends can be straightened with an adjustable wrench (Fig. 8.5). If a ring is really bent, replace it.

viii-5 BENT CRANKARM SPIDERS

If you installed a new chainring and are still seeing serious back-and-forth wobble, chances are good that the spider arms on the crank are bent. If the crank is new, this is a warranty item, so return it to your bike shop.

viii-6 CHAINRING REPLACEMENT

a. Double chainrings

Replacing either of the chainrings on a double (or the two largest chainrings on a triple) is easy (Fig. 8.7).

1. Unscrew the chainring bolts with a screwdriver (Fig. 8.6), with a 5mm Allen key, or on some bolts, a TORX T30 wrench. You may need to hold the nut on the backside with either a chainring-nut tool (Fig. 1.2) or a thin screwdriver (or, with some nuts, a 6mm hex key).

2. Install the new chainrings, lubricate the bolts and the little recesses that accept them in the chainring faces, and tighten them (Fig. 8.6).

WARPED

CHAINRINGS

—

BENT

CRANKARM

SPIDERS

—

CHAINRING

REPLACEMENT

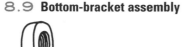

8.9 Bottom-bracket assembly

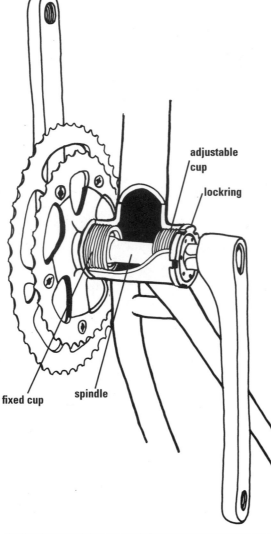

adjustable cup

lockring

fixed cup   spindle

The outer chainring has a protruding pin meant to keep the chain from falling down between it and the crankarm. Make sure this pin lines up under the crankarm and faces away from the bicycle. The middle (and inner ring on a triple) has a little bump protruding radially inward that is also to line up under the crankarm. And both (or all three) chainrings have recesses for the heads of the chainring bolts and nuts, so make sure that these recesses receive those parts and are not facing inward toward the spider. If the chainrings are rotated

relative to the crank or inverted, the shift ramps will not work.

NOTE: *Whenever you change the size of the outer chainring, you must reposition the front derailleur for proper chainring clearance, as described in Chapter 5, §v-5.*

b. To replace the inner chainring on a triple

1. Pull off the crankarm (§viii-1, Figs. 8.2 and 8.3).

2. With a 5mm Allen (or for some, a TORX T30) key, remove the bolts holding the chainring. They are threaded directly into the crankarm (Fig. 8.1B).

3. Install the new chainring, and lubricate and tighten the bolts. The inner rings each have a little bump protruding radially inward that lines up under the crankarm. Make sure that the heads of the chainring bolts and nuts are recessed down into the countersunk holes (in other words, make sure that the countersunk holes are not facing inward toward the spider).

NOTE: *Some cranks do not accept separate chainrings.*

ANOTHER NOTE: *Some triple cranks have chainrings that come off as a set; these are generally mountain cranks, but they can be used on a road bike. At the more expensive end, 1996–2002 Shimano XTR and 1997–2003 XT cranks rely on a slip-on spider system that allows you to slide off all three chainrings from the crankarm as a unit (Fig. 8.8). These are mountain bike cranks, but they can sometimes be found on road, touring, and cyclo-cross bikes. After removing a circlip (by prying it off with a screwdriver), a special lock-ring-remover tool loosens the chainring-spider–securing lockring; a female-threaded tool that goes on the crank bolt holds the lockring-remover tool in place (Fig. 8.8). Once the spider is off, you can interchange chainrings within the set or simply pop on a whole new*

8.10 Tightening and loosening non-drive-side bottom-bracket cup

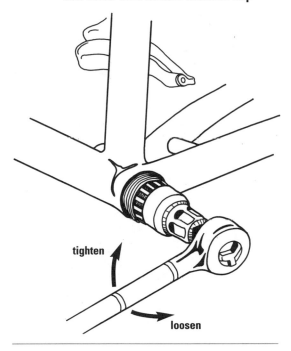

tighten

loosen

set. Inexpensive cranks often have chainrings riveted to the crank or riveted to each other and bolted to the crank as a unit. If these chainrings are damaged, you may have to replace the entire crankset.

4. Replace the crankarm (§viii-1, Fig. 8.2).

BOTTOM BRACKETS

Most bottom brackets simply thread into the frame's bottom-bracket shell and accept the crankarms (Fig. 8.9). Simple enough, but it's important to remember that not all bottom-bracket shells are the same.

Almost all current road bikes use English standard threads for the bottom bracket. That translates into a 1.370-inch diameter and a thread pitch of 24 threads per inch. These numbers are usually engraved on the bottom-bracket cups. If you are replacing a bottom bracket, make sure that the new cups have the same threads. It is important to remember that the drive side (right side) of an English standard bottom bracket has left-hand

threads. In other words, turning counterclockwise tightens the drive-side cup (Fig. 8.18). Meanwhile, the left cup has right-hand threads that are, therefore, tightened clockwise (Fig. 8.17).

Other threads you may run across are Italian (with a 36mm diameter, and note that both cups have right-hand threads), French, and Swiss (both of these come in 35mm diameter, but use different thread directions). The latter two thread patterns are very rare, although French threading was common until the early 1980s.

Currently, integrated-spindle bottom brackets with the bearings external to the bottom-bracket shell are all the rage. Additionally, there are a few bike brands with oversized, internally mounted bearings and oversized bottom-bracket shells to accept them, most notably Cannondale, Specialized, and Pinarello. The most common type of bottom bracket in the 1990s was the Shimano-style cartridge-bearing bottom bracket with splined cups (Fig. 8.10). The most common bottom bracket in the 1980s and before was the cup-and-cone style with loose ball bearings (Figs. 8.9 and 8.11). Another bottom-bracket type has a sealed cartridge bearing on either end secured by an adjustable cup and lock-ring at either end (Fig. 8.12).

From 1996 to 2003, Shimano's high-end bottom brackets, called Octalink, had a large "pipe" spindle with splined ends (Fig. 8.13), rather than square-taper ends. Most of these are the cartridge type shown in Figure 8.10 but with a large splined axle. The first generation of splined pipe-spindle Shimano Dura-Ace bottom brackets had four sets of loose, adjustable, and overhaulable bearings: two sets of tiny balls and two sets of needle bearings (Fig. 8.13).

To counter Shimano's patented Octalink designs,

8.11–8.17 Types of bottom brackets

8.11 Shimano-style cartridge with square taper spindle

8.12 Loose-bearing square taper

8.13 Adjustable cartridge-bearing, square taper

8.14 Shimano Dura-Ace Octalink loose-bearing splined-spindle

8.15 ISIS cartridge

8.16 Integrated spindle—Shimano shown

8.17 Mavic or Stronglight cartridge

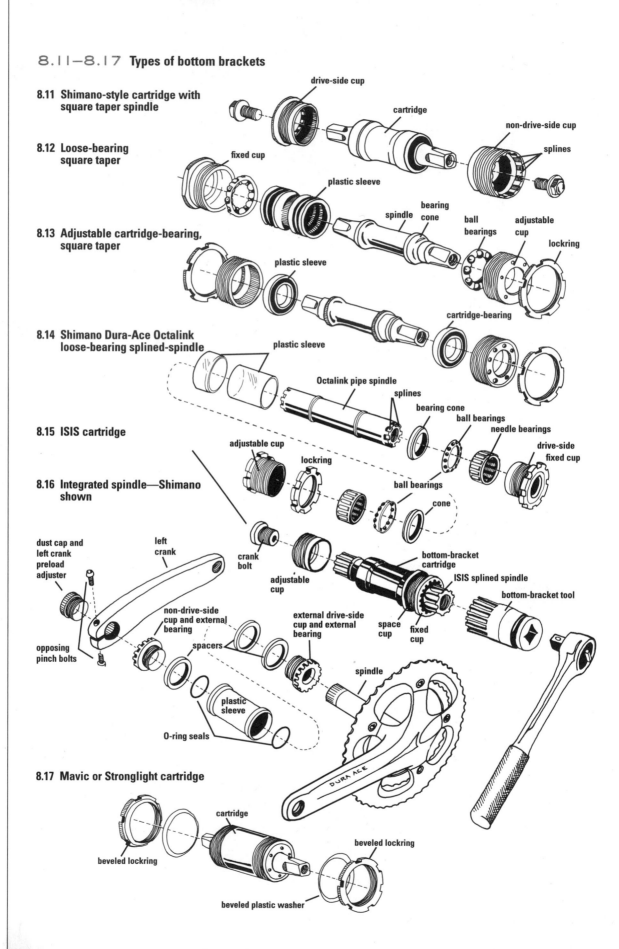

drive-side cup

cartridge

non-drive-side cup

splines

fixed cup

plastic sleeve

plastic sleeve

spindle

bearing cone

ball bearings

adjustable cup

lockring

cartridge-bearing

plastic sleeve

Octalink pipe spindle

splines

bearing cone

ball bearings

needle bearings

drive-side fixed cup

adjustable cup

lockring

ball bearings

cone

dust cap and left crank preload adjuster

left crank

crank bolt

adjustable cup

non-drive-side cup and external bearing

opposing pinch bolts

spacers

external drive-side cup and external bearing

bottom-bracket cartridge

ISIS splined spindle

space cup

fixed cup

bottom-bracket tool

spindle

plastic sleeve

O-ring seals

DURA ACE

beveled lockring

cartridge

beveled lockring

beveled plastic washer

BOTTOM

BRACKETS

which offer increased stiffness and lower weight than square-taper designs, a number of manufacturers banded together in the late 1990s to create the ISIS standard (Fig. 8.14). Like Octalink, ISIS has a larger-diameter splined spindle, but it features longer and deeper splines.

In 2003, Shimano upped the high-end ante again with the integrated-spindle design (Fig. 8.15), in which the right arm is permanently joined to the spindle, and the bearing cups place the bearings external to the bottom-bracket shell, making a larger spindle and larger bearings possible. Other manufacturers have followed suit but offer different attachment systems for the left arm and different spindle diameters, so their bearings are not usually interchangeable with Shimano's.

Some bottom brackets do not thread into the bottom-bracket shell. One rare type utilizes cartridge bearings held into an unthreaded bottom-bracket shell by snaprings in machined grooves. Another type includes a cartridge that is externally threaded on each end (Fig. 8.16); it slips into the bottom-bracket shell and is held in place by lockrings threaded onto the cartridge.

BOTTOM-BRACKET INSTALLATION

The most important item in bottom-bracket installation is to make sure that the axle length in the bottom bracket is correct. If it's incorrect, the chainrings will not line up well with the rear cogs (i.e., the chain line will be off; see §v-38 and §v-39 in Chapter 5). Some bikes come from the factory with the wrong length bottom bracket. No amount of fiddling with the derailleurs will get such a bike to shift properly. Get a bottom bracket specifically recom-

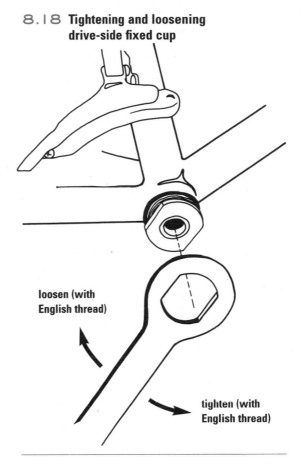

8.18 Tightening and loosening drive-side fixed cup

loosen (with English thread)

tighten (with English thread)

mended for your crankset, and double-check that it has the proper threading for your frame. Before installing a new bottom bracket of a brand and model different from your crank, see Figure 5.32, and read the chain-line sections (§v-38 and §v-39) at the end of Chapter 5.

With one-piece cartridge-style bottom brackets (Figs. 8.10 and 8.14) with cups that thread into the bottom-bracket shell, the axle length is not as critical, but for loose-bearing and integrated-spindle bottom brackets (Figs. 8.11, 8.13, and 8.15) to work properly, the threads on both sides of the frame's bottom-bracket shell must be lined up with each other, and the end faces of the shell must be parallel. If you have any doubts about your frame and are installing an expensive bottom bracket, it is a good idea to have the bottom-bracket shell tapped

BOTTOM-BRACKET INSTALLATION

8.19 Placing axle and drive-side bearings in bottom-bracket shell

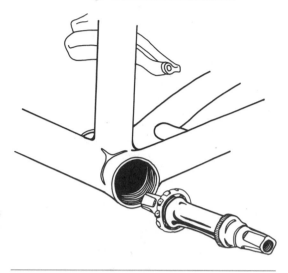

(threaded) and faced (ends cut parallel) by a qualified shop possessing the proper tools. Doing so will improve adjustment and freedom of movement with loose-bearing bottom brackets and will reduce both binding and the likelihood of creaking with integrated-spindle cranksets.

Always grease the threads when installing bottom brackets (or use an antiseize compound on them).

viii-7 SHIMANO OR CAMPAGNOLO SEALED CARTRIDGE-BEARING BOTTOM BRACKETS (AND CLONES)

Shimano- and Campagnolo-style sealed cartridge units (Fig. 8.10) are installed with a splined tool (Fig. 1.2), and the tool is different for the two manufacturers, although lots of other manufacturers use the Shimano tool. A Shimano-style cartridge-bearing bottom bracket can have either a square-taper axle (Fig. 8.10) or a large tubular axle with splined ends like the Octalink spindle in Figure 8.13 or the ISIS spindle in Figure 8.14. These instructions apply to cartridge-bearing bottom brackets like those shown in Figures 8.10 and 8.14, as well as to ones

with this type of cartridge body and a Shimano Octalink or ISIS splined spindle.

1. Thread the left cup (clockwise) in three to four turns by hand.

2. Slide the cartridge into the bottom-bracket shell, paying particular attention to the "right" and "left" markings on the cartridge. The cup with the raised lip is the drive-side cup (the cup shown on the left in Fig. 8.10). The drive-side cup is left-hand threaded on an English-thread bottom bracket and right-hand threaded on an Italian-threaded one.

3. By using the splined cup tool (for Shimano or Campagnolo) with either an open-end wrench or a ⅜-inch drive socket wrench on it, tighten the drive-side cup into the drive side of the bottom-bracket shell until the lip seats against the face of the shell (as in Fig. 8.17, except on the drive side instead of the nondrive side as illustrated). Recommended torque is high—see Appendix E.

NOTE: *Again, on most bikes, this drive-side cup will tighten counterclockwise. On Italian bikes, though, it will tighten clockwise.*

4. With the same tool, turn the left (nondrive) cup clockwise until it tightens against the cartridge (Fig. 8.17). The torque required is the same as for the right cup (see Appendix E). There is no adjustment of the bearings to be done; you can put on the crank now (§viii-1b).

viii-8 CUP-AND-CONE BOTTOM BRACKETS

Cup-and-cone (or "loose-ball") bottom brackets (Figs. 8.11 and 8.13) use ball bearings that ride between cone-shaped bearing surfaces on the axle and cup-shaped races in the threaded cups. One cup,

SEALED
CARTRIDGE-
BEARING
BOTTOM
BRACKETS
—
CUP-AND-CONE
BOTTOM
BRACKETS

called the fixed cup (the cup on the left in Fig. 8.11), has a lip on it and fits on the drive side (right side) of the bike. The other, called the adjustable cup (the right cup in Fig. 8.11), has a lockring that threads onto the cup and against the face of the bottom-bracket shell. The individual ball bearings are usually held together by a retaining cage, which varies in shape depending on bottom bracket. Some folks prefer to do without the retainer; it works fine either way.

In order for cup-and-cone bottom brackets to turn smoothly, it is important that the bearing surfaces of the cups be parallel. Because the cups thread into the bottom-bracket shell, the threads on both sides of the shell must be lined up with each other, and the end faces of the shell must be parallel. If you have any doubts about your frame, it is a good idea to have the bottom-bracket shell tapped (threaded) and faced (ends cut parallel) by a qualified shop possessing the proper tools.

1. Unless you have a fixed-cup tool, have a shop install the fixed cup for you. The shop tool assures that the cup goes in straight and very tightly. The tool pictured in Figure 8.18 can be used in a pinch, but it can let the cup go in crooked and will slip off before you get it really tight. The fixed cup must be very tight (see Appendix E for torque) so that it does not vibrate loose. Remember that English-threaded fixed cups are tightened counterclockwise.

2. Wipe the inside surface of both cups with a clean rag, and put a thin layer of clean grease on the bearing surfaces. Apply enough so that the balls will be half-covered; more than that will be wasted and will attract dirt.

3. Wipe the axle (also called a spindle) with a clean rag.

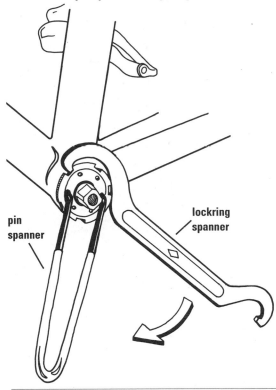

8.20 Tightening lockring; hold adjustable cup in place with pin spanner.

pin spanner

lockring spanner

4. Figure out which end of the bottom-bracket axle is the drive side. The drive side may be marked with an "R"; if not, you can tell by choosing the side with the longer end (when measured from the bearing surface). If there is writing on the axle, it will usually read right-side-up for a rider sitting on the bike. If there is no marking and no length difference, the axle orientation is irrelevant.

5. Slide one set of bearings onto the drive-side end of the axle (Fig. 8.19). If you're using a retainer cage, make sure you put it on right. The balls, rather than the retainer cage, should rest against the axle bearing surfaces. Because there are two types of retainers with opposite designs, you need to be careful to avoid binding, as well as smashing of the retainers. If you're still confused, there is one easy test: If it's in right, it'll

CUP-AND-CONE
BOTTOM
BRACKETS

turn smoothly; if it's in wrong, it won't. If you have loose ball bearings with no retainer cage, stick them into the greased cup. Most setups rely on nine balls; you can confirm that you are using the correct number by inserting and removing the axle and checking to make sure that they are evenly distributed in the grease with no extra gap for more balls.

6. Slide the axle into the bottom bracket so that it pushes the bearings into the fixed cup (Fig. 8.19). You can use your pinkie stuck through from the other side to stabilize the end of the axle as you slide it in.

7. Insert the protective plastic sleeve (shown in Figs. 8.11 and 8.13) into the shell against the inside edge of the fixed cup. The sleeve keeps dirt and rust from falling from the frame tubes into the bearings, so if you don't have one, get one.

8. Now turn your attention to the other cup. Place the bearing set into the greased adjustable cup. If you are using a bearing retainer, make sure it is properly oriented. If you are using loose balls, press them lightly into the grease so that they stay in place.

9. Without the lockring, slide the adjustable cup over the axle and tighten it clockwise by hand into the shell, being certain that it is going in straight. Screw the cup in as far as you can by hand—ideally, all the way until the bearings seat between the axle and cup.

10. Locate the appropriate tool for tightening the adjustable cup. Most cups have two holes that accept the ends, or pins, of an adjustable cup wrench called a "pin spanner" (Fig. 1.2). The other common type of adjustable cup has two flats for a wrench; on this type, you may use an adjustable wrench.

11. Carefully tighten the adjustable cup against the bearings, taking great care not to overtighten. Turn the axle periodically with your fingers to ensure that it moves freely. If it binds up, you have gone too far; back off a bit. The danger of overtightening is that the bearings can force dents into the bearing surfaces of the cups, and the bearings will never turn smoothly again.

12. Screw the lockring onto the adjustable cup, and select the proper tool for it. Lockrings come in different shapes, and so do lockring spanners; make sure yours mate properly with each other.

13. Tighten the lockring against the face of the bottom-bracket shell with the lockring spanner while holding the adjustable cup in place with a pin spanner (Fig. 8.20). If you turn the bicycle upside down, you can pull down harder on the wrenches.

14. As you snug the lockring against the bottom-bracket shell, check the axle periodically. The lockring can pull the cup out of the shell minutely and loosen the adjustment. The axle should turn smoothly without free play in the bearings. I recommend installing and tightening the drive-side crankarm onto the drive end of the axle (Fig. 8.2) at this time so that you can check for free play by wiggling the end of the crank; it will give you a better feel for any looseness in the system.

15. Adjust the cup so that the axle play is just barely eliminated. While holding the cup in place, tighten the lockring as much as you can (Fig. 8.20) so that the bottom bracket does not come out of adjustment while riding (recommended

torque is in Appendix E; tightening it as much as you can is about right). You may have to repeat this step a time or two until you get the ideal adjustment.

viii-9 INTEGRATED-SPINDLE BOTTOM BRACKETS

1. There will be a plastic sleeve attached to the right cup to keep contamination from falling onto the spindle inside of the frame. Leave this sleeve on when installing the cup.

2. After greasing their threads and starting them by hand first, tighten the right (drive-side) cup counterclockwise and the left cup clockwise by using the splined tool for the purpose, leaving the cup spacers in place. Torque is high (35–50 N·m), so reef on the tool pretty hard, because you are not likely to have a splined tool for this task that works with a torque wrench to measure it to spec.

3. Grease the face and internal bore of each bearing, as well as the left end and areas of the spindle that will contact the bearings. From the right side, push the spindle through the cups as far as you can (the spindle splines will protrude from the left bearing, and the right arm will be close to or contacting the right bearing).

4. Slip the left crank on the splines, ensuring that it is at 180 degrees from the right arm (Shimano IS spindles have two wider splines to ensure this).

5. Finish the installation according to the type of crank you have:

   (a) On Truvativ Giga X Pipe cranks and on FSA Mega Exo and carbon-fiber cranks, install the greased crank bolt and tighten the left arm with an 8mm hex key, the same as for a normal crank (torque varies but is relatively high; use 41–47 N·m for Truvativ). You're done, if you have one of these and you feel no end play in the bottom bracket.

   (b) On Shimano and FSA aluminum arms, tighten the left-side dust cap (not very tightly [0.4–0.7 N·m], just enough to pull the right and left cranks over against the bottom-bracket cups) with the special splined cap tool for Shimano and a hex key for FSA. Shimano's tool is just a round disc meant to be turned by hand to prevent overtightening it.

   (c) On Shimano and FSA aluminum arms, with a 5mm hex key, tighten the two opposing (greased) pinch bolts (to 10–15 N·m), by alternately tightening each one a quarter turn at a time. Check for play in the spindle.

6. Recheck the torque after one ride, as the crank may settle in and the bolts will need retightening. Periodically check the torque from then on.

viii-10 OTHER TYPES OF BOTTOM BRACKETS

LEVEL 2

The three bottom-bracket types just described probably represent about 95 percent of the road bikes in circulation. There are, however, a few variations worth mentioning.

a. Cartridge-bearing bottom brackets with adjustable cups

Cartridge-bearing bottom brackets with adjustable cups (Fig. 8.12) are reasonably easy to install. These come with an adjustable cup at each end. With this type, you simply install the drive-side cup and lockring, slide the cartridge bearing in (if it is not already pressed into the cup), slip the axle in, and then

INTEGRATED-
SPINDLE
BOTTOM
BRACKETS
—
OTHER
BOTTOM
BRACKETS

install the other bearing, cup, and lockring. Tighten each lockring while holding the adjustable cup in place with a pin spanner (Fig. 8.20). Adjust for free play as in §viii-8, steps 11–15.

The advantage of having two adjustable cups is that you can center the cartridge by moving it side to side in the bottom-bracket shell. If the chainrings end up too close or too far away from the frame (see chain-line discussion in §v-38 and §v-39 in Chapter 5), you can move one cup in and one out to shift the position of the spindle.

Sometimes cartridge-bearing bottom brackets bind up a bit during adjustment and installation. A light tap on each end of the axle usually seats them.

b. Stronglight (or Mavic) cartridge-bearing bottom brackets

Stronglight (or Mavic) cartridge-bearing bottom brackets (Fig. 8.16) require each end of the bottom-bracket shell to be chamfered at an angle to seat the angled lockrings. You need to go to a shop equipped with the correct cutting tool for this. Once the bottom-bracket-shell chamfer has been cut, you simply slip the cartridge into the shell, slide on one of the angled plastic rings from either end (pictured in Fig. 8.16), and screw on a lockring, angled side inward, from either side. Holding the cartridge with a pin spanner, tighten the lockrings on each side (Fig. 8.20). The beauty of these bottom brackets is that they work independently of the shell threads, and so they can be installed in shells with ruined threads or nonstandard threads. Mavic stopped producing them in 1995, but Stronglight now makes them.

c. Unthreaded bottom-bracket shell with snapring grooves

An unthreaded bottom-bracket shell with snapring grooves accepts only a bottom bracket that doesn't have cups (not pictured); snaprings retain the bearings. This type was popular at the beginning of the 1980s, but has virtually disappeared on new bikes. With a cupless bottom bracket, seat the cartridge bearings against the stops on either end of the axle. Install one snapring with snapring pliers into the groove in one end of the shell. Push the entire assembly of axle and two bearings in from the other side of the bottom-bracket shell. Install the other snapring, and you're done.

OVERHAULING THE BOTTOM BRACKET

A bottom-bracket overhaul consists of cleaning or replacing the bearings, cleaning the axle and bearing surfaces, and regreasing them. With any type, both crankarms must be removed (§viii-1).

viii-11 CARTRIDGE-BEARING BOTTOM BRACKETS

Standard cartridge-bearing bottom brackets (Fig. 8.10) are sealed units and cannot be overhauled. They must be replaced when they stop performing properly. Remove the cranks as in §viii-1. Remove the bottom bracket by unscrewing the cups with the splined cup tool (Fig. 8.17), and install a new bottom bracket as directed in §viii-7.

viii-12 CUP-AND-CONE BOTTOM BRACKETS

Cup-and-cone bottom brackets (Fig. 8.11) can be overhauled entirely from the nondrive side, after you have removed the crankarms as described in §viii-1.

1. Remove the lockring with the lockring spanner (as in Fig. 8.20, except the lockring spanner and the rotation direction will be reversed).

2. Remove the adjustable cup with the tool that fits yours (usually a pin spanner [Fig. 1.2], installed into the cup as in Fig. 8.20).

3. Leave the fixed cup in place, and check that it is tight in the frame by putting a fixed-cup wrench on it and trying to tighten it (counter-clockwise for English thread, clockwise for Italian) (Fig. 8.18).

4. Clean the cups and axle with a rag. There should be no need for a solvent unless the parts are glazed.

5. Clean the bearings with a citrus-based solvent, without removing them from their retainer cages. A simple way to do this is to drop the bearings in a plastic bottle, fill it with solvent, cap it, and shake it. A toothbrush may be required afterward, and a solvent tank is certainly handy if you have access to one. If your bearings are not shiny and in perfect shape, replace them. Balls with dull luster and/or rough spots or rust on them should be replaced.

6. Wash the bearings in soap and water to remove the solvent and any remaining grit. Towel them off thoroughly, and then let them dry completely. An air compressor is handy here.

7. Follow the installation procedure described in §viii-8.

8. Install the crankarms as in §viii-1, Figure 8.2.

viii-13 INTEGRATED-SPINDLE BOTTOM BRACKETS

Following the method of §viii-9, replace the cups and you are done! If you can get the bearing out of the cup (not likely), you could just replace the bearings, rather than the entire cups. If

ADVANTAGES OF A COMPACT-DRIVE DOUBLE CRANK

If you want lower gears for climbing, but you do not want a triple crank, which is heavier than a double and spaces the feet farther apart, consider a compact-drive double crank. A compact-drive road crank has a 110mm bolt-circle diameter, considerably less than the standard 130mm of Shimano and 135mm of Campagnolo. This smaller diameter allows the use of a 34-tooth inner chainring.

You can switch your crank from, say, a chainring with a tooth setup of 39-53 to 34-50 and lower your front derailleur accordingly. You generally will be replacing your bottom bracket as well, but it is possible that the new crank will work with your existing one, and you may wish to use the rest of your components just as they are (although you may want to shorten your chain by one link). However, the tighter curvature of the compact chainrings, and the larger 16-tooth jump (50 minus 34) versus the 14-tooth jump (53 minus 39) that you had before means that the double front derailleur you have been using will not shift as well. Ideally, you want a front derailleur meant for a compact road crank.

Campagnolo and FSA both make integrated systems; in other words, they both offer a compact crankset as well as a front derailleur specifically designed for it. IRD also makes a compact front derailleur intended for use on Shimano-equipped bikes with compact cranks from other manufacturers. I imagine that Shimano will have a compact-double system soon enough as well.

CRANKS AND BOTTOM BRACKETS

INTEGRATED-SPINDLE BOTTOM BRACKETS

not, you may be able to pry off the cover of the bearing and clean it out (Fig. 6.29); it may be worth a try.

viii-14 OTHER TYPES OF BOTTOM BRACKETS

If any cartridge-bearing bottom bracket becomes difficult to turn, the bearings must be replaced. If they are pressed into cups, then you may also have to buy new cups. Be doubly sure to get the correct size.

1. Reverse the installation procedure outlined in §viii-10a to remove the bottom bracket.

2. Replace the bearings.

3. Reinstall the bottom bracket (§viii-10a) and crankarms (§viii-1).

TROUBLESHOOTING CRANK AND BOTTOM-BRACKET NOISE

viii-15 CREAKING NOISES

Mysterious creaking noises can drive you nuts. Just as you think you have your bike tuned to perfection, a little noise comes along to ruin your ride. What's worse is that these annoying little creaks, pops, and groans can be a bear to locate.

Pedaling-induced noises can originate from almost anything connected to your crankset, including movement of the cleats on your shoes, loose crankarms on the bottom-bracket axle, loose chainrings, or poorly adjusted pedal or bottom-bracket bearings. Of course, noise could also originate from seemingly unrelated components like the seat, seatpost, frame, wheels, or handlebar.

Before spending hours overhauling the drivetrain, spend some time trying to isolate the source of the noise. Try different pedals and shoes and wheels. Pedal out of the saddle, and pedal without flexing the handlebar. If the source of the creak turns out to be the saddle, seatpost, pedals, wheels, or handlebar,

turn to the appropriate chapter for directions on how to correct the problem.

If the creaking is definitely in the crank area, here are some steps to resolve it.

1. Check to make sure that the chainring bolts are tight, and tighten them if they are not (Fig. 8.6).

2. If that does not solve the problem, make certain that the crankarm bolts are tight (Fig. 8.2). If they are not, the resulting movement between the crankarm and the bottom-bracket axle is a likely source of noise. If the crank is of a different brand than the bottom bracket, check with the manufacturers or your local shop to make sure that they are recommended for use together. Incompatible cranks and axles will never properly join and are a potential problem area.

3. Rusting can break the glue bond between a Shimano-style cartridge-bearing bottom bracket and one or both of its cups (Figs. 8.10 and 8.14), allowing movement between cartridge and cup. This movement can make creaking noises when pedaling. To quiet the noises, remove the cartridge, grease the inside of the cup(s) as well as the threads, and reinstall the bottom bracket.

4. The bottom bracket itself can creak owing to improper adjustment, lack of grease, cracked bearings, worn parts, or loose cups. All of these things require adjustment or overhaul procedures, outlined in the sections under the heading Bottom-Bracket Installation in this chapter. Many integrated-spindle designs are very sensitive to being out of parallel, and creaking can occur if the bottom-bracket shell is not perfectly tapped and faced. This is a job for a good bike shop.

5. If you have an unpainted titanium or aluminum

frame, check to make sure that the front-derailleur clamp is tight. The noise from a loose clamp while pedaling, especially under heavy load, can seem to emanate from the crankset.

6. Now for the bad news. If creaking persists, the problem could be rooted in the frame. Creaks can originate from cracks in and around the bottom-bracket shell. Or the threads in the bottom-bracket shell could be so worn that they allow the cups to move slightly. Neither of these is a good sign—unless, of course, you were hoping for an excuse to buy a new frame.

viii–16 CLUNKING NOISES

1. Crankarm play: Grab the crankarm and push on it side to side.

   (a) If there is play, tighten the crankarm bolt (Fig. 8.2; torque spec is in Appendix E).

   (b) If there is still crankarm play, and you have a cup-and-cone bottom bracket (Figs. 8.11 and 8.13) or a cartridge-bearing bottom bracket with a lockring on each side (Fig. 8.12), adjust the bottom-bracket axle-end play (steps 11–15, §viii-8).

   (c) If bottom-bracket adjustment does not eliminate crankarm play, or you have a non-adjustable cartridge-bearing bottom bracket (Fig. 8.10), the bottom bracket is loose in the frame threads. With a cup-and-cone bottom bracket, you can go back to §viii-8 and start over, making sure that the fixed cup is very tight. A cheater bar (extension tube) may need to be used on the fixed-cup wrench to tighten the fixed cup to high enough torque. Adjustable-cup lockrings need to be equally tight (Fig. 8.20),

once the axle-end play is adjusted properly.

   (d) The lockrings and fixed-cup flanges must be flush against the bottom-bracket shell all of the way around; if they are not, the bottom bracket must be removed, and the bottom-bracket shell must be tapped (threaded) and faced (cut parallel) by a shop equipped with the tools.

   (e) If the crankarm play persists or the bottom-bracket fixed cup or lockring will not tighten completely, then either the bottom-bracket cups are stripped or undersized, or the frame's bottom-bracket-shell threads are stripped or oversized. Either way, it's an expensive fix, especially the frame-replacement option! Get a second opinion if you reach this point. If you can find a Mavic or Stronglight cartridge-bearing bottom bracket (§viii-10b, Fig. 8.16), you can still use a frame with stripped threads.

2. Pedal-end play: Grab each pedal and wobble it to check for play. See the section on Overhauling Pedals in Chapter 9, if you find axle-end play.

viii–17 HARD-TO-TURN CRANKS

If the cranks are hard to turn, you need to overhaul the bottom bracket (see §viii-11 to §viii-14), unless you want to continue intensifying your workout or boost the egos of your cycling companions. The bottom bracket may be shot and need to be replaced.

viii–18 INNER CHAINRING DRAGS ON CHAINSTAY

If the inner chainring drags on the chainstay, it is possible that the bottom-bracket axle is too short or the square hole in the crankarm is so deformed that

CLUNKING

NOISES

—

HARD-TO-TURN

CRANKS

—

INNER

CHAINRING

DRAGS ON

CHAINSTAY

the crank slides on too far. If you have switched to a larger inner chainring and the chainring is too large, get a smaller one. A misaligned frame, with either bent chainstays or a twisted bottom-bracket shell, can cause chainring rub as well. A badly misaligned frame needs to be replaced.

With an adjustable cartridge-bearing bottom bracket (Fig. 8.12) with a lockring on each end, it is possible to fix the problem by offsetting the entire bottom bracket to the left (Fig. 8.20). If the bottom-bracket axle is too short, replace it with one of the correct length. If the square hole in the crank is badly deformed, replace the crankarm. There's no other cure; it will continue to loosen up and cause problems otherwise.

NOTE: *See §v-39 and Fig. 5.32 in Chapter 5 concerning the chain line to establish proper crank-to-frame spacing.*

INNER
CHAINRING
DRAGS ON
CHAINSTAY

CHAPTER 9

PEDALS

*Experience is that marvelous thing that enables
you to recognize a mistake when you make it again.*
—F. P. Jones

TOOLS

15mm pedal wrench

2.5mm, 3mm, 4mm, 5mm, 6mm, and 8mm hex keys

Phillips-head screwdriver

small flat-blade screwdriver

snapring pliers

8mm, 9mm, 10mm, 12mm, 20mm, and 22mm box wrenches

13mm cone wrench

Shimano, Look splined pedal-axle tools

grease

fine-tipped grease gun

chain lubricant

OPTIONAL

splined Campagnolo pedal-cap tool

TORX drivers

8mm socket wrench

speedplay grease fitting

threadlock compound

To best serve its purpose, a bicycle pedal needs only to be firmly attached to the crankarm and provide a stable platform for the shoe. A simple enough task, but you'd be amazed at the different approaches that have been taken to achieve this goal.

Still, for the purpose of our discussion, there are two basic types of road bike pedals: (1) The standard cage-type pedal, with or without a toeclip and strap, is the simplest and cheapest. A "quill" pedal is a standard pedal in which the cage is asymmetrical on the two sides (Fig. 9.1). The cage is thinner on the bottom side and curves up on the outboard end to improve cornering clearance. (2) "Clip-in"–type pedals (Fig. 9.2), retain the foot with spring-loaded clips (like a ski binding) and are almost universal on mid- to high-end road bikes. Clip-in pedals are sometimes called "clipless," because they have no toeclip.

Cage-type pedals are fairly common on lower-end bikes. They are relatively unintimidating for the novice rider, and the frame (or "cage") that surrounds the pedal provides a large, stable platform (Fig. 9.1). A symmetrical, mountain bike–style, cage-type pedal has an identical top and bottom, and it can be used with just about any type of shoe. If you mount toeclips on these without straps, your feet won't slide forward and will release easily in almost any direction.

One-sided road bike quill pedals (Fig. 9.1) are designed to be used exclusively with toeclips, because they cannot be pedaled upside-down very well. A toe strap keeps your foot on the pedal and also allows you to pull on the upward part of the pedal stroke, giving you more power, a fluid pedal stroke, and balanced muscle development. Of course, as you add clips and straps, the pedal becomes harder to enter and to exit, and running

9.1 Standard cage-type "quill" pedal with toeclip and strap

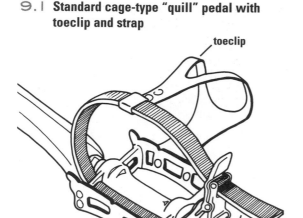

toeclip

tab

cage

strap

9.2 Clip-in pedal

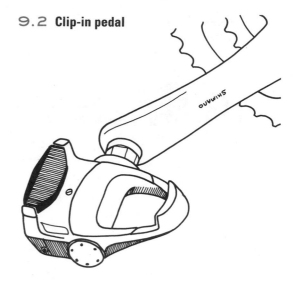

shoes with aggressive tread become increasingly difficult to use. A tab on the cage plate opposite the toeclip is there so that you can flip the pedal up with your toe in order to slide your foot into the toeclip.

Clip-in models (Figs. 9.2, 9.3, and 9.4) offer all of the advantages of a pedal firmly coupled to a stiff shoe by means of a slotted cleat mounted on the sole, snapped down onto the cage, and held in place with a toeclip and strap, yet they allow easier entry and exit from the pedal. Clip-in pedals are more expensive and require special shoes and accurate mounting of the cleats. Your choice of shoes is limited to stiff-sole models that accept cleats for your particular pedal. Once you have them properly mounted and adjusted, you will find that clip-in pedals waste less energy through flex and slippage and allow you to transfer more power directly to the pedals.

This chapter explains how to remove and replace pedals, how to mount the cleats and adjust the release tension with clip-in pedals, how to troubleshoot pedal problems, and how to overhaul and replace spindles on almost all road bike pedals. Incidentally, I use the terms "axle" and "spindle" interchangeably.

ix-1 PEDAL REMOVAL AND INSTALLATION

Note that the right pedal axle is right-hand threaded and the left is left-hand (reverse) threaded. Both unscrew from the crank in the pedaling direction. There's an interesting bit of history behind the threading of pedal axles this way. In the early days of cycling, fixed-gear bikes were the norm, and it was decided that if the pedal bearings were to seize up, the pedal should unscrew from the crank rather than tear up the rider's strapped-in feet. This isn't a concern on a modern bike, because the freewheel (on the rear hub) eliminates the bodily danger of a seized pedal, and the bearing quality makes seizing highly unlikely.

a. Removal

1. Slide a 15mm pedal wrench onto the wrench flats of the pedal axle (Fig. 9.3). Or, if the pedal axle is designed to accept it, you can use a 6mm or 8mm Allen wrench from the back side of the crankarm (Fig. 9.4). The latter is particularly handy on the road, because you probably won't be carrying a 15mm wrench. But if you are at home and the pedal is really tight, it will be eas-

9.3 Removing or installing pedal with 15mm wrench

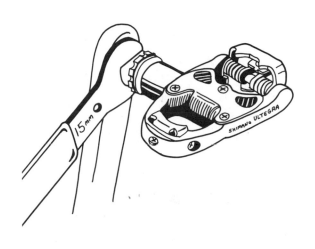

9.4 Removing or installing pedal with a 6mm Allen wrench

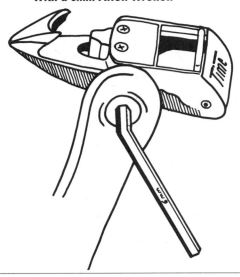

ier to use the standard pedal wrench, although many newer models have no wrench flats and only accept an Allen wrench.

2. Unscrew the pedal in the appropriate direction. The right, or drive-side, pedal unscrews counterclockwise when viewed from that side. The left-side pedal is reverse threaded, so it unscrews in a clockwise direction when viewed from the left side of the bike. Once loosened, either pedal can be unscrewed quickly by turning the crank forward with a 15mm pedal wrench engaged on the pedal spindle and the rear wheel off the ground.

b. Installation

1. Use a rag to wipe the threads clean on the pedal axle and inside the crankarm.

2. Apply a light coat of grease to the pedal threads.

3. Start screwing the pedal in with your fingers, clockwise for the right pedal, counterclockwise for the left.

4. Tighten the pedal with the 15mm pedal wrench (Fig. 9.3) or a 6mm or 8mm Allen wrench (Fig. 9.4). This step can be done quickly by turning

the cranks backward with a 15mm pedal wrench engaged on the pedal spindle.

SETTING UP CLIP-IN PEDALS

Setting up clip-in pedals involves installation and adjustment of the cleats on the shoes and adjusting the pedal-release tension.

There are a number of different "mounting platforms" for road bike pedals, and your shoe sole must be compatible with your pedal cleats. The original clip-in road bike pedal system was the Look, which has three M5-threaded holes arranged in a triangular pattern (Fig. 9.5) to accept a three-hole cleat (Fig. 9.10). The original Time pedal system required a flat surface with four smaller threaded holes (Fig. 9.6), and original Speedplay pedal cleats could be mounted on these as well. Original Shimano road bike pedals were made by Look and used the three-hole mounting system. Shimano Pedaling Dynamics, or SPD, began as a system for mountain bikes with tiny cleats (Fig. 9.9) that were easy to run with and less likely to clog with mud. SPD cleats mount with two side-by-side M5-thread screws,

9.5 Three-hole (Look) cleat drill pattern

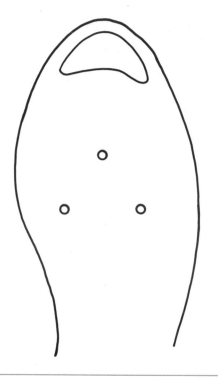

9.6 Original Time cleat drill pattern

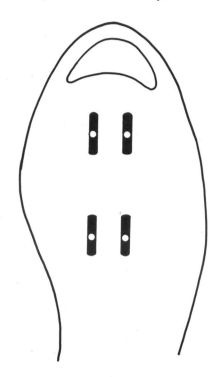

spaced 14mm apart. They screw into a movable threaded cleat-mounting plate behind two longitudinal grooves in the sole (Fig. 9.7). Crank Brothers cleats mount on this system as well. For their road bike, some riders prefer an SPD-compatible system that uses either a single-sided road bike pedal or a double-sided mountain bike pedal so that they are able to use a mountain bike shoe, which is far easier to walk in than a road bike cycling shoe.

Shimano's SPD-R pedal (since abandoned) required a shoe having a single lengthwise slot in the sole with an M5-threaded hole at either end moving on a threaded backing plate behind the slot (Fig. 9.8). (Diadora pedals have yet another mounting pattern, but they are no longer on the market and so are not included here.) Now, Shimano's SPD-SL road bike pedals and Ritchey, Time, and Speedplay road bike pedals have gone to the standard three-hole system. Pedal brands not mentioned in this

paragraph mount on one or several of these shoe-hole patterns.

Incidentally, many shoe and pedal manufacturers make adapter plates to fit various shoes and pedals to each other, so that if you have a favorite pair of shoes, it may be possible to make them work with an unrelated set of pedals.

ix-2 INSTALLING AND ADJUSTING PEDAL CLEATS ON THE SHOES

The cleat is important because its position determines the fore-and-aft, lateral (side-to-side), and rotational position of your foot. If the cleats aren't properly oriented, the misalignment could eventually cause hip, knee, or ankle problems.

1. Put the shoe on, and mark the position of the ball of your foot (the big bump behind your big toe) on the outside of the shoe. This mark will help you position the cleat so that the ball of

9.7 SPD cleat drill pattern

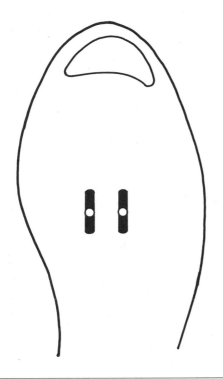

9.8 SPD-R cleat drill pattern

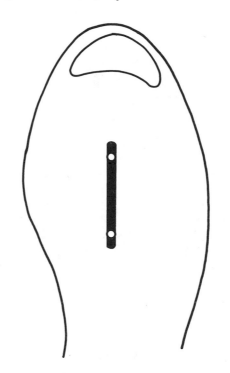

your foot will be straight above or just ahead of or behind the pedal spindle. Take the shoe off, and continue drawing the line straight across the bottom of the shoe.

NOTE: *On SPD-R cleats, the pontoon mounts on the rear bolt, pointing back.*

2. Grease the cleat screw threads, and screw the cleat that came with the pedals onto the shoe; this step usually requires a 4mm Allen wrench or a Phillips-head or standard screwdriver. Make sure you orient the cleat in the appropriate direction. Some cleats have an arrow indicating forward (Fig. 9.9); if yours do not, the instructions accompanying the pedals will specify which direction the cleat should point, and in some cases, on which shoe an asymmetrical cleat should be mounted. SPD and SPD-R cleats require rubber "pontoons" on a plate mounted under the cleat (Fig. 9.9). The pontoons guide

9.9 Cleat centered 1cm behind ball-of-foot line

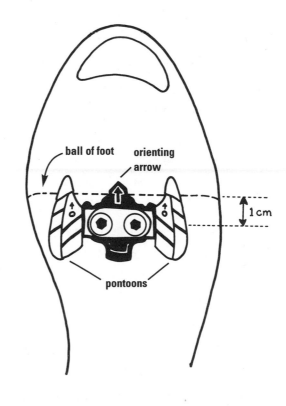

ball of foot   orienting arrow

1cm

pontoons

INSTALLING
AND
ADJUSTING
PEDAL CLEATS
ON SHOES

9.1O   **Look cleat with mark for pedal center**

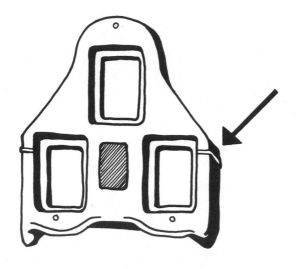

the small cleat into the pedal. The pontoons are not necessary on a mountain bike shoe as the relieved area in its tread will guide the cleat.

3. Position the cleat. Temporarily place it in the middle of its lateral- and rotational-adjustment range. Setting the fore-and-aft position requires knowing where the pedal spindle is positioned relative to the cleat. Many cleats have a mark on the side indicating the spindle position (Fig. 9.10). If your cleat has such a mark, line it up 0–1 centimeter behind the line you drew in step 1 across the shoe sole. With an SPD pedal, line up the mounting screws 0–1 centimeter behind the mark you made in step 1 (Fig. 9.9). With a Speedplay cleat, place the center of the hole in the middle of the cleat 0–1 centimeter behind the mark you made in step 1. If the cleat has neither centering marks nor is it SPD, you will have to tighten the screws and set the shoe in the pedal. When the shoe is level, you want the ball of the foot between 0 and 1 centimeter forward of the pedal spindle. Putting the ball farther forward is usually helpful to develop

power, while high-cadence spinning is usually enhanced with the ball of the foot farther back. If you know which type of rider you are, you can set the shoe as appropriate. Otherwise, split the difference and shoot for the middle of the range. Very small feet sometimes do better with the cleat farther forward on the shoe, placing the ball of the foot ahead of the spindle. Make sure you don't put an old-style Time rear cam on the wrong shoe, or you will not be able to release by twisting outward.

NOTE: *There are many SPD- and Look-style pedal clones under various brand names on the market. The cleat-mounting and tension-adjustment instructions for SPD or Look pedals generally apply to these models as well.*

4. Snug the screws down enough to prevent the cleat from moving when clipped in or out of the pedals, but don't tighten them fully. Follow the same steps with the other shoe.

5. To set the lateral cleat position, put the shoes on, sit on the bike, and clip into the pedals. Ride around a bit. Notice the position of your feet. Generally, the closer your feet are to the plane of the bike, the more efficient your pedaling will be, but you don't want them in so far that your ankles bump the cranks. Take the shoes off and adjust the cleats laterally, if necessary, to move the feet side to side. Get back on the bike and clip in again. Note that early Time pedals have no lateral cleat adjustment; recent Time models offer it by means of interchanging the left and right cleats.

6. To set the rotational cleat position, ride around some more. Notice if your feet feel twisted and uncomfortable. You may feel pressure on either

9.11 **Release-tension adjustment screw on Look pedal**

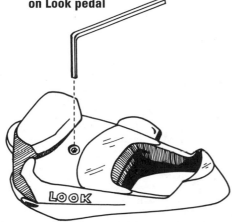

9.12 **Release-tension adjustment screw on Shimano SPD pedal**

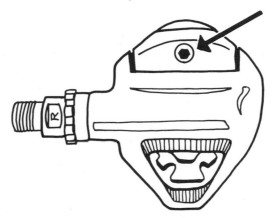

side of your heel from the shoe. If necessary, remove your shoes and rotate the cleat slightly. Most pedals now offer free-float, allowing the foot to rotate freely for a few degrees before releasing. Precise rotational cleat adjustment is less important if the pedal is free-floating. Some pedals have a dial on the back of the clip to set the amount of free-float rotation. Many companies also offer a number of cleat styles having increased or reduced (or eliminated) free-float range. I recommend starting with the greatest amount of free-float angle. You can reduce the float later if you desire. SPD-R cleats come in three styles: one with a wide tip for "fixed" operation and two narrower-tip models for different amounts of free-float. Vertical cleat play can be eliminated by raising rubber bumpers on the pedal body. Dura-Ace SPD-R pedals have a 3mm nut on the bottom of the pedal to push the bumper up, and Ultegra SPD-R pedals require removing three screws on the face of the pedal to interchange the two pads with thicker ones.

7. Once your cleat position feels right, trace the cleats with a pen or a scribe so that you can tell if the cleat stays put.

8. While holding the cleat in place, tighten the bolts down firmly. Hold the Allen wrench close to the bend so that you do not exert too much leverage and strip the bolts. There is little danger of overtightening with a screwdriver, but do take care that the blade (or Phillips tip) fits well in the screw slot (or Phillips cross). Push down firmly while tightening to avoid stripping the head of the screw.

NOTE: *If you have a small torque wrench, the recommended tightening torque for most cleat screws is 43–52 in-lbs (see Appendix E).*

9. When riding with new shoes or pedals, bring cleat-tightening tools along, because you may want to fine-tune the cleat adjustment over the course of a few rides.

ix-3 ADJUSTING RELEASE TENSION OF CLIP-IN PEDALS

If you find the factory-set release adjustment to be too loose or too restrictive, you can change it on many clip-in pedals; exceptions are Crank Brothers, Bebop, Diadora, Power, Speedplay, and Time (Fig. 9.4). The adjusting screws are usually located on or near the spring-loaded rear clip (Figs. 9.11 and

9.13 **Tool for removing Shimano pedal-axle assembly**

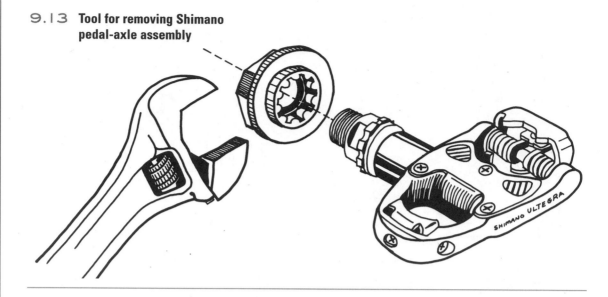

9.14 **A 22mm wrench fits the axle assembly of a Campagnolo ProFit pedal**

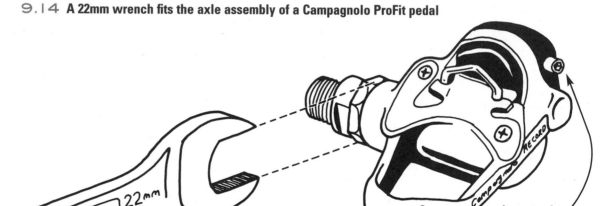

release-tension
adjustment screw

ADJUSTING RELEASE TENSION OF CLIP-IN PEDALS

9.12). The adjuster screws are usually operated with a small (usually 3mm) Allen wrench or a small screwdriver.

1. Locate the tension-adjustment screws. Older Looks have a screw (either slotted or 2.5mm or 3mm hex head) on top of the platform (Fig. 9.11); Look Anatomics and Campagnolo ProFits (Fig. 9.14) have a 3mm hex screw on the side. Look Keos and Shimano SPD-SLs have a 3mm hex screw on the top of the rear clip. Ritchey, Shimano SPD (Fig. 9.12), and SPD-R (Fig. 9.3) have a 3mm hex screw on the back of the clip.

NOTE: *There are many SPD- and Look-style pedal clones under various brand names on the market. The cleat-mounting and tension-adjustment instructions for SPD or Look pedals generally apply to these pedals as well.*

2. To loosen the tension adjustment, turn the screw counterclockwise; to tighten it, turn it clockwise (Figs. 9.11 and 9.12). It's the classic "lefty loosey, righty tighty" approach. There usually are click stops in the rotation of the screw. Tighten or loosen one click at a time (one-quarter to one-half turn), then ride the

bike to test the adjustment. Many types include an indicator that moves with the screw to show relative adjustment. Make certain that you do not back the screw out so far that it comes out of the spring plate or so far that it can vibrate loose; feel for at least the first "click" to hold it in place.

NOTE: *With Ritchey SPD-style pedals, you will decrease the amount of free-float in the pedal as you increase the release tension.*

OVERHAULING PEDALS

LEVEL 2

Like a hub or bottom bracket, pedal bearings and bushings need to be cleaned and regreased regularly.

There is a wide variation in road bike pedal designs. This book is not big enough to go into great detail about the inner workings of every single model. Speaking in general terms, pedal guts fall into two broad categories: those that have loose ball bearings (Figs. 9.15, 9.16, 9.24, and 9.25), and those that have cartridge bearings (Figs. 9.17–22).

Many pedals are closed on the outboard end and have a nut surrounding the axle on the inboard end (Figs. 9.13–9.17). The axle assembly installs into the pedal as a unit and is accessed by this inboard nut. Some axles are held in by a snapring (Figs. 9.18 and 9.19). The axle assemblies on older pedal designs (Fig. 9.24) and some new ones as well (Figs. 9.20 and 9.21) are accessed from the outboard end by removing a dust cap.

1. Remove the pedal from the bike (Figs. 9.3 and 9.4).

2. Before you start, figure out how the pedal is put together so that you will know how to take it apart; the following paragraphs and the illus-

trations on subsequent pages should help. In a few cases, the workings of the pedal guts may not be clear until you have completed step 1 in the overhaul process.

Most Shimano pedals have two sets of loose bearings and a bushing, which come out as a complete axle assembly (Fig. 9.16). You will see the tiny ball bearings at the small end of the axle (behind the wrenches in Fig. 9.23). Dura-Ace SPD-R (Fig. 9.15) and SPD-SL pedals have a set of ball bearings on each end of the spindle and a set of 6mm-inside-diameter (I.D.) needle bearings (not shown) just inboard of the outboard bearings.

Speedplay X/3 pedals have an inboard 10mm I.D. Teflon bushing and an outboard 6mm I.D. cartridge bearing. Speedplay X/5 pedals have an inboard needle bearing and an outboard cartridge bearing.

The Campagnolo Record ProFit (Fig. 9.14) pedal has one inboard and two outboard 17mm-outside-diameter (O.D.) cartridge bearings.

Look, Diadora, and older Time pedals have an inboard cartridge bearing (19mm, 24mm, and 24mm O.D., respectively) and one or two pressed-in outboard needle-bearing sets (not shown) (Figs. 9.17 and 9.18). Of the newer, carbon-composite-body pedals, Look Keos have a pair of 15mm O.D., inboard cartridge bearings and an 8mm I.D., outboard needle bearing, whereas Time RXS pedals have a 21mm O.D., inboard cartridge bearing and an 8mm I.D., outboard needle bearing.

Speedplay X/1, X/2, and Zero pedals have an inboard pressed-in needle bearing (not shown) and an outboard pair of cartridge bearings (Fig. 9.20).

Crank Brothers Quattros (Fig. 9.22) have two cartridge bearings: a large one on the inboard side and smaller one on the outboard side. This arrangement

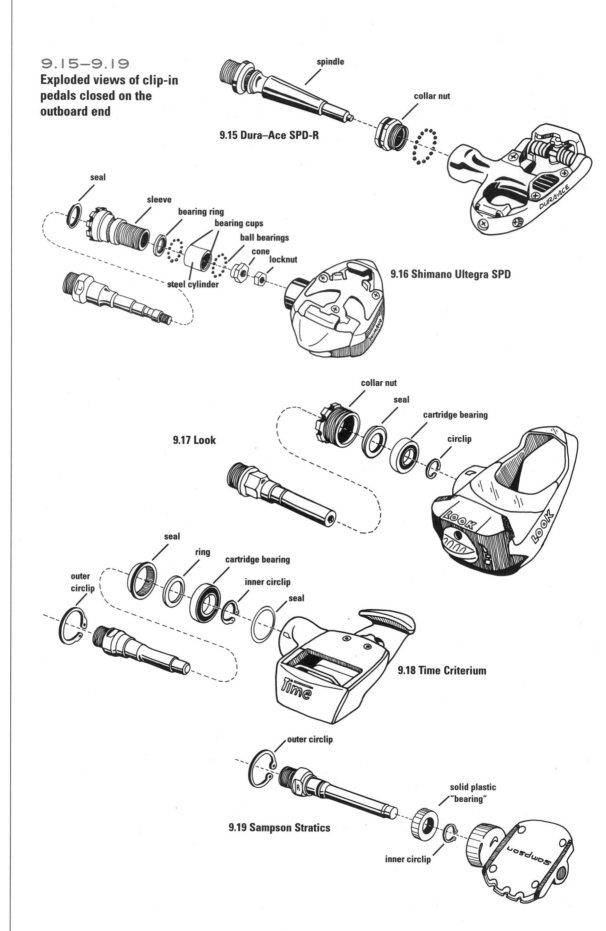

9.15—9.19
Exploded views of clip-in pedals closed on the outboard end

spindle

collar nut

9.15 Dura–Ace SPD-R

seal

sleeve

bearing ring

bearing cups

ball bearings

cone

locknut

steel cylinder

9.16 Shimano Ultegra SPD

collar nut

seal

cartridge bearing

circlip

9.17 Look

seal

ring

cartridge bearing

inner circlip

seal

outer circlip

9.18 Time Criterium

outer circlip

solid plastic "bearing"

9.19 Sampson Stratics

inner circlip

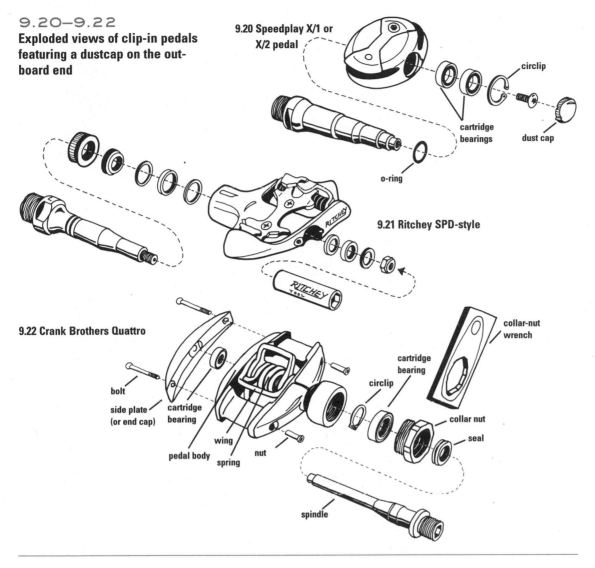

9.20—9.22

Exploded views of clip-in pedals featuring a dustcap on the outboard end

9.20 Speedplay X/1 or X/2 pedal

circlip

cartridge bearings

dust cap

o-ring

9.21 Ritchey SPD-style

9.22 Crank Brothers Quattro

collar-nut wrench

cartridge bearing

bolt

side plate (or end cap)

cartridge bearing

circlip

collar nut

seal

wing

pedal body   nut

spring

spindle

---

differs from that of Crank Brothers MTB pedals (Eggbeater, Candy, Mallet), which have one cartridge ball bearing (outboard) and one bushing (inboard). Also, the Quattro does not have a threaded end cap for regreasing the pedal (see §ix-5, step 1 note). This feature was eliminated to increase cornering clearance.

Sampson Stratics (Fig. 9.19) pedals have a 24mm outside diameter (O.D.) solid-plastic "bearing" on the inboard side and a plastic bushing inside the pedal body.

Ritchey SPD-style road bike pedals (Fig. 9.21) have two sets of pressed-in needle bearings, one with

an I.D. of 10mm and the other with an I.D. of 7mm.

Power Pedal axles (which only rotate in one direction) are not removable. The bearings are lubricated through the small grease fitting on the bottom of the pedal until clean grease squeezes out of the inboard side.

ix-4 OVERHAULING PEDALS CLOSED ON THE OUTBOARD END

1. Make sure your pedal does not have a dust cap or screw cover on the outboard end. If it does, skip to §ix-5. The exception is the Quattro (Fig.

9.22) which has a removable end cap but still is overhauled by unscrewing the inboard collar nut. Unless you have an old Time, Diadora, or Sampson pedal, remove the axle assembly by unscrewing the nut surrounding the axle ("the collar nut") where it enters the inboard side of the pedal (Figs. 9.13 and 9.14). You can usually just hold the pedal in your hand and unscrew the collar nut, but you may find that you will want to hold the pedal body in a padded vise while unscrewing the nut. The collar nut is often made of plastic and can crack if you turn it the wrong way, so be careful. Hold the pedal body with your hand or a vise while you unscrew the assembly. The fine threads take many turns to unscrew.

NOTE: *The threads on the pedal body are reversed compared to the crankarm threads on the axle. That means the right-axle assembly unscrews clockwise, and the left-axle assembly unscrews counterclockwise. It's confusing, but like English bottom-bracket threads, pedal bodies are threaded so that pedaling forward tightens the assembly.*

(a) Most Shimano pedals disassemble with a special plastic splined tool (Fig. 1.2), as do some Looks and Crank Brothers Quattros (Fig. 9.22). Use a large adjustable wrench or a vise to hold the tool (Fig. 9.13). Most other pedals take a 19mm, 20mm, or 22mm open-end wrench (Fig. 9.14). The collar nut on a Time RXS requires a special tool, but in its absence, the nut is easy to unscrew with a pair of pliers wrapped in cloth to avoid marring the nut's surface.

(b) Campagnolo ProFit (Fig. 9.14) and many Look pedal-axle assemblies unscrew with a 22mm open-end or box wrench; removal of

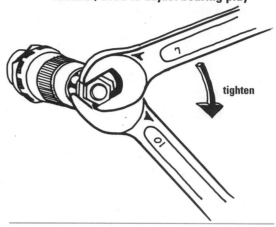

9.23 **Most Shimano axles have a cone and a locknut, used to adjust bearing play**

tighten

the Dura-Ace SPD-R (Fig. 9.15) and SPD-SL axle assemblies requires a 20mm wrench, and Look Keos take a 19mm wrench. Some older Look axles are accessed with a special Look splined tool similar to the one that unscrews most Shimano pedals (Fig. 9.13). Note that original Shimano clip-in road bike pedals are actually Looks with Shimano axle assemblies, and Campagnolo clip-in pedals prior to 1997 (other than an unfortunate attempt by Campagnolo itself in the late 1980s) are also Looks with Campagnolo axle assemblies.

(c) Older Time, Diadora, and Sampson pedal axles are retained by a snapring on the crank side (Figs. 9.18 and 9.19). Popping the snapring out usually requires inward-squeezing snapring pliers, but the snapring on a Time Impact requires only a thin screwdriver to remove, once you move the end of the snapring under the little notch in the inboard pedal-body face so that you can pry it up with the screwdriver. There is also a snapring on a Power Pedal, but there is no point in removing it, because the

OVERHAULING
PEDALS
CLOSED ON
OUTBOARD END

9.24 **Loose-bearing "quill" pedal exploded**

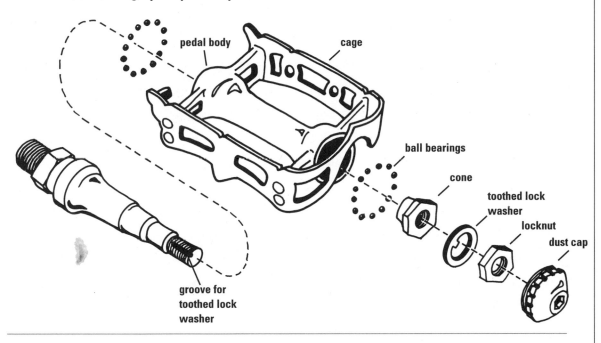

pedal body · cage · ball bearings · cone · toothed lock washer · locknut · dust cap · groove for toothed lock washer

clutch bearing and axle assembly are pressed in, and you will not be able to pull them out. With Time, Look, Sampson, or Diadora, skip to step 3.

2. Once you have removed the pedal body, take a look at the axle-bearing-bushing assembly. You will notice either one or two nuts on the thin end of the axle that serve to hold the bearings and/or bushings in place. Remove the nut or nuts as follows:

   (a) If the axle has a single nut on the end, simply hold the axle's large end with the 15mm pedal wrench and unscrew the little nut with a 9mm or 12mm wrench (or whatever fits it). The nut will be tight, because it has no locknut.

   (b) If the axle has two nuts on the end (Fig. 9.16), they are tightened against each other. To remove them, hold the inner nut with one wrench while you unscrew the outer nut with another (Fig. 9.23). On Shimano

pedals, the inner nut does double duty as the bearing cone; be careful not to lose the tiny ball bearings as you unscrew the cone!

3. Clean all of the parts as follows:

   (a) If it is a loose-bearing pedal, use a rag to clean the ball bearings, the cone, the inner ring that the bearings ride on at the end of the plastic sleeve (it looks like a washer), the bearing surfaces on either end of the little steel cylinder (or cylinders, in the case of Campagnolo Looks), the axle, and the inside of the plastic or aluminum axle sleeve (Fig. 9.16). To get the bearings really clean, wash them in the sink in soap and water with the sink drain plugged; the motion is the same as washing your hands, and results in both the bearings and your hands being clean for a sterile reassembly. Blot dry.

   (b) On a pedal with a cartridge bearing (Figs. 9.17–9.22), if the bearing is dirty or worn out, it is best to replace it. These units

OVERHAULING
PEDALS
CLOSED ON
OUTBOARD END

usually have steel bearing covers that cannot be pried off without damaging them, nor can the covers be replaced. Plastic cartridge-bearing covers can be pried off (Fig. 6.29) and the bearing regreased.

(c) Needle bearings (not visible in the figures because they are pressed inside) on Dura-Ace SPD-R/PD-7700 and SPD-SL/PD-7800, Look, Time, Diadora (Figs. 9.15, 9.17, and 9.18) can be cleaned with solvent and a thin toothbrush slipped inside the pedal-body bore. The needle bearings usually just need grease, though, because they are well isolated from dirt.

(d) On a Sampson (Fig. 9.19), just wipe down the axle, the plastic "bearing," and the pedal-body bore. Do the same for an inexpensive bushing-only pedal.

4. Lightly grease everything and reassemble the parts as they were, a simple process with bushings, cartridge bearings, and needle bearings, but not so simple with loose bearings!

(a) With a loose-bearing pedal, you have some exacting work to place the bearings on their races and screw the cone on while they stay in place. With most Shimano guts (Fig. 9.16), grease the bushing inside the axle sleeve, and slide the axle into the sleeve. Slide the steel ring, on which the inner set of bearings rides, down onto the axle and against the end of the sleeve. Make sure that the concave bearing surface faces away from the sleeve. Coat the ring with grease, and stick half of the bearings (usually 12) onto the outer surface of the ring. Slip the steel cylinder onto the axle so that one end

rides on the bearings. Make sure that all of the bearings are seated properly and that none are stuck inside of the sleeve.

(b) To prevent the bearings from piling up on each other and ending up inside the sleeve instead of on the races, grease the cone and start it on the axle a few threads. Place the remaining half of the bearings on the flanks of the cone. Being careful not to dislodge the bearings, screw the cone in until the bearings come close to the end of the cylinder without touching it. While holding the axle sleeve, push the axle inward until the bearings seat against the end of the cylinder. Make sure that the first set of bearings is still in place. Screw the cone in without dislodging the inboard bearings by avoiding turning the axle or the cylinder. Tighten the cone with your fingers only, and loosely screw on the locknut.

(c) Pre-1997 Look-style Campagnolo pedal guts are similar to Shimano, except that the bearing race is machined into the axle (rather than being a separate ring), and there are two cylinders, not one. Orient the cylinders so that their bearing races face outward, and otherwise follow the just-described steps.

(d) With Dura-Ace SPD-R/PD-7700 (Fig. 9.15) or Dura-Ace SPD-SL/PD-7800 pedals you needed to push back on the bearing cup (on the end of the 20mm nut that holds the axle into the pedal body) to remove the ball bearings in the first place. Grease the cup and push back on it again to allow enough space between the cup and the cylinder to set each of the 17 balls onto the edge of the cup with a small screwdriver.

5. Adjust the axle assembly. (For Time, Look, Diadora, and Sampson pedals, skip this step.)

(a) Pedals with a small cartridge bearing and a single nut on the end of the axle, such as Campagnolo Record ProFit, require that you tighten the nut against the cartridge bearing while holding the other end of the axle with the 15mm pedal wrench. Tighten it enough to remove play but not enough to bind the axle.

(b) On pedals with two nuts on the end of the axle, hold the cone or inner nut with a wrench and tighten the outer locknut down against it (Fig. 9.23). Check the adjustment for freedom of rotation, and be sure there is no lateral play. Readjust as necessary by tightening or loosening the cone or inner nut and retightening the locknut.

6. Replace the axle assembly in the pedal body. Smear grease on the inside of the pedal hole; this will ease insertion and act as a barrier to dirt and water. Screw the sleeve in with the same wrench you used to remove it (Figs. 9.13 and 9.14).

REMEMBER: *Pay attention to proper thread direction (see note in step 1)! Tighten carefully; it is easy to overtighten, which can crack a plastic nut.*

7. Put the pedals back on your bike, and go ride.

ix-5 OVERHAULING PEDALS WITH A DUST CAP ON THE OUTBOARD END

LEVEL 2

NOTE: *Assess the value of your pedals and your time before continuing. Well-made older classic quill racing pedals like Campagnolo (Figs. 9.1 and 9.24)*

deserve careful attention, but many non-clip-in pedals are not worth the effort of overhaul.

1. Remove the dust cover from the outboard end of the pedal with the appropriate tool. This could be a pair of pliers, a flat or Phillips screwdriver, a coin, an Allen wrench, or a splined tool made especially for your pedals; it's pretty easy to figure out which one is needed to remove the cap. Dig the dust cap out from SPD-style Ritcheys (Fig. 9.21) and Speedplay X/1, X/2, and Zero (Fig. 9.20) with a sharp pick or a sharpened nail (Ritchey pedals first require removal of a 2.5mm hex screw holding down the corner of the dust cap).

NOTE: *Speedplay bearings can be regreased without removing the axle and on newer models without removing the dust cap. On an older X/1 or X/2, remove the dust cap as just described in step 1, insert Speedplay's "Speedy Luber" grease-injection fitting, and squirt grease in with a fine-tip bicycle grease gun until it squirts out the other end. On newer X/1, X/2, X/3, X/5, or Zero, after removing the screw from the outboard end, pump grease in with a fine-tip grease gun while slowly turning the spindle until you see grease at the opposite end. Crank Brothers pedals other than the Quattro (Eggbeater, Candy, Mallet) have a similar feature, and the screw-in grease adapter (that screws in where the dust cap was and accepts the grease gun tip) comes with every pair of pedals.*

2. Hold the wrench flats on the inboard end of the axle with a pedal wrench, and unscrew the locknut with the appropriate-size socket wrench (or box wrench, if there is room for it).

(a) Ritchey road bike pedals require a deep, thin-wall 8mm socket; Ritchey makes a double-ended thin 8mm socket for the purpose that you can turn with an 8mm hex key in the other end.

(b) On a Speedplay X/1 or X/2 pedal, remove the TORX T15 or T20 screw on the outboard end under the dust cap (Fig. 9.20) with the appropriate TORX driver. You may have to heat the bolt with a soldering iron to soften the threadlock compound.

(c) On a Speedplay X/3 or X/5, carefully pry the two halves of the pedal apart with a knife or razor blade after removing the 2.5mm pedal-body screws from either side. Lift the axle assembly out and remove the 9mm locknut from the end of the spindle. Pull the bearings and bushing (all located in an alloy sleeve) and O-ring off the spindle. Clean and grease the parts, and replace the cartridge bearing and bushing if necessary. Reassemble the parts onto the axle, and tighten the locknut snugly against the bearing (35–40 in-lbs). When you reassemble the pedal, seal it from water by caulking the inside edges of the pedal-body halves and putting on a new O-ring.

3. Remove the axle. If it is a loose-bearing pedal (Fig. 9.24), hold the pedal over a rag to catch the bearings and then unscrew the cone. Keep the bearings from the two ends separate in case they differ in size or in number. Count them so that you can put the right numbers back in when you reassemble the pedal. The guts should look like Figure 9.24. If the pedal does not have loose bearings (Figs. 9.20 and 9.21), the procedure is different, as detailed next:

(a) With a Ritchey (Fig. 9.21) pedal, once you have removed the 8mm locknut, you can pull the axle out. The pedal has two pressed-in needle bearings inside. Scrub them with solvent and a rag or thin brush, if they are dirty. Removal of bad needle bearings requires a special tool to pull them out.

(b) With a Speedplay X/1, X/2, or Zero pedal (Fig. 9.20), you pull the axle out and reinstall the TORX screw in the end of the axle. Remove the little snapring from the outboard end of the pedal bore with inward-squeezing snapring pliers. Push the axle back in and carefully push the cartridge bearings out. The cartridge bearings are easily replaceable, but if the needle bearings are in bad shape, you will have to buy a new pedal body from Speedplay with the needle bearings already pressed in. You can clean them as just described for Ritchey pedals.

(c) With Ritchey or Speedplay pedals, dry and grease the needle bearings and put the pedals back together by reversing the process of disassembly. Do not overtighten the Ritchey locknut; remove bearing play, but don't bind the axle. Put threadlock compound on the Speedplay TORX end bolt, and tighten it snugly (35–40 in-lbs). Then skip to step 11.

4. With a rag, clean the bearings, cones, and bearing races. Clean the inside of the pedal body by pushing the rag through with a screwdriver. If there is a dust cover on the inboard end of the pedal body, you can clean it in place, or pop it out with a screwdriver and clean it separately.

5. If you want to get the bearings really clean, wash them in a plugged sink with soap and water. The motion is the same as washing your hands, and

OVERHAULING
PEDALS WITH
DUST CAP ON
OUTBOARD END

9.25 **Dropping in bearings**

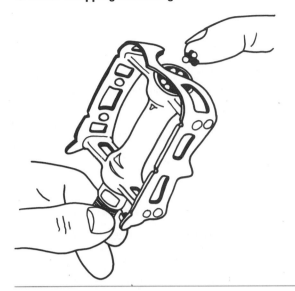

9.26 **Lubricate the springs and cleat contact areas**

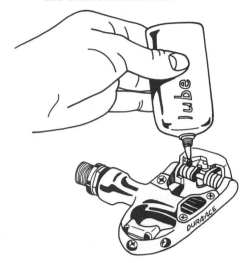

it results in both the bearings and your hands being clean for a sterile reassembly. Blot dry.

6. If you removed it, press the inboard dust cover back into the pedal body. Smear a thin layer of grease in the inboard bearing cup and replace the bearings. Once all of the bearings are in place, there will be a gap equal to about half the diameter of one bearing.

7. Drop the axle in and turn the pedal over so that the outboard end is up. Smear grease in that end, and replace the bearings (Fig. 9.25).

8. Screw the cone in until it almost contacts the bearings, then push the axle straight in to bring the cone and bearings together; this prevents the bearings from piling up and getting spit out as the cone turns down against them. Without turning the axle (which would knock the inboard bearings about), screw the cone in until it is finger-tight.

9. Slide on the washer and screw on the lock nut. While holding the cone with a cone wrench, tighten the lock nut (similar to Fig. 9.23, but you will be holding the cone with a 13mm or

similar cone wrench, not the pictured 10mm standard open-end wrench).

10. Check that the pedal spins smoothly without play. Readjust as necessary by tightening or loosening the cone and retightening the locknut.

11. Replace the dust cap.

12. Install the pedals and go for a ride.

TROUBLESHOOTING
PEDAL PROBLEMS

ix-6 CREAKING NOISE WHILE PEDALING

1. The shoe cleats need grease on the tip, or they are loose and need to be tightened, or they are worn and need to be replaced (see §ix-2).

2. Pedal bearings and pedal-body threads need cleaning and lubrication (see the Overhauling Pedals section in this chapter and especially §ix-4 and §ix-5).

3. The noise is originating from somewhere other than the pedals (see Troubleshooting Crank and Bottom-Bracket Noise in Chapter 8 or Appendix A).

ix-7 RELEASE OR ENTRY WITH CLIP-IN PEDALS IS TOO EASY OR TOO HARD

1. Release tension needs to be adjusted. See Adjusting Release Tension of Clip-In Pedals, §ix-3.

2. Pedal-release mechanism needs to be cleaned and lubricated. Clean off mud and dirt, and drip chain lubricant on the springs and a dry lubricant (like White Lightning) on the cleat-contact surfaces of the clips (Fig. 9.26).

3. The cleats themselves need to be cleaned and lubricated. Clean off dirt and mud, oil the springs, and put a dry chain lubricant or dry grease like pure Teflon on the contact ends of the cleats.

4. The cleats are worn out. Replace them (§ix-2).

5. The clips on the pedal are bent or the guide plates on top of the pedal are worn, bent, broken, or missing. Straighten bent clips if you can, or replace them. If you can't repair or replace the clips, you may have to replace the entire pedal. On Speedplays, the top and bottom metal plates may need replacing.

6. If it is hard to clip into your pedals, check the metal cleat guide plate at the center of an SPD-type pedal. It is held on with Phillips screws, and they may be loose or have fallen out, or the guide plate can be bent or broken. Tighten loose mounting screws and replace missing or damaged guide plates.

7. If you have small feet, and it is hard to get in and out of a pedal that has a large cleat (Look and copies, Campagnolo) or a large adapter plate, the curvature of your shoe sole may be so extreme that the center of the cleat hits the center of the pedal before the ends have clipped in. The fix may be as simple as removing the little rubber plug from under your Look cleat. You may also need to shim the front and rear of the cleat away from the shoe, or file down the center of the cleat.

ix-8 YOU EXPERIENCE KNEE AND JOINT PAIN WHILE PEDALING

1. Cleat rotational misalignment often causes pain on the sides of the knees (see §ix-2). Loosen and realign your cleats the way your feet want to be oriented when pedaling.

2. You need more rotational float. Consider a pedal that offers more float (or replace fixed cleats with floating ones, or adjust your Look pedals for more float).

3. If your foot naturally needs to tip inward for proper pedaling mechanics, yet your shoe and cleat tip your feet farther out (this correction is built into some shoes), then there is likely to be an increase in the tension on the iliotibial (I-T) band, the tendon connecting the hip and calf. This will eventually cause pain on the outside of the knee. You need to see a specialist, because you may need custom orthotics for your shoes to correct the problem.

4. Fatigue and improper seat height can also contribute to joint pain. Pain in the front of the knee right behind the kneecap can indicate that your saddle is too low. Pain in the back of the leg behind the knee suggests that your saddle is too high.

CAUTION: *If any of these problems result in chronic pain, consult a specialist.*

RELEASE OR

ENTRY TOO

EASY OR HARD

—

KNEE AND

JOINT PAIN

WHILE

PEDALING

CHAPTER 10

SADDLES AND SEATPOSTS

I do most of my work sitting down. That's where I shine.
—Robert Benchley

TOOLS

**4mm, 5mm, and
  6mm hex keys**
screwdriver
grease

OPTIONAL

soft hammer
**securely mounted
  vise**
penetrating oil
hacksaw
flex hone
electric drill
cutting oil

After a few hours on the bike, I can pretty much guarantee that you will be most aware of one component on your bike: the saddle. It is the part of your bike with which you are most . . . uh. . . intimately connected. Nothing can ruin a good ride faster than a poorly positioned or uncomfortable saddle.

The seatpost connects the saddle to the frame. A few bicycles, such as the Softride, employ a flexible beam attached to the front of the frame instead of a seatpost. These are covered separately at the end of this chapter.

x-1 SADDLES

Most bike saddles are made up of a flexible plastic shell, some padding, a cover, and a pair of rails (Fig. 10.1). Not much to it, which perhaps explains why there are countless variations on this theme: Some have extra thick padding or high-tech gel cushions; some have depressions, holes, or splits in the shell to reduce pressure on sensitive areas; some reduce weight with rails made of titanium, hollow steel, or even braided carbon fiber; others have synthetic covers, covers made from Kevlar, or covers made from the finest full-grain leather money can buy.

You can expect to spend anywhere from $20 to $200 for a decent saddle, yet price may not be the best indicator of what makes a saddle really good—namely, comfort. My best advice is to ignore weight, fashion, and looks, and choose a saddle that is comfortable. I could go on for pages about hi-zoot gel padding, scientifically designed shells that support some parts and don't contact others and flex just right, as well as all sorts of factors that engineers consider when designing a saddle. None of it would count for squat if, after reading it, you ran out and bought a saddle that turned out to be a giant pain in the rear. People are different and saddles are different. Try as many as you can before buying one.

The current marketing war raging over saddles that are designed to prevent male impotency (Fig. 10.2) can blind a consumer's ability to select appropriately. If you buy a saddle out of fear, and it is uncomfortable, you have done yourself a disservice. Don't take it on faith or scientific studies that such a saddle must be protecting you, even if you don't particularly like it; if it hurts or you get numb, it isn't working for you. What works for one person won't necessarily work for another.

Determine which saddle shape and design is the most comfortable for your body. Then—and only then—start looking at things like titanium rails, fancy covers, and all of the other things that improve a saddle. Some people can only find comfort on 400-gram saddles with tons of thick padding. Others can ride for hours on a skinny little sub–150-gram saddle. It's a matter of preference. Any decent bike shop worth its weight in titanium should let you try a saddle for a while before locking you into a sale. And keep in mind that the position of the saddle can be as important as the shape.

Brooks and Ideale saddles have no plastic shell, foam padding, or cover. They are constructed from a single piece of thick leather attached to a steel frame with large brass rivets (Fig. 10.3). This was the main type of saddle up until the 1980s. Brooks still makes them this way, updated with titanium rails in some models. This sort of saddle requires a long break-in period and frequent applications of a leather-softening compound that comes with the saddle or from a

IO.I Modern lightweight saddle

IO.2 Saddle designed to not contact the perineum

IO.3 Brooks leather saddle

shoe store. As is the case with a lot of old bike parts, you either love 'em or you hate 'em. If you're not familiar with them by now, you'll probably hate 'em, so go out and buy a nice comfortable modern saddle (Figs. 10.1 or 10.2).

A saddle with a plastic shell and foam padding requires little maintenance, except to keep it clean. Check periodically that the rails are not bent or cracked (a clear sign that you need to replace your saddle).

10.4 Saddle adjustments

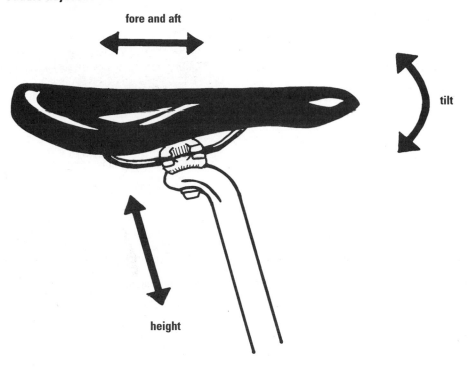

fore and aft

tilt

height

x-2 SADDLE POSITION

Even if you have found the perfect saddle, it can still feel like a medieval torture device if it isn't properly positioned. Saddle placement is the most important part of finding a comfortable riding position. Not only does saddle position affect how you feel on the bike, but it affects your control and efficiency as well. With the saddle in the right place, you suddenly become a much better rider. See Appendix C, §C-3 for a detailed explanation of setting saddle and handlebar position. The following are some short guidelines.

There are three basic elements to saddle position: tilt, fore-and-aft position, and saddle height (Fig. 10.4). Proper saddle height (Fig. 10.4) is key to effectively transferring power to the pedals. The ideal height on a road bike places your leg in a 90 to 95 percent extension when you're riding. If your frame is the correct size, you should have no trouble achieving this without pulling the post out beyond

its height-limit line. Appendix C has more detail on this sizing factor.

A common cause of numb crotch and butt fatigue (and even sore arms and shoulders) is an improperly tilted saddle (Fig. 10.4). The general rule of thumb is that you should keep the saddle level when you first install it. After a while, some people find that they prefer a slight upward or downward tilt to their saddles. I strongly recommend against making that tilt much more than ¼ inch. Too much upward tilt places too much of your body weight on the nose of the saddle. Too much downward tilt will cause you to slide down the saddle as you ride. That puts unnecessary pressure on your arms, back, and shoulders as they fight to oppose the forward slide.

Fore-and-aft position (Fig. 10.4) determines where your butt sits on the saddle (or get a new one, if it is too wide for you), the position of your knees relative to the pedals, and how much of your weight is transferred to your hands. Regardless of manufacturer, all saddles are designed to have your butt centered over the widest part. If this is not where you sit, reposition the saddle. You want to have a comfortable bend in your arms, without feeling too cramped or stretched out. If you find that your neck and shoulders feel tighter than usual and your hands are going numb, then redistribute your weight by moving the saddle back.

Fore-and-aft saddle position also affects how your legs are positioned relative to the pedals. Ideally, your position should be such that your knee pushes straight down on the forward pedal when the crankarms are in a perfectly horizontal position. Appendix C explains how to determine this precisely.

Butt pain is intimately connected to handlebar position, as are other aches and pains. The shorter the upper-body reach and higher the handlebar, the more weight will go on the butt. On the other hand, the longer the reach and lower the bar, the more the pelvis rotates forward, and the pressure point moves from the sit bones to the soft tissue of the perineum and genital area. As a general rule, a novice rider will want a shorter reach and higher bar, and perhaps a correspondingly wider saddle, than an experienced rider. Once again, consult Appendix C.

x-3 SEATPOST MAINTENANCE

A standard seatpost requires little maintenance other than removing it from the frame every few months. Wipe down the seatpost, regrease it, dry out and grease the inside of the frame's seat tube, and then reinstall the seatpost. This procedure keeps it clean and able to move freely if you want to adjust it. It also should prevent the seatpost from getting stuck in the frame (a very nasty and potentially seri-

---

° PRO TIP

CARBON SEATPOSTS

Carbon-fiber seatposts are susceptible to breakage if the pinch-bolt assembly digs in and cuts some fibers or makes a notch in the post. Some carbon seatposts, like Campagnolo, come with a special binder clamp meant to distribute the clamping force. Make sure you use it if your post comes with one. Without one, you can also reverse the binder clamp that surrounds the top of your seat tube so that its slot is not lined up with the seat tube slot.

Carbon seatposts often slip down. If you have this problem, make sure there is no grease on the post. A carbon post cannot corrode in place, so grease to prevent seizure is unnecessary, and it is often damaging to the clear coat on the seatpost.

---

ous problem), and it will prevent a steel seat tube from rusting out from the inside. The procedures for installing a new seatpost and for removing a stuck seatpost are outlined later in this chapter.

Regularly check any seatpost for cracks or bends so that you can replace it before it breaks with you on it.

Because suspension seatposts are rare on road bikes, maintenance of them is not covered here, but it is covered in *Zinn & the Art of Mountain Bike Maintenance.*

x-4 INSTALLING A SADDLE

Remember the heavy steel posts with the skinnier section on top that you had on bikes as a kid (or on a cheap adult bike)? Those seatposts had a single

CHAPTER 10   207

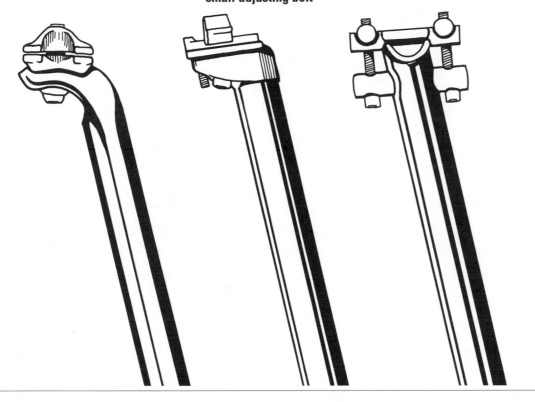

10.5 Single-bolt seatpost **10.6** Single-bolt seatpost with small adjusting bolt **10.7** Two-bolt seatpost

horizontal bolt that pulled together a number of knurled washers with ears to hold the saddle rails. They are cheap to make, being simply a steel tube with some washers and a bolt, but they do not hold up well to adult use. If they fail, and you upgrade the post, you may have to upgrade the saddle as well, if it has flat, rather than round-cross-section, rails.

Much more secure (and generally lighter) is a post with one or two vertical bolts holding an aluminum clamshell together. Most posts have either one (Fig. 10.5) or two (Figs. 10.6 and 10.7) bolts for clamping the saddle. Two-bolt posts usually rely on one of two systems. In one, the two bolts work together by pulling the saddle into the clamp (Fig. 10.7). On others, a smaller second bolt holds the tilt angle (Fig. 10.6). It is reasonably easy to figure out how to remove, install, and adjust the saddle, no matter what kind of post you have.

x-5 SADDLE INSTALLATION ON SEATPOST WITH A SINGLE VERTICAL BOLT

Posts with a single vertical bolt (Fig. 10.5) usually have a two-piece clamp that fastens onto the saddle rails. On most models, saddle tilt is controlled by moving the clamp and saddle along a curved platform. Before you tighten the clamp bolt, make sure there is not a second, much smaller bolt (or "setscrew") that adjusts seat tilt. If one is present, skip to the next section (§x-6).

1. Loosen the bolt until there are only a couple of threads still holding onto the upper clamp.

2. Turn the top half of the clamp 90 degrees and slide in the saddle rails. Do it from the back where the space between the rails is wider. You might need to remove the top clamp piece completely from the bolt if it is too large to fit between the rails. If you do disassemble the clamp, pay

SADDLE
INSTALLATION
ON SEATPOST
WITH SINGLE
VERTICAL BOLT

10.8 **Saddle installation on single-bolt seatpost**

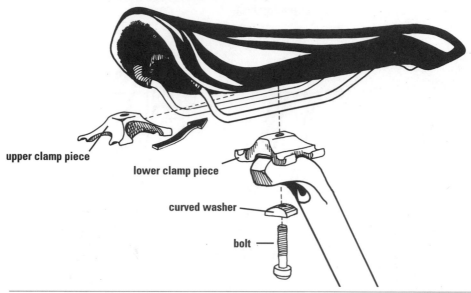

upper clamp piece

lower clamp piece

curved washer

bolt

10.9 **Saddle installation on two-bolt seatpost**

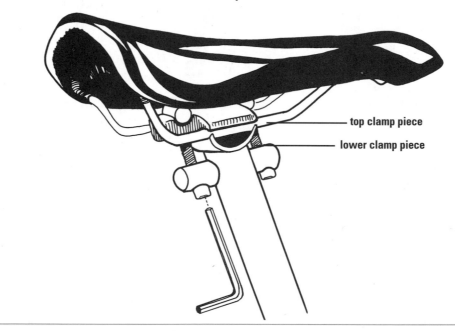

top clamp piece

lower clamp piece

SADDLE
INSTALLATION
WITH LARGE
CLAMP BOLT
AND SMALL
SETSCREW

attention to the orientation of the parts so that you can put it back together the same way.

3. Set the seat rails into the grooves in the lower part of the clamp, and set the top clamp piece on top of the rails (Fig. 10.8). Slide the saddle to the desired fore-and-aft position.

4. Tighten the bolt and check the seat tilt. Readjust if necessary.

x–6 SADDLE INSTALLATION ON SEATPOST WITH LARGE CLAMP BOLT AND SMALL SETSCREW

This post type is illustrated in Figure 10.6.

1. Loosen the large bolt until the top part of the clamp can be moved out of the way or removed so that you can slide the saddle rails into place.

2. Set the saddle rails between the top and bottom

sets of grooves in the seat clamp. Slide the saddle to the desired fore-and-aft position. Tighten the large bolt.

3. To change saddle tilt, loosen the large clamp bolt, adjust the saddle angle as needed by turning the setscrew, and retighten the clamp bolt. Repeat until the desired adjustment is reached.

CAUTION: *Do not use the setscrew to make the clamp tight! Do not adjust the setscrew unless the clamp bolt is loose!*

NOTE: *On these types of seatposts, the setscrew may be vertical or horizontal. On posts with a vertical setscrew (Fig. 10.6), the screw is usually adjacent to the clamp bolt. A horizontal setscrew can be placed at the top front of the seatpost, pushing back on the clamp. With such a setscrew, push down on the back of the saddle with the clamp bolt loose to make sure the clamp and setscrew are in contact. Another type of post has a horizontal tilt-adjusting bolt that passes crosswise through a slot in the seatpost clamp. On this type, the saddle can be fully tightened down, yet the tilt-adjust screw can be loosened and the saddle tipped differently and retightened without adjusting the clamp bolt.*

x-7 INSTALLING SADDLE ON SEATPOST WITH TWO EQUAL-SIZED CLAMP BOLTS

This post type is illustrated in Figure 10.7.

1. Loosen or remove one or both of the bolts to open the clamp enough to slide the saddle rails into the grooves of the clamp.

2. Slide the saddle to the desired fore-and-aft position. Tighten down one or both of the clamp bolts completely.

3. Loosen one clamp bolt and tighten the other to change the tilt of the saddle (Fig. 10.9). Repeat as necessary.

10.10 **Seatpost installation into the frame**

4. Complete by tightening both bolts.

x-8 SEATPOST INSTALLATION INTO THE FRAME

1. Check for irregularities, burrs, and other problems inside the seat tube visually and with your finger; if there are some, you may need to sand or otherwise clean up inside the seat tube. It may be necessary for a bike shop to ream the seat tube if a post of the correct size will not fit.

2. Unless you have a carbon-filter seatpost, grease the seatpost and the inside of the seat tube. Do not grease carbon seatposts (see Pro Tip). Grease the seatpost binder bolt. If you are using a sleeve or shim to adapt an undersized seatpost to fit the frame, grease it inside and out, and insert it.

3. Insert the seatpost (Fig. 10.10), and tighten the binder bolt. Some binder bolts are tightened with a wrench (usually a 5mm hex key), and

INSTALLING SADDLE WITH TWO EQUAL-SIZED CLAMP BOLTS

—

SEATPOST INSTALLATION INTO FRAME

10.11 Saddle on Softride beam

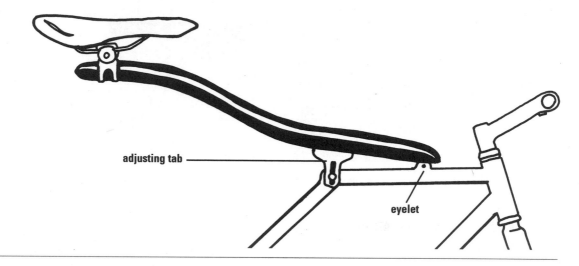

adjusting tab

eyelet

some require two wrenches (usually two 5mm hex keys or two open-end wrenches).

4. After the saddle is attached, adjust the seat height to your desired position. It is a good idea to mark this height on the post with an indelible marker or a piece of tape. This way, if you remove it, you can just slide it right back into the proper place.

IMPORTANT: *Periodically remove the seatpost, invert the bike to drain water out of the seat tube, and let it dry out. The frequency depends on the conditions you are riding in. With a steel frame, spray oil (or better yet, "Frame Saver") into the seat tube to arrest the rusting process. Regrease the post and the inside of the seat tube, and then reinstall it.*

x-9 INSTALLING A SOFTRIDE SUSPENSION BEAM ONTO FRAME

The frame must be built to accept the beam, or you must purchase a retrofit kit from Softride to install it on a standard frame.

1. Attach the beam to the front frame-mounting bracket with a steel pin. The underside of the beam's nose has a small steel eyelet that fits between two tabs on the bracket, which is located on the top of the frame's top tube (Fig. 10.11). With a soft hammer, tap the included pin through the bracket, through the eyelet on the bottom of the beam, and out through the hole in the other side of the bracket.

2. Attach the beam to the rear frame-mounting bracket, located a few inches behind the front eyelet. The rear mount on the beam consists of two curved tabs separated by the width of the frame's mounting bracket that extend down. Long, curved slots in each tab (Fig. 10.11) are used to adjust the saddle height. Pass the bolt through one of the rectangular washers (with its knurled side pointing inward) and into the slot of one tab. Then pass it through the round end cap of the cylindrical frame mount, the frame mount itself, and out through the second end cap, the other oval tab hole, and the other rectangular washer. Screw on the nut after lining up the offset end-cap holes so that they fit into the mounting bracket with the bolt in place.

3. Swing the beam up to the desired height, with the fixing bolt loose. For starters, set it about an

inch higher than what your normal seat height would be, to offset the beam's flex. If you reach the end of the adjustment in the bracket tab slots and the seat is still not as high as you need it to be, rotate the rear frame-mount end caps. The caps' offset holes offer two height positions for this very reason.

4. Tighten the fixing bolt. Readjust saddle height as needed.

x–10 REMOVING A STUCK SEATPOST

LEVEL 3

You are having this difficulty because you did not follow the "important" note in §x-8. This is a level 3 job because of the risk involved. It may be best to entrust this job to a shop, because if you make a mistake, you run the risk of destroying your frame. If you're not 100 percent confident in your abilities, go to someone who is—or at least to someone who will be responsible if they screw it up.

1. Remove the seat-lug binder bolt. Sounds easy enough.

2. Squirt penetrating oil around the seatpost, and let it sit overnight. To get the most penetration, remove the bottom bracket (Chapter 8), turn the bike upside down, squirt the penetrating oil in from the bottom of the seat tube, and let it sit overnight.

3. The next day, stand over the bike and twist the saddle.

4. If step 3 does not free the seatpost, warm up the seat-lug area with a hair dryer to expand it. Discharge the entire cartridge of a CO_2 inflator at the joint of the seatpost and the seat collar to freeze it and shrink it. (Alternatively, ice the exposed seatpost with a plastic bag filled with crushed ice.) Now try twisting as in step 3.

5. If step 4 does not free the seatpost, you will need to move into the difficult and risky part of this procedure.

   (a) You will now sacrifice the seatpost. Remove the saddle and all of the clamps from the top of the seatpost. With the bike upside down, clamp the top of the seatpost into a large bench vise that is bolted to a very secure workbench.

   (b) Congratulations, you have just ruined your seatpost. Don't ever ride it gain.

   (c) Perform the heat/ice or CO_2 trick from step 4. Grab the frame at both ends, and begin to carefully apply a twisting pressure. Be aware that you can easily apply enough force to bend or crack the frame, so be careful. If the seatpost finally releases, it often makes such a large "pop" that you will think that you have broken many things!

6. If that did not work, cut off the seatpost a few inches above the seat lug and clamp the top of it in a vise. Warm up the seat-lug area with a hair dryer to expand it. Discharge the entire cartridge of a CO_2 inflator down inside the seatpost to freeze it and shrink it. Now try twisting as in step 4.

7. If step 5 or 6 does not work, you need to go to a machine shop and get the post reamed out of the seat tube.

If you still insist on getting it out yourself, you should really sit down and think about it for a while. Will the guy at the machine shop really charge you so much money that it is worth the risk of completely destroying your frame yourself?

Do you still insist on doing this yourself? Okay, but don't say I didn't warn you.

Take a hacksaw and cut off the post a little more than an inch above the frame. (Now you really have destroyed your seatpost, so I don't have to warn against riding it again.) Remove the blade from the saw and wrap a piece of tape around one end. Hold on to the taped end and slip the other end into the center of the post. Carefully—very carefully—make two outward cuts about 60 degrees apart. Your goal is to remove a pie-shaped wedge from the hunk of seatpost stuck in your frame. Be careful; this is where many people cut too far and go right through the seatpost into the frame. Of course, you wouldn't do that, would you?

Once you've made the cut, pry or pull this piece out with a large screwdriver or a pair of pliers. Be careful here, too. A lot of overenthusiastic home mechanics have damaged their frames by prying too hard.

Once the wedge is out, work the remaining piece out by curling in the edges with the pliers to free more and more of it from the seatpost walls. It should eventually work its way out.

With the post out of the frame, clean the inside of the seat tube thoroughly. A flex hone, sold in auto parts stores (or rented at rental stores) for reconditioning brake cylinders, is an excellent tool for the purpose. Turn the frame upside down, put the hone in your electric drill, and be sure to use plenty of honing fluid or cutting oil as you work. If you do not know how to use a hone, it may be best to take the frame to a bike shop to have the job done or try sandpaper wrapped around your fingers.

Inasmuch as removing a stuck post is so miserable that no one wants to do it twice, I'm certain that I do not need to remind you to grease the new post

thoroughly before inserting it in the frame, and check it regularly thereafter as previously outlined.

x-11 TROUBLESHOOTING PROBLEMS IN THE SEAT AND SEATPOST

a. Loose saddle

Check the bolts. They are probably loose. Tighten the bolts and set the desired saddle tilt, after setting fore-and-aft saddle position (§x-2). Check for any damage to the clamping mechanism, and replace the post if necessary. If you need help, look up the instructions that apply to your seatpost.

b. Stuck seatpost

This can be a serious problem. Follow the instructions in §x-10 carefully, or you might damage your frame.

c. Saddle squeaks with each pedal stroke

The problem can come from the smooth leather or plastic moving against metal parts or from grit in the rail attachments.

1. On saddles that extend low on the sides, contact of the leather overlapping the saddle shell with the seatpost clamp or rails is likely the culprit. Greasing the contact area will eliminate the noise. Also, roughing up the leather at the contact point with metal will quiet it down, because smooth leather sliding on metal can squeak. Another approach, borrowed from the horsey set, is to sprinkle the squeaky leather with talcum powder.

2. Also try squirting chain lube into the three points where the rails are inserted into the plastic shell of the saddle, in case some grit working at the rails is making the noise.

d. Creaking noises from the seatpost

A seatpost can creak from movement of the clamp

holding the saddle. Another possible creak source is movement of the shaft back and forth against the sides of the seat tube while you ride. Pull the post from the frame and regrease the post and seat tube.

1. Some frames use a collar to adapt the seat tube to a certain seatpost diameter. Remember that the internal diameter of the seat tube is larger below the collar. I have seen bikes that creaked because the bottom of the seatpost rubbed against the sides of the seat tube below the extension of the collar. You can solve that problem by shortening the seatpost a bit with a hacksaw. If you do saw off the post, make sure that you still have at least 3 inches of seatpost inserted in the frame for security.

2. Similarly, movement between the frame, sizing shims, and the post can cause creaking. Greasing all of these parts well should eliminate the noise.

3. If the creaking originates from the post head where the saddle is clamped, check the clamp bolts. Lubricate the bolt threads, and you will be able to tighten them a bit more.

4. Shock-absorbing seatposts can squeak as they move up and down. Try greasing the sides of the inner shaft. Grease the elastomers inside, too.

e. Seatpost slips down

Tighten the seat-lug binder bolt. If the seat lug is pinched closed, and the post still slips down, you may be using a seatpost with an incorrect diameter, or the seat tube on your bike may be oversized or has stretched. Double-check the seat-tube diameter with calipers, or ask your local shop to do so.

Try putting a larger seatpost in the frame, and replace yours if you find one that fits better. If the next size up is too big, you may need to shim your existing post. Cut a 1-inch by 3-inch piece of aluminum from a pop can. Pull the seatpost out, grease it and the pop-can shim, and insert both back into the frame. Bend the top lip of the shim over to prevent it from disappearing inside the frame. You may need to experiment with various shim dimensions until you find a piece that will go in with the seatpost and will also prevent slippage. Fortunately, they're cheap.

With a carbon-fiber seatpost, make sure first of all that there is no grease on it (see Pro Tip). Second, if you must tighten the clamp more, make sure it is not forcing the corners of the seat-tube slot into the seatpost, creating damage and the possibility of breakage. Use an offset-clamp binder or turn the binder around so its slot does not line up with the seat tube's slot (see Pro Tip).

On a titanium frame with an integral seat binder (one that is welded to the seat tube, as opposed to an external clamp), the seat tube will stretch if the binder is chronically overtightened. If the post is slipping because the binder slot has closed up, contact the frame manufacturer for assistance. You might be able to rescue the situation by filing the slot and binder wide enough to keep it from pinching closed (a tedious job, but titanium will yield to a normal metal file). Plug the seat tube with a greasy rag to keep metal filings from falling into the bottom bracket, and suspend the frame upside down to encourage the filings to go elsewhere.

By the way, don't try this until you get the go-ahead from the frame builder; attacking the frame in this manner will undoubtedly void the warranty in the absence of explicit authorization. If filing isn't recommended, you will probably have to return the frame to the manufacturer for more comprehensive repair.

CHAPTER 11

STEMS, HANDLEBARS, AND HEADSETS

I may not have gone where I intended to go,
but I think I have ended up where I intended to be.
—Douglas Adams

4mm, 5mm, and 6mm hex keys

32mm headset wrenches (two)

hammer

screwdriver

hacksaw

flat file

round file

glue stick

electrical tape

grease

citrus solvent

OPTIONAL

star-nut installation tool

threadless saw guide

channel-lock pliers

securely mounted vise

crown-race slide punch

crown-race remover

headset press

headset-cup remover

head-tube reamer

crown-race facer

On a bike, you maintain or change your direction by applying force to your handlebar. If everything works properly, variations in that pressure will result in your front wheel's changing direction. Pretty basic, right? Right, but it is the series of parts between the handlebar and the wheel that makes that simple process possible. The parts of the steering system are illustrated in Figure 11.1. In this chapter, we'll cover most of that system by going over stems, handlebars, and headsets.

STEMS

The stem connects to the fork's steering tube (which is either 1 inch or 1⅛ inches in diameter; see Fig. 14.1) and clamps around the handlebar, which has one of two standard diameters: 26.0mm or 31.8mm (although Cinelli handlebars used to be 26.4mm, and many low-end handlebars are 25.4mm clamp diameter). Stems come in one of two basic types: for (1) threaded (Figs. 11.1–11.4) or

(2) threadless (Figs. 11.5–11.7) fork steering tubes.

As of this writing, most high-end road bikes have 1⅛-inch-diameter unthreaded forks, although those took over from 1-inch threadless forks, which were preceded by a century of road bikes with 1-inch threaded forks. With all of that history and so many old bikes still in circulation, the majority of forks on road bikes out there are still threaded, which means that the steering tube on the fork has external threads at the top onto which the headset screws for attachment and adjustment. Stems for threaded steering tubes (Figs. 11.2–11.4) have a "quill," which extends down into the steering tube of the fork, and a shaft, or extension, which connects to the handlebar. The stem binds to the inside of the steering tube by means of a conical plug (Fig. 11.2) or angularly truncated cylindrical wedge (Fig. 11.3) pulled up by a long stem expander bolt that runs through the quill (Fig. 11.4).

Unthreaded steering tubes, which debuted on

I I . I   Parts of the steering system

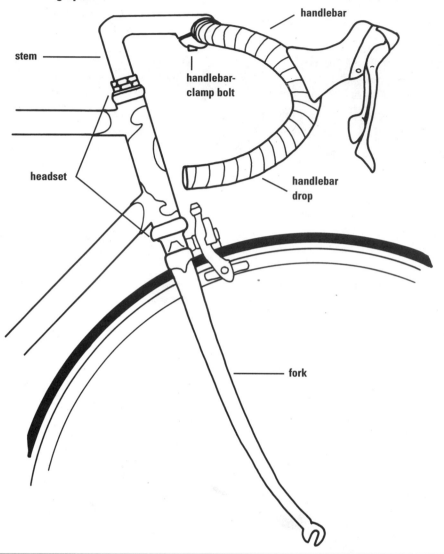

stem

handlebar

handlebar-
clamp bolt

headset

handlebar
drop

fork

**I I .2   Forged aluminum quill road stem with
expander plug**

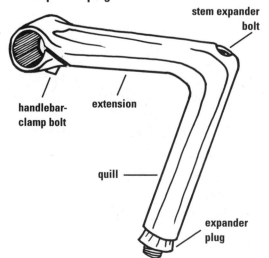

stem expander
bolt

handlebar-
clamp bolt

extension

quill

expander
plug

**I I .3   Welded quill-type stem with expander
wedge**

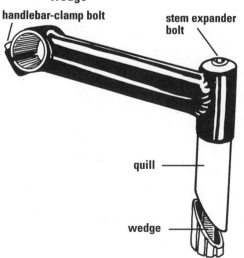

handlebar-clamp bolt

stem expander
bolt

quill

wedge

mountain bikes, have become standard on road bikes as well. Stems for unthreaded steering tubes (Fig. 11.5) have a clamping collar in place of the quill. Because the steering tube has no threads, the top headset cup merely slides on and off when the clamping collar is loosened. In this case, the stem plays a dual role. It clamps around the steering tube to connect the handlebar to the fork, and it also keeps the headset in proper adjustment by preventing the top headset cup from sliding up the steering tube (Figs. 11.6 and 11.7). If you have a 1-inch diameter threadless steering tube (the old standard) and a stem for a 1⅛-inch threadless steering tube (the current standard), you can get a slotted aluminum reduction bushing (normally supplied with a new stem) to allow the stem to be used with the 1-inch steering tube.

Traditionally, the shaft of a road bike stem that attaches to the handlebar extends out from the fork steering tube at an angle of about 73 degrees so that, when installed on the bike, the extension is horizontal (Figs. 11.1 and 11.4). Stems on track bikes historically tended to be angled downward when mounted

11.4 Cutaway of threaded headset system, showing expander-plug binding stem inside steering tube

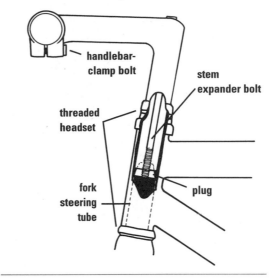

11.5 Threadless stem

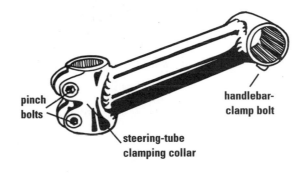

11.6 Threadless headset and stem cutaway

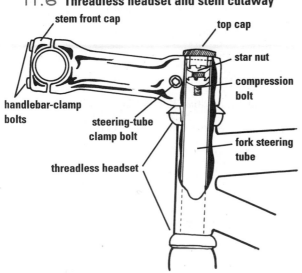

11.7 Threadless-headset cup held in place by stem

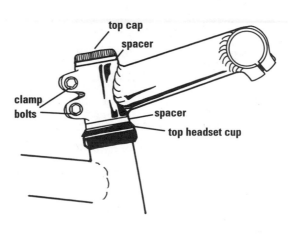

STEMS, HANDLEBARS, AND HEADSETS

STEMS

11.8 Loosening stem wedge

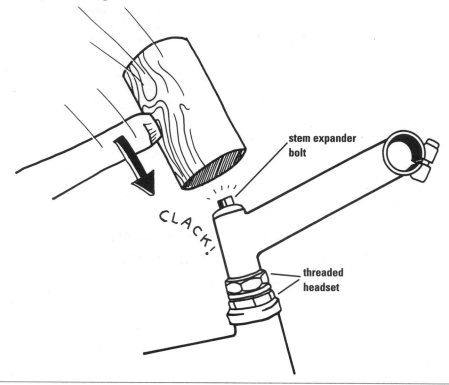

CLACK!

stem expander
bolt

threaded
headset

REMOVAL,

INSTALLATION,

AND

ADJUSTMENT

OF QUILL STEM

IN THREADED

FORK

on the bike. Stems with 90-degree angles and greater, resulting in an upward angle on the assembled bicycle (Figs. 11.6, 11.7, and 11.8), are becoming commonplace on road bikes and even on track bikes.

xi-1 REMOVE QUILL-TYPE STEM FROM THREADED FORK

1. Unscrew the stem-fixing bolt on the top of the stem about three turns or so. Most stem bolts take a 6mm Allen wrench. Some stems have a rubber plug on top of the stem that must be removed to get at the stem bolt.

2. Tap the top of the bolt down with a mallet or hammer (Fig. 11.8) to disengage the plug or wedge from the bottom of the quill. If the head of the bolt is recessed down in the stem so that a hammer cannot get at it, leave the Allen wrench in the bolt and tap the top of the Allen wrench until the wedge is free.

3. Pull the stem out of the steering tube. If the stem will not budge, see §xi-6a.

xi-2 INSTALL AND ADJUST HEIGHT OF QUILL STEM IN THREADED FORK

LEVEL 2

1. Generously grease the stem quill, the expander-bolt threads, the outside of the wedge or conical plug, and the inside of the steering tube. If this is the first time you've done this, I know what you're thinking: "Why put grease on something that I want to wedge together?" Don't worry; the grease won't prevent the wedge from keeping the stem tight. What the grease will do is prevent the parts from seizing or rusting together so that you can't get them apart again.

2. Thread the expander bolt through the stem and into the wedge or plug until the bolt pulls

the plug or wedge into place, but not so far as to prevent the stem from inserting into the steering tube.

3. Slip the stem quill into the steering tube (Fig. 11.4) to the depth you want. Make sure the stem is inserted beyond its height-limit line. Tighten the bolt until the stem is snug but can still be turned.

4. Set the stem to the desired height, line it up with the front wheel, and tighten the bolt. It needs to be tight, but don't overdo it. You can over-tighten the stem bolt to the point that it puts a bulge in the steering tube, so be careful.

xi-3 REMOVE CLAMP-TYPE STEM FROM THREADLESS STEERING TUBE

1. Loosen the horizontal clamp bolt(s) (Fig. 11.7) securing the stem around the steering tube.

2. With a 5mm (usually) Allen wrench, unscrew and remove the adjusting bolt (or "compression bolt" because it compresses the headset into the proper bearing adjustment) in the headset top cap (Fig. 11.9). The fork can now fall out, so hold the fork as you unscrew the bolt.

NOTE: *Some threadless headsets do not use a top cap. For instance, DiaTech threadless headsets have a collar beveled internally on the top and bottom to adjust headset compression. Without a top cap, as soon as you loosen the stem, the fork can slip out.*

3. With the bike standing on the floor, or while holding the fork to keep it from falling out, pull the cap and the stem off the steering tube. Leave the bike standing until you replace the stem, or slide the fork out of the frame, keeping track of all headset parts.

4. If the stem will not budge, see §xi-6b.

11.9 Loosening and tightening compression bolt on threadless headset

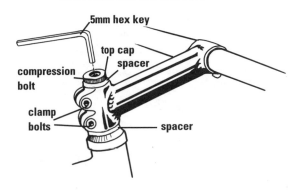

---

xi-4 INSTALL AND ADJUST HEIGHT OF STEM ON THREADLESS STEERING TUBE

LEVEL 2

Installing and adjusting the height of a stem on a threadless fork is much more complicated than installing and adjusting the height of a standard stem in a threaded fork. That's why this step is listed with a level 2 designation. Because the stem is integral to operation of the headset (Fig. 11.7), any change to the stem position alters the headset adjustment.

1. Stand the bike on its wheels, so that the fork does not fall out. Grease the top end of the steering tube if it is steel or aluminum, and leave it dry if it is carbon fiber. Loosen the stem-clamp bolts and grease their threads. Slide the stem onto the steering tube.

2. Set the stem height to the desired level. If you want to place the stem in a position higher than directly on top of the headset, you must put some spacers between the bottom of the stem clamp and the top piece of the headset (Fig. 11.7). No matter what, there must be contact (either directly or through spacers) between the headset and the stem. Otherwise, the headset will be loose.

STEMS, HANDLEBARS, AND HEADSETS

REMOVAL,
INSTALLATION,
AND
ADJUSTMENT
OF STEM
ON/FROM
THREADLESS
STEERING TUBE

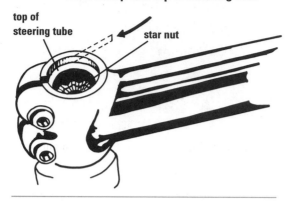

11.10 Measuring distance between stem clamp and top of steering tube

top of steering tube

star nut

INSTALL AND
ADJUST
STEM ON
THREADLESS
STEERING TUBE

3. Check the steering-tube length: In order to adjust the threadless headset, the top of the stem clamp (or spacers placed above it) should overlap the top of the steering tube by 3–6mm (⅛–¼ inch) (Fig. 11.10). If it does, skip ahead to step 4.

NOTE: *Most new stems available have a 1⅛-inch clamp size, and they come with a simple split shim (a short piece of tubing with a slot down one side) that you can slide over a 1-inch steering tube to make the stem fit on a fork of that size. With this type of stem and shim on a 1-inch steering tube, you can usually use spacers under the stem sized for a 1-inch steering tube, as long as they are wide enough to contact the entire bottom edge of the stem. However, above the stem, you may need to use a spacer and a headset top cap meant for a 1⅛-inch steering tube, in order to push the stem down properly and to aesthetically match the top of the stem.*

4. If the top spacer or the top of the stem clamp overlaps the top of the steering tube by more than 6mm (¼ inch), the steering tube is too short to set the stem height where you have it. If you have spacers below the stem, remove some until the top edge of the stem clamp overlaps the top of the steering tube by 3–6mm. If you cannot or do not wish to lower the stem any farther, you

PRO TIP

SPACERS WITH CARBON STEERING TUBES

If your fork has a carbon steering tube, always place one spacer above the stem (Fig. 11.7). That way, the entire stem clamp is clamped onto the steering tube and there is no chance for the upper part of the clamp to pinch the end of the tube. This is a good idea to do with a steel or aluminum steering tube as well.

If you want to raise your handlebar up high, be careful about using too many spacers below the stem; consult the owner's manual for your fork for recommendations for maximum spacer stack height. It's preferable to use an up-angled stem, rather than a down-angled one with a lot of spacers below it. And of course, make sure the expander plug inside the steering tube (which prevents the stem clamp from crushing the carbon steering tube) is supporting the area under the stem clamp.

will need a fork with a longer steering tube or a stem with a shorter clamp or a stem that is angled upward more to achieve the desired handlebar height. Stems for threadless steering tubes with clamps of differing lengths are available, as are stems of varying angles. Replacing the stem is a lot cheaper and easier than replacing the fork.

5. If the steering tube is too long, there are several steps you can take:

   (a) If the top of the steering tube is less than 3mm (⅛ inch) below the top spacer or the top edge of the stem clamp (or if the steering tube sticks up above the top of the stem clamp), you have a choice. If you want the option to raise the stem for a higher handlebar position, stack some headset spacers on top of the stem clamp until the spacers overlap the top edge of the steering tube by at least 3mm.

(b) If, on the other hand, you are sure you will never want the stem any higher, you can cut off the excess tube. First, mark the steering tube along the top edge of the spacer above the stem clamp (or the stem clamp itself if you are not heeding my advice to always have at least a single thin spacer above the stem). Remove the fork from the bike. Make another mark on the steering tube 3mm below the first mark. Place the steering tube in a padded vise or bike-stand clamp. By using the lower mark as a guide, cut the excess steering tube off with a hacksaw.

(c) In steel and aluminum steering tubes that have already been installed in a bike, there is a star nut (Figs. 11.6 and 11.18) that is inserted inside the steering tube (Fig. 11.10). You screw the compression bolt through the top cap into it to adjust the headset bearings (but not to retain the headset; the stem-clamp bolts do that). If the star nut is already inside the steering tube, and it looks like the saw is going to hit it, you must move the star nut down before cutting. See step 6 for instructions on how to push the star nut in deeper. (Carbon-fiber fork steering tubes have either a glue-in support insert with a star nut inside, or an expandable steering-tube support insert with an integrated anchor

for the top-cap bolt [Fig. 11.21]; in either case, the insert must be removed before cutting the steering tube.)

(d) Make your cut straight. Measure twice; cut once! Mark it straight by wrapping a piece of tape around the steering tube and cutting along it. If you are not sure your cut will be straight, start it a little higher and file it down flat to the tape line. If you really want to be safe, use a tool specifically designed to help you make a straight cut; Park Tool's "threadless saw guide" will do the trick. Remember that you can always shorten the steering tube a little more, but you cannot make it longer! Use a round file on the inside of the tube and a flat file on the outside to remove any metal burrs left by the hacksaw or cutter.

(e) When you have completed cutting and deburring, put the fork back in, replacing all headset parts the way they were originally installed (Fig. 11.18). Return to step 1 in this section.

6. Check that the edges of the star-shaped nut are at least 12mm below the top edge of the steering

---

PRO TIP

CUTTING CARBON STEERING TUBES

If you are cutting a carbon-fiber steering tube, cut three-fourths of the way through and then turn the steering tube over and cut from the other side to meet your first cut. This method will prevent you from cutting right through and peeling back the last few layers of carbon at the bottom.

INSTALL AND ADJUST STEM ON THREADLESS STEERING TUBE

tube. The nut must be far enough down that the bottom of the headset top cap does not hit it once the adjusting bolt is tightened. If the nut is not in deeply enough, you need to drive it deeper into the steering tube after removing the stem, in the case of a steel or aluminum steering tube. In the case of a carbon steering tube, you set the expander plug inside the steering tube under the stem clamp by tightening its bolt with a hex key. This part is a must to prevent crushing the carbon steering tube with the stem clamp.

(a) Driving the star nut deeper into a metal steering tube is best done with the star-nut installation tool (Fig. 1.3 in Chapter 1). The tool threads into the nut, and you hit it with a hammer until it stops; the star nut will now be set 15mm deep in the steering tube. If you do not have this tool, go to a bike shop and have the nut set for you. If you insist on doing it yourself, read the next paragraph. Just remember that it is easy to mangle the star nut if you do not tap it in straight.

(b) Pushing the star nut in deeper without a star-nut installation tool requires three steps: (1) Put the adjusting bolt through the top cap and thread it six turns into the star nut. (2) Set the star nut over the end of the steering tube and tap the top of the bolt with a mallet; use the top cap as a guide to keep it going in straight. (3) Tap the bolt in until the star nut is 15mm below the top of the steering tube.

NOTE: *If the wall thickness of the steering tube is greater than standard, the stock headset star nut will not fit in, and it will bend when you try to install it. Even pros sometimes ruin star nuts. It's not a big prob-*

lem, because replacements can be purchased separately. If yours goes in crooked, take a long punch or rod, set it on the star nut, and drive it all of the way out of the bottom of the steering tube. Dispose of the star nut, and get another.

If the internal diameter (I.D.) of the steering tube is undersized (standard I.D. is 22.2mm [⅞ inch] on a 1-inch steering tube, 25.4mm [1 inch] on a 1⅛ inch steering tube, and 28.6mm [1⅛ inch] on a 1¼ inch steering tube), you cannot use the stock star nut from the headset for that size. Get a correctly sized star nut at a bike shop or from the fork manufacturer. In a pinch, you can make a big stock star nut fit by bending each pair of opposite leaves of the star nut toward each other with a pair of channel-lock pliers to reduce the nut's width. Now you can insert the nut; be aware that it may not grip as well as a properly sized one.

7. Install the headset top cap on the top of the stem clamp (or spacers you set above it). Grease the threads of the top-cap compression bolt, and screw it into the star nut inside the steering tube with a 5mm hex key (Fig. 11.9).

8. Adjust the headset. The steps are outlined in §xi-15.

xi-5 STEM MAINTENANCE AND REPLACEMENT SCHEDULE

A bike cannot be controlled if the stem breaks, so make sure yours doesn't break. Aluminum has no fatigue endurance limit, which means that any aluminum part regularly stretched or flexed will eventually fail. Steel and titanium parts repeatedly stressed more than about one-half of their tensile strength will eventually fail as well. Aluminum may fail suddenly; steel and titanium tend to crack first and then tear over time.

What this means is that stems and handlebars are not permanent accessories on your bike. Replace them before they fail on you.

Clean the stem regularly. Whenever you clean it, look for corrosion, cracks, and bent or stressed areas. If you find any, replace the stem immediately. If you crash hard on your bike, especially hard enough to bend the handlebar, replace the stem and possibly your fork—and the bar, of course. Err on the side of caution.

Italian stem maker 3T recommends replacing stems and handlebars every four years. If you rarely ride the bike, this is overkill. If you ride hard and ride often, every four years may not be frequent enough. Do what is appropriate for you, and be aware of the risks.

xi-6 REMOVING A STUCK STEM

LEVEL 3

A stem can get stuck into (or onto) the steering tube owing to poor maintenance. Regular maintenance involves periodically regreasing the stem and steering tube to enable the parts to slide freely when disassembled. The grease also forms a barrier to sweat and water.

If the stem is really stuck, be careful as you try to remove it; you can—quite easily, in fact—ruin the fork as well as the stem and the headset trying to get it out. In fact, you're better off having a shop work on it, unless you really know what you are doing and are willing to accept the risk of destroying a lot of expensive parts.

a. Removing a stuck stem from a threaded fork

1. Unscrew the stem bolt on top of the stem three turns or more. Smack the bolt (or the Allen wrench in the bolt) with a mallet or hammer (Fig. 11.8) to completely disengage the wedge.

2. Grasping the front wheel between your knees,

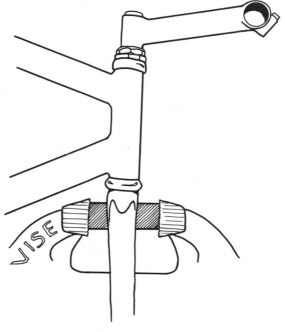
11.11 Clamping fork crown in vise

make one last attempt to free the stem by twisting back and forth on the bar. Don't use all of your strength, because you can ruin a fork and front wheel this way.

3. If the stem didn't budge, squirt penetrating oil around the stem where it enters the headset. Let the bike sit for several hours and add more penetrating oil every hour or so.

4. Turn the bike over, and squirt penetrating oil into the bottom of the fork steering tube so that it runs down around the stem quill. Let the bike sit for several hours and add more penetrating oil every hour or so.

5. Now that it is totally soaked in penetrating oil, try step 2 again.

6. If that does not work, remove the stem expander bolt and discharge a CO_2 cartridge inflator inside the stem quill to shrink it with cold. Now try step 2 again.

7. If the stem does not come free this time, you have to go to your workbench and use that

11.12 Spreading the stem clamp to free a stuck stem

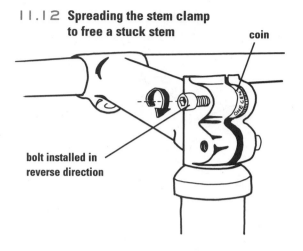

coin

bolt installed in
reverse direction

11.13 Removing handlebar tape

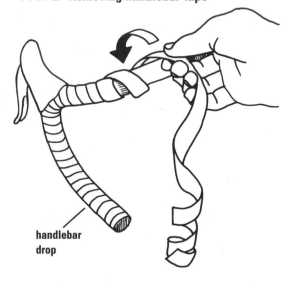

handlebar
drop

heavy-duty vise. It's solidly mounted, isn't it? Good, because it will need to be.

8. Remove the front wheel (Chapter 2) and the front brake (Chapter 7). Put pieces of wood on each side of the vise. Clamp the fork crown into the vise (Fig. 11.11).

9. Grab both ends of the handlebar and twist back and forth. Again, try discharging a CO_2 cartridge inflator inside the stem quill to shrink it with cold. The stem will generally come free with a very loud pop. If this doesn't work, you may have to saw off the stem just above the

headset and have the bottom of the stem reamed out of the steering tube by a machine shop. In this case, unscrew the headset and remove the fork; don't take the bike to a machine shop as an assembly. I told you that you should have gone to a bike shop before getting to this point!

b. Removing a stuck stem from a threadless fork

1. Remove the top cap (Fig. 11.9) and the bolts clamping the stem to the steering tube.

2. Thread the clamp bolts in from the other side. Spread the stem clamp by inserting a coin into the slot between each bolt end and the opposing unthreaded half of the binder lug (Fig. 11.12). Tighten each bolt against each coin so that it spreads the clamp slot open wider. The stem should come right off the steering tube now.

NOTE: *If the stem is the type that comes with a single bolt in the side of the stem shaft ahead of the steering tube (Fig. 11.6), loosen the bolt a few turns and tap it in with a hammer to free the wedge. It might require some penetrating oil and perhaps some heat to expand it to free this type of stem from around the steering tube.*

3. If it still will not come free, you may have to use a vise, following instructions 6 and 7 in the previous section on freeing a quill-type stem. Failing that, your last resort is to saw through the steering tube at the base of the stem clamp, and replace the stem, fork, and headset.

HANDLEBARS

I am generally referring here to standard road bike drop bars (Fig. i.1), but most of these comments also apply to the "cow horn" style of handlebar common on triathlon and time-trial bikes (Fig. i.2).

xi-7 HANDLEBAR REMOVAL

a. From a stem with a single handlebar-clamp bolt

Stems with a single handlebar-clamp bolt are shown in Figures 11.1–11.5.

1. Remove the handlebar tape (Fig. 11.13), at least from one side.

2. Remove the brake levers (Chapter 7).

3. Loosen the bolt on the stem clamp surrounding the bar (Fig. 11.1). This usually takes a 5mm Allen wrench.

4. Pull the bar out, working the bend around through the stem. If the bar won't budge, or if it will budge but it appears that you will tear up the bar's finish working it out through the stem, or if the bend in the bar will not pass through the stem clamp, you need to open the stem clamp a bit more. On many stems, you can do this by removing the clamp bolt, threading it back in from the opposite side with a coin inserted into the clamp slot, and tightening the bolt against the coin to spread the clamp. (Opening a stem clamp in this way—but from a steering tube—is illustrated in Fig. 11.12.)

b. From a stem with a removable front stem cap

Stems with a removable front stem cap are shown in Figures 11.6 and 11.19.

1. Completely remove the bolts holding on the front stem cap. There can be two (Fig. 11.6), three, or four bolts, depending on model.

2. Pull off the stem cap, and the handlebar will now drop off the stem. Makes it easy, eh, having a removable front cap?

xi-8 HANDLEBAR INSTALLATION

1. Remove the handlebar stem-clamp bolt (or bolts), grease the threads, and replace it (them). Grease the inside of the stem clamp, and grease the clamping area in the center of the bar. Grease keeps the parts from seizing over time and also will prevent squeaks from developing later.

2. Install the bar and rotate it to the position you find most comfortable. The old-school way was to set a drop bar so that the bottom flat section (the "drop"; see Figs. 11.1 and 11.15) was horizontal. Pro riders tend to have their drops aimed down and back toward the rear brake or the rear hub, but the setting you choose is entirely a matter of personal preference.

3. Tighten the bolt or bolts that clamp the bar to the stem to the recommended torque—see the torque table in Appendix E. This step is particularly important with expensive, lightweight stems and bars. You can pinch and thereby weaken a lightweight handlebar by overtightening, and the high-strength tubing will crack right by the stem. Light stems come with ever-smaller bolts with ever-finer threads, and overtightening can strip the threads inside the aluminum (or magnesium, etc.) stem. If you don't have a torque wrench and you have a lightweight stem with small bolts (e.g., M5 or M6 bolts, which take 4mm and 5mm hex keys, respectively), use a short hex key so that you can't get much leverage. Proper torque is even more important with carbon-fiber handlebars. Also, make sure that there is the same amount of space between the stem and either edge of the front plate on a front-opening stem. Any stem whose clamp gap(s) gets pinched nearly closed when tightened around the bar needs to be replaced, along with the handlebar.

xi-9 HANDLEBAR MAINTENANCE AND REPLACEMENT SCHEDULE

A bike cannot be controlled without a handlebar, so you never want one to break on you. Do not look at the bar as a permanent accessory on your bike. All handlebars will eventually fail. The trick is not to be riding them when they do.

Keep the bar clean. Regularly inspect it (under the tape!) for cracks, crash-induced bends, corrosion, and stressed areas. If you find any sign of wear or cracking, replace the bar. Never straighten a bent handlebar! Replace it! If you crash hard on your bike, consider replacing the bar even if it looks fine. If the bar has taken an extremely hard hit, it's a good idea to replace it rather than gamble on its integrity.

The Italian stem and bar manufacturer 3T recommends replacing stems and bars every four years. As with a stem, if you rarely ride the bike, this is overkill. If you ride hard and ride often, every four years may not be frequent enough. Do what is appropriate for you, and be aware of the risks.

xi-10 WRAPPING HANDLEBAR TAPE

You need both hands free and the bar rigidly held. Clamping the bike in a bike stand or holding it in a stationary trainer should do the trick, but you may need to stabilize the front wheel between your knees or with a strap around the down tube and rim or a bar-holder from the seatpost to the handlebar. Again, before wrapping, clean the bar and inspect it for cracks, crash-induced bends, corrosion, and stressed areas. If you find any sign of wear or cracking, replace the bar. Tape down concealed brake and shift cables in a few places with electrical tape or strapping tape (Fig. 11.14) (Pre-1984 or so brake levers have no concealed cables; the brake cable comes out of the top of

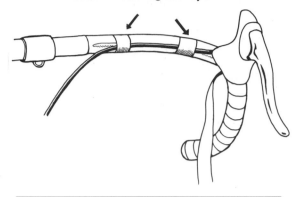

11.14 Tape cables to the bar before installing bar tape

the lever.) Shimano STI levers have concealed brake cables and exposed shift cables. Both the shift cables and brake cables are concealed on Campagnolo Ergopower or Mavic Mektronic levers. Tape the cables down where they will be the most comfortable on your hands. Some handlebars have creases in them for the cables; tape the cables down so that they stay in the creases. Shimano STI brake cables go along the front of the handlebar. Campagnolo Ergopower shift cables go along the front of the bar, and the brake cables go around the back of the bar; or, my preference is to route both the brake cable and the shift cable from the Ergopower along the front of the handlebar.

If your handlebar tape does not have an adhesive back surface covered with a paper backing strip, smear some Glue Stick on the bar around the outside of all of its bends. These areas are where the handlebar tape tends to creep and separate; the glue will help keep that from happening.

Handlebar tape sets usually come with two short pieces. These are to cover the brake-lever-clamp bands. Peel back the edge of the rubber hood on the brake lever, wrap the little tape piece around the clamp band and insert each end under the hood. You may want to tape the ends down with some Scotch

HANDLEBAR

MAINTENANCE

AND

REPLACEMENT

SCHEDULE

—

WRAPPING

HANDLEBAR

TAPE

tape. Leave the hoods peeled back so that you can wrap the bar tape up onto the edge of the lever body and then cover it with the skirt of the rubber hood.

Peel back the paper backing on the tape and start wrapping at the end of the bar from the inside out. Overlap the end of the bar by more than about an inch, so that you can push the excess in with the end plug later. Lightweight bars tend to have thin walls and consequently a large inside diameter, and many end plugs will not fit tightly in them. In this case, the extra tape sticking out will fill the extra space. Alternatively, you can put the plugs in first and simply start wrapping right at the ends of the bar with no overlap. In this case, you can wrap some electrical tape around the insertion prongs of the plug until it fits tightly and won't rattle out.

To have a long-lasting tape job, you always want to wrap from the end of the bar so that each wrap holds down the inner edge of the prior one. Wrapping from the center of the bar and finishing at the end plug is a mistake, because your hands will constantly peel back the edge of each tape wrap because your hands will push outward on those edges as you ride. The tape will look bad and get torn quickly.

Pull the tape tightly as you wrap, but not enough to break it. Overlap each wrap about one-quarter to one-half of its width (Fig. 11.15). Use as much overlap as you can to increase padding and decrease the chance of the tape slipping enough to reveal the handlebar. The amount of overlap will depend on the length of the tape, the width and drop depth of the bar, and the amount you stretch the tape as you wrap.

When you get to the bulged section of the bar that clamps into the stem, you should have just run out of tape. If you have more, you can rewrap part of the bar with more overlap, or you can cut off the

11.15 Wrapping handlebar tape

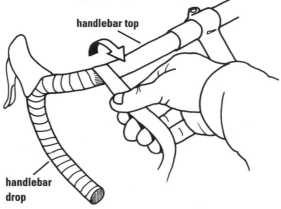

handlebar top

handlebar drop

excess. If the tape doesn't make it to the bulge, you can rewrap part of the bar with less overlap. If you want to end with only a narrow piece of sticky tape holding it down, you can trim the end of the bar tape to a point, and hold it down with a single width of electrical tape wrapped around a couple of times. You can follow with the decorative tape piece that came with the bar tape. Otherwise, just wrap around the bar a number of times with electrical tape, going wide enough with it to completely cover the square-cut end of the bar tape. Cut or break the electrical tape so that it ends under the bar.

Push the plugs into the ends of the bar, using them to push in the extra tape you left sticking off of the ends of the bar. Most plugs are now simply that—cylindrical plastic plugs. Old-school end plugs have an expanding device in them; you tighten a screw on the end, and it pulls a wedge into its internally tapered inner end, expanding it out against the walls of the handlebar.

xi-11 INSTALLING A CLIP-ON AERO BAR

Open the clamps that attach around the handlebar by removing the bolts with a hex key.

NOTE: *I will refer to the bike's handlebar when a*

11.16 Installing clip-on aero bars

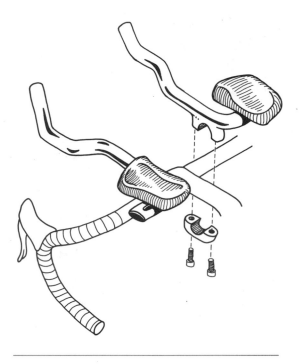

clip-on is attached to it as the "base bar."

Clip-ons (clip-on aero bars) generally mount on the bulge of the base bar, right next to the stem. If the clip-on you have chosen mounts on the thinner-diameter section of the base bar, you will have to peel back some handlebar tape from the section adjacent the bulge.

For starters, set the clip-on bar level or angled upward slightly. Bolt the clip-on clamps around the base bar (Fig. 11.16). You want the bolts tight enough that the clip-on bar won't slip when you hit a bump or pull on it, but you also don't want to crush the base bar. See the torque table in Appendix E.

Set the elbow pads in a medium-width position. The pad is often held onto the elbow support with a hook-and-loop fastener such as Velcro; pulling off the pad will reveal the adjusting bolt. Ideally, you want the elbow pad positioned under your elbow or slightly forward of it, and you want the clip-on to be of such a length that your hands grasp the ends comfortably with the elbows on the pads.

INSTALLING A

CLIP-ON

AERO BAR

—

SETTING STEM

AND BAR

POSITIONS

—

HEADSETS

xi-12 SETTING STEM AND BAR POSITIONS

Setting handlebar height and reach is very personal. Much depends on your physique, your flexibility, your frame, your riding style, and a few other preferences. This subject is covered in depth in Appendix C. Here are some brief suggestions.

- I recommend setting a drop handlebar so that the flat section below the bend (the "drop"—Figs. 11.1 and 11.5) is horizontal or aimed slightly downward toward the rear hub.

- If you stand a lot when you climb, you will want the bar low enough that you can use your arms efficiently when gripping the brake levers and pulling.

- A low, stretched-out position is better aerodynamically. A low position puts the top of the handlebar about 6–12cm lower than the top of the saddle. With your hands on the drops, a stretched-out position places your elbow at least 2 inches in front of your knee at the top of the pedal stroke.

- If you are using an aero (clip-on) bar, you want to find a position that maximizes both comfort and aerodynamic efficiency. The lower and more aerodynamic you are trying to be, the more forward you will want to position your saddle to open up the angle between your torso and your thigh. When setting the reach to the bar, a good rule of thumb is to position your elbow pads so that your ear is over the bend in your elbow. As for width, the narrower the elbow pads, the more aerodynamic you will be. Work on getting lower only after you have gotten comfortable and efficient with a narrow position.

HEADSETS

There are two basic types of headsets: threaded (Fig. 11.17) and threadless (Fig. 11.18). Road headsets have

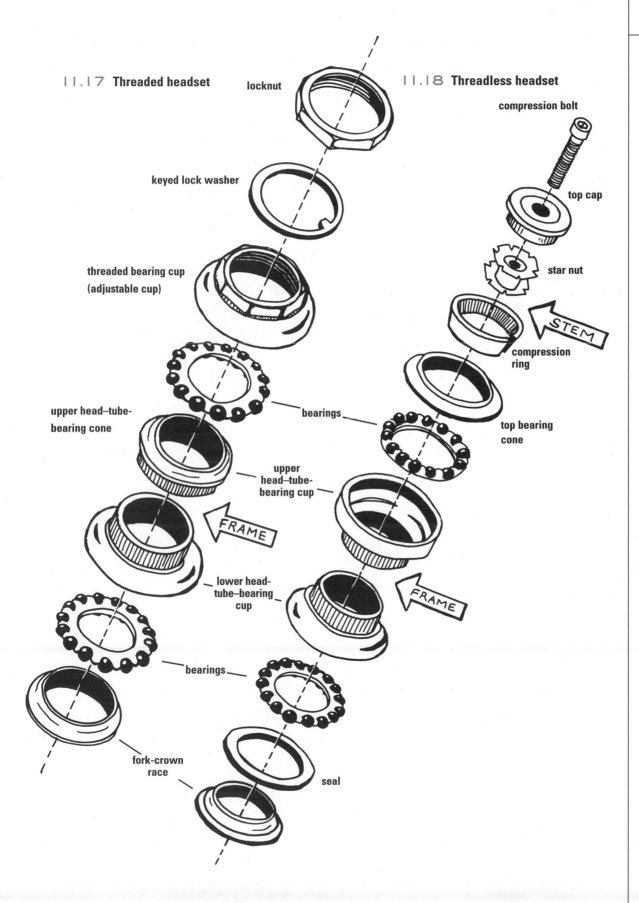

11.17 **Threaded headset**

locknut

keyed lock washer

threaded bearing cup
(adjustable cup)

upper head–tube-
bearing cone

bearings

upper
head–tube-
bearing cup

lower head-
tube–bearing
cup

bearings

fork-crown
race

seal

FRAME

11.18 **Threadless headset**

compression bolt

top cap

star nut

STEM

compression
ring

top bearing
cone

FRAME

STEMS, HANDLEBARS, AND HEADSETS

HEADSETS

11.19 Cane Creek Zero-Stack internal headset with press-in cups (cutaway)

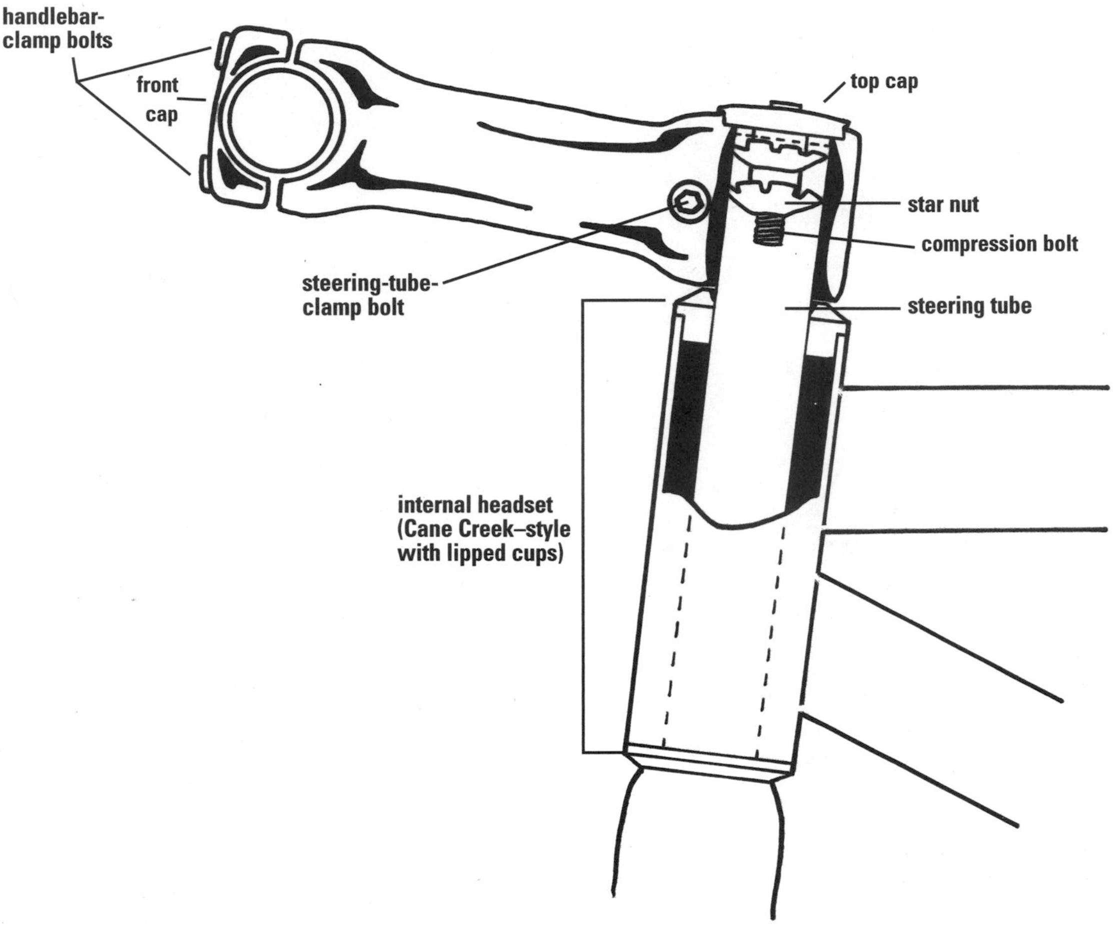

handlebar-clamp bolts

front cap

top cap

star nut

compression bolt

steering-tube-clamp bolt

steering tube

internal headset
(Cane Creek–style
with lipped cups)

traditionally come in the 1-inch-diameter size, but now the standard for road bikes is the 1⅛ inch headset.

The top bearing cup on a threaded headset has wrench flats, a keyed lock washer stacked on top of it, and a locknut that covers the top of the steering tube. That locknut tightens against the keyed lock washer and threaded cup (see Fig. 11.17). Extra spacers may be included under the locknut. A brake-cable hanger (Fig. 7.8) may be included under the locknut on a cyclo-cross or touring bike with cantilever brakes, or on 1970s or earlier bike with center-pull brakes (Fig. 7.3)

The Dia-Compe (now Cane Creek) AheadSet was the first threadless headset (Fig. 11.18), which is

a lighter system because it eliminates the stem quill, bolt, and wedge. The AheadSet connection between the handlebar and the stem is more rigid, too. Of course, fork manufacturers prefer threadless headsets, because they do not have to thread their forks and/or offer various lengths of fork steering tubes; steering-tube diameter becomes the only variable.

On an unthreaded headset, the top cup or cone and a conical compression ring slide onto the steering tube (Figs. 11.18, 11.20, 11.22, and 11.23). The stem clamps around the top of the steering tube, above the compression ring. When its conical base is pressed into the beveled edges of the hole through the top cup or cone, the compression ring keeps the

11.20 **Campagnolo Hiddenset drop-in-style integrated headset system (exploded)**

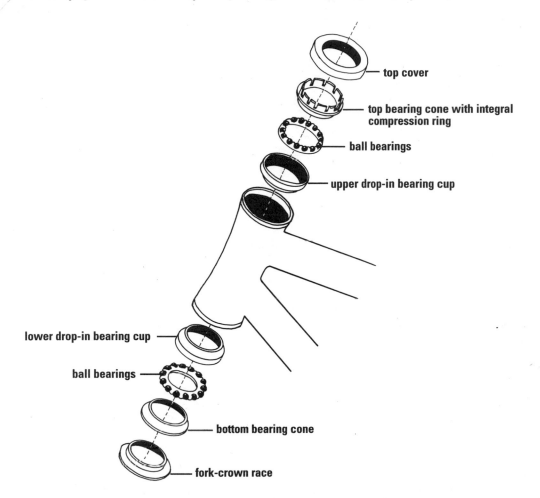

- top cover
- top bearing cone with integral compression ring
- ball bearings
- upper drop-in bearing cup
- lower drop-in bearing cup
- ball bearings
- bottom bearing cone
- fork-crown race

top cup or cone centered on the steering tube.

A "star nut"—a nut with two layers of sharp, spring-steel teeth sticking out from it (originally dubbed the "Star Fangled Nut" by Dia-Compe)—fits into an aluminum, steel, or titanium steering tube and grabs its inner walls (Figs. 11.6 and 11.19). On a carbon-fiber steering tube, an expandable insert (Fig. 11.21) or glue-in tubular insert with integrated star nut replaces the standard star nut and serves the dual purpose of protecting the steering tube from being crushed by the stem clamp and of anchoring the top-cap compression bolt.

A top cap sits atop the stem clamp and pushes it down to adjust the headset by means of the long

11.21 **Inserting an expandable support plug into a carbon-fiber fork steering tube**

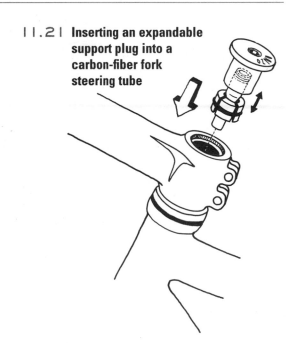

HEADSETS

11.22 Exploded cupless (drop-in) internal cartridge-bearing headset

11.23 Exploded Cane Creek Zero-Stack style press-in internal headset with lipped cups

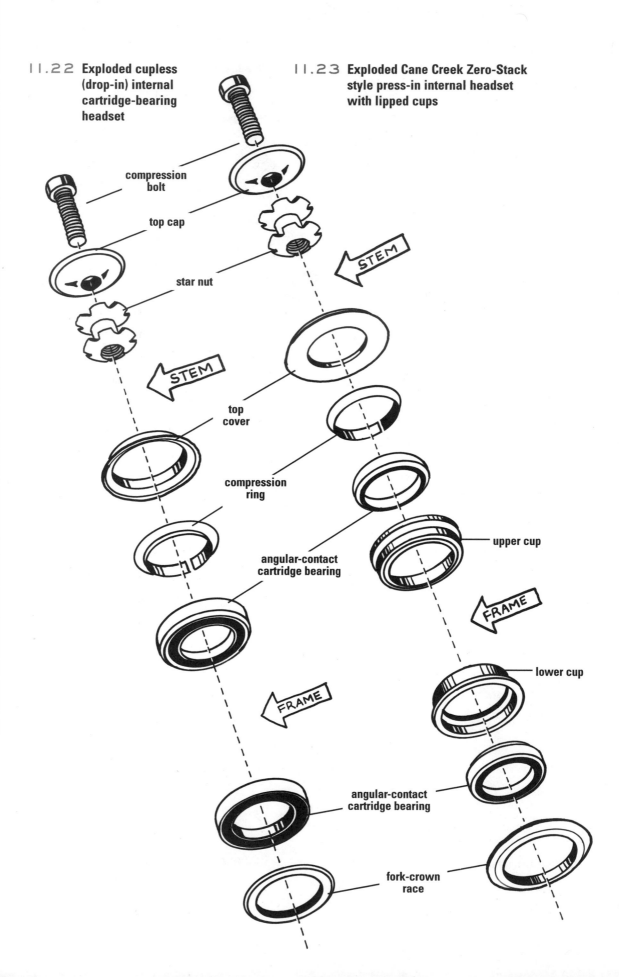

compression bolt

top cap

star nut

STEM

STEM

top cover

compression ring

angular-contact cartridge bearing

upper cup

FRAME

FRAME

lower cup

angular-contact cartridge bearing

fork-crown race

II.24 Needle bearings

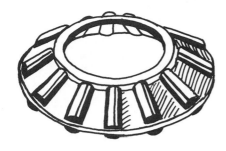

II.25 Lower parts of cartridge-bearing headset

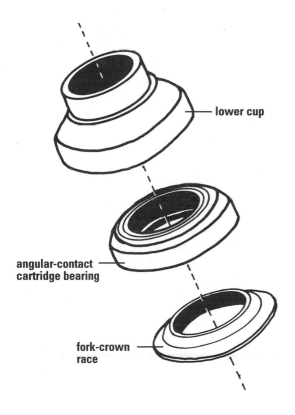

lower cup

angular-contact cartridge bearing

fork-crown race

compression bolt threaded into the star nut (Figs. 11.6 and 11.19) or into the crush-prevention insert in a carbon steering tube (Fig. 11.21). The stem clamped around the steering tube holds the headset in adjustment (Fig. 11.7).

The latest generation of headset is the threadless internal type, or "integrated headset," concealed inside the frame's steering tube (Figs. 11.19 and 11.20). Whereas standard threaded and threadless headsets have bearing cups above and below the ends of the head tube (Figs. 11.17 and 11.18), integrated headsets have bearings seated inside the head tube. Some types of integrated headsets have no press-in cups; the bearings either roll on bearing cups that just drop into the flared head tube and rest on machined shelves within the head tube itself (Fig. 11.20), or the headset simply has angular cartridge bearings that drop into the same style of flared head tube and rest without a cup on those machined shelves within the head tube (Fig. 11.22). Other types of internal headsets have cups with thin flanges that extend out to the edges of the head tube (Figs. 11.19 and 11.23). Otherwise, integrated headsets are identical to, and are adjusted the same as, original threadless headsets.

Many headsets—threaded or threadless—use individual ball bearings held in some type of steel or plastic retainer or "cage" (Figs. 11.17, 11.18, and 11.20) so that you are not chasing dozens of separate balls around when you work on the bike. A variation on this (Stronglight and Ritchey) has needle bearings held in conical plastic retainers (Fig. 11.24) riding on conical steel bearing surfaces.

Cartridge-bearing headsets usually employ "angular contact" bearings (Figs. 11.22, 11.23, and 11.25), since normal cylindrical cartridge bearings (Fig. 6.29) cannot take the side forces encountered by the bottom bearing of a headset. Each angular contact cartridge bearing is a separate, sealed, internally greased unit.

xi-13 CHECK HEADSET ADJUSTMENT

If the headset is too loose, it will rattle or clunk while you ride. You might even notice some "play" in the fork as you apply the front brake. If the headset is too tight, the fork will be difficult to turn or feel rough to rotate.

1. Check for headset looseness by holding the front brake and rocking the bike forward and back. Try it with the front wheel pointed straight ahead and then with the wheel turned at 90 degrees to the bike. Feel for back-and-forth movement (or "play") at the lower head cup with your other hand. If there is play, you need to adjust the headset because it is too loose. If the headset is loose, skip to the appropriate adjustment section, §xi-14 or §xi-15.

2. Check for headset tightness by turning the handlebar back and forth with the front wheel off the ground. Feel for any binding or stiffness of movement. Also, check for the chunk-chunk-chunk movement to fixed positions characterizing a pitted headset (if you feel this, you need a new headset; skip to §xi-18). Lean the bike to one side and then the other; the front wheel should turn as the bike is leaned (be aware that cable housings can resist the turning of the front wheel). Lift the bike by the saddle so that it is tipped down at an angle with both wheels off the ground. Turn the handlebar one way and let go of it. See if it returns to center quickly and smoothly on its own. If the headset does not turn easily on any of these steps, it is too tight, and you should skip to the appropriate adjustment section, §xi-14 or §xi-15.

3. If the headset is a threaded model, try to turn the top nut and the threaded cup by hand. They should be so tight against each other that they can only be loosened with wrenches. If you can tighten or loosen either part by hand, even if it passed tests one and two, you still need to adjust the headset; go to §xi-14.

xi-14 ADJUSTING A THREADED HEADSET

LEVEL 2

The secret to good adjustment is simultaneously controlling the steering tube, the adjustable cup, and the locknut as you tighten the latter two together.

NOTE: *Perform the adjustment with the stem installed. Not only does it give you something to hold onto that keeps the fork from turning during the installation, but there are slight differences in adjustment when the stem is in place as opposed to when it is not. Tightening the stem bolt inside a threaded steering tube can sometimes bulge the walls of the steering tube slightly (Fig. 11.4), just enough for it to shorten the steering tube and tighten a previously perfect headset adjustment.*

1. Following the steps outlined in §xi-13, determine whether the headset is too loose or too tight.

2. Put a pair of headset wrenches that fit the headset on the headset's top nut (which I will also call the "locknut") and top bearing cup (or "threaded cup" or "adjustable cup"). Headset nuts come in a wide variety of sizes, so make sure you have purchased the proper size. The standard wrench size for a road bike is 32mm. Place the wrenches so that the top one is slightly offset to the left of the bottom wrench. That way you can squeeze them together to free the nut (Fig. 11.26).

NOTE: *People with small hands or weak grip will need to grab each wrench out at the end to get enough leverage.*

3. Hold the lower wrench in place and turn the top wrench counterclockwise about one-quarter turn to loosen the locknut. It may take considerable force to break it loose, because it is generally tight to keep the headset from loosening up.

4. If the headset was too loose, turn the lower (or

11.26 Offseting the headset wrenches to loosen the locknut

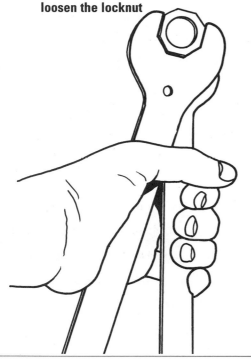

11.27 Offsetting the wrenches to tighten the locknut

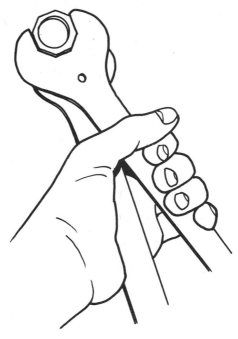

threaded) cup clockwise about one-sixteenth of a turn while holding the stem with your other hand. Be careful when tightening the cup; overtightening it can ruin the headset by pressing the bearings into the bearing surfaces and make little indentations. The headset then stops at the indentations rather than turning smoothly, a condition known as a "pitted" or "brinelled" headset.

(a) If the headset was too tight, loosen the threaded cup counterclockwise one-sixteenth of a turn while holding the stem with your other hand.

(b) If the headset was too tight, loosen the threaded cup counterclockwise one-sixteenth of a turn while holding the stem with your other hand. Loosen it until the bearings turn freely, but not to the point where any play develops.

5. Holding the stem, tighten the locknut clockwise with a single wrench. Make sure that the threaded cup does not turn while you tighten the locknut. If it does turn, either you are missing the keyed lock washer separating the cup and locknut (Fig. 11.17), or the washer you have is missing its key. In this case, remove the locknut (the stem has to come out first) and replace the keyed lock washer. Put the locknut on the steering tube so that the key engages the longitudinal groove in the steering tube. Thread on the locknut, install the stem, and redo the adjustment procedure.

NOTE: *You can adjust a headset without a keyed lock washer by working both wrenches simultaneously, but it is trickier, and the headset often will then come loose while you are riding.*

6. Check the headset adjustment again. Repeat steps 4 and 5 until the headset is properly adjusted.

7. Once the headset is properly adjusted, place one wrench on the locknut and the other on the

STEMS, HANDLEBARS, AND HEADSETS

ADJUSTING
A THREADED
HEADSET

threaded cup. Tighten the locknut (clockwise) firmly against the washer(s) and threaded cup to hold the headset adjustment in place (Fig. 11.27).

8. Check the headset adjustment again. If it is off, follow steps 2–7 again. Once it is adjusted properly, make sure the stem is aligned with the front wheel before riding.

NOTE: *If you constantly get what you believe to be the proper adjustment and then find it to be too loose after you tighten the locknut and threaded cup against each other, the steering tube may be too long, causing the locknut to bottom out. Remove the stem and examine the inside of the steering tube. If the top end of the steering tube butts up against the top lip of the locknut, the steering tube is too long. Remove the locknut and add another spacer.*

If you don't want to add another spacer, file 1mm or 2mm from the steering tube. Be sure to deburr it inside and out, and avoid leaving filings in the bearings or steering-tube threads. Replace the locknut and return to step 5.

Wheels Manufacturing makes a headset locknut called the "Growler." It replaces the locknut and will not come loose, even on bumpy terrain. It threads on like a normal locknut and is adjusted the same way. The only difference between a Growler and a standard locknut is that the Growler is split on one side and has a pinch bolt bridging the split. Once the headset is adjusted, you tighten the pinch bolt to keep the locknut from unscrewing.

xi-15 ADJUSTING A THREADLESS HEADSET

Adjusting a threadless headset—whether it is the new integrated type (Figs. 11.19, 11.20, 11.22, and 11.23) or the external type (Figs. 11.6 and 11.18)—is much easier than adjusting a threaded one. It's a level 1 procedure and usually only takes a 5mm Allen wrench.

a. First steps

1. Check the headset adjustment (§xi-13). Determine whether the headset is too tight or too loose.

2. Loosen the bolt(s) that clamp the stem to the steering tube.

3. Adjust the headset. Be careful not to overtighten the compression bolt, which will put too much pressure on the bearings and eventually pit the headset. If you're using a torque wrench, Dia-Compe recommends a tightening torque on this bolt of 22 in-lbs, which is a very low torque. This is a good place to start, but your headset may require a different torque for proper adjustment.

   (a) If the headset is too tight, loosen the compression bolt on the top cap about one-sixteenth of a turn (Fig. 11.28). This step usually takes a 5mm hex key, but on many expander inserts for carbon-fiber steering tubes (Fig. 11.21), the top cap itself is turned with a 6mm hex key.

   (b) If the headset is too loose, tighten the compression bolt on the top cap about one-sixteenth of a turn (Fig. 11.28) by using either a 5mm hex key or a 6mm hex key, as just explained for some carbon-fiber forks.

NOTE: *Not all threadless stems are adjusted with the top-cap system. DiaTech threadless headsets have no top cap. Instead, a clamping collar below the stem adjusts headset tension. The stem is first clamped in place. The collar is beveled on the inside from both ends, and it slides down an externally beveled ring above it as you tighten the clamp screw to put pressure on the headset. As soon as you loosen the stem, the headset comes out of adjustment.*

ADJUSTING A THREADLESS HEADSET

b. Adjustment problems

If the cap does not move down and push the stem down, redo step 2, making sure the stem is not stuck to the steering tube. If the stem won't budge, go to §xi-6b earlier in this chapter.

Another hindrance occurs if the conical compression ring (Figs. 11.18, 11.20, 11.22, and 11.23) is stuck to the steering tube, preventing adjustment via the top-cap bolt. Remove the top cap, stem, spacers, and headset top cover first to address this problem.

- With most (i.e., non-Campagnolo) compression rings, which are simply cone-shaped pieces split on one side, you need only tap the steering tube down with a mallet and then push the fork back up to free the compression ring. Grease the ring and the steering tube, and reassemble.

- With a Campagnolo threadless headset (either an integrated "Hiddenset"—Fig. 11.20, or a standard

external one), the compression ring is plastic and is conical on both ends. Its bottom end presses into the beveled hole in the top cone, but its turreted top end is also conical and presses into the hole in the headset top cover that is beveled toward the bottom. Pushing down on the top

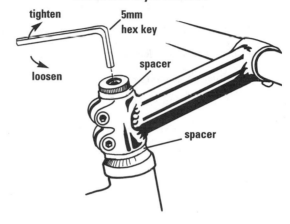

11.28 Loosening and tightening the compression bolt on a threadless-style headset

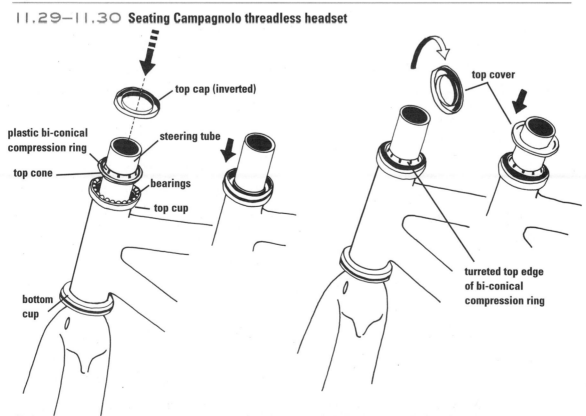

11.29–11.30 Seating Campagnolo threadless headset

ADJUSTING A

THREADLESS

HEADSET

cover (via the compression bolt pushing down on the stem) simply pinches the compression ring tighter in its place, rather than pushing it down. Instead, what you must do is flip the top cover upside down (Fig. 11.29) so that the nonbeveled end of its through-hole is against the turreted top edge of the compression ring, and push the compression ring down to preload the headset bearings by seating the top cone into them. Then, flip the top cap back over (Fig. 11.30), put it back in place, and reassemble the spacers, stem, top cap, and compression bolt.

If neither the stem nor the compression ring is stuck, yet the cap still does not push the stem down, the steering tube may be so long that it is hitting the lip of the top cap and preventing the cap from pushing the stem down. The steering tube's top should be 3–6mm below the rim of the stem clamp (Fig. 11.10) or 3–6mm below the rim of the spacer(s) above the stem. If the steering tube is too long, add a spacer above or below the stem, or use a flat file to make the steering tube shorter. Some top caps have thicker edge lips than others and require more space down to the top of the steering tube to avoid bottoming out on it.

Another thing that can thwart adjustment is if the star nut is not installed deeply enough, so that the cap bottoms out on the star nut. The highest point of the star nut should be 12–15mm below the top of the steering tube. With metal steering tubes, tap the star nut deeper with a star-nut installation tool, or put the bolt through the top cap, thread it five turns into the star nut, and gently tap it in with a soft hammer; the top cap is used to keep the star nut going in straight. Some top caps have taller center sections than others and require deeper insertion

of the star nut to avoid bottoming out on it.

With carbon steering tubes, first loosen the aluminum expander with a 5mm hex key (Fig. 11.21). Next, unscrew its top cap a turn or two with a 6mm hex key. By hand, push the assembly in farther until the top cap stops it, and reexpand the plug with a 5mm hex key. Finally, tighten the top cap down (22 in-lbs of torque is standard) against the top of the stem to adjust the headset.

Once you have fixed the cause of the adjustment problem, return to step 1.

c. Final steps

4. Tighten the steering-tube clamp bolt, or bolts, on the stem. If using a torque wrench, Dia-Compe recommends a tightening torque of 130 in-lbs.

5. Recheck the headset adjustment. Repeat steps 2–4 if necessary. With some integrated headsets, you may need a shim under the top cup so that the edges of the top cap do not drag and scrape on the top end of the head tube.

6. If the headset is adjusted properly, make sure the stem is aligned straight with the front wheel, and go ride.

xi-16 OVERHAUL THREADED HEADSET

LEVEL 2

Like any other bike part with bearings, headsets need periodic overhauls. If you use your bike regularly, you should probably overhaul a loose-bearing headset once a year. Headsets with sealed cartridge bearings usually never need to be overhauled; if a bearing fails, you either replace the bearing (such as the Shimano shown in Fig. 11.25) or, if the headset has pressed-in bearings (like Chris King and Dia-Compe's "S" series, Fig. 11.31), you replace the entire cup. If you have a Shimano cartridge-bearing headset, continue with these instructions. If you are replacing a Chris King or Dia-Compe "S" headset cup, move on to the instructions for headset removal.

A bike stand is highly recommended when overhauling a headset.

1. Disconnect the front-brake cable (Chapter 7), and remove the stem by loosening the stem bolt three turns, tapping the bolt down with a hammer to free the wedge (Fig. 11.8), and pulling it out.

2. Either turn your bike upside down or be prepared to catch the fork as you remove the upper part of the headset. To remove the top headset cup, unscrew the locknut and threaded cup with headset wrenches: Place one wrench on the locknut and one on the threaded cup. Loosen the locknut by turning it counterclockwise. It's easiest if the top wrench is angled just to the left of the lower wrench, and you squeeze them together (Fig. 11.26). Unscrew the locknut and the cup from the steering tube. The headset washer or washers will slide off the steering tube as you unscrew the threaded cup.

3. Pull the fork out of the frame.

4. Remove any seals that surround the edges of the cups. Make a point of remembering the position and orientation of each.

5. Remove the bearings from the cups. If the balls are loose, be especially careful not to lose any. Separate top and bottom sets if they are of different sizes.

6. Clean or replace the bearings.

   (a) With standard ball-bearing or needle-bearing headsets, put the bearings in a jar or old water bottle along with some citrus-based solvent. Shake. If the bearings from

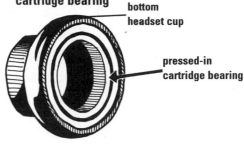

11.31 Chris King-style pressed-in cartridge bearing

bottom headset cup

pressed-in cartridge bearing

the top and bottom are of different sizes, keep them in separate containers to avoid confusion.

   (b) With sealed cartridge bearings, check to see whether they turn smoothly. If they do not, buy new ones. Either way, skip to step 8.

7. Blot the bearings dry with a clean rag. Plug the sink, and wash the bearings in soap and water in your hands, just as if you were washing your palms by rubbing them together. This helps keep your hands clean for the assembly steps as well. Rinse bearings thoroughly and blot them dry. Let them air dry completely.

8. Wipe all of the bearing surfaces with clean rags. Wipe the steering tube clean, especially the threads, and wipe the inside of the head tube clean with a rag stuck to the end of a screwdriver.

9. Inspect all bearing surfaces for wear and pitting. If you see pits (separate indentations made by bearings in the bearing surfaces), you need to replace the headset. If that's the case, skip to §xi-18.

10. Apply grease to all bearing surfaces. A thin film will do, especially if you are using sealed cartridge bearings.

11. Turn the bike upside down in the bike stand. Place a set of bearings in the top cup and a set in the cup on the lower end of the head tube.

STEMS, HANDLEBARS, AND HEADSETS

OVERHAUL

THREADED

HEADSET

Make sure you have the bearing retainer right side up so that only the bearings contact the bearing surfaces. If you have installed the retainer upside down, it will come in contact with one of the bearing surfaces, and the headset will not turn well. This is a bad thing, because assembling and riding it that way will turn the retainer into jagged chunks of broken metal. To be safe, double and triple check the retainer placement by turning each cup pair in your hand before proceeding.

(a) Most headsets have the bearings set up symmetrically top and bottom (Fig. 11.17). This way, the top piece of each pair is a cup, and the bottom piece is a cone; the bearing retainer rides the same way in both sets. Some headsets, however, place both cups facing outward from the head tube (Fig. 11.18), so that the bearing retainers are asymmetrical on either end of the head tube. Also, watch for asymmetry in ball size; Ritchey and recent Campagnolo headsets have smaller balls on top than in the bottom.

NOTE: *Stronglight, Ritchey, and similar needle-bearing headsets come with two pairs of separate conical steel rings. These are the bearing surfaces that sit on either side of each needle bearing (Fig. 11.24). You will find that one conical ring of each set is smaller than the other ring. Place the smaller one on the lower surface supporting the bearing: for the bottom bearing, place the smaller ring on the fork-crown race and, for the top bearing, place the smaller ring on the cup on top of the head tube.*

(b) If you have loose ball bearings with no bearing retainer, stick the balls into the grease in the cups one at a time, making sure that you replace the same number you started with in each cup.

12. Reinstall any seals that you removed from the headset parts.

13. Drop the fork into the head tube so that the lower headset bearing set seats properly (Fig. 11.32).

14. Screw the top cup, with the bearings in it, onto the steering tube. Keeping the bike upside down at this point not only keeps the fork in place, it also prevents grit from falling into the bearings as you thread the cup on.

15. Turn the bike upright. Slide on the keyed lock washer (Fig. 11.17). Align the key in the groove of the steering-tube threads. Screw on the lock-nut with your hand.

16. Grease the stem quill and insert it into the steering tube (Fig. 11.4). Make certain that it is in deeper than the imprinted limit line. Align the stem with the front wheel and tighten the stem bolt.

17. Adjust the headset as outlined in §xi-14.

xi–17 OVERHAUL THREADLESS HEADSET

LEVEL 2

These instructions apply to both integrated (Figs. 11.19, 11.20, 11.22, and 11.23) and external (Figs. 11.6 and 11.18) threadless headsets.

Like any other bike part with bearings, headsets need periodic overhauls. If you use your bike regularly, you should probably overhaul your loose-bearing headset once a year. Headsets with cartridge bearings (Figs. 11.25 or 11.31) need less frequent overhaul; some angular-contact bearings can be disassembled and cleaned and some cannot. With those that cannot, if a bearing fails, you either

OVERHAUL
THREADLESS
HEADSET

11.32 **Setting fork in head tube to seat bearings**

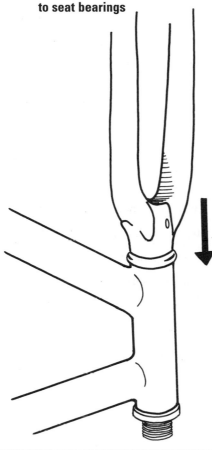

replace the bearing or, if it has press-in bearings (like Chris King and Dia-Compe's "S" series, Fig. 11.31), you replace the entire cup (§xi-20).

Either place the bike upside down in the work stand or be ready to catch the fork when you remove the stem.

1. Disconnect the front brake (Chapter 7), and unscrew the top-cap bolt (Fig. 11.28) and the stem-clamp bolt, or bolts. Remove the top cap and the stem.

2. Remove the top headset cup by sliding the top cup, conical compression ring (Fig. 11.18), and any spacers off the steering tube. It may take a tap with a mallet on the end of the steering tube, followed by pushing the fork back up, to free the compression ring.

3. Pull the fork from the frame.

4. Remove any seals that surround the edges of the cups. Remember the position and orientation of each.

5. Remove the bearings from the cups. Be careful not to lose any. Separate top and bottom sets if they are of different sizes.

6. If your bearings are the type that will not come apart, check to see if they turn smoothly. If they do not, buy new ones. Skip to step 8. Otherwise, clean or replace the bearings:

    (a) With standard ball-bearing or needle-bearing headsets, put the bearings in a jar or old water bottle along with some citrus-based solvent. Shake. If the bearings from the top and bottom are of different sizes, keep them in separate containers to avoid confusion. Blot the bearings dry with a clean rag.

    (b) Some cartridge bearings (Fig. 11.25) can be pulled apart and cleaned. Over a container to catch the balls, hold the bearing so that the beveled outer surface that fits into the cup faces down, and push up on the bearing's inner ring. The bearing should come apart—the inner ring will pop up and out with the bearings stuck to its outer surface. It may take a little rocking of the inner ring as you push up. If the bearing does not come apart, first pry off the plastic seal covering the bearings with a knife or razor blade, as in Chapter 6, Figure 6.29, and then try again. Wipe the bearings and bearing rings and seals with a clean rag.

7. Blot the bearings dry with a clean rag. Plug the sink, and wash the bearings in soap and water

in your hands, just as if you were washing your palms by rubbing them together. Your hands will get clean for the assembly steps as well. Rinse bearings thoroughly and blot them dry. Let them air dry completely.

8. Wipe all of the bearing surfaces with clean rags. Wipe the steering tube clean.

9. Inspect all bearing surfaces for wear and pitting. If you see pits (separate indentations made by bearings in the bearing surfaces), you need to replace the headset. If so, skip to §xi-18.

10. Apply grease to all bearing surfaces. If you are using sealed-cartridge bearings, apply grease conservatively.

11. Turn the bike upside down in the bike stand.

   (a) Place a set of bearings into the top cup and a set into the cup on the lower end of the head tube.

   (b) With a Campagnolo or other integrated headset with drop-in bearing cups (Fig. 11.20), place a bearing cup into the seat in the bottom of the head tube. Place a greased set of ball bearings into the cup, with the bearing retainer oriented properly (see step 11d for tips on determining proper bearing orientation).

   (c) With a cupless integrated headset (Fig. 11.22), set a bearing into the seat in the bottom of the head tube itself. See step 11e regarding orientation.

   (d) With loose-ball headsets, make sure you have the bearing retainer right side up so that only the bearings contact the bearing surfaces (note the different upper-cup styles and bearing orientations in Figs. 11.17 and 11.18). If you have installed the

retainer upside down, it will come in contact with one of the bearing surfaces, and the headset will not turn well. This is a bad thing, because assembling and riding it that way will turn the retainer into jagged chunks of broken metal. To be safe, double- and triple-check the retainer placement by turning each cup pair and bearing in your hand before proceeding. Most loose-ball headsets have the bearings set up identically top and bottom (Fig. 11.17). The top piece of each pair is a cup, and the bottom piece is a cone; the bearing retainer rides the same way in both sets. Some headsets, however, place both cups (and hence the bearing retainers) facing outward from the head tube (Fig. 11.18).

NOTE: *If you have loose ball bearings with no bearing retainer, stick the balls into the grease in the cups one at a time, making sure that you replace the same number you started with in each cup.*

   (e) With angular-contact cartridge bearings, the beveled end faces into the cup (Fig. 11.25) or into the seat machined inside of the head tube (Fig. 11.22).

12. Reinstall any seals that you removed from the headset parts.

13. Drop the fork into the head tube so that the lower headset bearing set seats properly (Fig. 11.32).

14. With a Campagnolo or other integrated headset with drop-in cups (Fig. 11.20), place a bearing cup into the seat in the top of the head tube. Otherwise, skip this step.

15. Slide the top cup or cone, with the bearings in it, onto the steering tube. Keep the bike upside down at this point; doing so not only keeps the

fork in place, it also prevents grit from falling into the bearings as you put the cup on.

16. Grease the compression ring and slide it onto the (greased) steering tube, so that the narrower end slides into the conical space in the top of the top cup or cone or angular-contact cartridge bearing (Figs. 11.18, 11.22, or 11.23).

NOTE: *On a Campagnolo threadless headset (integrated or external), there is a plastic bi-conical compression ring inserted into the top bearing cone (Fig. 11.20), and it acts like a normal split compression ring, to center the top cone over the bearings. The upper edge of the plastic compression ring is notched like a turreted castle tower in case you accidentally pull it out of the cone and wonder which way it goes back in. Above this part comes the top bearing cover, whose inner edge is beveled for the turreted top conical edge of the plastic compression ring. To preload the bearings, you must first install the top bearing cover upside down (Fig. 11.29) and then push down on it to preload the bearings by pushing the top cone down. If you install the top bearing cover in its standard orientation before the cop cone and plastic compression ring are slid down far enough to preload the bearings, the beveled inner edge of the top bearing cover will pinch the turreted upper conical edge of the plastic compression ring in place and not allow it to slide down farther. Once you have pushed the bearing cone down fully in this manner, flip the top bearing cover right side up and put it in place over the cone and compression ring (Fig. 11.30).*

17. Slide on any spacers you had under the stem.

18. Slide the stem on, and tighten one stem-clamp bolt to hold it in place.

19. Turn the bike over. Check that the stem clamp or the top spacer above the stem extends 3–6mm above the top of the steering tube (Fig. 11.10) and that the star nut is 12–15mm down in the steering tube. If they are, install the top cap on the top of the stem clamp and steering tube, and screw the bolt into the star nut (Fig. 11.28).

20. If the steering tube is too long, remove the stem. Add a spacer or file the steering shorter until the stem clamp overlaps it by 3–6mm. If the steering tube is too short, remove spacers from below the stem, if there are any. If there are no spacers to remove, try a new stem with a shorter clamp.

21. Adjust the headset (§xi-15).

xi-18 REMOVING THE HEADSET

LEVEL 3

1. Remove the front brake. Open the headset and remove the fork and bearings by following steps 1–5 in either §xi-16 or §xi-17, depending on headset type.

2. Remove the bearings:

    (a) If you have a cupless integrated headset (Fig. 11.22) with bearings seated on steps machined into the head tube itself, just pull the bearings out and skip to step 6.

    (b) With a Campagnolo Hiddenset (Fig. 11.20), pull out both the bearing cups and the bearings from either end of the head tube and skip to step 6.

    (c) With a headset with cups pressed into the head tube (Figs. 11.17, 11.18, or 11.23), just pull out the bearings, unless they are pressed into the cups as in Figure 11.31.

3. For a headset with cups pressed into the head tube (Figs. 11.17, 11.18, 11.19, or 11.23), slide the solid end of the headset-cup remover (sometimes called a headset "rocket," a wonderfully

11.33 Inserting headset-cup removal tool (or "rocket")

11.34 Removing headset cup

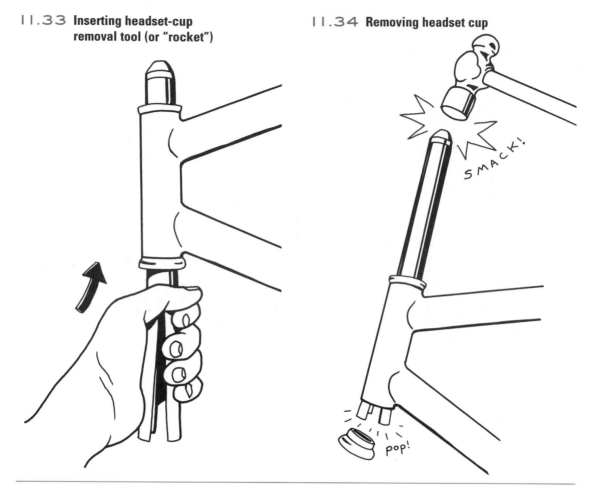

evocative name, as you'll see) through one end of the head tube (Fig. 11.33). As you pull the headset-cup remover through the head tube, the splayed-out tangs on the opposite end of the tool will pull through the cup and spread out.

4. Strike the solid end of the cup remover with a hammer, and drive the cup out (Fig. 11.34). Be careful as you do this, as the remover, or rocket, is liable to launch the cup across the room if hit with sufficient force.

5. Remove the other cup by placing the cup remover into the opposite end of the head tube and repeating steps 3 and 4 on the opposite end of the end tube.

6. Old, steel road bike fork crowns with 1-inch steering tubes in them are narrower than the diameter of the headset fork-crown race, so that you can elegantly remove the crown race with a U-shaped crown-race remover (step 6a) or an appropriately sized bench vise (step 6b). For forks whose crown race is not larger in diameter than the crown, skip to steps 6c and 6d.

(a) To use an old-school U-shaped crown-race remover, stand the fork upside down on the steering tube. Place the U-shaped crown-race remover so that it straddles the underside of the fork crown and its ledges engage the front and back edges of the crown race. Smack the top of the crown-race remover with a hammer to knock the race off (Fig. 11.35).

(b) To use a bench vise, slide the fork into the vise, straddling its center shaft. Tighten the

11.35 Removing fork-crown race with a crown-race remover

11.36 Removing fork-crown race with a vise

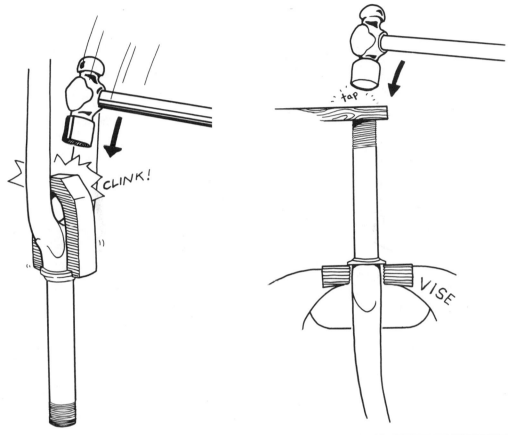

REMOVING

THE HEADSET

vise so that its faces ever-so-lightly contact the front and back of the fork crown with the lower side of the crown race sitting on top of them. Put a block of wood on the top of the steering tube to pad it. Strike the block with a hammer to drive the fork down and knock the crown race off (Fig. 11.36).

(c) If the fork crown is larger in diameter than the fork-crown race, and you don't have the slick tool mentioned in step 6d, you will need to knock the race off with a screwdriver—preferably an old, cheap screwdriver that you no longer use to drive screws. Turn the fork upside down so that the top of the steering tube is sitting on the workbench, or clamp the steering tube

horizontally in a vise between a pair of V-blocks. If there are notches at the front and back of the fork crown under the bearing race, place the blade of a large screwdriver into the notch on one side of the crown so that it butts against the bottom of the headset fork-crown race. If there is no notch, work the screwdriver blade under the race however you can; you may need to first drive a thin blade between the race and fork crown to open a gap. Tap the handle of the screwdriver with a hammer to drive the crown race up the steering tube a bit (Fig. 11.37). Move the screwdriver to the other side of the crown, and tap it again to move that side of the crown race

11.37 **Removing fork-crown race with a screwdriver**

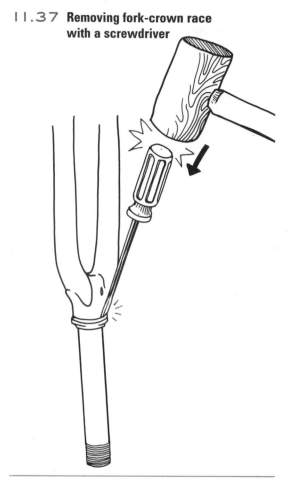

up a bit. Continue in this way, alternately tapping either side of the crown race up the steering tube, bit by bit, until it gets past the enlarged section of the steering tube and slides off.

(d) If you are fortunate enough to have a Park Universal Crown-Race Remover (Fig. 1.4), use it! First back the screw on the top off enough that the tool will slide down over your steering tube until the blades are below the fork-crown race. Using the screws at its base, finger-tighten the blades in under the fork-crown race until they stop. Then tighten the handle of the long screw on top to pull the crown race off its seat.

xi-19 FRAME AND FORK PREPARATION PRIOR TO INSTALLATION OF HEADSET

The frame and fork need to be properly prepared for the headset prior to installation. One assumes that new frames and forks are properly prepared prior to sale, but this is not always so, and if they are not, your headset will bind up at some steering angles and be too loose at others. Proper frame and fork preparation requires tools only some shops possess.

1. If this is a new frame (or one that has "eaten" headsets in the past), ream and face the head tube. If you do not have the tools for this, have a bike shop equipped with the proper tools do it for you. Reaming makes the head tube ends perfectly round inside and of the correct diameter for the headset cups to press in. Facing makes the ends of the head tube parallel so that the bearings can turn smoothly and uniformly. The tool that simultaneously reams and faces the end of the head tube is pictured in Figure 1.4 in Chapter 1.

2. If this is a frame for a cupless integrated headset (Fig. 11.22) or a Campagnolo Hiddenset (Fig. 11.20), and the bearing seats are badly machined inside the head tube so that the bearings are not parallel, it will eat bearings in a hurry. Fortunately, many shops now have a tool to recut the bearing seats so that they are parallel.

3. The base of the steering tube also needs to be turned down to the correct diameter for the crown race. The crown-race seat on the fork crown must be faced in a way that places the crown race parallel to the head tube cups and perpendicular to the steering tube.

   (a) With today's carbon-fiber forks, you generally do not want to run a cutter over the crown-race seat and risk cutting any fibers. On the other hand, you can be fairly confident that the crown race is perpendicular to the steering tube, whose base should also be the right diameter. As carbon forks are molded, rather than welded or brazed together, it is easier to control these dimensions during manufacturing, rather than requiring a postmanufacture machining step as metal forks generally do. The same goes with any type of suspension fork, as their parts are generally machined before assembly.

If the crown-race seat is oversized or untrue, many shops have a tool that simultaneously machines down the outer dimension of the base of the head tube while cutting the crown-race seat flat and perpendicular to the steering-tube axis.

4. The fork steering tube (threaded or threadless) must also be cut to the proper length. Remember, you can always go back and cut more off. You can't go back and add any, so be careful! You can wait until the headset (and stem and spacers, in the case of a threadless headset) is installed. Or you can figure out the length first.

(a) The safest way to make sure you don't cut the steering tube too short is to install the headset first (§xi-20). Once a threaded headset is assembled, you can measure the amount of excess length as in Figure 11.38, remove the top nut, and trim that much length off the top of the steering tube, deburring it inside and out afterward. Determining the steering-tube length for an already-installed threadless headset is detailed in §xi-4.

11.38 Measuring amount of steering tube to cut

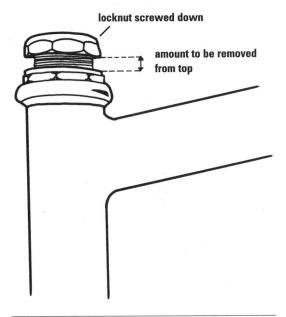

locknut screwed down

amount to be removed from top

(b) If you choose to cut the steering tube before installing the headset and are using a threaded headset, you need to know the headset's stack height. The headset stack height is often listed in the headset owner's manual, or a bike shop can look it up in Barnett's Manual or Sutherland's Manual. Armed with this number, measure the length of the frame's head tube and add the headset stack-height to this length. If you are adding extra spacers or brake-cable hangers between the headset nuts, add their thickness in as well. The resulting value represents the length that the steering tube must be. If the steering tube is already more than 3–5mm shorter than this sum, you need to find another headset with a shorter stack height (or, if you have included spacers, remove as many as needed).

(c) If the steering tube is longer than this sum, you can cut the tube down to size. Measure

STEMS, HANDLEBARS, AND HEADSETS

FRAME
AND FORK
PREPARATION
FOR HEADSET
INSTALLATION

twice and mark the cut line well, so you only have to cut once. Thread the headset adjustable cup onto the steering tube well below the cut point, and then cut the steering tube to the correct length with a hacksaw, following a thread for straightness. Use a flat file to square off the cut, and a round file to remove the burrs the hacksaw left on the inside and outside edges of the steering tube end. Then unscrew the adjustable cup, which, as it comes off the steering tube, will dress the threads.

(d) You can follow much the same steps if you are using a threadless headset. Add the headset stack-height to the length of the steering tube, the spacers, and the stem clamp, and subtract 3mm from the total. This is the length the steering tube should be from fork crown to top. I recommend not cutting until the headset is assembled and the stem is installed so that you can see if you want some more spacers under the stem to raise your bar higher.

(e) If you do not know the headset stack height, or if you're afraid you'll cut the steering tube too short, or if you want to see how it goes together before you cut it down, continue with the installation and assembly. When you are ready, cut it to 3–6mm below the top edge of the stem.

xi-20 INSTALL HEADSET

There is really no good way to install a headset without a headset cup press and a fork-crown-race punch (Fig. 1.3 in Chapter 1). For some inte-

11.39 Setting fork-crown race

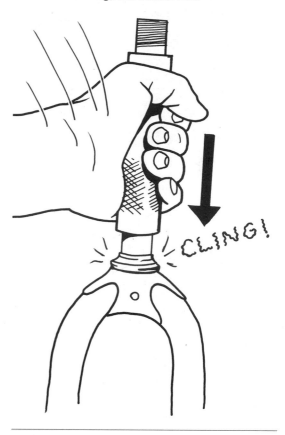

grated headsets, you need only the latter tool. If you do not have the necessary tools, it is better to take the parts to a bike shop for installation.

1. Put a thin layer of grease on the ends of the headset cups that will be pressed into the head tube, in the fork-crown-race bore, inside the ends of the head tube itself, and on the base of the steering tube.

2. Slide the fork-crown race down on the fork steering tube until it hits the enlarged section at the bottom. Slide the crown-race punch up and down the steering tube, pounding the crown race down until it sits flat on top of its seat on the fork crown (Fig. 11.39). Some crown-race punches are longer and closed on the top and are meant to be hit with a hammer rather than be slid up and down by hand. Hold

11.40 Pressing in headset cups with a headset press

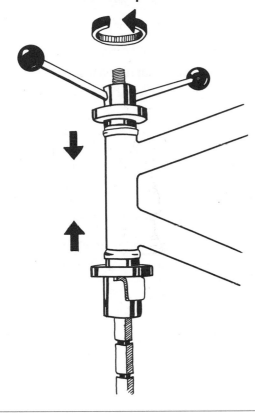

the fork up against the light to see if there are any gaps between the crown race and the crown.

NOTE: *Thin crown races can be bent or broken by the crown-race punch. Chris King, Park, and Shimano all offer support tools that sit over the race and distribute the impact from the punch. The Park punch, for instance, has three interchangeable ends (for each steering-tube diameter). Hold the crown race against each of the three to see which one will best support the race while you strike the punch with a hammer.*

3. By hand, place the headset cups into the ends of the head tube. Slide the headset-press shaft through the head tube. Press the button on the detachable end of the tool and slide it onto the shaft until it bumps into one of the cups (Fig. 11.40). This same method, and often the same press, can be used for internal (Fig. 11.23) and

external (Figs. 11.17 and 11.18) headsets with cups. You must make sure with internal cups that the press only makes contact with the outer cup flange and not the bearing seat. Find the nearest notch on the shaft and release the button. Some headset presses use a system of spacers and cones on both ends of the cups. Follow the instructions to set yours up properly. Whatever you do, be certain that the parts that make contact with the cups are not touching the precision surfaces the bearings roll in.

NOTE: *Dia-Compe "S" and Chris King headsets have bearings that are pressed into the cups and cannot be removed (Fig. 11.31). If you use a headset press that pushes on the center of the cups, you will ruin the bearings. You need a press that pushes the outer part of the cup and does not touch the bearings. Chris King makes tool inserts for this that fit most headset presses, and Park has a headset press with large, flat ends for the purpose. On the other hand, some thin aluminum headset cups can be mashed by pushing on the outside of the cup with the flat surface of a headset press; stop pressing as soon as they reach the ends of the head tube. Otherwise, these cups need press inserts pushing on the edges of the bearings to support them under high loads.*

4. Hold the lower end of the cup press shaft with a wrench. That will keep the tool from turning as you press in the cups. Tighten the press by turning the top handle clockwise (Fig. 11.40). Keep tightening the tool until the cups are fully pressed into the ends of the head tube. Examine them carefully to make sure there are no gaps between the cups and the ends of the head tube.

NOTE: *You can easily crush thin headset cups with a flat-surface headset press, so be careful and stop when the cups reach the head tube.*

TROUBLE-

SHOOTING

STEM,

HANDLEBAR,

AND HEADSET

PROBLEMS

5. Liberally apply grease to all bearing surfaces. If you are using sealed cartridge bearings, a thin film will do.

6. Assemble and adjust the headset, following the directions in §xi-16 and §xi-14 for a threaded headset and those in §xi-17 and §xi-15 for a threadless one.

xi-21 TROUBLESHOOTING STEM, HANDLE-BAR, AND HEADSET PROBLEMS

a. Bar slips

Tighten the pinch bolt on the stem that holds the bar, but not beyond the maximum allowable torque (see Appendix E). With a front-opening stem, make sure that there is the same amount of space between the stem and the front plate on both edges of the front plate. With any stem, if the clamp closes on itself without holding the bar securely, check that the bar is not deformed or smaller diameter than the stem was made to fit and the stem clamp is not cracked or stretched. Replace any questionable parts. You can slide a shim made out of a beer can between the stem and bar to hold it better, but replacing parts is a safer option; there is always a reason why parts that are meant to fit together no longer do! With superlight stems and bars, you cannot just keep tightening the small clamp bolts like you can the larger bolts on heavy stems because you will strip threads and/or cause bar and stem failures.

b. Bar makes creaking noise while you are riding

Loosen the stem clamp, grease the area of the bar that is clamped in the stem, slide the bar back in place, and tighten the stem bolt. Also, sanding the hard anodized surface inside the stem clamp and on the clamping area of the bar can sometimes eliminate creaking. If the bar has a sleeved center section, rather than a bulged section, the bar could be creaking inside the sleeve. There's no cure for this; replace the bar.

c. Clip-on bar slips

Tighten the clip-on's clamp bolts.

d. Stem not pointed straight ahead

Loosen the bolt (or bolts) securing the stem to fork steering tube, align the stem with the front wheel, and tighten the stem bolt (or bolts) again. With a threaded headset, the bolt you are interested in is a single vertical bolt on top of the stem; loosen it about two turns, and tap the top of the bolt with a hammer to disengage the wedge on the other end from the bottom of the stem (Fig. 11.8). With a threadless headset, there are one (Fig. 11.6), two (Fig. 11.7), or three horizontal bolts pinching the stem around the steering tube that need to be loosened to turn the stem on the steering tube. Do not loosen the bolt on the top of the stem cap (Fig. 11.28); you'll have to readjust the headset if you do.

e. Fork and headset rattle or clunk when you are riding

The headset is too loose. Adjust the headset (§xi-14 or §xi-15).

f. Stem + bar + fork assembly does not turn smoothly but instead stops in certain fixed positions

The headset is pitted and needs to be replaced. See §xi-18 and §xi-19.

g. Stem + bar + fork assembly does not turn freely

The headset is too tight. The front wheel should swing easily from side to side when leaning the bike or lifting the front end. Adjust the headset (§xi-14 or §xi-15, depending on type).

h. Stem is stuck in or on fork steering tube.

See §xi-5.

**Phillips and
flat-blade
screwdrivers**

electrical tape

CHAPTER 12

CYCLING COMPUTERS

*For a list of all the ways technology has failed to
improve the quality of life, please press three.*
—Alice Kahn

A cycling computer can be a useful tool if it is set up correctly, and if you want the information. On the other hand, it can give you incorrect information if not set up properly, and it can also give you information you might be better off not having.

xii-1 WHY HAVE A CYCLING COMPUTER?

Most likely, you ride a bike because you love riding. Or at least that is why you started. If having a computer on your handlebar adds to your pleasure, then by all means use one.

You may love watching yourself eat up the miles on a long ride. Or you may get a thrill from seeing how fast you can go downhill. Timing yourself periodically on a favorite loop may bring satisfaction as your times drop with improving fitness. You may like watching your cadence or working on keeping your pedaling rate in a certain range. An altimeter feature may be fun to watch in the mountains.

You may have a specific workout schedule with which a heart monitor and/or a power meter can assist you in realizing your goals more rapidly. Effectiveness of interval training can be enhanced, because duration, speed, and intensity of the intervals (and, at least as important, the intensity of the rest periods between intervals and the intensity of recovery rides between interval days) can be monitored and even stored for later playback with a power meter (see §xii-3) and/or a computer with heart-monitor analysis software.

On the other hand, if you start using your computer to tell you whether you have ridden "far enough," "fast enough," "hard enough," or "correctly" today, or this week, or this year, then you may want to reconsider. We all are probably compulsive enough in our work that we don't need to be compulsive in our play as well. My intention in writing this book is to add to your enjoyment of cycling, and I am not interested in your judging yourself harshly

12.1 Rolling out the wheel to measure its circumference

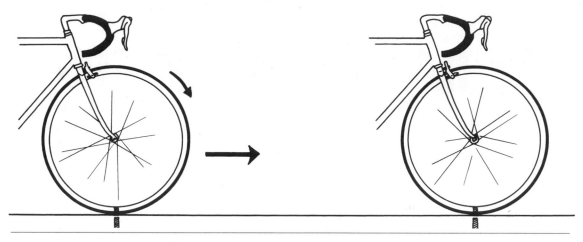

about what you have or have not done on a bike. It can be an insidious feature of a cycling computer that what started as a fun way to monitor yourself becomes a way in which you beat yourself up. And it can creep up on you. Bike riding can devolve slowly from fun to drudgery without your noticing, until riding a certain way becomes another thing you "have to do." Yank the computer off your bike if you see this happen.

xii-2 SETTING UP A CYCLING COMPUTER

Computers vary from brand to brand, and, without having this book become an unmanageably large, dry tome, I can't go into the exact details of which buttons to push when for which computer. But I can give you some general guidelines that work for setting up any computer, and you can get the specifics about which buttons to push from the owner's manual or from a friendly guy or gal at the bike shop.

a. Measure the circumference
of the wheel and tire

1. Properly inflate the tire mounted on the wheel that will carry the magnet (usually the front), and wrap a piece of tape across the rim and around the tire in one spot.

2. Put a piece of tape crosswise on a hard floor or driveway, and set the wheel on it so that the tape around the tire is lined up over it (Fig. 12.1).

3. Holding the ends of the axle, roll the wheel forward one revolution until the piece of tape is at the bottom again.

4. Put another piece of tape on the floor lined up with the tape on the tire (Fig. 12.1).

5. With a tape measure, find the distance from the leading edge of one piece of tape on the floor to the other. This is the circumference of the inflated tire. Your computer needs this information to properly measure speed and distance, because it is counting revolutions of the wheel and must know the distance covered with each revolution.

6. In the computer owner's manual, either you will find a way to enter the circumference, or you will find a table of code numbers corresponding to ranges of circumference and instructions on how to enter the proper code number.

b. Install the computer and sensor

1. Snap the computer bracket around the handlebar next to the stem (Fig. 12.2). If it fits too loosely onto the bar, wrap the bar at that spot

with one of the rubber pieces that come with the computer or with layers of electrical tape. If your handlebar has an oversized (31.8mm) diameter, and your computer only has a strap for a standard-diameter bar (26.0mm), you will need to get an oversized mounting strap from the computer manufacturer, or you will need to rig something up to hold your computer with zip-ties. If you have a handlebar (or integrated carbon handlebar-stem combination) with an ergonomic flat top surface, you can generally get a little computer-mount piece from the handlebar manufacturer. If you have an aero bar (Fig. 11.16), the real estate on the top of your base handlebar will be too cluttered for a computer, and you wouldn't be able to see a computer mounted on the base bar when you are on the aero bar. Mount the computer on the stem or on a cross-member of the aero bar, or buy and install a computer-mounting stub for your aero bar.

2. Tighten the screw to secure the mount, and snap the computer onto the mount.

3. If the computer has a wire to the sensor, wrap the wire around the front-brake cable to take up slack, and strap the sensor around the fork blade.

   (a) To give yourself more flexibility later, don't wrap the sensor around and around the brake wire. Instead, first attach the bracket to the bar and the sensor to the fork. Start twisting the computer wire around the brake cable, from the middle of its slack length, and secure it in the center with tape or a zip-tie. Raising the handlebar then does not require disconnecting the sensor and unwinding it; you merely cut the tape

12.2 Position the computer where you can read it easily

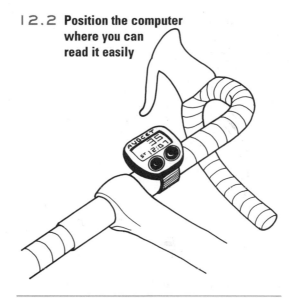

12.3 Attaching a Shimano Flight Deck shifting sensor to the STI brake/shift lever

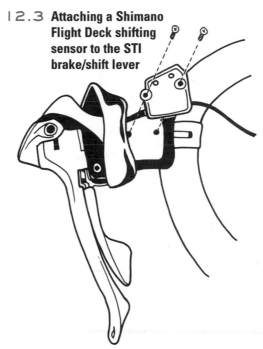

or zip-tie to release the wire (or just untwist it, leaving the zip-tie connected).

(b) With a wireless computer, you need only strap the sensor to the fork blade.

(c) The sensor usually mounts to the inside of the fork leg about midway down, but the position may need to be changed later for optimal clearance with the wheel magnet. There is usually a built-in zip-tie

SETTING UP
A CYCLING
COMPUTER

12.4 Slotted wheel magnet

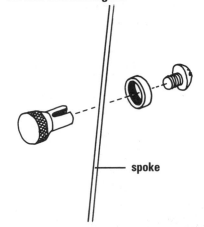

spoke

12.5 Plastic wheel-magnet holder that folds around two spokes

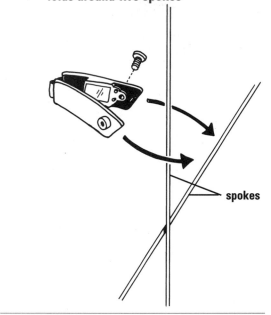

spokes

12.6 Snap-on wheel magnet

SNAP

spoke

on the sensor, or separate zip-ties are used to hold the sensor. Older Avocet computer sensors mount around the dropout, not on the fork leg.

(d) Secure the wire to the fork with tape or zip-ties.

4. Shimano and Campagnolo cycling computers also have wires that must be connected to the brake levers, because they sense when you shift (Fig. 12.3). You will have to remove a plastic cover piece from the lever and replace it with the piece attached to the computer wire.

(a) That cover is on the inboard side of a Shimano lever. Unscrew it and screw in the new one attached to the Flight Deck computer (Fig. 12.3).

(b) On a Campagnolo lever, you pull out the plastic cover plug on the underside of the lever body (i.e., on the side against the handlebar). That plastic cover plug is shown in the far lower right of Figure 5.23B. (There is a similar plastic plug in Fig. 5.23A, but eight-speed levers are not compatible with ErgoBrain computers.) The shift sensor for a Campagnolo ErgoBrain computer snaps in where the plug came out, and you make sure the little push button is visible through the kidney-shaped hole on the inboard side of the lever body. To reach down in there and contact that little button, you then snap a little, kidney-shaped plastic button (included) with a spring attached to its underside into the hole, paying attention to the "R" or "L" markings on the snap-in button.

(c) With both Campagnolo and Shimano

computers, there are bumps on the rubber lever-cover hoods that line up with the buttons so that you can control the computer without your hands leaving the brake levers.

5. Attach the wheel magnet to the spokes. Some magnets have a slotted holder with a collar and a screw to tighten against the spoke (Fig. 12.4). Other magnets sit in a plastic housing that wraps around the spoke and is retained by a screw (Fig. 12.5), or they come in a plastic housing that snaps onto the spoke (Fig. 12.6). To fit the magnet on aero spokes, either use the plastic folding-type holder shown in Figure 12.5 or one like that in Figure 12.6 but specifically for the aero spoke size you have. Also, many wheelsets with aero spokes come with a magnet to fit the spokes. Any small magnet will do; you can also file the slot wider in a slotted magnet holder like the one in Figure 12.4. For a wheel without wire spokes, you can tape a refrigerator magnet onto a disc wheel or onto the side of a composite spoke or rim.

6. Make sure the wheel magnet passes close to the sensor. If the computer does not indicate a speed when you spin the wheel, the positions of the sensor and/or the magnet need to be changed. Many sensors have a scribed line indicating where the magnet should pass (some sensors have lines at either end, giving you a couple of options). Make sure the magnet passes by the line and that it is close to the sensor (1 to 5mm away), but it doesn't touch (Fig. 12.7). You may need to slide the sensor and the magnet up or down. Older Avocet computer magnet rings live in a plastic housing that snaps onto the hub. If

12.7 Position the magnet close to the sensor and align with one of its scribed lines

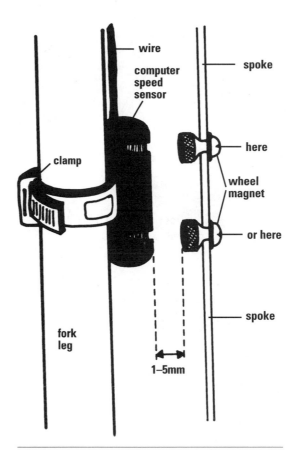

the hub flange is too far inboard, the sensor will not respond to the magnet, and you will need to clip a second magnet over the first one. If the clips are not in the right spots to fit the hub, you can snip the clip tabs off and lace the magnet to the spokes with wire or twist-ties.

7. If the computer has a separate cadence sensor and magnet, the magnet usually goes on the crankarm, and the sensor mounts to the chainstay. Campagnolo computers have a cadence magnet that you can stick inside the 6mm hex-key hole on the end of the pedal spindle. Shimano computers calculate cadence from wheel speed and gear size, so you need no magnet on the crankarm and sensor on the chainstay.

SETTING UP

A CYCLING

COMPUTER

12.8 **Replacing the computer battery**

xii-3 POWER METERS AND HEART MONITORS

The four primary power meters on the market are the SRM, the Power Tap, the Polar, and the Ergomo.

The SRM power meter has strain gauges built into the spider arms on the right crank. The meter gets the strain-gauge data via a wireless pick-up near the bottom bracket and converts the strain into torque and then to power output. You need a special right crankarm from SRM.

The Power Tap has strain gauges built into an oversized rear hub. Torque on the hub is communicated wirelessly to a sensor on the seatstay. You need a special Power Tap rear hub.

The Polar system has a sensor on the chainstay that detects the musical pitch of the chain to determine the tension on it.

The Ergomo measures the force on the bottom bracket. You need a special Ergomo bottom bracket for it.

Stand-alone heart monitors or heart monitors built into power-measuring computers require no additional hookups on the bike, just a strap around your chest.

xii-4 DIAGNOSING COMPUTER PROBLEMS

a. No display or battery indicator appears on computer screen

The battery probably needs to be replaced. Some computers have a battery not only in the computer (Fig. 12.8) but also in the sensor, so check both places. Some computers have two batteries in the computer itself. A bike shop (or a camera store) should have a battery to match.

If the battery is not the problem, check for broken wires.

b. Computer is on, but speed does not register

1. The wheel magnet may be missing, or it may be too far from the sensor as it passes by. Adjust the positions of the sensor and the magnet so that the magnet passes close by the scribed line on the sensor but does not touch it (Fig. 12.7).

2. On a wireless computer, the sensor may be too far from the computer head. Move the sensor farther up the fork, and, of course, move the wheel magnet correspondingly farther radially outward on the wheel so that it still passes close by the sensor (Fig. 12.7).

c. Cadence reading does not display

Check that your computer does have a cadence feature. If so, check that the sensor and magnet on the crank and frame pass closely by each other.

d. Computer reads wrong speed and distance

The wrong wheel size may have been entered. Follow the owner's manual for the button-pushing sequence to find the number programmed into the computer for wheel size. See §xii-2a for measuring wheel circumference.

e. Can't find computer owner's manual

Here are a number of options:

1. Check with a bike shop for a new manual.

2. Get the contact information for the manufacturer or distributor from the bike shop, and contact the company directly.

3. Check the computer maker's Web site for an on-line owner's manual or to order a new one.

4. Learn from a friend or shop employee who knows how to work your computer. Take notes.

CYCLING COMPUTERS

DIAGNOSING
COMPUTER
PROBLEMS

CHAPTER 13

WHEEL BUILDING

If you think you can or think you can't, you're right.
—Henry Ford

TOOLS

screwdriver
spoke wrench
truing stand
wheel-dishing tool
spoke prep or
  grease

OPTIONAL
linseed oil

Congratulations. You have arrived at the task most often used to gauge the talents of a bike mechanic. Next to building a frame or fork, building a good set of wheels is the most critical, and creative, of a bike mechanic's tasks. Despite the air of mystery surrounding the art of wheel building, the construction of a good set of bicycle wheels is actually a straightforward task.

Clearly, wheels are the central component of a bike. For any bike to perform well, its wheels must be well made and properly tensioned. Once you learn how, it is quite rewarding to turn a pile of small parts into a set of strong and light wheels upon which you can corner and descend with confidence. You will be amazed at what they can withstand, and you will no longer go through life thinking that building wheels is something just the "experts" do. With practice and patience, you can build wheels at your house that are as good as any custom-made set, and far superior to those built by machine.

This is not meant to be an exhaustive description of how to build all types of wheel spoking patterns; there are entire books written on the subject—justifiably so, by the way, because the bicycle wheel is an artful engineering miracle that deserves thoughtful exegesis. (If you are interested in a more comprehensive treatment of the subject of wheel building, I recommend *Barnett's Manual* by John Barnett, *The Art of Wheelbuilding* by Gerd Schraner, or *The Bicycle Wheel* by Jobst Brandt.)

You can, however, build great wheels following the methods presented here. The first part describes how to build a wheel laced in the classic "three-cross" spoking pattern, in which each spoke crosses three other spokes (Fig. 13.1) A later section (§xiii-7) details how to build a radially spoked front wheel or a rear wheel spoked radially on one side and three-cross on the other side. So let's get started.

I3.I The complete wheel with three-cross spoke pattern

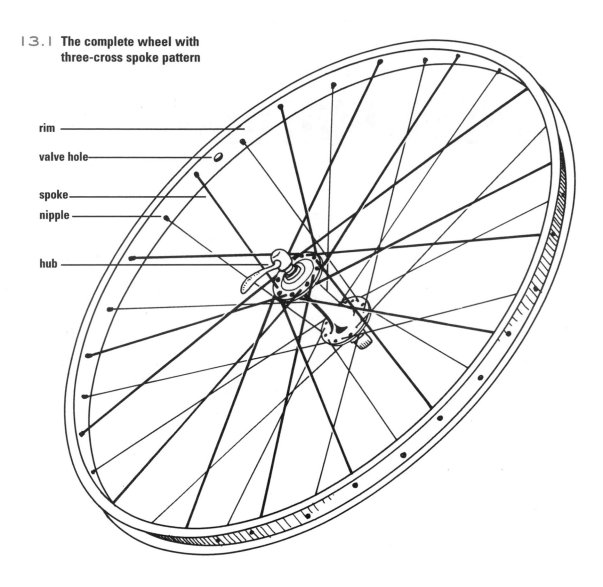

rim

valve hole

spoke

nipple

hub

I3.2 Spoke and nipple

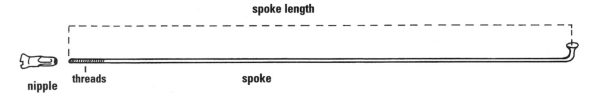

spoke length

nipple   threads   spoke

xiii-1 PARTS

Gather the parts you need: a rim, a hub (make sure that the hub has the same number of holes as the rim), and properly sized spokes and nipples to match. Make sure you have the right size spoke wrench for those nipples as well. I suggest getting the spokes from your local bike shop. That way, a mechanic can help make sure you get the right spoke lengths (Fig. 13.2) and can counsel you on which gauge (thickness) of spoke to select, as well as which rim makes sense for your weight, budget, and the kind of riding you plan on doing. Remember when you calculate spoke length to specify that you will be using a three-cross spoking pattern (unless you are building a radial wheel—see §xiii-7).

NOTE: *If you are replacing a rim on an old wheel, do not use the old spokes unless it is a very new wheel you just dented on a pothole or train track. You won't save much money reusing the old spokes, and the rounded-out nipples and weakened spokes will soon make you wish you had bought a new set.*

xiii-2 LACING THE WHEEL

For the sake of brevity and clarity, I do not mention using spoke prep compound with every instruction to thread a nipple onto a spoke. Although the use of thread compound is not mandatory, I think that the wheel is improved with it. It encourages the nipples to thread on more smoothly, it takes up some of the slop between the spoke and nipple threads, and its thread-locking ability discourages the nipples from vibrating loose. But better yet than spoke prep is to use DT Pro Lock nipples, which contain a two-component adhesive in the nipple thread to prevent the spoke-nipple connection from loosening under the effect of operating loads (loading and unloading of the wheel during riding), ensuring constant spoke tension.

The spoke prep is applied to the spoke threads before the nipples are put on. You do not want too much, as it will be hard to adjust the nipples months and years down the road; you just want the spoke prep in the valleys of the threads. You can get the right amount if you dip the threads of a pair of spokes into the prep compound, and then take two more dry spokes and roll the threads of all four spokes together with your fingers. With DT Pro Lock nipples, you don't have to do any of this, but you also want to complete the wheel in one sitting. Like epoxy glue, you will be bursting little beads of the two glue components inside the nipple. So if you get

it done while the glue is viscous, the nipples will hold better than if you let them harden and then turn them again in ensuing days.

In the absence of spoke prep, at least dip the threads of each spoke in grease. Grease accomplishes everything spoke prep does, save for locking the threads.

1. Divide your spokes into two separate groups, one set for each side of the hub flange, and rubber band each set together. If you are building a rear wheel, you should be working with two different spoke lengths, because spokes on the right-hand side, or drive side, are almost always shorter. For a radial front wheel, skip to §xiii-7.

2. Hold the rim on your lap with the valve hole away from you. Note that the holes alternate being offset upward or downward from the rim centerline.

NOTE: *If you are building a rear wheel with an OCR (off-center rear) rim drilled off center (e.g., Ritchey OCR, Bontrager ASYM, Campagnolo asymmetrical), make sure that you orient the rim so that the spoke holes are offset to the left (nondrive) side (see Fig. 13.3). The rim is meant to reduce wheel dish, so that offsetting the nipples to the left reduces the otherwise very steep angle at which drive-side spokes normally hit the rim. The balanced left-to-right spoke tension should increase the lifetime of the wheel, and the lower spoke angle moves the drive-side spokes away from the rear derailleur. So with an OCR rim (Fig. 13.3), have the spoke holes offset downward, toward your lap.*

3. Hold the hub in the center of the rim, with the right side of the hub pointing up. On a rear hub, the right side is the drive side. Front hubs are symmetrical; pick a side to be the right side. In the illustrations, the right side has the nut end of the quick release.

13.3 **"OCR" (off-center rear) rim laced correctly**

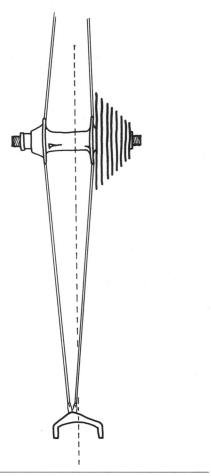

13.4 **First half of right-side spokes placed in hub**

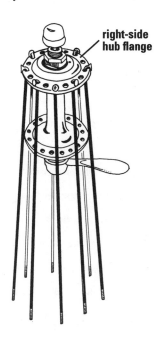

right-side
hub flange

a. First set of spokes

4. Drop a spoke down into every other hole in the top (right side) hub flange, so that the spoke heads are facing up (Fig. 13.4) Make sure if it's a rear wheel that you put the shorter spokes on the right (drive) side. On some (older) hubs, half of the holes you are looking at will be countersunk deeper into the hub flange to provide a radius less stressful on the spoke elbow, so don't use those holes— use their neighbors. That said, most hubs anymore have the same countersinking on all holes to prepare for the possible eventuality of building a completely symmetrical, radially spoked wheel.

5. Put a spoke into the first hole counterclockwise from the valve hole and screw the nipple on three turns (Fig. 13.5). Notice that this hole is offset upward (on an OCR rim, this means that the hole is offset upward from the centerline of the spoke holes, not the centerline of the rim). If the first hole counterclockwise from the valve hole isn't offset upward, you have a misdrilled rim, and you must offset all instructions one hole.

6. Working counterclockwise, put the next spoke on the hub into the hole in the rim four holes away from the first spoke, and screw a nipple on three turns. There should be three open rim holes between these spokes, and the hole you put the second spoke into should also be offset upward.

7. Continue counterclockwise around the wheel in the same manner. You should now have used half of the rim holes that are offset upward, and there should be three open holes between each spoke (Fig. 13.6).

8. Flip the wheel over.

13.5 First spoke, right side up

valve hole

next spoke
of the
first set

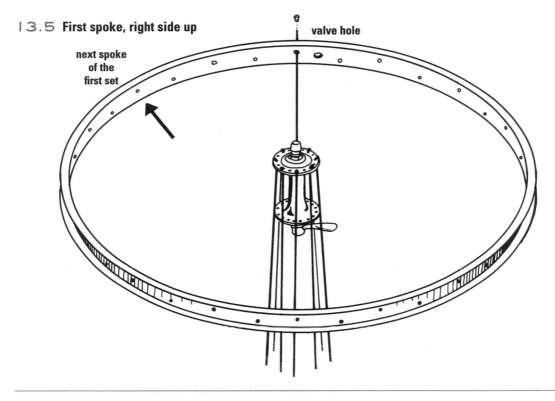

b. Second set of spokes

9. Sight across the hub from one hub flange to the other. Notice that the holes in one flange do not line up with the holes in the other; each hole lines up between two holes on the opposite flange (Fig. 13.7).

10. Drop a spoke down through the hole in the top flange that is immediately clockwise from the first spoke you installed (the spoke that is just clockwise from the valve hole).

11. Put this new spoke into the second hole clockwise from the valve hole, next to the first spoke you installed (Figs. 13.8 and 13.9). This hole will be offset upward from the rim centerline.

12. Thread the nipple on three turns.

13. Double check to make sure that the spoke you just installed starts at a hole in the hub's top (left side) flange that is one-half-a-hole space clockwise from the hole in the lower flange where the first spoke you installed started. When you look

at the wheel from the side, these two spokes (your first spoke and the one you just installed) should not cross each other and should look like they are trending slightly away from each other so that their trajectories continued outward would keep diverging and would never cross each other, even far beyond the rim (Fig. 13.9). In wheel-building parlance, these two spokes are called "diverging parallel" spokes.

14. Drop a spoke down through the hole in the top (left side) hub flange two holes away in either direction, and continue around until every other hole has a spoke hanging down through it (Fig. 13.8).

15. Working counterclockwise, take the next spoke from the hub and put it in the rim hole that is three holes counterclockwise from the valve hole. This hole should be offset upward and four holes to the left of the spoke you just installed. Thread the nipple on three turns.

13.6 First set of spokes laced

13.7 Spoke-hole offset

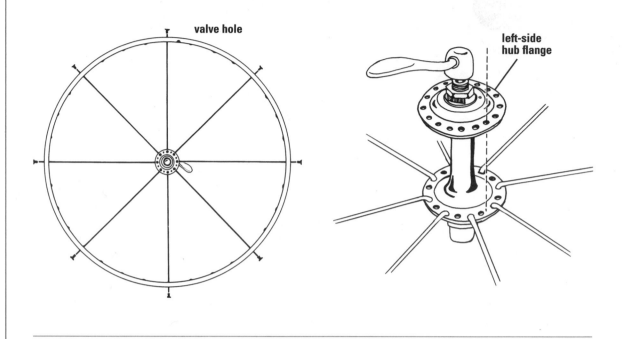

13.8 Lacing second set

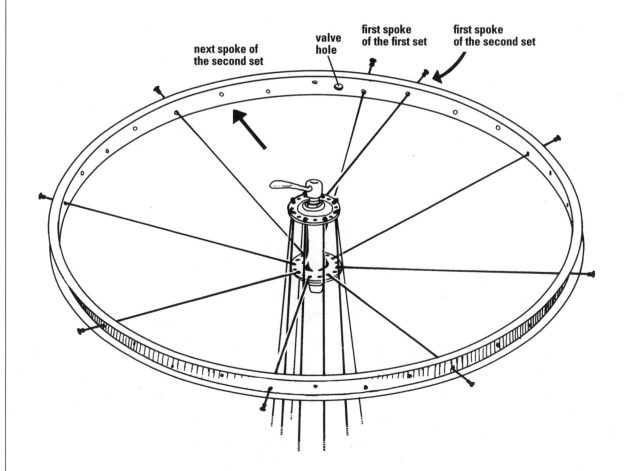

13.9 "Diverging parallel" spokes

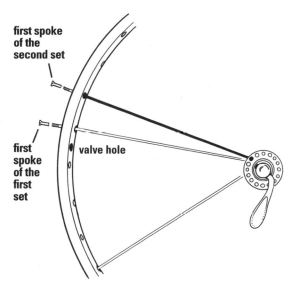

first spoke
of the
second set

first
spoke
of the
first
set

valve hole

13.10 Second set of spokes laced

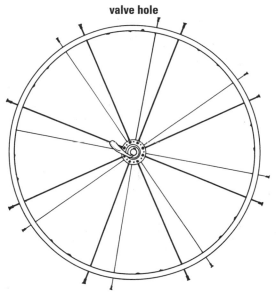

valve hole

16. Follow this pattern counterclockwise around the wheel (Fig. 13.10). You should have now used half of the rim holes that are offset upward, as well as half of the total rim holes. The second set of spokes should all be in upwardly offset holes, one hole clockwise from each spoke of the first set.

c. Third set of spokes

17. Drop spokes through the remaining holes on the right side of the hub, from the inside out (Fig. 13.11). Remember: if it's a rear wheel, these spokes should be shorter than the spokes used on the left side.

18. Flip the wheel over, grabbing the spokes you've just dropped through to keep them from falling out.

19. Fan the spokes out, so that they cannot fall back down through the hub holes.

20. Grab the hub shell and rotate it counterclockwise as far as you can (Fig. 13.12).

21. Pick any spoke on the top (right-hand) hub

flange that is already laced to the rim. Now find the spoke five hub holes away in a clockwise direction.

22. Take this new spoke, cross it under the spoke you counted from (the one five holes away), and stick it into the rim hole two holes counterclockwise from that spoke (Fig. 13.13). Thread a nipple on three turns.

23. Continue around the wheel, doing the same thing (Fig. 13.14). You may find a spoke or two that doesn't reach quite far enough. If that's the case, at a point about an inch from the spoke elbow, push down on the spoke to help it reach.

24. Make sure that every spoke coming out of the upper side of the top flange (the spokes that come out toward you with their spoke heads hidden from view) crosses over two spokes and under a third. All three of these "crossing" spokes come from the underside of the same flange and have their spoke heads facing toward you. These "crossing" spokes begin one, three, and five hub

13.11 Placing third set of spokes in hub

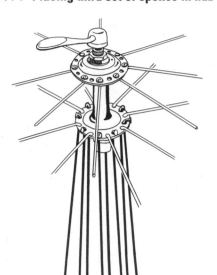

13.12 Rotating hub counterclockwise

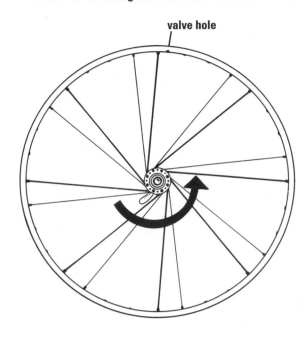

valve hole

13.13 Lacing third set of spokes

first spoke of
the third set

valve hole

first spoke of
the first set

next spoke
of the third set

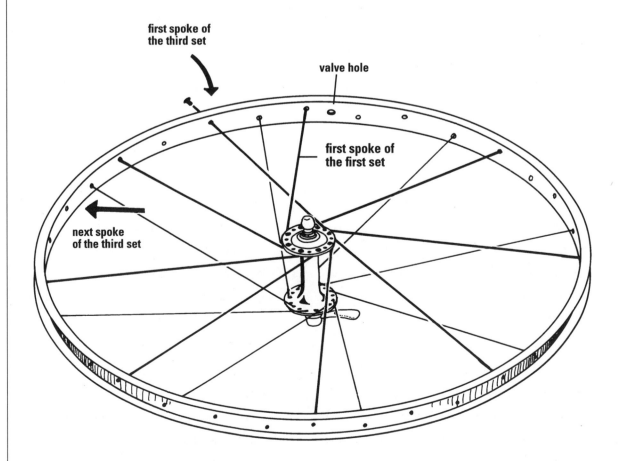

13.14 Third set laced

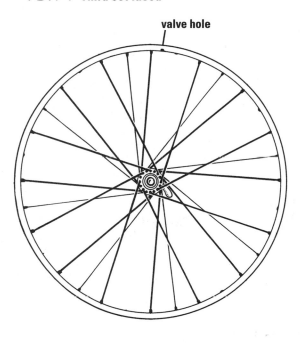

valve hole

holes counterclockwise from the spoke that you just inserted into the rim (Fig. 13.14). This is called a "three-cross" pattern because every spoke crosses three others on its way to the rim (over, over, under). Every upwardly offset hole should now be occupied on the rim.

d. Fourth set of spokes

25. Drop spokes down through the remaining hub holes in the bottom flange from the inside out (like Figure 13.11, but with the other side of the hub up).

26. Flip the wheel over, grabbing the spokes to keep them from falling back down through the holes.

27. Fan the spokes out.

28. Pick any spoke on the top (left-hand) hub flange that is already laced to the rim. Now find the spoke five hub holes away in a counterclockwise direction.

29. Take that spoke, cross it over two spokes and under the spoke you counted from. Stick the

spoke into the rim hole two holes clockwise from the spoke it crosses under (Fig. 13.15). Thread a nipple on three turns.

30. Continue around the wheel, doing the same thing until the wheel is laced like Figure 13.1. You may find that some spokes don't reach far enough. If that's the case, at a point about an inch from the spoke elbow, push down on the spoke to help it reach.

31. Make sure that every spoke coming out from the upper side of the top flange (the spokes that come out toward you with their spoke heads hidden from view) crosses over two spokes and under a third (Fig. 13.1). All three of these "crossing" spokes come from the underside of the same hub flange and have their spoke heads facing you. The "crossing" spokes begin one, three, and five hub holes clockwise from each spoke emerging from the top of the upper (left) hub flange (Fig. 13.1). Every hole should now be occupied on the rim. When you look at the wheel from the side, the valve hole should be between two spokes (your first spoke and the first spoke of the fourth set) that do not cross each other but whose trajectories look like they are trending slightly toward each other. In other words, if these spokes were to continue infinitely outward, their trajectories would eventually cross far beyond the rim (Fig. 13.16). In wheel-builder speak, these two spokes are called "converging parallel" spokes. Lacing the spokes this way around the valve hole will provide the maximum possible space between the spokes for the pump head when inflating the tire.

13.15 **Lacing fourth set of spokes**

next spoke of
the fourth set

valve hole

first spoke of
the fourth set

NOTE: *If this is a rear wheel, the spokes coming out of the outside of the hub flange on both sides oppose the clockwise twist the chain applies on the cogs. See §xiii-6 for more on this subject.*

xiii-3 TENSIONING THE WHEEL

1. Put the wheel in the truing stand.

2. Tighten each nipple with a spoke wrench until only three threads are visible beyond the bottom of the nipple (see Figs. 13.17–13.20 for rotation direction). From now on, every time you tighten or loosen a spoke nipple, turn it back the opposite direction one-eighth turn afterward. This unwinds the twist in the spoke that your tightening or loosening had just caused.

3. Using your thumb, press the spokes coming out-ward from the outer side of the hub flanges down at the elbow to straighten their line to the rim. Spokes coming out of the inner side of the flange do not need this.

4. Go around the wheel, tightening each nipple a half-turn. Do this uniformly, and only a half-turn, so that the wheel is not thrown out of true.

5. Check to see if the spokes are tight enough to give a tone when plucked. Squeeze pairs of spokes together and compare with a good wheel with spokes of the same gauge; your wheel should have considerably less tension at this point.

6. Repeat steps 4 and 5 until the spokes all make a tone but are under less tension than an existing, good wheel. Final tensioning will come with the remainder of the truing process.

13.16 "Converging parallel" spokes

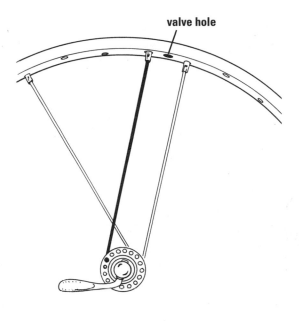

valve hole

---

xiii-4 TRUING THE WHEEL

a. Lateral true

Side-to-side trueness is the most obvious wheel parameter when you spin a wheel.

1. Make sure the hub axle has no end play. If it does, adjust the hub (see Hub adjustment in Chapter 6, §vi-16d).

2. (Optional) Put a drop of linseed oil around the top of each nipple where it seats in the rim to lubricate the contact area between it and the inside of the rim hole.

3. Set the truing stand feelers so that one of them scrapes the side of the rim at the worst lateral wobble (Figs. 13.17 and 13.18).

4. Ending a few spokes on either side of where the rim scrapes, tighten the spokes coming from the opposite flange of the hub and loosen the spokes coming from the same-side flange of the hub (Figs. 13.17 and 13.18). Start with a quarter-turn on nipples at the center of the scraping area and decrease the amount you turn each nipple as you move away in either direction. This step pulls the rim away from the feeler. If it does the opposite, you are turning the nipples the wrong direction. Remember: you normally turn something to the right to tighten and to the left to loosen, but tightening and loosening spoke nipples at the bottom of the wheel is the opposite of what you would normally do (Figs. 13.17–13.20). This is because the nipple head is underneath your spoke wrench. Try opening a jar that is upside down, and you will immediately understand the principle involved.

5. Work around the wheel in this way, bringing in the feelers as the wheel gets truer.

13.17 Adjusting spokes to pull rim to the right

13.18 Adjusting spokes to pull rim to the left

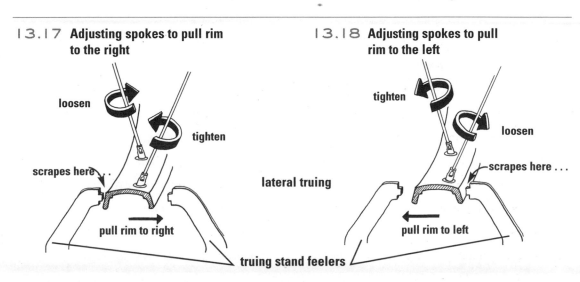

loosen

tighten

scrapes here . .

pull rim to right

lateral truing

tighten

loosen

scrapes here . . .

pull rim to left

truing stand feelers

13.19 **Radial truing: pull rim in**

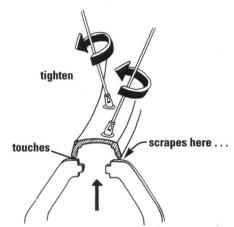

tighten

touches   scrapes here . . .

13.20 **Radial truing: let rim out**

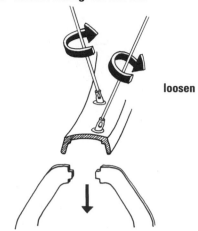

loosen

b. Radial true

While not as obvious as side-to-side trueness, out-of-roundness is more important to the longevity of the wheel, because, as Portia Masterson, former owner of the Self Propulsion bike shop in Golden, Colorado, so eloquently puts it, "uniformity of tension is the key to durability." Radial truing can also be somewhat slow and frustrating work. If you find yourself running out of patience for this job, step away for awhile and then start again when you feel fresh and ready.

6. Set the truing-stand feelers so that they now contact the circumference of the rim, rather than the sides.

7. Bring the feelers in until they scrape against the highest spot on the rim (Fig. 13.19).

8. Tighten the spokes a quarter-turn where the rim scrapes. This will pull the rim inward. Decrease the amount of each turn (to an eighth-turn and less) as you move away from the center of the scraping area.

9. Work around the wheel this way, bringing the feelers in as the wheel becomes rounder.

10. Wherever there is a dip in the rim, loosen the spokes (Fig. 13.20). If the spokes are too tight at

this point, they will be hard to turn and creak and groan as you turn them. When the spokes become hard to turn (i.e., the nipples feel on the verge of rounding off), loosen all of the spokes in the wheel a quarter-turn before continuing. Compare tension with a good wheel with the spokes of the same gauge; tension at this point should still be lower in the wheel you are building.

xiii-5 DISHING (CENTERING) THE WHEEL

1. Place the dishing tool across the right side of the wheel, bisecting the center (Fig. 13.21).

2. Tighten or loosen the dishing gauge screw until the gauge contacts the outer face of the axle-end nut (Fig. 13.21).

3. Flip the wheel over.

4. Place the dishing tool across the other side of the wheel.

5. Check the gap of the dishing gauge with this axle end-nut face (Fig. 13.22). Any gap between the dishing gauge and the axle end-nut face indicates the amount the rim is offset from the centerline of the wheel. If there is no gap, but an overlap instead, reset the dishing gauge on this side (the previously overlapped side). Then flip

it over and check the other side (i.e., repeat steps 3, 4, and 5 on the opposite side).

6. Put the wheel back in the truing stand.

7. Pull the rim toward the center (reducing the gap between the dishing tool and the axle end face) by tightening the spokes on the opposite side of the wheel from the axle end that had the gap between it and the dishing gauge. Tighten a half-turn each—no more. If the spokes start getting really tight (they will creak a lot when tightening, the nipples will start rounding off, and the spokes will feel much tighter than the spokes in a comparable wheel), then loosen the spokes uniformly on the opposite side of the wheel.

8. Recheck the wheel with the dishing gauge by repeating steps 1–5.

9. If the dish is still off (there is still a gap between the dishing gauge and the end nut when you flip it over), repeat steps 6–8 until the dish is correct (the gap is zero).

10. Stress the spokes by squeezing each pair together with your hands (Fig. 13.23). They will make a "ping" noise as they unwind.

13.21 Using the dishing tool to check the centering of the rim relative to the axle ends

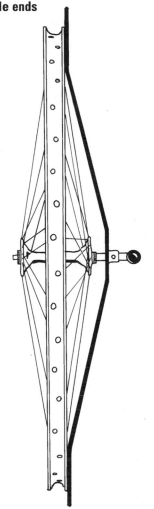

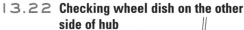

13.22 Checking wheel dish on the other side of hub

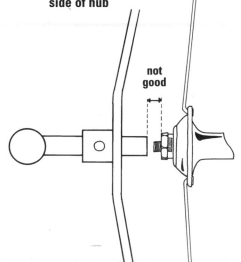

not good

13.23 Relieving tension

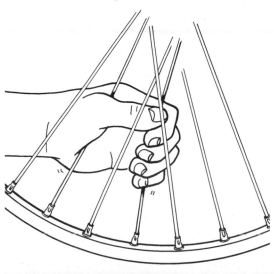

(a) Leaning on the wheel is a quicker way to prestress it, but this method has the potential to wreck the wheel if you are not careful. To proceed, set the axle end on the workbench and carefully press down on the rim with your hands at the 9 o'clock and 3 o'clock positions. This pressure will affect an area of about three spokes on each side, so rotate the wheel three spokes, press down again, rotate three more spokes in the same direction, press down again, and so on. After you finish one side, flip the wheel over and do the other side. Do not press down with all your might; while a well-built wheel's lateral strength is impressive, it is still easy to destroy your work with too much pressure.

(b) If prestressing throws the wheel way out of true, the spokes are probably too tight. Loosen them all one-eighth turn. Note, though, that some loss of wheel "trueness" is normal. If the loss is minor, you can overlook it and continue with step 11.

11. Repeat Truing the Wheel (steps 1–10), followed by Dishing the Wheel (§xiii-5), prestressing the spokes frequently as you go. Keep improving the accuracy of the build this way.

12. Bring up the tension to that of a comparable wheel by making small tightening adjustments to every nipple, adjusting dish and true after each time around, until the wheel is as you want it.

13. If the rim is oily, wipe it down with a citrus-based biodegradable solvent.

14. Congratulate yourself on building your wheel, and show it off to your friends.

xiii-6 COMMENTS ON WHEEL BUILDING

Your wheel has some features that you won't find on machine-built wheels. Most significantly, on your rear wheel, the "pulling spokes" are to the outside. In plain speak, this means that you have a spoking pattern that best resists the twisting force on the hub produced by pedaling forces on the chain.

To explain, in the wheel you've built, half of the spokes are called "pulling" or "dynamic" spokes, and the other half are called "static" spokes (this is true of any spoking pattern except radial). The pulling spokes are the ones directed in such a way that a clockwise twist on the hub increases the tension in them. If you look at the wheel from the drive side, you will see what I am talking about.

You will also see that the static spokes do not oppose a clockwise twist on the hub. In fact, their tension decreases when you stomp on the pedals.

By placing all of the pulling spokes so that they come from the inside of the hub flanges out (i.e., the spoke heads are on the inward side of the flanges), we have attached the spokes doing the most work the farthest outward on the hub, reducing the fatigue on them and increasing their ability to oppose forces acting on the rim. The reasoning is that the spokes whose tension changes the most during the working of the wheel should be the ones that are lying across the hub flange with the heads on the inside of the flange. Tension changes lead to spoke breakage due to fatigue, and the weakest part of a spoke is at its elbow. If there is more contact between the spoke elbow and the flange, there is less stress on the spoke elbow. Also, the spokes under the most stress should have the widest "stance" (if you want to resist being knocked over, you plant your feet farther apart), because they come from the outside of the flanges and are thus farthest apart at their elbows.

13.24 Radially spoked front wheel

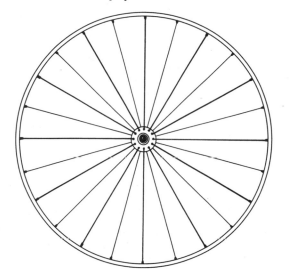

13.25 Radial/three-cross rear wheel

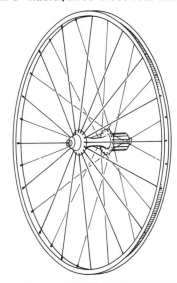

If you choose the appropriate parts for your weight and riding style, and have the proper spoke tension, then you should have a strong wheel that will last a long time. Congratulations!

xiii-7 RADIALLY SPOKED WHEELS

With the advent of stronger rim materials and stiffer rim cross sections, radially spoked wheels (Fig. 13.24) have become popular. They are simple to build, and radial spoking offers a number of advantages.

A radially spoked wheel is vertically stiffer than a crossed one, because radial spokes allow little opportunity for spokes to absorb energy in the spoking pattern. The radial wheel can be stiffer laterally, too, because all of the spokes can come to the outside of the hub flange and increase the pulling angle to the rim.

A radial wheel is lighter, because the spokes are shorter. Further weight can be removed with fewer spokes, and radial spoking allows any even spoke count to be used (with nonradial patterns, the spoke count must be a multiple of four). And radial spoking allows the use of direct-pull hubs and nail-head spokes (straight spokes without elbows), eliminating

a potential weak spot in the spokes.

Radially laced spokes line up behind each other and thus improve the aerodynamics of the wheel. Aero-shaped spokes can improve the aerodynamics even further, but using aero-shaped spokes in a standard hub often requires slotting the hub holes with a jeweler's file to get the spoke through. If you do this yourself, make sure you only file downward from the hole, toward the meat of the flange. Slotting upward toward the edge greatly weakens the hub and invites the spoke to rip through.

Speaking of torn hub flanges, the warranty of some hubs is voided when spoked radially; Shimano, for one, has this stipulation. The stress is greater on hub holes with radial spoking because the spoke tension in a radial wheel is often higher and because there is less material resisting the hub's tearing out when the spoke is pulling straight outward than if it is pulling at an angle along the hub flange.

A completely radial wheel can only be used on the front. On the rear, the drive side (or the nondrive side, if the hub shell is oversized and stiff) must still have a crossing pattern to oppose the twist on the hub caused by the chain (Fig. 13.25).

a. How to lace a radial front wheel

Drop all of the spokes from the inside of each flange outward, or from the outside of the flange inward, and lace them straight to the rim.

b. How to lace a rear wheel with a radial left side and a three-cross drive side

First lace the drive side following the instructions in §xiii-2a, steps 4 through 7, and §xiii-2c, steps 17 through 24. Now lace the left-side spokes outward through the hub flange, or inward through the hub flange, and straight to the rim.

The tensioning and truing steps are the same as for standard three-cross wheels, but radial-spoke tension should be higher to help prevent the spokes from vibrating loose.

xiii-8 WHEELS FOR BIG RIDERS

Building wheels for heavy and tall riders requires greater lateral and vertical stiffness. The weight of the rider can more readily bend and laterally flex the rim, but it creates another problem as well. The heavier rider detensions the spokes at the bottom of the wheel more by making the rim more D-shaped at the bottom as it rolls. If the spokes are under less tension, or if the nipple flanges periodically lose contact with the bases of the rim holes, the nipples can unscrew, and the wheel will fall apart. To achieve the higher strength required, you can add the following characteristics.

First, the spoke count needs to be high; 36 or more spokes is highly preferable for riders over 190 pounds. The spokes need to be heavier, because thicker spokes have less stretch as well as less breakage. Although 14- or 15-gauge (2.0mm or 1.8mm) double-butted spokes will probably have no more breakage than straight 14-gauge (2.0mm) spokes (because most breakage occurs at the nipple or the elbow, where butted spokes are thick), butted spokes will stretch more, allowing spoke loosening.

The deeper the rim, the higher its hoop strength (vertical stiffness and strength). Unfortunately, most deep aero rims are also thinner to reduce weight and hence lose some strength. Very-deep-section rims work with low spoke counts because of this high hoop strength. The strongest wheel is a deep-section rim drilled for more spokes.

With eight-, nine-, and ten-speed rear wheels, dish is high (one side is flatter than the other), meaning that there is a great tension difference between spokes on the two sides. The loose spokes on the left can unscrew, especially under high pedaling forces, and the tight spokes on the right can break. As the chain twists the cogs clockwise, the spokes opposing the twist (the "pulling spokes") get tighter, while the tension in the "static spokes" is reduced and they can unscrew.

Using radial spokes on the left side (see §xiii-7) can counteract the problem of grossly uneven tension. With a radial left side, the chain winding up the hub always tightens all of the left-side spokes, rather than loosening half of them as happens with a crossing pattern.

An off-center rim, such as a Ritchey OCR, can also help by reducing the wheel dish. The rim holes are offset to the left side (Fig. 13.3), so that the drive-side spokes come to the rim at a lower angle and can work with lower tension. The left-side spokes come to the rim at a higher angle and can be under higher tension without forcing the use of dangerously high tensions on the drive side. Before lacing an off-center rim, make sure you read the note in step 2 of §xiii-2.

CHAPTER 14

FORKS

Someday we'll look back on this moment and plow into a parked car.
—Evan Davis

The fork serves a number of purposes. Most obviously, it connects the front wheel to the handlebar. Of course, the fork allows the bike to be steered, and it supports the front brake.

The fork also offsets the front hub some distance forward of the steering axis (Fig. 14.1). This offset distance (called "fork rake," R in Fig. 14.1), combined with the steering axis (the "head angle," q in Fig. 14.1) and the wheel size (the radius, r, in Fig. 14.1), determine how your bike is going to handle and steer.

All forks—even rigid road forks (Fig. 14.2) provide at least a minimum amount of suspension by allowing the front wheel to move up and down. The steering axis angles the fork forward from vertical, while the front hub is offset farther forward yet, and these things make it possible for any fork to flex along its length and absorb vertical shocks.

Virtually every road bike fork is made up of a simple combination of components: the steering tube, the fork crown, the fork legs (sometimes called "blades"), and the fork ends (also called "dropouts" or "fork tips"). Figure 14.2 illustrates these parts on a rigid fork. Forks for cyclo-cross bikes and some touring bikes also have cantilever or V-brake posts (Fig. 14.3). Road bike forks are manufactured from steel, aluminum, carbon fiber, titanium, and countless mixes of these materials.

xiv-1 FORK INSPECTION

For the most part, forks are pretty durable, but they do break occasionally. A fork failure can ruin your day, because the means of control of the bike is eliminated. Such loss of control usually precedes the rapid acceleration of your body downward onto the road, resulting in substantial pain.

Ever since I first opened my frame-building shop, people have regularly brought in what has grown to be an amazing collection of broken forks of all types to show me or in hopes that I could repair them.

14.1 Front-end geometry of a bicycle

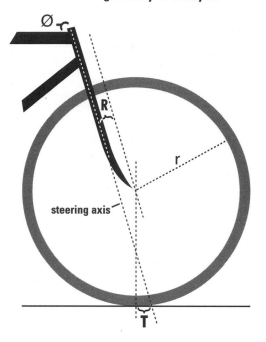

14.2 Rigid fork

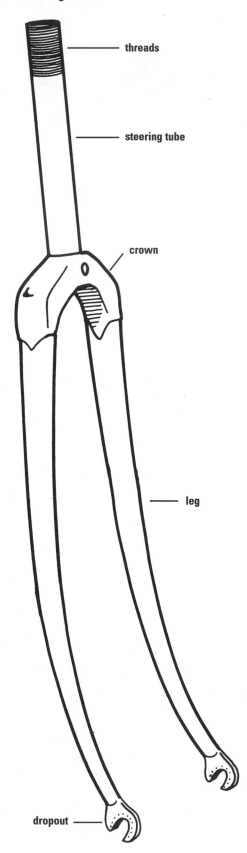

Some of the forks had broken with catastrophic consequences. Some had steering tubes broken either at the fork crown or in the threads. Others had fork crowns that broke or separated (releasing a fork leg or two), fork legs that folded, cantilever posts that snapped, and front dropouts that bent over or broke off. You can go a long way toward preventing problems like these by regularly inspecting your fork.

With that in mind, get into the habit of checking your fork regularly for any warning signs of impending failure. Obvious things to look for include bends, cracks, and stressed paint. On carbon forks, look for cut or torn fibers or loose glue bonds on the dropouts, fork crown, or steering tube.

If you have crashed your bike, give the fork an especially thorough inspection. If you find any indication that the fork has been damaged, replace it. A new fork is cheaper than emergency room charges, brain surgery, or an electric wheelchair.

When you inspect a fork, remove the front wheel, wipe any dirt off, and look under the crown and

FORK INSPECTION

14.3 **Cyclo-cross fork**

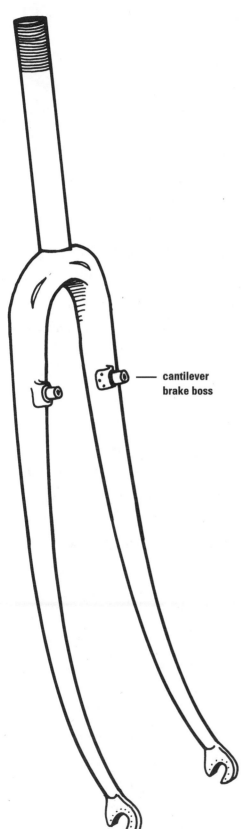

cantilever
brake boss

14.4 **Types of fork damage**

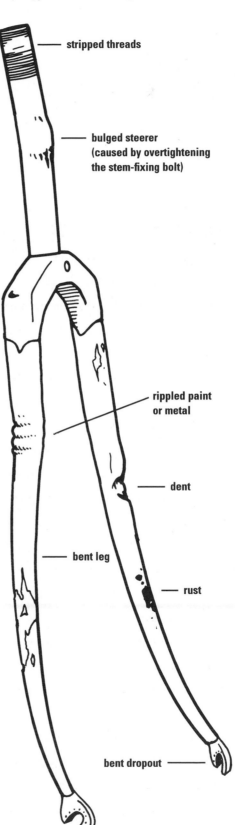

stripped threads

bulged steerer
(caused by overtightening
the stem-fixing bolt)

rippled paint
or metal

dent

bent leg

rust

bent dropout

FORK

INSPECTION

between the fork legs. Carefully examine all of the outside areas. Look for any areas where the paint or finish looks cracked or stretched. Look for bent parts, from little ripples in fork legs to bent dropouts (Fig. 14.4). Skewed or broken cantilever posts are something to look for on cyclo-cross and touring forks (Fig. 14.3).

Put the wheel back in and watch to see if the fork legs twist when you tighten the hub into the dropouts. Check to make sure that a true wheel centers under the fork crown. If it doesn't, turn the wheel around and put it back in the fork to determine whether the misalignment is in the fork or the supposedly true wheel. If the wheel lines up off to one side when it is in one way and off the same amount to the other side when it is in the other way, the wheel is off, and the fork is straight. If the wheel is skewed off to the same side in the fork no matter which direction you place the wheel, the fork is misaligned.

I recommend overhauling your headset annually (Chapter 11, §xi-16 and §xi-17); when you do, carefully examine the steering tube for any signs of stress or damage. Check for bent, cracked, or stretched areas, stripped threads (Fig. 14.4), a bulging threaded steering tube where the stem expands inside or a crimped threadless steering tube where the stem clamps around its top. Look for cracks on a carbon steering tube where the stem is clamped on, and make sure that there is an expandable or glue-in support inside the steering tube under the stem clamp.

With a threaded fork, hold the stem up next to the steering tube to make sure that, when your stem is inserted to the depth you have been using it, the bottom of the stem is always more than an inch below the bottom of the steering-tube threads. If the stem is expanded in the treaded region, you are ask-

ing for trouble; the threads cut the steering-tube wall thickness down by about 50 percent, and each thread offers a sharp breakage plane along which the tube can cleave.

xiv-2 FORK DAMAGE

If your inspection has uncovered some damage that does not automatically require fork replacement, here are some guidelines to go by and means of repair.

a. Dents

Not all fork dents threaten the integrity of the fork. A small dent in a steel fork usually poses little risk; a large dent (Fig. 14.4) demands attention (replace the fork). Carbon forks don't tend to dent. If yours has a dent, that is a cause for concern, but you would usually see shattered clear coat and perhaps separated fibers in the area as well.

b. Fork misalignment

Within limits, a rigid steel fork can be realigned if it is slightly off center (see §xiv-3b). Aluminum, carbon-fiber, and titanium cannot be realigned. Don't try it!

c. Stripped steering-tube threads

If the threads on the steering tube are damaged (Fig. 14.4) so that the headset slips when you try to tighten it, you need to replace the fork. If the steering tube is bulged, it also needs to be replaced, because it can split.

On a steel fork, you can have a frame builder replace the steering tube, but it is hardly worth it.

d. Obvious bend, ripple, or crease in fork legs

Replace the fork if ripples and bends are obvious (Fig. 14.4). The poor handling and potential breakage pose too great a threat to your safety to be worth saving a few bucks.

14.5 Measuring dropout spacing

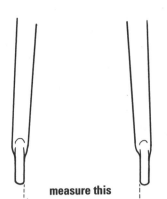

measure this

14.6 Installing dropout-alignment tool and bending the dropout with it

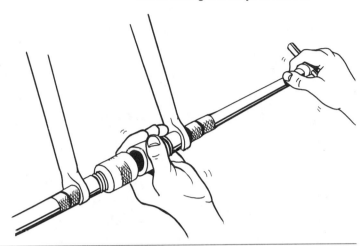

e. Bent or stripped cantilever bosses

Some cantilever studs can be unscrewed with an 8mm open-end wrench and replaced. It is a good idea to use a thread-locking compound on the threads of the new mount.

On many touring and cyclo-cross forks, the entire cantilever boss is welded on (Fig. 14.3). Bent or stripped cantilever bosses on such forks usually mean that you have to buy a new fork. If you have a frame builder in your area, he or she may be able to weld or braze a new one on a steel, titanium, or aluminum fork. You will also need to repaint the fork; all that work may cost more than a new fork, by the way.

xiv-3 MAINTAINING ROAD FORKS

LEVEL 3

Beyond touching up the paint on steel forks and performing regular inspections, the only maintenance procedure for a rigid road fork is to check the alignment (§xiv-3a) if your bike is handling badly. You can perform minor realignment on a steel fork if you find that it is off center, but note that it is risky enough to qualify as a level 3 job. Do not try to realign titanium, carbon-fiber, or aluminum forks.

a. Check fork alignment

You will need a ruler, a true front wheel, and dropout-alignment tools (Fig. 1.4). If you have an aluminum, titanium, or carbon-fiber fork, this procedure is diagnostic only, because you should not try to realign any of these forks. Checking the alignment may help explain bike-handling problems.

If you find the alignment to be off more than a couple of millimeters in any direction with any fork other than a steel unsuspended one, you will need a new fork. If the fork is new, misalignment should be covered by the warranty.

If a steel fork is more than 8mm off in any direction, you ought to get a new fork. If the dropouts of a steel fork are slightly bent, you can realign them. You can also take a moderately bent (less than 8mm off) steel fork to a frame builder or a bike shop for realignment. Make sure that whomever you take it to is properly equipped with a fork jig or alignment table and is well versed in the art of "cold setting" (a fancy term for bending) steel forks.

1. Remove the fork from the bike (Chapter 11, §xi-16 and §xi-17).

2. With the front wheel out, measure the spacing

14.7 Correct dropout alignment

14.8 Incorrect dropout alignment (dropout is twisted or right fork leg is bent back)

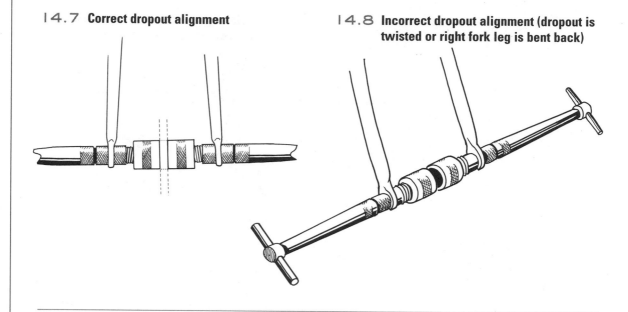

between the faces of the dropouts (Fig. 14.5). Adult bikes should have a spacing of 100mm between the inner surfaces of the dropouts. (Some low-end kids' bikes have narrower spacing—about 90mm or so. But if that's the type of bike you are working with, don't bother checking alignment; it isn't worth the trouble.) Remember that you are measuring the distance between the flat surfaces that meet the hub-axle faces (and not between wheel-retaining nubs that protrude inward from the dropouts on some forks). Dropout spacing as wide as 102mm and as narrow as 99mm is acceptable. Beyond that in either direction means a trip to the bike shop for a new fork. If you have a steel fork, you can take it to a bike shop or frame builder for alignment.

3. Clamp the steering tube of the fork in a bike stand or between V-blocks in a vise. Install the dropout-alignment tools (Fig. 14.6). The tools are made so that they can be used on either the fork or the rear triangle of the bike, and thus they have two axle diameters and spacers for use in the wider rear dropouts. Move all of the spacers to the outside of the dropouts so that only the cups of the tools are placed inside of the dropouts. Install the tools so that the shafts are seated up against the tops of the dropout slots. Tighten the handles down.

4. Ideally, the ends of the cups on the dropout-aligning tools should be parallel and lined up with each other (Fig. 14.7). The cups of Campagnolo dropout-alignment tools are non-adjustable and are nominally 50mm in length; the ideal space between their ends is 0.1–0.5mm. The cups on Park dropout-aligning tools (illustrated in Figures 14.6, 14.7, and 14.8) are adjustable in length, so that you can bring the faces up close to each other no matter what the dropout spacing. If they are lined up with each other, and the dropouts are spaced between 99mm and 102mm apart, continue to step 5. If a steel rigid fork's dropouts are not lined up straight across with each other (Fig. 14.8), and the dropouts are within the 99–102mm spacing range, skip to §xiv-3b to align them.

14.9 **Correct alignment of wheel valve hole in a straight fork**

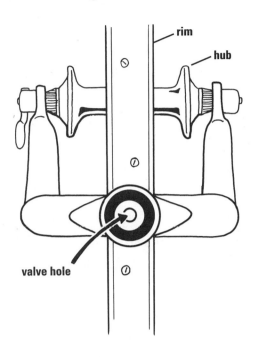

rim

hub

valve hole

14.10 **Sighting through steering tube to check fork alignment**

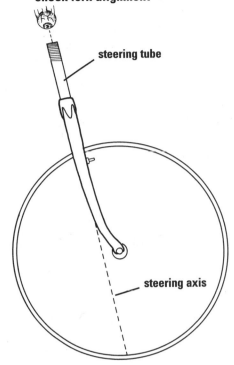

steering tube

steering axis

NOTE: *It is very important that the dropout faces are parallel before continuing with step 5, or the rest of the alignment procedures will be a waste of time. Clamping the hub into misaligned dropouts will force the fork legs to twist. If the dropouts are misaligned, any measurement of the side-to-side and fore-and-aft alignment of the fork legs will not be accurate.*

5. Remove the tire from the front wheel. Make sure the wheel is true and properly dished (Chapter 13, §xiii-4 and §xiii-5).

6. Install the wheel in the fork. Make sure the axle is seated against the top of the dropout slot on either side, and make sure the quick-release skewer is tight. Lightly push the rim from side to side to make certain that there is no play in the front hub. If there is play, you first must adjust the hub (Chapter 6).

7. Look down the steering tube and through the valve hole to the bottom side of the rim (Fig.

14.9). The steering tube should be lined up with this line of sight through the wheel (Fig. 14.10).

(a) When you are sighting through the steering tube and the valve hole, you should see the same amount of space between either side of the rim and the sides of the steering tube. You should also see the center of the bottom side of the rim through the valve hole.

(b) Turn the wheel around and install it again so that what was the right end of the axle is now the left and vice versa. Sight through the steering tube and the wheel valve hole again.

(c) Placing the wheel in the fork both ways corrects for deformation in the axle or any wobble in the wheel. If the wheel is true and dished properly, and the axle is in good shape, the wheel should line up exactly as it did before. If it does not line

14.11 Checking fore-and-aft alignment of forks

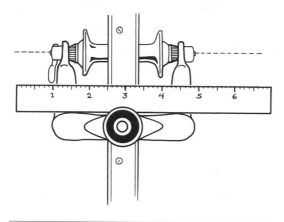

up, but is off by the same amount to one side as it is to the opposite side when the wheel is turned around, the wheel is off and the fork is fine side-to-side.

(d) If this test indicates that the fork is as much as 2–3mm off to the side, that is close enough; continue on. If it is off by more than 3mm, get a new fork or have it aligned by a frame builder (if it is steel, that is; do not try to realign suspension, titanium, carbon-fiber, or aluminum forks).

NOTE: *If you are sighting through the wheel in this way and you cannot see the bottom side of the rim through the valve hole because the hub is in the way, the fork has big problems. In order for the bike to handle properly, the fork must have some forward offset of the front hub from the steering axis. This offset, or "rake," is usually around 4–5cm. If you sight through the steering tube and see the front hub, the fork is bent backward so much that it has little or no offset! If this is the case, you need a new fork.*

8. With the wheel still in the fork, place a ruler on edge across the fork blades just below the fork crown (Fig. 14.11). Make sure the ruler is perpendicular to the steering tube.

9. Holding the ruler in place, lift the fork toward a light source so that you are sighting across the ruler and the front hub toward the light. The ruler's edge should line up parallel with the fronts of the dropouts (or with the axle ends sticking out of either end of the hub) (Fig. 14.11). This test will tell you whether one fork leg is bent back relative to the other one. If the two line up parallel or very close to that, the fork alignment has checked out completely, and you can put the fork back in the bike. If one fork leg is considerably behind the other, you need to get a new fork or have this one aligned. If the dropout-alignment tools also indicated that one dropout was ahead of the other (Fig. 14.8), then the fork legs alone could be bent, and not the dropouts.

b. Align dropouts on rigid steel fork

You can only do this with a steel, nonsuspension fork!

Dropouts are easy to tweak out of alignment; simply pulling the bike off a roof rack and failing to lift it high enough to clear the rack skewer will do it. Forks can also come with misaligned dropouts to start with.

If the dropout is bent more than 7 degrees or so, or if the paint is cracked at the dropout where it is bent, it may be dangerous to bend it back. Replace the fork.

1. Install dropout-alignment tools and check alignment as described in steps 3 and 4 of §xiv-3a. If one alignment tool is ahead of the other (Fig. 14.8), it could indicate that (a) the dropouts are bent, (b) one fork leg is ahead of the other (which you checked for in §xiv-3a, steps 8 and 9, or (c) a combination of both problems.

2. If the dropouts are not aligned, and the fork spacing is between 99mm and 102mm, and step

9 of §xiv-3a indicated that both fork legs are parallel, then you can align the dropouts. If the fork spacing is wider than 102mm or less than 99mm, there is no point in aligning the dropout faces, because you must bend the fork legs as well to correct the spacing. Without an alignment table or fork jig, you cannot do this accurately. You should get a new fork, or have a qualified mechanic or frame builder align your steel fork. If your fork spacing is between 99mm and 102mm, clamp the crown or unicrown of the fork very tightly between two wood blocks in a well-anchored vise.

3. Grab the end of the dropout-alignment tool handle with one hand and the cup of the tool with the other (Fig. 14.6). Bend each dropout until the open faces of the dropout-alignment tools are parallel and the edges line straight up with each other (Fig. 14.7).

4. Remove the tools, and continue with §xiv-3b, step 5.

xiv-4 FORK UPGRADES

You may be able to improve the ride of your bike by replacing the fork. There are a number of reasons to do this. To lighten the bike and add gee-whiz value, you could get a carbon-fiber fork. To stiffen the ride, you could get a steel fork. To lighten the bike and get a more rigid fork-to-bar connection, you could switch to a threadless system (see Chapter 11 on headsets for the difference between threaded and threadless systems). And to reduce aerodynamic drag, you could get an aero fork.

Make sure you get a fork with the same length steering tube as your old fork (unless you are also switching to a threadless system, in which case you will just get a long, unthreaded steering tube). Chapter 11 covers the installation of the headset.

The crowns on many carbon forks are so thick that they require an extra-long brake nut to be able to reach the brake bolt. Such a nut should be supplied with the fork.

FORKS

FORK
UPGRADES

CHAPTER 15

FRAMES

Duct tape is like The Force.
It has a light side, a dark side, and it holds the universe together.
—Carl Zwanzig

2.5mm, 3mm, 4mm, and 5mm hex keys

a true rear wheel

oil

grease

OPTIONAL

derailleur-hanger-alignment tool

string

ruler

dropout-alignment tools

metric taps

bottom-bracket tap set

electric drill

drill-bit set

16mm wrench

8mm open-end wrench

P ay close attention to the frame, because it is what holds your entire bike together. It is one item that is nearly impossible to fix on the road, and if it fails, the consequences can be serious.

xv-1 FRAME DESIGN

The traditional rigid "double-diamond" design of a road bike frame relies on a "front triangle" and a "rear triangle" (Fig. 15.1); never mind that the front triangle is not actually a triangle—or much of a diamond, for that matter.

Referring to Figure 15.2, the angle of the seat tube relative to the horizontal (the "seat angle") determines the fore-and-aft position of the rider relative to the pedals. It also plays a role in determining the weight distribution on the wheels. And seat angle partially dictates the length of the chainstays, because the more tipped-back the seat tube is, the farther back the rear wheel will have to be to avoid hitting it.

For a given top-tube length and front-end geometry, the seat angle also dictates whether your feet hit the front wheel or not when pedaling around a tight, low-speed turn (the interference is called, quaintly these days, "toe-clip overlap"). And unless the frame tubing is altered to compensate, the vertical and lateral compliance of the rear of the bike will increase with decreasing seat angles and correspondingly longer chainstays.

The angle of the head tube relative to the horizontal (the "head angle")—in combination with the fork rake (explained at the beginning of Chapter 14) and wheel diameter—determines much of the steering and handling characteristics of the bike. These two items also dictate in large part how much shock is absorbed by the fork.

The height of the bottom bracket above the ground determines how much clearance you will have for your pedals when rounding a turn. (Low

I5.I The frame and its parts

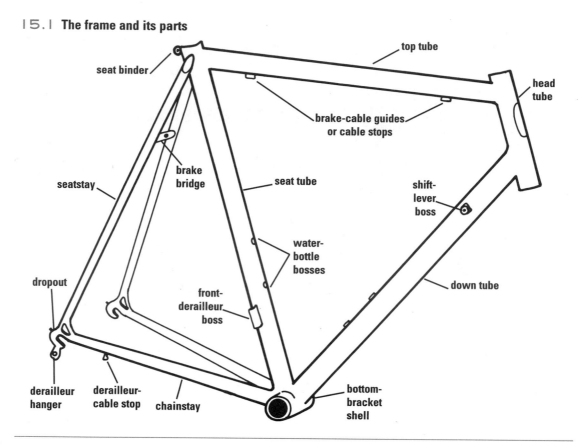

bottom brackets impart a feeling of stability. Compromises between cornering clearance and stability are often made by frame builders, especially in pro-level bikes where it is assumed the rider will have sufficient experience to always corner with the inner crank up.) Along with the seat-tube length and angle, the bottom-bracket height also helps determine the stand-over clearance your crotch has over the top tube.

The top-tube length—along with the stem length, seat angle, and seat fore-and-aft position on the seatpost—determines your reach to the handlebar.

The seat-tube length (or "frame size") determines the amount of seatpost extension you will get for a given seat height, as well as the minimum seat height possible on the bike. It also is one of the variables determining stand-over height.

The wheel base is the distance between the wheel axles. It determines the minimum possible turning radius.

Some frames are designed for improved aerodynamic performance and have wing-shaped tubes and a low-profile design to reduce air drag.

On modern road bike frames, the shift-lever boss on the down tube shown in Figure 15.1 is generally replaced by a threaded shift-cable stop to accept a barrel adjuster, and this is usually located either on the head tube or on the down tube near the intersection of these two tubes.

xv-2 FRAME MATERIALS

A materials evolution has accompanied the development of the bicycle ever since its birth. Wood was the material of choice for the first bikes, but was soon replaced by steel, aluminum, and even bamboo. Steel, aluminum, and carbon composites are the materials

15.2 Frame dimensions

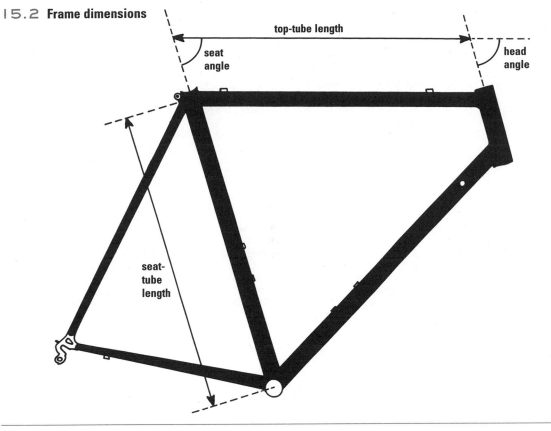

seat angle

top-tube length

head angle

seat-tube length

most commonly used to build frames today, but titanium, magnesium, and metal matrix composites account for a significant share at the more expensive end. Bicyclists are reaping benefits from the end of the Cold War by riding on parts made of materials produced by former defense contractors looking for new markets after their gravy train dried up.

Because the materials used in road bike frames come in a variety of grades with varying costs and physical properties, let's assume for the following discussion that I am talking about the highest grades used in bicycles. For example, the aluminum used in pop cans and window frames is much weaker than the 7000-series aluminum used in high-end bicycle-frames.

Steel has the highest modulus of elasticity (a principal determinant of stiffness) as well as the highest density and tensile strength of any of the metals commonly used in frames. Aluminum has a much lower modulus, density, and tensile strength than steel; titanium has a modulus, density, and tensile strength between the two. With good frame design and construction combined with intelligent selection of tube properties, diameters, shapes, and wall thicknesses, long-lasting frames with comparable stiffness-to-weight and/or strength-to-weight ratios can be built from any of these metals.

Butting of metal tubing reduces weight by putting thicker material at the tube ends and thinning the center sections. "Double-butted" means that both ends are thicker than the center section, whereas "triple-butting" and "quad-butting" refer to gradation steps in the thickness at the ends.

Alloying and heat-treating of most metals make a huge difference in their tensile strengths. Low-carbon steel (like gas pipe) is soft and easy to bend

FRAME

MATERIALS

and break. High-carbon steels alloyed with chromium, molybdenum, and other materials are far stronger; heat-treating makes them stronger yet. The same goes for aluminum. One improvement in aluminum for bicycles is alloying it with the element scandium, which raises aluminum's strength considerably. Most aluminum frames require a postweld heat-treatment step, or they will be soft and breakable.

Titanium alloyed with 3 percent aluminum and 2.5 percent vanadium (3Al/2.5V) is far stronger than commercially pure (CP) titanium, which is 98 percent titanium. Titanium alloyed with 6 percent aluminum and 4 percent vanadium (6Al/4V) is stronger yet but is rarely drawn into tubing, so 6/4 bike tubes are generally made from rolled and welded sheet, which can reduce aesthetics and ultimate strength somewhat. Titanium, like steel, requires no postweld heat treatment, but it must be welded in an inert-gas atmosphere or it will oxidize and become extremely brittle.

Advertising claims touting one frame-tubing material over another can be misleading, because you may not know whether a manufacturer is comparing its material with the high-strength alloyed forms of competitors' materials. If scandium-alloyed aluminum is compared with commercially pure titanium, for example, it comes off looking much better than if it were compared with hardened 6/4 or 3/2.5 titanium, but the consumer just sees "titanium" listed in the advertisement.

Carbon-fiber, boron-fiber, and similar composite frame materials consist of fibers embedded in a resin (plastic) matrix. These materials can be very light, very strong, and very stiff. Bikes can be built by gluing carbon-fiber tubes into lugs (usually made of carbon fiber or aluminum), by gluing several large, molded subassemblies together, or by molding the frame in a single piece ("monocoque" construction).

The big advantage of carbon composites is that extra composite fabric can be added into sections of the mold to add thickness precisely where extra strength is needed. The tricky part is holding the composite parts together in a frame that does not come apart.

Metal-matrix composite frame materials contain additions of ingredients that improve mechanical properties (usually tensile strength). These additions are not alloying materials (i.e., they are not melted together with the metal), because that would generally contaminate the metal. Rather, particles of sand-like materials (aluminum oxide, silicon oxide, etc.) are worked into the metal (usually aluminum) without melting the particles. The trick with metal-matrix composites is making them weldable without weakening the frame at the joints.

Frame builders endlessly experiment with all sorts of exotic materials that offer mechanical advantages. Beryllium, for example, was commonly used in the defense industry. Its light weight and low density coupled with high strength and stiffness made it an ideal material to use on the nose cones of nuclear missiles. Well, they're not making too many of those any more, so a few folks have tried building bikes out of the stuff. It works great but has the drawback of being poisonous if ingested or inhaled; I advise against trying to taste or snort a beryllium frame.

xv-3 FRAME INSPECTION

You can avoid potentially dangerous frame failures by inspecting your frame frequently. If you find damage, and you are not sure how dangerous the

15.3 Checking derailleur-hanger alignment

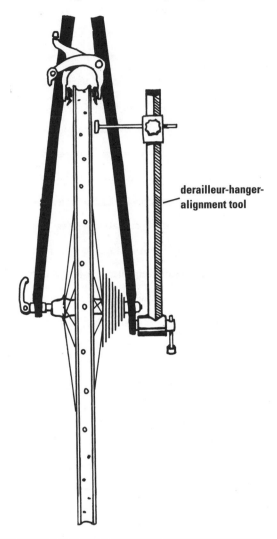

derailleur-hanger-alignment tool

bike may be to ride, take it to a bike shop for advice.

1. Clean the frame every few rides, so that you can spot problems early.

2. Inspect all tubes for cracks, bends, buckles, dents, and paint stretching or cracking, especially near the joints where stress is highest. If in doubt, take it to an expert for advice.

3. Inspect the rear dropouts and the welds or glue joints around the brake bridge and chainstay bridge (the little cross-tube between the chainstays just behind the bottom bracket on some frames) for cracks (see Fig. 15.1 for names and

locations of frame parts). Check to be sure the dropouts (and brake posts and cable hangers on cyclo-cross and touring frames) are not bent. Some dropouts and brake posts bolt on and are replaceable, and some cable hangers are glued in and replaceable. Otherwise, badly bent or broken dropouts, brake posts, and cable hangers need to be replaced; a frame builder in your area may be able to do the job.

4. Remove the seatpost every few months and invert the bike to remove any water that might have collected in the seat tube, and let it dry out. On steel frames, look for deeply rusted areas. Look and feel for rust inside, or for rust falling out. I recommend squirting oil or a rust-preventing spray for bicycle-frames (like Frame Saver) inside the tubes periodically. With thin-walled steel tubing, the time between commencement of rusting and of rusting through can be short. Often, you will see bubbles in the paint, for example, around the bottom-bracket joints or on the back of the seat tube. Although bubbles can indicate paint problems, they often indicate that the seat tube has pinholes rusted through it under the paint. Remember to grease both the seatpost and the inside of the seat tube when you reinsert the seatpost. After sanding off the rust, touch up any external areas where the paint has come off with touch-up paint or nail polish (hey, it's available in lots of cool colors).

5. Check that a true and properly dished rear wheel sits straight in the frame, centered between the chainstays and seatstays and lined up in the same plane as the front triangle. Check that tightening the hub skewer does not result in bowing or twisting of either the chainstays or the seatstays.

CHECK AND
STRAIGHTEN
REAR-
DERAILLEUR
HANGER
—
CHECK FRAME
ALIGNMENT
AND ADJUST
DROPOUT
ALIGNMENT

15.4 **Checking frame alignment with a string**

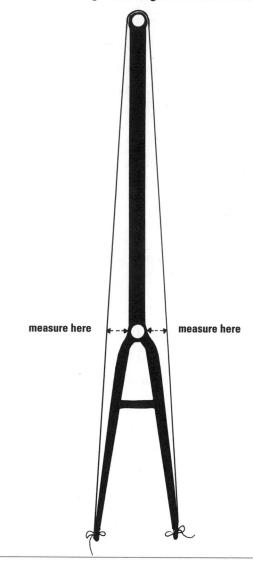

measure here   measure here

15.5 **Measuring dropout width**

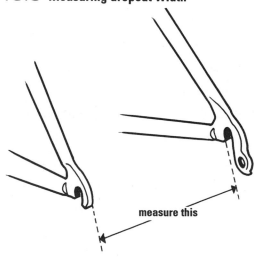

measure this

xv-4 CHECK AND STRAIGHTEN REAR-DERAILLEUR HANGER

1. If you have a derailleur-hanger-alignment tool (Fig. 1.4), thread it into the derailleur hanger on the right dropout (Fig. 15.3).

2. Install a true rear wheel in the frame.

3. Swing the tool around, measuring the spacing between its arm and the rim all of the way around. The arm of the tool should be the same distance from the rim at all points. Some tools, like the one shown in Figure 15.3, have a setscrew extending from the arm that you can adjust to check the spacing; others require you to measure the gap with a ruler or caliper.

4. If the tool has play in it, keep it pushed inward lightly as you perform all of the measurements, or you will get inconsistent data.

5. If the spacing between the tool arm and the rim is not consistent (within a millimeter or two all of the way around), carefully bend the hanger by pulling outward lightly on the arm of the tool where it is closest to the rim.

6. If the derailleur hanger is severely bent, you may not be able to align it without breaking it (you may even have trouble threading the tool in, because the threaded hole will be ovalized). If you have a replaceable bolt-on dropout, replace it.

7. If the threads or the hanger itself are really screwed up, and you do not have a replaceable dropout, see §xv-7b for other derailleur hanger options.

xv-5 CHECK FRAME ALIGNMENT AND ADJUST DROPOUT ALIGNMENT

Exacting alignment checks require a precision surface plate, an uncommon

15.6 Using dropout-alignment tools on rear dropouts

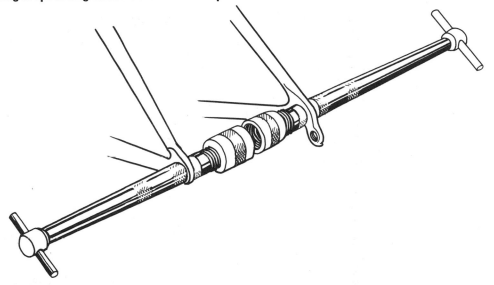

tool in the home workshop. Thus, the following meth-ods for determining frame alignment are inexact, but sufficient for determining gross alignment woes.

If you find problems more severe than moder-ately bent dropouts or a misaligned derailleur hanger, do not attempt to correct them. Adjusting frame alignment, if it can be done at all, should only be performed with an accurate frame-alignment table by someone who is practiced in its use.

1. With the frame clamped in a bike stand, tie the end of a string to one rear dropout. Stretch it tightly around the head tube, and tie it sym-metrically to the other dropout (Fig. 15.4).

2. Measure from the string to the seat tube on each side (Fig. 15.4). The measurement should be the same within 1mm.

3. Put a true and properly dished rear wheel in the frame and check that it lines up in the same plane as the front triangle. Make certain that the wheel is centered between the seatstays and chainstays. If you have dropouts with tip screws that thread in from the back of the dropout, turn one or the other of them so that your true wheel

lines up straight behind the seat tube (centered between the chainstays). The hub should slide easily into the dropouts without requiring you to pull outward or push inward on the dropouts. Tightening the hub quick release should not result in bowing or twisting of frame members.

4. Remove the wheel and measure the spacing between the dropouts (Fig. 15.5). For eight-, nine-, or ten-speed rear hubs, this spacing should be 130mm. Measure the width of the rear hub with a caliper to see what the rear-end spac-ing of the frame should be. If the spacing on the frame is 1mm less or 1.5mm more than nomi-nal, it is acceptable. For instance, if you have a frame whose rear spacing should be 130mm, acceptable spacing is 129mm to 131.5mm.

5. If you have dropout-alignment tools, put them in the dropouts so that their shafts are fully seated into the dropouts (Fig. 15.6). If you have dropouts with tip screws that thread in from the back of the dropout, you can remove them and seat the dropout-alignment tools all of the way to the rear of the dropout slots. Alternatively, you can leave

them installed, and before installing the dropout-alignment tools, turn one or the other of them until a true wheel lines up straight behind the seat tube. Arrange the tool spacers (and the cups, if they are adjustable) so that the faces of the cups are within a millimeter of each other. Tighten the handles on the tools. The tool cups should line up straight across from each other, with their faces exactly parallel. If the tools do not align, one or both dropouts are bent. If you have replaceable dropouts, go ahead and replace one or both of them. If you have a composite or bonded rear triangle of any kind, there is nothing you can do about the problem if the bike is not equipped with replaceable dropouts. If the bike has a steel rear triangle, you can align the dropouts by bending them carefully with the dropout-alignment tools. Hold the cup of the tool with one hand and push or pull on the handle with the other. Aluminum or titanium rear dropouts can sometimes be aligned, but it is something you should have a shop do. Titanium is hard to bend because it keeps springing back, and you run a great risk of breaking aluminum by bending.

CAUTION: *Never heat the dropouts (or any part of the frame) for alignment purposes. Doing so could irreparably change the strength, temper, or hardness of the part and lead to further damage.*

xv-6 CORRECTING FRAME DAMAGE

Other than alignment items already covered in this chapter, the only frame problems you can correct are damaged threads, chipped paint, and small dents. Broken braze-ons and bent, broken, or deeply dented tubes call for a new frame or require a frame builder to perform the repair.

xv-7 FIXING DAMAGED THREADS

a. Retapping and using a new bolt

A road bike frame has threads in the bottom-bracket shell, the water-bottle bosses, and the rear-derailleur hanger. In addition, some bikes have a threaded seat binder, some have cantilever brake posts, and some have a small threaded hole in the bottom of the bottom-bracket shell to which a derailleur-cable guide is bolted.

1. If any threads on the frame are stripped or cross-threaded, try chasing through the threads with the appropriate thread tap. Then replace the bolt or bottom-bracket cup with a new one. Whenever you retap any threads, use oil on the tap (use canola vegetable oil on titanium threads). Specific thread-cutting oil is not necessary on old threads because they are already cut. The following tap sizes are commonly found on most road bikes:

Water-bottle bosses and the hole for a plastic shift-cable guide:	M5 (5mm x 0.8)
Hole under bottom-bracket shell for derailleur-cable guide:	M5 (5mm x 0.8)
Seat binders and brake posts:	M6 (6mm x 1)
Derailleur hanger:	M10 (10mm x 1)
Bottom-bracket shells, English thread:	1.37 inches x 24 tpi (threads per inch)

NOTE: *Remember, the drive-side (right side) English bottom-bracket threads are left-hand threaded; the other side is right-hand threaded.*

Bottom-bracket shells, Italian thread:	36mm x 24tpi

NOTE: *Remember, Italian bottom-bracket shells are right-hand threaded on both ends.*

CORRECTING
FRAME
DAMAGE
—
FIXING
DAMAGED
THREADS

2. Turn the tap forward (clockwise) a bit, then turn it back, then forward (two steps forward and one back), etc., to prevent the tap from binding and possibly breaking. Be aware that taps are made of very hard and brittle steel. If you put any side or twisting forces on small taps, they can easily break. If the tap breaks, you'll have a real mess; the broken tap in the hole is harder than the frame and it's impossible to drill the broken tap out. If you break off a tap in the frame, do not try to get it out yourself. Take it to a bike shop, a machine shop, or a frame builder before you break off what little is left sticking out. Unless you put the tap in crooked, breaking one should not be a problem when retapping damaged frame threads because these threads will be so worn; getting the tap to find any metal to bite into will probably be your biggest problem.

IMPORTANT NOTE: *Tapping a bottom-bracket shell requires expertise. If you have never done it before and want to do it yourself, get some expert supervision. In addition to making sure that you place the correct tap in the correct end of the shell, you must also be certain that the taps go in straight. Most bottom-bracket taps have a shaft between the two taps to keep them parallel to each other (see Fig. 1.4). They must both be started at the same time from both ends. If you mess up the threads, you can ruin your frame. So if in doubt, ask an expert.*

b. Other specific remedies

1. **Damaged water-bottle bosses.** Some bike shops have a tool that rivets bottle bosses into the frame. Check for this possibility first, because you can avoid a new paint job that way. But note that these riveted bosses tend to

15.7 Inserting Dropout Saver in damaged derailleur hanger

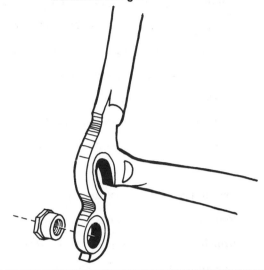

loosen up over time, especially if the bottle-cage bolts are overtightened. Otherwise, take the bike to a frame builder to get a new boss welded or brazed in.

2. **Damaged threads in rear-derailleur hanger.** Some bikes have replaceable rear dropouts or derailleur hangers that bolt onto the frame. If your bike doesn't, one option is to use a "Dropout Saver" derailleur-hanger backing nut (Fig. 15.7) made by Wheels Manufacturing and available at bike shops. The Dropout Saver is simply a sleeve threaded the same as the dropout, with 16mm wrench flats. You drill out the hole in the damaged derailleur hanger with a $^{15}\!/_{32}$-inch drill bit, push the Dropout Saver in from the back side, and screw in the derailleur. Dropout Savers come in two lengths, depending on the thickness of the dropout. Another option is to saw off the derailleur hanger with a hacksaw and use a separate derailleur hanger from a cheap bike that fits flat against the outside of the dropout and is held in by the hub-axle bolts or quick

release. You could have the dropout replaced by a frame builder (i.e., have a new one welded or brazed on), or as a final option, you could always get a new frame.

3. **Damaged seat binders.** Drill out the threads and install a quick release or a bolt and nut. Seat-binder threads rarely get stripped, however; it is usually the bolt that is the problem, and that's easy to replace.

4. **Damaged bottom-bracket-shell threads.** You can use an old-style Mavic (now Stronglight) bottom bracket (Chapter 8, §viii-10b, Fig. 8.16), if you can still find one, because it does not depend on the threads in the shell to anchor it. Mavic stopped producing these bottom brackets in 1995, but Stronglight took up making them. You must have a shop bevel the ends of the bottom-bracket shell with a special Mavic cutting tool. If the shop has the cutting tool, it likely will have the tools to install the bottom bracket as well.

5. **Damaged bottom-bracket cable-guide threads.** A new hole in the bottom of the bottom bracket can be drilled and tapped, or the stripped hole can be tapped out with larger threads for a larger screw. Make sure the screw you use is short enough that it does not protrude into the inside of the bottom-bracket shell.

6. **Damaged brake posts and bosses.** Some brake posts are replaceable; they have wrench flats (usually 8mm) at the base, and they thread into a boss welded to the frame. If the posts are not of this type, you will have to ask a frame builder to install a new boss.

REPAIR
CHIPPED PAINT
AND SMALL
DENTS
—
MAINTENANCE
OF PIVOTLESS
SUSPENSION
FRAME

xv-8 REPAIR CHIPPED PAINT AND SMALL DENTS

Fixing paint chips is simply a matter of cleaning the area and applying a bit of touch-up paint. Sand any chipped paint or rust completely away before repainting. Use a touch-up paint made for your bike, model paint of a similar color, or fingernail polish.

Small dents can be filled with automotive body putty, but there is little point to filling them if you are only doing a paint touch-up, because the repaired area probably won't look that great anyway.

There are plenty of frame painters around the country who can fill dents, repaint frames, and even match original decals. Many of them advertise in bike magazines or can be found on the Internet.

xv-9 MAINTENANCE OF PIVOTLESS SUSPENSION FRAME

Suspension frames are rare on road bikes, but the majority of those that do exist have no pivots on which suspension members rotate. Instead, they rely on the flexibility of various frame members. Suspension frames without moving pivots fall into two broad categories: beam bikes, where the saddle is mounted not on a seatpost but rather out on the end of a long cantilevered beam (Fig. 10.11), and bikes with a shock that depend on the flexure of the chainstays, rather than the pivoting of a rear swingarm.

The beam suspension with the longest heritage is the Softride "viscoelastic" flexible composite beam (Fig. 10.11), and many frame builders have offered frames for it. Zipp and Softride beams also exist that do not flex along their length, but rather at the mount on the frame. Softride and Zipp beams themselves are generally maintenance free; the mounting points on the frame feel high forces and are candidates for failure, though. Inspect the beam-mounting points on the frame periodically for fatigue indications (stretched, bulged, or cracking metal or paint). Installation and replacement of the Softride flexible beam is covered in Chapter 10, §x-9.

Another simple and lightweight rear-suspension design relies on the flexure of the chainstays coupled with a small shock behind the seat tube or radically curved seatstays. It is a good idea to check the chainstays frequently for indications of fatigue (stretched, bulged, or cracking metal or paint) as well as the seatstays and shock-mounting points. If a shock is used, it should be kept lubricated and tuned to your weight and riding style.

FRAMES

MAINTENANCE
OF PIVOTLESS
SUSPENSION
FRAME

APPENDIXES

It is better to know some of the questions than all of the answers.
—James Thurber

APPENDIX A

TROUBLESHOOTING INDEX

This index is intended to assist you in finding and fixing problems. If you already know wherein the problem lies, consult the Table of Contents for the chapter covering that part of the bike. If you are not sure which part of the bike is affected, this index can be of assistance. It is organized alphabetically but, because people's descriptions of the same problem vary, you may need to look through the entire list to find your symptom.

This index can assist you with a diagnosis and can recommend a course of action. Following each recommended action are listed chapter numbers to which you can refer for the repair procedure.

SYMPTOM	LIKELY CAUSES	ACTION	CHAPTER
bent wheel	1. maladjusted spokes	true wheel	6
	2. broken spoke	replace spoke	6
	3. bent rim	replace rim	13
bike pulls to one side	1. wheels not true	true wheels	6
	2. tight headset	adjust headset	11
	3. pitted headset	replace headset	11
	4. bent frame	replace or straighten	15
	5. bent fork	replace or straighten	14
	6. loose hub bearings	adjust hubs	6
	7. low tire pressure	inflate tires	2, 6
bike shimmies at high speed	1. frame cracked	replace frame	15
	2. frame bent	replace or straighten	15
	3. wheels way out of true	true wheels	6

SYMPTOM	LIKELY CAUSES	ACTION	CHAPTER
bike shimmies	4. loose hub bearings	adjust hubs	6
at high speed (cont.)	5. headset too loose	tighten headset	11
	6. soft frame/heavy rider	replace frame	15
	7. poor frame design	replace frame	15
bike vibrates	see "chattering and vibration		
when braking	when braking" in Strange Noises		
brake doesn't stop bike	1. maladjusted brake	adjust brake	7
	2. worn brake pads	replace pads	7
	3. wet rims	keep braking	7
	4. greasy rims	clean rims	7
	5. sticky brake cable	lube or replace cable	7
	6. steel rims in wet	use aluminum rims	13
	7. brake damaged	replace brake	7
	8. sticky or bent brake lever	lube or replace lever	7
brake rubs on rim	1. brake misaligned	adjust brake	7
	2. untrue wheel	true wheel	6, 13
chain falls off in front	1. maladjusted front derailleur	adjust front derailleur	5
	2. chain line off	adjust chain line	8
	3. chainring bent or loose	replace or tighten	8
chain jams in front	1. dirty chain	clean chain	4
between chainring	2. bent chainring teeth	replace chainring	8
and chainstay (called	3. chain too narrow	replace chain	4
chain suck)	4. chain line off	adjust chain line	8
	5. stiff links in chain	free links, lube chain	4
chain jams in rear	1. maladjusted rear derailleur	adjust derailleur	5
	2. chain too wide	replace chain	4
	3. small cog not on spline	re-seat cogs	6
	4. poor frame clearance	return to dealer	15
chain skips	1. tight chain link	loosen tight link	4
	2. elongated (worn) chain	replace chain	4
	3. maladjusted derailleur	adjust derailleur	5
	4. worn rear cogs	replace cogs & chain	6, 4
	5. dirty or rusted chain	clean or replace chain	4
	6. bent rear derailleur	replace derailleur	5
	7. bent derailleur hanger	straighten hanger	15

SYMPTOM	LIKELY CAUSES	ACTION	CHAPTER
chain skips (cont.)	8. loose derailleur jockey wheel	tighten jockey wheel	5
	9. bent chain link	replace chain	4
	10. sticky rear shift cable	replace shift cable	5
chain slaps chainstay	1. chain too long	shorten chain	4
	2. weak rear derailleur spring	replace spring or derailleur	5
	3. terrain very bumpy	ignore noise; use lg chainring	n/a
derailleur hits spokes	1. maladjusted rear derailleur	adjust derailleur	5
	2. broken spoke	replace spoke	6
	3. bent rear derailleur	replace derailleur	5
	4. bent derailleur hanger	straighten or replace	15
knee pain	1. poor shoe cleat position	reposition cleat	9
	2. saddle too low or high	adjust saddle	10
	3. clip-in pedal has no float	get floating pedal	9
	4. foot rolled in or out	replace shoes or get orthotics	n/a
pain or fatigue when riding, particularly in the back, neck, and arms	1. incorrect seat position	adjust seat position	10
	2. too much riding	build up miles gradually	
	3. incorrect stem length	replace stem	11
	4. poor frame fit	replace frame	15
pedal(s) move laterally clunk, click, or twist while pedaling	1. loose crankarm	tighten crank bolt	8
	2. pedal loose in crank	tighten pedal to crank	9
	3. bent pedal axle	replace pedal or axle	9
	4. loose bottom bracket	adjust bottom bracket	8
	5. bent bottom bracket axle	replace bottom bracket or axle	8
	6. bent crankarm	replace crankarm	8
	7. loose pedal bearings	adjust pedal bearings	9
pedal entry difficult (with clip-in pedals)	1. spring tension set high	reduce spring tension	9
	2. cleat guide loose or gone	tighten or replace	9
pedal release difficult (with clip-in pedals)	1. spring tension set high	reduce spring tension	9
	2. loose cleat on shoe	tighten cleat	9
	3. dry pedal spring pivot	oil spring pivots	9
	4. dirty pedals	clean and lube pedals	9
	5. bent pedal clips	replace pedals or clips	9
	6. dirty cleats	clean, lube cleats	9

SYMPTOM	LIKELY CAUSES	ACTION	CHAPTER
pedal release too easy	1. release tension too low	increase release tension	9
(with clip-in pedals)	2. cleats worn out	replace cleats	9
rear shifting	1. maladjusted derailleur	adjust derailleur	5
working poorly	2. sticky or damaged cable	replace cable	5
	3. loose rear cogs	re-seat and tighten cogs	6
	4. worn rear cogs	replace cogs and chain	6, 4
	5. worn/damaged chain	replace chain	4
	6. see also "chain jams in rear" and "chain skips," above		
resistance	1. tire rubs frame or fork	adjust axle; true wheel	2, 6
while coasting	2. brake drags on rim	adjust brake	7
or pedaling	3. tire pressure too low	inflate tire	2, 6
	4. hub bearings too tight	adjust hubs	6
	5. hub bearings dirty/worn	overhaul hubs	6
	6. mud packed around tires	clean bike	2
resistance	1. bottom bracket too tight	adjust bottom bracket	8
while pedaling only	2. bottom bracket dirty/worn	overhaul bottom bracket	8
	3. chain dry/dirty/rusted	clean/lube or replace	4
	4. pedal bearings too tight	adjust pedal bearings	9
	5. pedal bearings dirty/worn	overhaul pedals	9
	6. bent chainring rubs frame	straighten or replace	8
	7. true chainring rubs frame	adjust chain line	8
stiff steering	1. tight headset	adjust headset	11
tire bulged	1. broken casing threads	replace tire	6
	2. slipped tubular tire	reglue tire and line up valve stem	6
tire pinch flats	1. insufficient pressure	pump tire higher	6
	2. tire diameter too small	replace with larger tire	6
tire valve-stem	1. tube slipped in tire	deflate and slide tire around rim	6
angled sharply	2. slipped tubular tire	reglue tire and line up valve stem	6

STRANGE NOISES

Weird noises can be hard to locate; use this to assist in locating them.

SYMPTOM	LIKELY CAUSES	ACTION	CHAPTER
creaking noise	1. dry handlebar/stem joint	grease inside stem clamp	11
	2. loose seatpost	tighten seatpost	10
	3. loose shoe cleats	tighten cleats	9
	4. loose crankarm	tighten crankarm bolt	8
	5. cracked frame	replace frame	15
	6. dry, rusty seatpost	grease seatpost	10
	7. see "squeaking," below	see "squeaking," below	
clicking noise	1. cracked shoe cleats	replace cleats	9
	2. cracked shoe sole	replace shoes	9
	3. loose bottom bracket	tighten BB	8
	4. loose crankarm	tighten crankarm	8
	5. loose pedal	tighten pedal	9
chattering and vibration when braking	1. bent or dented rim	replace rim	13
	2. loose headset	adjust headset	11
	3. brake pads toed out	adjust brake pads	7
	4. wheel way out of round	true wheel	6
	5. greasy sections of rim	clean rim	6
	6. loose brake pivot bolts	tighten brake bolts	7
	7. rim worn through & ready to collapse	replace rim ASAP!	13
clunking from fork	1. headset loose	adjust headset	11
rubbing or scraping noise when pedaling	1. crossed chain	avoid extreme gears	5
	2. front derailleur rubbing	adjust front derailleur	5
	3. chain ring rubs frame	longer bottom bracket or,	8
		move bottom bracket over	8
rubbing, squealing, or scraping noise when coasting or pedaling	1. tire dragging on frame	straighten wheel	2, 6
	2. tire dragging on fork	straighten wheel	2, 6
	3. brake dragging on rim	adjust brake	7
	4. dry hub dust seals	clean and lube dust seals	6
squeaking noise	1. dry hub or BB bearings	overhaul hubs or BB	6, 8
	2. dry pedal bushings	overhaul pedals	9
	3. squeaky saddle	grease edge of leather	10
	4. rusted or dry chain	lube or replace chain	4

STRANGE NOISES (continued)

Weird noises can be hard to locate; use this to assist in locating them.

SYMPTOM	LIKELY CAUSES	ACTION	CHAPTER
squeaking noise (cont.)	5. squeaky seatpost clamps	tighten seatpost clamp	10
	6. seatpost squeaking inside seat tube	shim or shorten seatpost	10
squealing noise	1. brake pads toed out	adjust brake pads	7
when braking	2. greasy rims	clean rims and pads	7
	3. loose brake arms	tighten brake pivot bolt(s)	7
ticking noise	1. wheel magnet hits sensor	move computer sensor	12
when coasting	2. badly glued tubular	reglue tire	6
ticking noise	1. glue on rim sidewall	clean rim with solvent	6
when braking	2. gouge in rim sidewall	sand rough spot	6
	3. high rim seam junction	ignore, or sand seam	6

APPENDIX B

GEAR CHART

This gear table is based on a 700C × 28mm tire (671mm diameter). Your gear-development numbers may be slightly different if the diameter of the fully inflated rear tire, with your weight on it, is not 671mm. Unless your bike has 650C, 24-inch, or some other nonstandard-size wheels, these numbers will be very close.

If you want to have accurate gear-development numbers for the tire you happen to have on at the time, at a certain inflation pressure, then measure the tire diameter very precisely with the following procedure. You can come up with your own gear chart by plugging your tire diameter into the gear-development formula below the chart on the following pages or by multiplying each number in this chart by the ratio of the tire diameter divided by 671mm (the tire diameter I used). Even easier, go to Tom Compton's interactive gear chart at www.analyticcycling.com/GearChart_Page.html.

MEASURING TIRE DIAMETER

1. Sit on the bike with the tire pumped to your desired pressure.

2. Mark the spot on the rear rim that is at the bottom, and mark the floor adjacent to that spot.

3. Roll forward one wheel revolution, and mark the floor again where the mark on the rim is again at the bottom (Fig.12.1).

4. Measure the distance between the marks on the floor; this is the tire circumference at pressure with your weight on it.

5. Divide this number by π (π= 3.14159) to get the diameter.

NOTE: *This roll-out procedure is also the method to measure the wheel size with which to calibrate your bike computer, except that the procedure will be done on the front wheel for most computers (see Fig. 12.1).*

NUMBER OF TEETH ON FRONT CHAINRING

	28	29	30	31	32	33	34	35	36	37	38	39	40	41
11	67.2	69.6	72.0	74.4	76.9	79.3	81.7	84.1	86.5	88.9	91.3	93.7	96.1	98.5
12	61.6	63.8	66.0	68.2	70.4	72.6	74.8	77.1	79.3	81.5	83.7	85.9	88.1	90.3
13	56.9	58.9	61.0	63.0	65.0	67.1	69.1	71.1	73.2	75.2	77.2	79.3	81.3	83.3
14	52.8	54.7	56.6	58.5	60.4	62.3	64.2	66.0	67.9	69.8	71.7	73.6	75.5	77.4
15	49.3	51.1	52.8	54.6	56.4	58.1	59.9	61.6	63.4	65.2	66.9	68.7	70.4	72.2
16	46.2	47.9	49.5	51.2	52.8	54.5	56.1	57.8	59.4	61.1	62.7	64.4	66.0	67.7
17	43.5	45.1	46.6	48.2	49.7	51.3	52.8	54.4	55.9	57.5	59.1	60.6	62.2	63.7
18	41.1	42.6	44.0	45.5	47.0	48.4	49.9	51.4	52.8	54.3	55.8	57.2	58.7	60.2
19	38.9	40.3	41.7	43.1	44.5	45.9	47.3	48.7	50.1	51.4	52.8	54.2	55.6	57.0
20	37.0	38.3	39.6	40.9	42.3	43.6	44.9	46.2	47.6	48.9	50.2	51.5	52.8	54.2
21	35.2	36.5	37.7	39.0	40.3	41.5	42.8	44.0	45.3	46.5	47.8	49.1	50.3	51.6
22	33.6	34.8	36.0	37.2	38.4	39.6	40.8	42.0	43.2	44.4	45.6	46.8	48.0	49.2
23	32.2	33.3	34.5	35.6	36.8	37.9	39.1	40.2	41.3	42.5	43.6	44.8	45.9	47.1
24	30.8	31.9	33.0	34.1	35.2	36.3	37.4	38.5	39.6	40.7	41.8	42.9	44.0	45.1
25	29.6	30.6	31.7	32.8	33.8	34.9	35.9	37.0	38.0	39.1	40.2	41.2	42.3	43.3
26	28.4	29.5	30.5	31.5	32.5	33.5	34.5	35.6	36.6	37.6	38.6	39.6	40.6	41.7
27	27.4	28.4	29.4	30.3	31.3	32.3	33.3	34.2	35.2	36.2	37.2	38.2	39.1	40.1
28	26.4	27.4	28.3	29.2	30.2	31.1	32.1	33.0	34.0	34.9	35.9	36.8	37.7	38.7
29	25.5	26.4	27.3	28.2	29.2	30.1	31.0	31.9	32.8	33.7	34.6	35.5	36.4	37.3

NUMBER OF TEETH ON REAR COG (vertical axis label)

GEAR FORMULA:

Gear = (number of chainring teeth) x (tire diameter) ÷ (number of cog teeth)

If you want the gear in inches, put in the tire diameter in inches.

To find out how far you get with each pedal stroke (gear rollout), multiply the gear by π (3.14159).

NUMBER OF TEETH ON FRONT CHAINRING

42	43	44	45	46	47	48	49	50	51	52	53	54	55	56
100.9	103.3	105.7	108.1	110.5	112.9	115.3	117.7	120.1	122.5	124.9	127.3	129.7	132.1	134.5
92.5	94.7	96.9	99.1	101.3	103.5	105.7	107.9	110.1	112.3	114.5	116.7	118.9	121.1	123.3
85.3	87.4	89.4	91.4	93.5	95.5	97.5	99.6	101.6	103.6	105.7	107.7	109.7	111.8	113.8
79.3	81.1	83.0	84.9	86.8	88.7	90.6	92.5	94.3	96.2	98.1	100.0	101.9	103.8	105.7
74.0	75.7	77.5	79.3	81.0	82.8	84.5	86.3	88.1	89.8	91.6	93.3	95.1	96.9	98.6
69.3	71.0	72.6	74.3	75.9	77.6	79.3	80.9	82.6	84.2	85.9	87.5	89.2	90.8	92.5
65.3	66.8	68.4	69.9	71.5	73.0	74.6	76.1	77.7	79.3	80.8	82.4	83.9	85.5	87.0
61.6	63.1	64.6	66.0	67.5	69.0	70.4	71.9	73.4	74.8	76.3	77.8	79.3	80.7	82.2
58.4	59.8	61.2	62.6	64.0	65.3	66.7	68.1	69.5	70.9	72.3	73.7	75.1	76.5	77.9
55.5	56.8	58.1	59.4	60.8	62.1	63.4	64.7	66.0	67.4	68.7	70.0	71.3	72.6	74.0
52.8	54.1	55.4	56.6	57.9	59.1	60.4	61.6	62.9	64.2	65.4	66.7	67.9	69.2	70.4
50.4	51.6	52.8	54.0	55.2	56.4	57.6	58.8	60.0	61.2	62.4	63.6	64.8	66.0	67.2
48.2	49.4	50.5	51.7	52.8	54.0	55.1	56.3	57.4	58.6	59.7	60.9	62.0	63.2	64.3
46.2	47.3	48.4	49.5	50.6	51.7	52.8	53.9	55.0	56.1	57.2	58.3	59.4	60.5	61.6
44.4	45.4	46.5	47.6	48.6	49.7	50.7	51.8	52.8	53.9	54.9	56.0	57.1	58.1	59.2
42.7	43.7	44.7	45.7	46.7	47.8	48.8	49.8	50.8	51.8	52.8	53.9	54.9	55.9	56.9
41.1	42.1	43.1	44.0	45.0	46.0	47.0	47.9	48.9	49.9	50.9	51.9	52.8	53.8	54.8
39.6	40.6	41.5	42.5	43.4	44.3	45.3	46.2	47.2	48.1	49.1	50.0	50.9	51.9	52.8
38.3	39.2	40.1	41.0	41.9	42.8	43.7	44.6	45.5	46.5	47.4	48.3	49.2	50.1	51.0

APPENDIX C

ROAD BIKE FITTING

f you are getting a new bike, get one that fits you properly. Fit should be the primary consideration when selecting a bike; you can adapt to heavier bikes and bikes not painted your favorite color, but your body will soon protest if you ride on one that doesn't fit. The simple need to protect your more sensitive parts should keep you away from a bike without sufficient stand-over clearance (Fig. C.1), but there are a lot of other factors to consider as well. You'll want to make certain that your bike has enough knee to handlebar distance (Fig. C.2) to ensure that you don't bang your knees on the handlebar, that your neck and back are not in agony after a long ride, and that your weight is distributed over the wheels evenly. And, if you are racing triathlon and time trials, aerodynamics and efficient positioning on an aero handlebar will be important. An improperly sized bike will cause you to ride with less efficiency and more discomfort. So, take some time with this appendix and find out how you can pick a properly sized bike for you.

I've outlined two methods for finding your frame size. The first is a simple method of checking your fit to fully assembled bikes at a bike shop. The second is a bit more elaborate, because it involves taking body measurements. This more detailed approach will allow you to calculate the proper frame dimensions whether the bike is assembled or not.

C-1 SELECTING THE SIZE OF A BUILT-UP BIKE

a. Stand-over clearance

Stand over the bike's top tube and lift the bike straight up until the top tube hits your crotch. The wheels should be at least 1 inch off the ground to ensure that you can jump off the bike safely without hitting your crotch. On a bike with sloping top tube, there is no maximum measurement. On a bike with a level top tube, unless the frame has been built with a head tube with extra extension above the top tube to lift the stem higher, you probably don't want any more than 3 or 4 inches of stand-over.

NOTE: *If you have 2 inches of stand-over clearance over one bike, do not assume that another bike with the same listed frame size will also offer you the same*

C.1 Stand-over clearance and bottom-bracket height

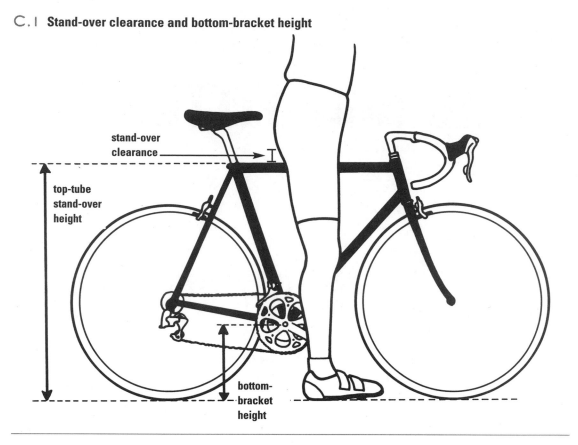

stand-over clearance

top-tube stand-over height

bottom-bracket height

---

stand-over clearance. *Manufacturers measure frame size by using a variety of methods. They also may slope their top tubes differently and use different bottom-bracket heights (Fig. C.1), all of which affect the final stand-over height of the bike and hence your stand-over clearance.*

All manufacturers measure the frame size up the seat tube from the center of the bottom bracket, but the top of the measurement varies. Some manufacturers measure to the center of the top tube ("center-to-center" measurement), some measure to the top of the top tube ("center-to-top"), and others measure to the top of the seat tube (also called "center-to-top"), even though there is wide variation in the length of the seatpost collar above the top tube. Obviously, each of these methods will yield a different "frame size" for the same frame.

No matter how the frame size is measured, the stand-over height of a bike depends on the slope of the top tube. Road bikes made in the last millennium generally have level top tubes, but top tubes that slant up to the front are becoming increasingly more common, and stand-over clearance above a sloping tube is obviously a function of where you are standing. With an up-angled top tube, stand over it a few inches forward of the nose of the saddle, and then lift the bike up into your crotch to measure stand-over clearance.

Stand-over height is also a function of bottom-bracket height above the ground (Fig. C1), but there is normally no substantial variation in this measurement between sizes and brands of road bikes.

Unless the manufacturer lists the stand-over height in its brochure and you know your inseam length, you need to actually stand over the bike.

C.2 **Knee-to-handlebar clearance**

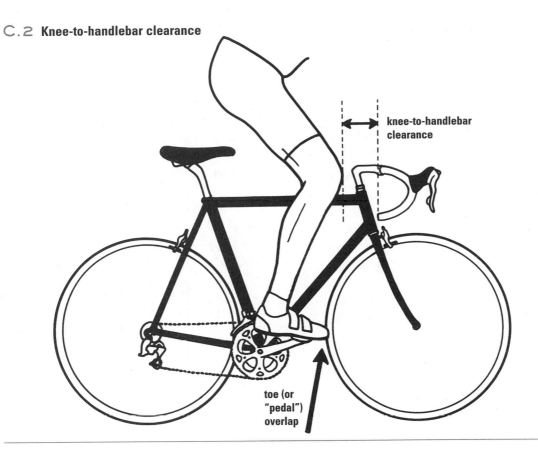

knee-to-handlebar
clearance

toe (or
"pedal")
overlap

ANOTHER NOTE: *If you are short and cannot find a frame size small enough to get at least one inch of stand-over clearance, consider a bike with 650C (24-inch) wheels rather than 700C.*

b. Knee-to-handlebar clearance

Make sure your knee cannot hit the handlebar (Fig. C.2). Check this standing out of the saddle and with the front wheel turned slightly, to make sure that the knee will not hit when you are in the most awkward pedaling position you might use.

c. Handlebar reach and drop

Ride the bike. See if the extension of your arms and torso feels comfortable to you when holding the bar on the flat section adjacent to the stem clamp, on top of the brake hoods, or in the drops. Make sure it is easy to grab the brake levers. Make sure your knees do not hit your elbows as you pedal (Fig. C.5). Make sure that the stem can be raised or lowered enough to achieve a comfortable handlebar height.

NOTE: *Threadless headsets allow very limited adjustment of stem height. Large changes in height require a change in stems.*

d. "Pedal overlap"

"Pedal overlap" is a misnomer, because you are actually interested in whether your toe, not the pedal, can hit the front tire when you are turning sharply at low speeds. Sitting on the bike with the crankarms horizontal and your foot on the pedal, turn the handlebar and check that your toe does not hit the front tire (Fig. C.2). Toe overlap is to be avoided for any kind of slow-speed riding, or else making a slow, tight turn in a parking lot can put you on your nose. Toe overlap is not an issue for most riding, because the speeds are high enough on the road that turning the bike does not require turning the front wheel at enough of an angle to hit your foot.

C-2 CHOOSING A FRAME SIZE FROM BODY MEASUREMENTS

You will need a second person to assist you.

By taking three easy measurements (Fig. C.3), most people can get a very good frame fit. When designing a custom frame, I go through a more complex procedure than this, involving more measurements. For picking an off-the-shelf bike, the following method works well. You can download a measurement ("order") form to use at www.zinncycles.com as well as use the "Fit" calculator on that Web site to automatically make the following calculations.

a. Measure your inseam

Spread your stocking feet about 2 inches apart, and measure up from the floor to a broomstick held level and lifted firmly up into your crotch. You can also use a large book and slide it up a wall to keep the top edge horizontal—as you pull it up as hard as you can—into your crotch. You can mark the top of the broomstick or book on the wall and measure up from the floor to the mark.

b. Measure your inseam-plus-torso length

Hold a pencil horizontally in your sternal notch, the U-shaped bone depression just below your Adam's apple. Standing up straight in front of a wall, mark the wall with the horizontal pencil. Measure up from the floor to the mark.

c. Measure your arm length

Hold your arm out from your side at a 45-degree angle with your elbow straight as in Figure C.3. Measure from the sharp bone point directly behind your shoulder joint (the posterior tip of the acromion) to the wrist bone on the little-finger side of your arm.

d. Find your frame size

Subtract 27.5 to 32cm (10.8 to 12.6 inches) from your inseam length (how to select the proper length

C.3 Body measurements

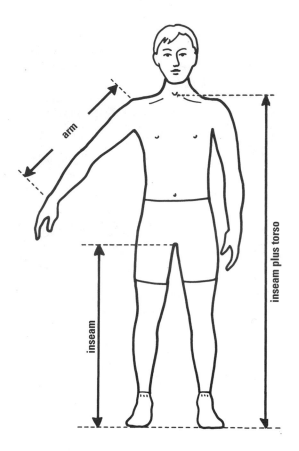

to subtract for you is explained later in this section). The resulting calculated length is your frame size (also known as seat-tube length) measured along the seat tube from the center of the bottom bracket to the top of the top tube (Fig. C.4). If the frame you are interested in has a sloping top tube, you need a bike with a shorter seat tube. In the case of a sloping top tube, project a horizontal line back to the seat tube (or seatpost) from the top of the top tube at the center of its length (Fig. C.4). Mark the seat tube or seat post at this line. Measure from the center of the bottom bracket to this mark; this length should be 27.5 to 32cm less than your inseam measurement.

Also, if the bike has a bottom bracket higher than 27cm (10.6 inches), subtract the additional bottom-bracket height from the seat-tube length as well.

C.4 Bike dimensions on sloping-top-tube road bike

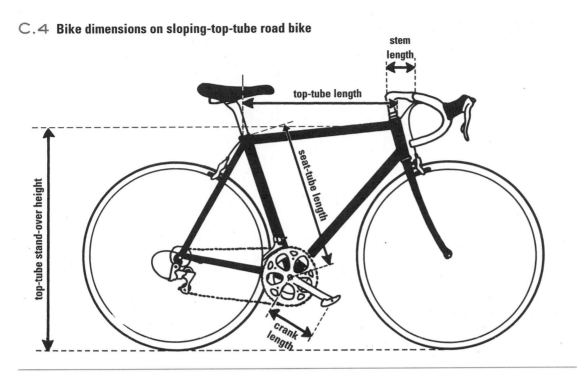

Generally, smaller riders will want to subtract close to 27.5cm from their inseam measurement, whereas taller riders will subtract closer to 32cm. Because an average bottom-bracket height on a road bike is 26.5cm, subtracting any less than 27.5cm could result in less than one inch (2.5cm) of stand-over clearance. But there is considerable range here. The top-tube length is more important than the frame size, and, if you have short torso and arms, you can use a small frame to get the right top-tube length, as long as you can raise your handlebar as high as you need it.

If you are short and cannot find a bike small enough for you to get at least an inch of stand-over clearance (Fig. C.1), consider one with 650C (26 inches) or even 24-inch wheels rather than 700C wheels.

NOTE: *A step-through frame (i.e., "women's" frame, "mixte frame," or "girl's bike") having a steeply up-angled top tube meeting near the bottom-bracket shell makes seat-tube length irrelevant for determining stand-over clearance. With a step-through bike, the only considerations will be horizontal and vertical reach to the handlebar.*

e. Find your top-tube length

To find your torso length, subtract your inseam measurement (found in step 1) from your inseam-plus-torso measurement (found in step 2). Add this torso length to your arm-length measurement (found in step 3). To find the top-tube length, multiply this arm-plus-torso measurement by a factor between 0.47 and 0.485. If you are a casual rider, use 0.47; if you are an aggressive and flexible rider, use 0.485. If you are between these riding levels, use a factor between these values. This top-tube length is measured horizontally from the center of the seat tube to the center of the head tube (Fig. C.4).

But if this is a bike you plan to set up exclusively with an aero handlebar and race in draft-illegal triathlons or time trials, you will generally want a longer top tube. Use 0.495 as the multiplier to find the top tube in this case. If the seat angle on the bike you will be using for this purpose is not very steep—less than 75 degrees—you will likely need to add more length yet to the top tube. This type of setup would be appropriate if you will be pushing your saddle all of the way forward or using a forward-offset seatpost to position yourself in a forward position. Because the forward-set saddle will consume much of your reach to the handlebar, you will need more top-tube length to stretch out properly. The longer top tube will also ensure a more even weight distribution over the wheels and prevent you from using a stem and bar so long that you will be hanging way out over the front of the bike with too much of your weight on the front wheel.

NOTE: *On a sloping-top-tube bike, the actual horizontal top-tube length is greater than the length found by measuring along the top tube.*

f. Find your stem length

Multiply the arm-plus-torso length you found in step 5 by 0.09 to 0.11 to find the stem length (Fig. C.4). Again, a casual rider will multiply by 0.09 or so, while an aggressive, flexible rider will multiply by closer to 0.11. The product is a starting stem length. Finalize the stem length (Fig. C.4) once you are sitting on the bike and see what feels best.

g. Determine crankarm length

Generally, road crankarms come in 2.5mm length increments (Fig. C.4) from 165mm to 180mm—although 167.5mm is often hard to find. Longer than 175mm can usually only be found on high-end cranks, and Campagnolo has stopped making crankarms longer than 175mm in any model. It is possible to find 185mm and even 200mm and longer or 160mm or shorter from some small manufacturers—see www.zincycles.com for more on this.

Frame size you determined in step 4	Appropriate stock crank length (in mm)
less than 46cm	165mm or shorter
47–49cm	167.5
50–53	170
54–57	172.5
58–60	175
61–63	177.5
64 or larger	180 or longer

Given that there is no consensus on ideal crank length, I will give you a simple selection method that works well when buying stock-sized bikes and cranks.

If your riding is focused on time trials, triathlons, or hill climbing, try 2.5mm longer than the recommendations given here.

I have done numerous crank-length tests for *VeloNews*, and the results show that (1) there is no one crank length that works for a given body size and (2) standard stock crank lengths are arbitrary. It is worth experimenting to see what you like.

h. Choosing handlebar width and drop

Your handlebar should be the same width or slightly wider than the distance from the center of the top of one upper-arm bone—the humerus—to the other. You can hold the front of the bar up to your shoulders and see if each side meets in the center of the top of each humerus or slightly overlaps the outside of your arms. That way, your arms will support your shoulders straight in line, and your chest will be able to open for efficient breathing.

If you are a small person, you will want a shallow drop bar, whereas a big person will want a deep drop. If you have small hands, look for a bar with a bend specifically made to reduce the reach to an STI or Ergopower brake lever.

C-3 POSITIONING OF SADDLE AND HANDLEBAR

The frame fit is only part of the equation. Except for the stand-over clearance, a good frame fit is relatively meaningless if the seat setback, seat height, handlebar height, and handlebar reach are not set correctly for you.

a. Saddle height

When your foot is at the bottom of the stroke, lock your knee without rocking your hips. Do this sitting on your bike on a trainer with someone else observing. Your foot should be level, or the heel should be slightly higher than the ball of the foot. Another way to determine seat height is to take your inseam measurement (according to the method in §C-2a) and multiply it by 1.09; the product is the length from the center of the pedal spindle (when the pedal is down) to one of the points on the top of the saddle where your butt bones (ischial tuberosities) contact it. Adjust the seat height (Chapter 10) until you get it the proper height.

NOTE: *These two methods yield similar results, although the measurement-multiplying method is dependent on the thickness of your shoe sole and pedal platform and is thrown off if these are not of standard thickness. Either method yields a biomechanically efficient pedaling position.*

b. Saddle setback

Sit on your bike on a stationary trainer with your cranks horizontal and your forward foot at the usual angle that it is at when you are pedaling. Have a friend drop a plumb line from the front of your knee cap. You can use a heavy ring or washer tied to a string for the plumb line. The plumb line (the "knee over pedal" line in Fig. C.5) should hit the end of the crankarm (or pass up to 2cm behind

it); you will need to lean the knee inward to get the string to hang clear. If the front of the kneecap is over the end of the crankarm, the center of rotation of the knee will be over the center of rotation of the pedal. A saddle positioned fore-and-aft in this manner encourages smooth pedaling at high rpm, whereas positioning yourself so that the line falls up to 2cm behind the crank end encourages powerful seated climbing.

Slide the saddle back and forth on the seatpost (Chapter 10) until you achieve the desired fore-and-aft saddle position. Set the saddle level or very close to it. Recheck the seat height in step 1, because fore-and-aft saddle movements affect seat-to-pedal distance as well.

For draft-illegal-triathlon and time-trial purposes, most riders using an aero handlebar will want to position their saddle considerably farther forward than just recommended, however. Being forward will allow the shoulders to drop low and out of the wind without restricting the hips and having the knees hit the chest—or swing outward to avoid hitting. If it is a frame built for triathlon and/or time trials (Fig. i.2), it will generally have a steep—maybe 76- to 78-degree—seat angle, making the forward seat position easy to accomplish. If not, you may need to get a forward-position seatpost, but this may make your reach to the handlebar too short or require such a long stem that you will be hanging dangerously far out over the front wheel. Set the fore-and-aft seat position so that you are not constricted at the hips when your shoulder joint is the same level as, or just higher than, your hip joint. You may need to tip the saddle very slightly downward and even perhaps turn it a few degrees from straight ahead to find some more crotch comfort. Speed can be painful.

ROAD BIKE FITTING

C.5 Saddle and stem positioning

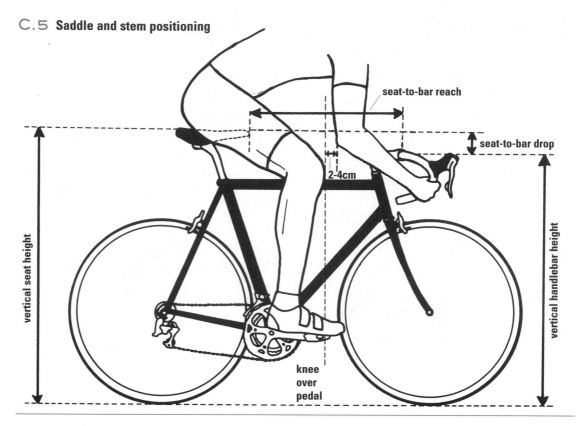

seat-to-bar reach

seat-to-bar drop

2-4cm

vertical seat height

vertical handlebar height

knee over pedal

c. Handlebar height

Measure the handlebar height relative to the saddle height by measuring the vertical distance of the saddle and bar up from the floor (Fig. C.5). How much higher the saddle is than your bar, or vice versa, depends on your flexibility, your riding style, your overall size, and the type of terrain over which you prefer to ride.

Aggressive and/or tall riders will prefer to have their saddle 10cm or more higher than their handlebar. Shorter riders will want proportionately less drop, as will less aggressive riders and riders who do most of their riding in the mountains, as a higher handlebar is easier on the back on long, steep climbs. Generally, people beginning at road bike riding will like their bars high and can lower them as they gain flexibility and become more comfortable with the bike.

If in doubt, start with 4cm of drop and vary it from there. The higher the bar, the more weight is carried on your butt, and the more wind resistance you can expect. Change the bar height by raising or lowering the stem (Chapter 11) or by switching stems and/or bars.

Again, threadless headsets allow only limited stem-height adjustment without substitution of a differently angled stem.

For time trials and draft-illegal triathlons on flat or rolling terrain, you will want your aero bar elbow pads low enough to get your back close to parallel with the ground (Fig. C.6). This setup will make a significant aerodynamic difference, but you may take a while to get used to the setup, and it may be too low for you to produce much power in, so you should work the handlebar height down gradually. Also, you may find a position that is this low impossible to maintain for an Ironman distance or other long event.

C.6 Aero bar position

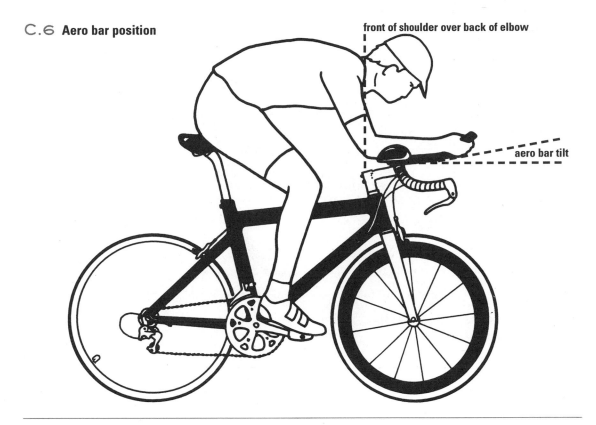

front of shoulder over back of elbow

aero bar tilt

d. Setting handlebar reach

The reach from the saddle to the handlebar is also very dependent on personal preference. More aggressive riders will want a more stretched position than will casual riders. This length is subjective, and I usually need to look at the rider on the bike and get a feel for how he or she would be comfortable and efficient.

A useful starting place is to drop a plumb line from the back of your elbow with your arms bent in a comfortable riding position. This plane determined by your elbows and the plumb line should be 2–4cm horizontally ahead of each knee at the point in the pedal stroke when the crank arm is horizontal and forward (Fig. C.5). The idea is to select a position that you find comfortable and efficient; pay attention to what your body wants.

Vary the saddle-to-bar distance by changing stem length (Chapter 11), not by changing the seat fore-

and-aft position (see C-3b), which is based on pedaling efficiency and not on reach.

On aero bars, set the reach so that a plumb bob from the front of your shoulder comes out over the back of your elbow (Fig. C.6). This will position your upper arms to be angled slightly forward.

NOTE: *There is no single formula for determining handlebar reach and height. The all-too-common method of placing your elbow against the saddle and seeing if your fingertips reach the handlebar is close to useless. Similarly, the oft-suggested method of seeing if the handlebar obscures your vision of the front hub is not worth the brief time it takes to look, being dependent on elbow bend and front-end geometry. Another method involving dropping a plumb bob from the rider's nose is dependent on the handlebar height and elbow bend and thus does not lend itself to a prescribed relationship for all riders.*

e. Other settings for aero handlebars

The elbow pads should be positioned for comfort, and in the case of racing in time trials and draft-illegal triathlons on flat or rolling terrain, they should be placed close to each other for aerodynamics so that the elbows are in front of the knees or yet farther in.

For fore-and-aft placement, the farther forward from your elbows the pads are, the greater the leverage that will smash the pads against your forearms. Achieving pad support under the elbows can be accomplished by using aero bars with the pads cantilevered back behind the bars—toward the rider—or by using a shorter stem and a longer aero bar. Having the pads farther back does not make you faster, but it may offer you more comfort.

Tightly spaced elbows make a big difference in aerodynamic efficiency. Wind-tunnel tests consistently show that narrowness of knee and elbow placement makes a very large difference. But if you can't find a comfortable position to breathe in and pull hard and handle the bike well with narrowly spaced elbow pads, move them out until you can.

The tilt of the aero bar is a matter of personal preference. Wind-tunnel tests have shown time and again that many different angles appear to be equally efficient aerodynamically. Start with none (level) or with a moderate up-angle to the bar, perhaps 5 or 10 degrees (Fig. C.6).

APPENDIX D

GLOSSARY

adjustable cup the nondrive-side cup in the bottom bracket. This cup is removed for maintenance of the bottom-bracket spindle and bearings, and it adjusts the bearings. The term is sometimes applied to the top headset cup as well.

AheadSet a style of headset that allows the use of a fork with a threadless steering tube. Also called a "threadless headset." The name is a trademark of Dia-Compe and Cane Creek.

Allen key (or Allen wrench or hex key) a hexagonal wrench that fits inside a hexagonal hole in the head of a bolt.

anchor bolt (cable anchor bolt, cable-fixing bolt) a bolt securing a cable to a component.

axle the shaft about which a part turns, usually on bearings or bushings.

axle overlock dimension the length of a hub axle from dropout to dropout, referring to the distance from locknut face to locknut face.

ball bearing a set of balls, generally made out of steel, rolling in a track to allow a shaft to spin inside a cylindrical part. May also refer to one of the individual balls.

barrel adjuster a threaded cable stop that allows for fine adjustment of cable tension. Barrel adjusters are commonly found on rear derailleurs, shifters, and brake levers.

BB (see "bottom bracket").

bearing (see "ball bearing").

bearing cone a conical part with a bearing race around its circumference. The cone presses the ball bearings against the bearing race inside the bearing cup.

bearing cup a polished, dish-shaped surface inside of which ball bearings roll. The bearings roll on the outside of a bearing cone that presses them into their track inside the bearing cup.

bearing race the track or surface the bearings roll on. It can be inside a cup, on the outside of a cone, or inside a cartridge bearing.

binder bolt a bolt clamping a seatpost in a frame, a bar end to a handlebar, a handlebar inside a stem, or a threadless steering tube inside a stem clamp.

bonk (1) v. to run out of fuel for the (human) body so that the ability to continue further strenuous activity is impaired. (2) n. the state of having such low blood sugar from insufficient intake of calories that the ability to perform vigorous activity is impaired.

bottom bracket (or BB) the assembly that allows the crank to rotate. Generally the bottom-bracket assembly includes bearings, an axle, a fixed cup, an adjustable cup, and a lockring.

bottom-bracket drop the vertical distance between the center of the bottom bracket and a horizontal line passing through the wheel-hub centers. Drop is equal to the wheel radius minus the bottom-bracket height.

bottom-bracket shell the cylindrical housing at the bottom of a bicycle frame through which the bottom-bracket axle passes.

brake the mechanical device that decelerates or stops the motion of the wheel (and hence of the bicycle and rider) through friction.

brake boss (or brake post or pivot; or cantilever boss, post, or pivot) a fork- or frame-mounted pivot for a brake arm.

brake bridge the cross tube between the seatstays to which a rear road brake is bolted.

brake caliper brake part fixed to the frame or fork containing moving parts attached to brake pads that stop or decelerate a wheel.

brake pad (or brake block) a block of rubber or similar material used to slow the bike by creating friction on the rim, hub-mounted disc, or other braking surface.

brake post (see "brake boss").

brake shoe the metal pad holder that holds the brake pad to the brake arm.

braze-on boss a generic term for most metal frame attachments, even those welded or glued on.

brazing a method commonly used to construct steel bicycle frames. Brazing involves the use of brass or silver solder to connect frame tubes and attach various "braze-on" items including brake bosses, cable guides, and rack mounts to the frame. Although rarely done, it is also possible to braze aluminum and titanium.

bushing a metal or plastic sleeve that acts as a simple bearing on pedals, suspension forks, suspension swing arms, and jockey wheels.

butted tubing a common type of frame tubing with varying wall thicknesses. Butted tubing is designed to accommodate high-stress points at the ends of the tube by being thicker there.

cable (or inner wire) wound or braided wire strands used to operate brakes and derailleurs.

cable anchor (see "anchor bolt").

cable anchor bolt (see "anchor bolt").

cable end a cap on the end of a cable to keep it from fraying.

cable-fixing bolt an anchor bolt that attaches cables to brakes or derailleurs.

cable hanger cable stop on a stem, headset washer, fork-, or seatstay arch used to stop the brake-cable housing for a cantilever or U-brake.

cable housing a metal-reinforced exterior sheath through which a cable passes.

cable stop (or cable-housing stop) a fitting on the frame, fork, or stem at which a cable-housing segment terminates.

cage two guiding plates through which the chain travels. Both the front and rear derailleurs have cages. The cage on the rear also holds the jockey pulleys. Also, a water-bottle holder.

caliper (see "brake caliper" and "measuring caliper").

Campagnolo Italian bicycle-component company.

Cane Creek American bicycle-component company and originator of the threadless headset. Originally known as Dia-Compe USA.

cantilever boss (see "brake boss").

cantilever brake a cable-operated rim brake consisting of two opposing arms, pivoting on frame- or fork-mounted posts. Pads mounted to each brake arm are pressed against the braking surface of the rim via cable tension from the brake lever.

cantilever pivot (see "brake boss").

cantilever post (see "brake boss").

cartridge bearing ball bearings encased in a cartridge consisting of steel inner and outer rings, ball retainers, and, sometimes, bearing covers.

cassette the group of cogs that mounts on a freehub.

cassette hub (or freehub) a rear hub that has a built-in freewheel mechanism to which the rear cogs are attached.

chain a series of metal links held together by pins and used to transmit energy from the crank to the rear wheel.

chain line the imaginary line connecting the center of the middle chainring with the middle of the cogset. This line should, in theory, be straight and parallel with the vertical plane passing through the center of the bicycle. The chain line is measured as the distance from the center of the seat tube to the center of the middle chainring of a triple crank, or, in the case of a double crank, to the center plane midway between the two chainrings.

chain link a single unit of bicycle chain consisting of four plates with a roller on each end and in the center.

chainring a multiple-tooth sprocket attached to the right crankarm.

chainring-nut tool (or chainring-nut spanner) a tool used to secure the chainring nuts while tightening the chainring bolts.

chainstays frame tube on a bicycle connecting the bottom-bracket shell to the rear dropout (and hence to the rear-hub axle).

chain suck the dragging of the chain by the chainring past the release point at the bottom of the chainring. The chain can be dragged upward until it is jammed between the chainring and the chainstay.

chain whip (or chain wrench) a flat piece of steel usually attached to two lengths of chain. This tool is used to remove the rear cogs on a freehub or freewheel.

chase, wild goose (see "goose chase, wild").

circlip (or snapring or Jesus clip) a C-shaped snapring that fits in a groove to hold parts together.

clincher rim a rim with a high sidewall and a "hook" facing inward to constrain the bead of a clincher tire.

clincher tire a tire with a "bead" to hook into the rim sides. A separate inner tube is inserted inside the tire.

clip-in pedal (or clipless pedal) a pedal that relies on spring-loaded clips to grip a cleat attached to the bottom of the rider's shoe, without the use of toe clips and straps.

clipless pedal (see "clip-in pedal").

cog a sprocket located on the drive side of the rear hub.

cone a threaded conical nut that serves to hold a set of bearings in place and also provides a smooth surface upon which those bearings can roll. Can refer to the conical (or male) member of any cup-and-cone ball-bearing system (see also "bearing cone").

crankarm the lever attached at the bottom-bracket spindle and to the pedal used to transmit a rider's energy to the chain.

crankarm anchor bolt (or crank bolt or crankarm-fixing bolt) the bolt attaching the crank to the bottom-bracket spindle on a cotterless drive train.

crank bolt (see crankarm anchor bolt).

crank length the distance measured along the crank between the centerline of the bottom-bracket spindle and the centerline of the pedal axle.

crankset the assembly that includes a bottom bracket, two crankarms, chainring set, and accompanying nuts and bolts.

cross three a pattern used by wheel builders that calls for each spoke to cross three others in its path from the hub to the rim.

cup a cup-shaped bearing surface that surrounds the bearings in a bottom bracket, headset, or hub (see "bearing cup").

derailleur a gear-changing device that allows a rider to move the chain from one cog or chainring to another while the bicycle is in motion.

derailleur hanger a metal extension of the right rear dropout through which the rear derailleur is mounted to the frame.

diamond frame the traditional bicycle frame shape.

disc brake a brake that stops the bike by squeezing brake pads attached to a caliper mounted to the frame or fork against a circular disc attached to the wheel.

dish a difference in spoke tension on the two sides of the rear wheel adjusted such that the rim is centered in the frame or fork.

dishing centering the rim by adjusting spoke tension in a wheel.

dishing tool a tool to check the centering of a rim on a wheel.

double a two-chainring drivetrain setup (as opposed to a three-chainring, or "triple," one).

down tube the frame tube that connects the head tube and bottom-bracket shell together.

drivetrain the crankarms, chainrings, bottom bracket, front derailleur, chain, rear derailleur, and freewheel (or cassette).

drop (1) the vertical distance between the center of the bottom bracket and a horizontal line passing through the wheel hub centers (see also "bottom-bracket drop"). (2) the difference in height between two parts. (3) a terrain discontinuity you may or may not want to ride off of. (4) something not to do with your tools.

dropouts the slots in the fork and rear triangle where the wheel axles attach.

dual-pivot sidepull brake a sidepull brake whose arms pivot at two points rather than one.

DT (a.k.a. DT Swiss) manufacturer of spokes, other bicycle components, and tools.

dust cap a protective cap keeping dirt out of a part.

elastomer a urethane spring sometimes used in suspension forks and rear shocks. Also called an "MCU."

Ergopower an integrated road brake/shift lever manufactured by Campagnolo.

expander bolt a bolt that, when tightened, pulls a wedge up inside or alongside the part into which the bolt is anchored to provide outward pressure and secure said part inside a hollow surface. Expander bolts are found inside quill stems and some handlebar-end plugs and handlebar-end shifters.

expander wedge a part threaded onto an expander bolt and usually used to secure a quill stem inside the fork steering tube or handlebar-end plugs or handlebar-end shifter inside a handlebar. An expander wedge is threaded down its center axis to accept the expander bolt and is either cylindrical in shape and truncated along an inclined plane or conical in shape and truncated parallel to its base.

ferrule a cap for the end of cable housing.

fixed cup the nonadjustable cup of the bottom bracket located on the drive side of the bottom bracket.

flange the largest diameter of the hub where the spoke heads are anchored.

fork the part that attaches the front wheel to the frame.

fork crown the cross piece connecting the fork legs to the steering tube.

fork ends (see "dropouts").

fork rake (or rake) the perpendicular offset distance of the front axle from an imaginary extension of the steering-tube centerline (see "steering axis"). Also called "wheel offset" or simply "offset."

fork tips (see "dropouts").

frame the central structure of a bicycle to which all of the parts are attached.

freehub (see "cassette hub").

freewheel the mechanism through which the rear cogs are attached to the rear wheel on a derailleur bicycle. The freewheel is locked to the hub when turned in the forward direction, but it is free to spin backward independently of the hub's movement, thus allowing a rider to stop pedaling and coast as the bicycle is moving forward.

friction shifter a traditional (nonindexed) shifter attached to the frame or handle bar. Cable tension is maintained by a combination of friction washers and bolts.

front triangle (or main triangle) the head tube, top tube, down tube, and seat tube of a bike frame.

girl's bike (see "step-through frame").

goose chase, wild (see "wild goose chase").

granny ring the lowest gear on the bike in which the chain is on the inner (of three) front chainring and the largest rear cog.

Grip Shift a trademarked twist shifter of the SRAM Corporation that is integrated with the handlebar grip of a bike. The rider shifts gears by twisting the grip (see also "twist shifter").

handlebar the curved tube, connected to the fork through the stem, that the rider grips in order to turn the fork and thus steer the bicycle. The brake levers and shift levers are attached to it.

head angle the acute angle formed by the centerline of the head tube and the horizontal.

headset the bearing system consisting of a number of separate cylindrical parts installed into the head tube and onto the fork steering tube that secure the fork and allow it to spin and swivel in the frame.

headset cup (see "bearing cup").

headset top cap (see "top cap").

head tube the front tube of the frame through which the steering tube of the fork passes. The head tube is attached to the top tube and down tube and contains the headset.

hex key (see "Allen key").

hub the central part of a wheel to which the spokes are anchored and through which the wheel axle passes.

hub brake a disc, drum, or coaster brake that stops the wheel with friction applied to a braking surface attached to the hub.

hydraulic brake a type of brake that uses oil pressure to move the brake pads against the braking surface.

index shifter a shifter that clicks into fixed positions as it moves the derailleur from gear to gear.

inner wire (see "cable").

integrated headset a headset in which the bearing seats are integrated into the head tube (rather than requiring separate headset cups) and the bearings are completely concealed inside of the head tube.

Jesus clip (see "circlip").

jockey wheel (or jockey pulley) a circular, cog-shaped pulley attached to the rear derailleur that is used to guide, apply tension to, and laterally move the chain from rear cog to rear cog.

link a pivoting steel hook on a V-brake arm that the cable-guide "noodle" hooks into (see also "chain link").

locknut a nut that serves to hold the bearing adjustment in a headset, hub, or pedal.

lockring a large, thin circular locknut. On a bottom bracket, the outer ring that tightens the adjustable cup against the face of the bottom-bracket shell. On a freehub, the lockring holds the cogs on.

lock washer a notched or toothed washer that serves to hold surrounding nuts and washers in position.

master link a detachable link that holds the chain together. The master link can be opened by hand without a chain tool.

Mavic French bicycle-component company. Subsidiary of Salomon, which is a subsidiary of Adidas.

measuring caliper tool for measuring the outside dimensions of an object or the inside dimensions of a tube or hollow object by means of movable jaws.

Mektronic Mavic electronic rear-derailleur system.

mixte frame (see "step-through frame").

mounting bolt a bolt that mounts a part to a frame, fork, or component (see also "pivot bolt").

needle bearing steel cylindrical cartridge with rod-shaped rollers arranged coaxially around the inside walls.

nipple a thin nut designed to receive the end of a spoke and seat it in a hole in a rim.

noodle curved cable-guide pipe on a V-brake arm that stops the cable housing and directs the cable to the cable anchor bolt on the opposite arm.

outer wire (see "cable housing").

outer wire stop (see "cable stop").

pedal platform the foot pushes on to propel the bicycle.

pedal overlap the overlapping of the toe with the front wheel while pedaling.

pin spanner a V-shaped wrench with two tip-end pins to fit into holes in a lockring; often used for tightening the adjustable cup of the bottom bracket or other lockrings.

pivot a pin about which a part rotates through a bearing or bushing. Found on brakes and derailleurs.

pivot bolt a bolt on which a brake or derailleur part pivots.

preload (bearings) to adjust the bearings to rotated freely without endplay in the axle. This allows them to turn most freely once loaded.

Presta valve thin, metal tire valve that uses a locking nut to prevent air from escaping out of the inner tube or tire.

quick release (1) the tightening lever and shaft used to attach a wheel to the fork or rear dropouts without using axle nuts. (2) a quick-opening lever and shaft pinching the seatpost inside the seat tube, in lieu of a wrench-operated bolt. (3) a quick cable release on a brake. (4) a fixing mechanism that can be quickly opened and closed, as on a brake cable or wheel axle. (5) any anchor bolt that can be quickly opened and closed by a lever.

quill the vertical tube of a stem for a threaded headset system that inserts into the fork steering tube. It has an expander wedge and bolt inside to secure the stem to the steering tube.

quill pedal a pedal with a cage supporting the foot on only the top side, and whose cage plate is a single continuous piece that curves up to a point at the outboard end of the pedal to protect the side of the foot from being scraped on the road (Fig. 9.1). This type of pedal is meant to be used with a toeclip. The cage offset toward the top and curved upward at the outer end also serves to increase pedaling clearance when the rider leans the bike over when riding around a corner, as well as eliminating the excess weight of cage plates extending downward where they would never be used because of the toeclip on the top. A quill pedal will generally also have a tab on its trailing cage plate so that the rider can flip the pedal upright with the toe of the shoe in order to slide the foot into the toeclip.

race a circular track on which bearings roll freely.

Rapidfire shifter an indexing shifter manufactured by Shimano for use on mountain bikes with two separate levers operating each shift cable.

rear triangle the rear part of the bicycle frame, including the seatstays, the chainstays, and the seat tube.

rebound damping the diminishing of speed of return of a spring by hydraulic or mechanical means.

rim the outer hoop of a wheel to which the tire is attached.

Ritchey American bicycle and bicycle-component company.

saddle (or seat) a platform made of leather and/or plastic upon which the rider sits.

saddle rails the two metal rods supporting the saddle; the seatpost is clamped to these rods.

Schrader valve a high-pressure air valve with a spring-loaded air-release pin inside. Schrader valves are found on some bicycle inner tubes and air-sprung suspension forks as well as on adjustable rear shocks and automobile tires and tubes.

sealed bearing a bearing enclosed in an attempt to keep contaminants out (see also "cartridge bearing").

seat (see "saddle").

seat angle the acute angle formed by the centerline of the seat tube and the horizontal.

seatpost the tube (inserted into the frame) that supports and secures the saddle.

seatstay a frame tube on a bicycle connecting the seat tube or the rear shock to the rear dropout (and hence to the rear-hub axle).

seat tube the frame tube to which the seatpost (and, usually, the cranks) are attached.

sew-up tire (see "tubular tire").

shim a thin element inserted between two parts to

ensure that they are the proper distance apart. On bicycles, a shim is usually a thin washer and can be used to space a disc-brake caliper away from the frame or fork or to space a bottom-bracket cup away from the frame's bottom-bracket shell.

Shimano Japanese bicycle-component company and maker of Dura-Ace and Ultegra component lines as well as SPD (pedals), and STI (shifting system).

sidepull cantilever brake (see "V-brake").

skewer (1) a long rod. (2) a hub quick release. (3) a shaft passing through a stack of elastomer bumpers in a suspension fork.

Slime tire sealant consisting of chopped fibers in a liquid medium that can be injected inside a tire or inner tube to flow to and fill small air leaks.

snapring (see "circlip").

socket a cylindrical tool with a square hole in one end to mount onto a socket-wrench handle and with hexagonal walls inside the opposing end to grip a bolt head or nut to turn it.

socket wrench a cylindrical wrench handle with a ratcheting square head extending at right angles to the handle onto which sockets or other wrench bits for turning bolts or nuts are installed. Also called "socket-wrench handle" or simply "wrench handle."

spacer on a bicycle, generally a thick washer, cylindrical in shape, intended to space two parts farther apart. Spacers can be found between the headset and the stem and between the stem and the top cap on a threadless steering tube, or between the upper bearing cup and the top nut on a threaded steering tube. Spacers may also be used to space a bottom-bracket cup away from

the frame's bottom-bracket shell.

spanner a wrench in primarily British parlance.

spider a star-shaped piece of metal that connects the right crankarm to the chainrings.

spline one of a set of longitudinal grooves and ridges designed to interlock two mechanical parts together.

spokes metal rods that connect the hub to the rim of a wheel.

spring an elastic contrivance that, when compressed, returns to its original shape by virtue of its elasticity. In bicycle suspension applications, the spring used is normally either an elastic polymer cylinder, a coil of steel or titanium wire, or compressed air.

spring preload the initial loading of a spring so that part of its compression range is taken up prior to impact.

sprocket a circular, multiple-toothed piece of metal that engages a chain (see also "cog" and "chainring").

SRAM American bicycle-component company. Owner of Sachs, Avid, and Truvativ bicycle-component companies.

stand-over clearance (or stand-over height) the distance between the top tube of the bike and the rider's crotch when standing over the bicycle.

star nut (or star-fangled nut) a pronged nut that is forced down into the steering tube and that anchors the headset top-cap bolt to adjust a threadless headset.

steering axis the imaginary line about which the fork rotates.

steering tube the vertical tube on a fork that is attached to the fork crown and that fits inside the head tube and swivels within it by means of the headset bearings. A steering tube can be threaded or threadless, meaning that the top headset cup can either screw onto the steering tube or slide onto it, and the stem can either (1) insert inside the steering tube and clamp with an expander wedge (threaded) or (2) clamp around the steering tube (threadless). Also called "steerer" or "forksteerer."

stem connection element between the fork steering tube and the handlebar. An archaic word for stem is also "gooseneck."

stem length the distance between the center of the steering tube and the center of the handlebar measured along the top of the stem.

step-through frame (or women's frame or girl's bike or mixte frame) a bicycle frame with a steeply up-angled top tube connecting the bottom of the seat tube to the top of the head tube. The frame design is intended to provide ease of stepping over the frame and ample stand-over clearance.

STI (Shimano Total Integration) an integrated brake/shift lever manufactured by Shimano.

straddle cable short segment of cable connecting two brake arms together.

straddle-cable holder (see "yoke").

swingarm the movable rear end of a rear-suspension frame.

threaded headset a headset whose top bearing cup and top nut above it screw onto a threaded steering tube.

threadless headset (see "AheadSet").

three cross (see "cross three").

thumb shifter a thumb-operated shift lever attached on top of the handlebars.

tire bead the edge of the tire that seats down inside of the rim. The bead's diameter is held fixed to established standards by means of a strong, stretch- and tear-resistant material—usually either steel or Kevlar. These strands alone are also referred to as the "bead."

tire lever a tool to pry a tire off of the rim.

tire sealant (see "Slime").

toe overlap (or toeclip overlap) (see "pedal overlap").

top cap the round top part of a headset that has a bolt passing through it that screws into the star nut to apply downward pressure on the stem to properly load and adjust the headset bearings on a threadless steering tube.

top tube the frame tube that connects the seat tube to the head tube.

torque the rotational analogue of force. Torque is a vector quantity whose magnitude is the length of the radius from the center of rotation out to the point at which the force is applied, multiplied by the magnitude of the force directed perpendicular to the radius. On bicycles, we are primarily interested in (1) the tightening torque applied to a fastener (this value can be measured with a torque wrench—see Appendix E) and (2) the torque applied by the rider on the pedals to propel the rear wheel and hence the bicycle.

torque wrench a socket-wrench handle with a graduated scale and an indicator to show how much torque is being applied as a bolt is being tightened.

TORX wrench a tool with a star-shaped end that fits in the star-shaped hole in the head of a TORX bolt.

triple a term used to describe the three-chainring combination attached to the right crankarm.

Truvativ a bicycle-component manufacturer. Subsidiary of SRAM.

tub (see "tubular tire").

tubular (see "tubular tire").

tubular rim a rim for a tubular tire. A tubular rim is generally double-walled and concave on top. It is devoid of hook sides that constrain the beads of a clincher tire.

tubular tire a tire without a bead. The tube is surrounded by the tire casing, which is sewed together on the bottom. A layer of cotton tape is usually glued over the stitching, and rim cement is applied to the base tape and the rim to bond the tire to the rim (also called "tubular," "sew-up," and in British parlance, "tub").

twist shifter a cable-pulling derailleur control handle surrounding the handlebar adjacent the hand grip; it is twisted forward or back to cause the derailleur to shift (see also "Grip Shift").

unicrown a manufacturing method of nonsuspended (i.e., rigid) forks in which the fork legs curve toward each other and are welded directly to the steering tube.

V-brake (sidepull cantilever brake) a cable-operated cantilever rim brake consisting of two vertical brake arms that can pivot on frame- or fork-mounted bolts when pulled together by a horizontal cable. A brake pad is affixed to each arm, and there is a cable link and cable-guide pipe on one arm and a cable anchor on the opposite arm.

welding the process of melting two metal surfaces in order to join them.

wheel base the horizontal distance between the two wheel axles.

wheel dish (or wheel dishing) (see "dish" or "dishing").

wheel-dishing tool (see "dishing tool").

wheel-retention tabs cast-in or separate fixtures at the fork ends designed to prevent the front wheel from falling out if the hub quick-release lever of axle and nuts are loose.

wheelset a pair of wheels for the front and rear of the bicycle.

wild goose chase (see "chase").

women's frame (see "step-through frame").

wrench a tool having jaws, a shaped insert, or a socket to grip the head of a bolt or a nut to turn it. In British parlance, also called a "spanner."

yoke the part on a cantilever or U-brake attaching the brake cable to the straddle cable.

Zinn author of this book; not to be confused with Zen.

APPENDIX E

TORQUE TABLE

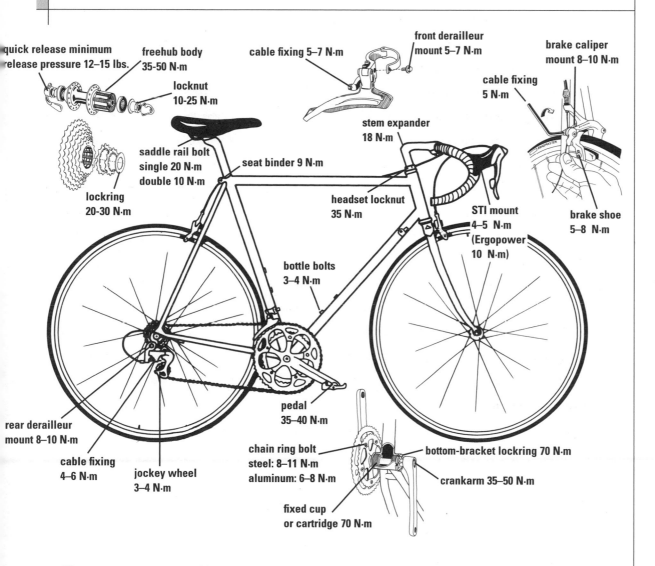

quick release minimum release pressure 12–15 lbs.

freehub body 35-50 N·m

locknut 10-25 N·m

cable fixing 5–7 N·m

front derailleur mount 5–7 N·m

brake caliper mount 8–10 N·m

cable fixing 5 N·m

saddle rail bolt single 20 N·m double 10 N·m

seat binder 9 N·m

stem expander 18 N·m

lockring 20-30 N·m

headset locknut 35 N·m

STI mount 4–5 N·m (Ergopower 10 N·m)

brake shoe 5–8 N·m

bottle bolts 3–4 N·m

rear derailleur mount 8–10 N·m

cable fixing 4–6 N·m

jockey wheel 3–4 N·m

pedal 35–40 N·m

chain ring bolt steel: 8–11 N·m aluminum: 6–8 N·m

bottom-bracket lockring 70 N·m

crankarm 35–50 N·m

fixed cup or cartridge 70 N·m

One of the single biggest sources of mechanical problems (and breakage risk) is over-tightening or undertightening of fasteners, particularly on lightweight equipment. It is great to have the feel for what is tight enough, but many people do not have this, and feel really should only sup-plement torque measurement. With some parts, particularly today's superlight stems and handlebars, it is incredibly important to tighten them to exact torque specification or you could have a stem or handlebar break while you are riding, which results in an immediate and terrifying loss of control of the bicycle. Even "old guard" mechanics, with their "feel" from years of practice, often overtighten the small, light bolts on lightweight stems.

That said, I also recommend that you develop a feel for bolt tightness. On small bolts, even if you are using a torque wrench, choke up on the wrench so you can feel with your fingers how hard you are twisting it. *Torque = Force X Radius*, and since you are reducing the radius at which you apply the force, you have to apply more force to get the same torque on the bolt, so you are aware of the effort it takes. You don't get this sensation when tightening a small bolt by pulling from the end of a long lever where it takes little force to apply a lot of torque. Don't worry about throwing off the torque reading by choking up, as long as you are pulling smoothly. Most torque wrenches have a spring inside to balance the torque on the square bit drive, and this spring action is independent of hand position (the spring pulls from the end of the wrench, and it is the tension on this spring that determines the reading measured by the wrench, irrespective of where you grab the wrench as long as you don't grab its head).

There is also danger to undertightening fasteners. The handlebar in an undertightened stem clamp can come loose and twist, or an undertightened brake cable can pull free when you really yank hard on the brakes. Also, an undertightened bolt suffers more fatigue during use than one that is preloaded.

The standard method of calculating torque specifications is to load the fastener to 80 percent of its yield strength. When you have a rigid joint, this method works. High bolt preload assures that the fastener is always in tension to prevent metal fatigue in the fastener. However, many bike parts are not rigid, and high torques can overcompress or crush compo-nents. This is especially important when you are using parts of different brands, eras, or materials together. For instance, a stem manufacturer's torque specification for a handlebar clamp may not have anticipated that a carbon handlebar would be used, and what would work for an aluminum bar could crush the carbon one. There is no springback in a rigid joint, but if parts flex under tightening (a handlebar is a good example), that flex may provide the preload that the bolt needs at a considerably lower torque setting than if it were bolted through solid steel parts.

Modern torque wrenches usually have a twist knob at the base of the handle to pull tension on the internal spring. You read the torque setting on a vernier scale or against a line on an indicator window on the side of the handle. When the set torque is reached, the head of the wrench snaps over to the side to alert you. Alternatively, a beam-type torque wrench has a needle arm parallel to the wrench shaft that moves across a scale.

You actually need two torque wrenches for working on bikes. The big one cannot measure torques accurately for small bolts. The little one cannot tighten a bottom bracket or crank bolt enough because it does not have a long enough handle, and its scale does not go up high enough.

Using a torque wrench is not a guarantee against a screwup; it simply reduces the chances of one. First, you must make sure that the torque setting you are going for is the one recommended for the bolt you are tightening. This torque table in this appendix includes a lot of bolts, but it obviously cannot include all bolts from all manufacturers, so if you can consult your owner's manual, do it.

Second, lubrication of the bolt, temperature, and a wide variety of other variables will affect torque readings as well. Bicycle bolts generally assume lubrication or threadlock (which provides lubrication before it dries) on the threads, but often not under the bolt head. Lubricating under the bolt head allows the bolt to turn further at the same torque setting than the same bolt without lubrication under the head, and it thus increases the tension on the bolt.

Third, the torque reading will depend on if the bolt is turning or you are starting a stationary bolt into motion, since its coefficient of static friction will be higher than its coefficient of dynamic (sliding) friction. If you try to determine the torque of a bolt by checking what torque setting is required on the handle to unscrew the bolt, you will have estimated a higher torque than the actual one, particularly if the bolt has been in place for some time and has corrosion or dirt around it.

Fourth, the reading on the torque wrench assumes that the head is centered over the bolt; the torque reading will be low if you have a radius multiplying the torque. For instance, measuring tightening torque on a pedal axle (if not using a 6mm hex key in the hex hole in the axle end) requires a "crow's foot" 15mm open-end wrench attachment on a torque wrench. The crow's foot creates an offset between the axle centerline and the tool head centerline, which, if lined up straight with the torque wrench, multiplies the torque setting displayed on the wrench handle (i.e., it will make the wrench—the Radius—effectively longer). The decimal by which you must multiply the torque reading on the wrench to determine the actual torque applied to the bolt will usually be imprinted on the crow's foot. You must use this torque multiplication factor if you have the crow's foot extending straight out from the torque wrench. If you keep the crow's foot at 90 degrees from the torque wrench, provided the crow's foot is short relative to the length of the torque wrench, you can use the torque settings on the wrench (since the hypotenuse and the long side of the right triangle will be close to the same length).

Finally, torque wrenches are not 100 percent accurate, and their accuracy changes over time with wear on the internal spring. Most torque wrenches can be calibrated; there will be a bolt attached to the spring that can be screwed in or out to adjust the reading on the wrench to match a known torque. Ultimately, your feel and common sense are also necessary to ensure safety.

It will be worth your while to review §ii-16 (in Chapter 2) to help you develop a feel for bolt tightness. Whether or not you have "the touch," a torque wrench is a wonderful thing, as long as you know how tight the bolt is supposed to be.

Listed below are tightening torque recommendations of many bike component manufacturers. Where there is only a maximum torque listed, you can figure around 80–90 percent of that number for the minimum torque.

Most torques are for steel bolts; where possible, aluminum and titanium bolts are described as such in the table. Note that it is particularly important to use a copper-filled lubricant like Finish Line "Ti-Prep" on titanium bolts to prevent them from binding and galling; the same goes for installing any bolt into threads in a titanium component or bike frame.

CONVERSION BETWEEN UNITS

The following table is in inch-pounds (in-lbs) and in Newton-meters (N·m) (the latter being the one which I find to be easier to use, since the numbers tend to be nice, round one- or two-digit numbers). Divide these in-lb settings by 12 to convert to foot-pounds (ft-lbs). Multiply in-lb settings by 0.113 to convert to Newton-meters (N·m). Multiply kgf-cm settings by 0.098 to convert to Newton-meters (N·m). Multiply kgf-cm settings by 0.098 to convert to Newton-meters.

BOLT SIZES

M5 bolts are 5mm in diameter and take a 3mm or 4mm hex key (except on derailleurs, where they often take a 5mm hex key or an 8mm box wrench).
M6 bolts are 6mm in diameter and generally take a 5mm hex key.
M7 bolts are 7mm in diameter and generally take a 6mm hex key.
M8 bolts are 8mm in diameter and generally take a 6mm hex key.
M10 bolts are 10mm in diameter and on bikes will likely take a 5mm or 6mm hex key (rear derailleur mounting bolt).

The designation M in front of the bolt size number means millimeters and refers to the bolt shaft size, not to the hex key that turns it; an M5 bolt is 5mm in diameter, an M6 is 6mm, and so on, but it may not have any relation to the wrench size. For instance, an M5 bolt usually takes a 4mm hex key (or in the case of a hex-head style, an 8mm box-end or socket wrench), but M5 bolts on bicycles often accept non-standard wrench sizes. M5 bolts attach bottle cages to

the frame, and while some accept the normal 4mm hex key, many have a rounded "cap" head and take a 3mm hex key or sometimes a 5mm hex key. The M5 bolts that clamp a front derailleur around the seat tube, or that anchor the cable on a front or rear derailleur, also take a non-standard hex key size, namely a 5mm. And M5 disc-brake-rotor bolts often take a *Torx* T25 key. Conversely, the big single pinch bolts found on old stems usually take only a 6mm hex key, but they may be M6, M7, and even M8.

Generally, tightness can be classified in three levels:

1. Snug (10–30 in-lbs, or 1–3 N·m): small setscrews, bearing preload bolts (such as on threadless-headset top caps) and screws going into plastic parts need to be snug.

2. Firmly tightened (30–80 in-lbs, or 3–9 N·m): this refers to small M5 bolts, like shoe cleat bolts, brake and derailleur cable anchor bolts, derailleur band clamp bolts, small stem faceplate or stem steerer clamp bolts. Some M5 and M6 seatpost clamp bolts need to be firmly tightened.

3. Tight (80–240 in-lbs, or 9–27 N·m): wheel axle nuts, old-style single-bolt stem bolts (M6, M7 or M8), some seatpost binder bolts and seatpost saddle clamp bolts need to be tight.

4. Really tight (280–600 in-lbs, or 31–68 N·m): crank arm bolts, pedal axles, cassette-lockring bolts, and bottom-bracket cups are large parts that need to be really tight or they will creak or come loose.

ROAD BIKE FASTENER TORQUE TABLE
(unit conversion factors are at the end of below table)

BOTTOM BRACKETS AND CRANKS	inch-lbs		N·m	
	min	max	min	max
Shimano Crankarm Fixing Bolt (M8 steel)	305	391	34	44
Shimano Crankarm Fixing Bolt (Octalink/Hollowtech)	305	435	35	50
Shimano Left Crankarm Fixing Cap (Hollowtech 2)	4	6	0	1
Shimano Left Crankarm Fixing Bolts (M5 for Hollowtech 2)	88	132	10	15
Shimano Chainring Fixing Bolt	70	95	8	11
Shimano sealed cartridge bottom bracket cups	435	608	50	70
Shimano integrated-spindle (Hollowtech 2) bearing cups	305	435	35	50
Shimano loose-ball-bearing bottom bracket fixed cup	609	695	69	79
Shimano loose-ball-bearing bottom bracket lockring	609	695	69	79
Campagnolo Crankarm Fixing Bolt (M8 steel)	283	336	32	38
Campagnolo sealed cartridge bottom bracket cups		619		70
Campagnolo Chainring Fixing Bolt		71		8
FSA M8 steel crankarm fixing bolt	304	347	34	39
FSA M12 steel crankarm fixing bolt	434	521	49	59
FSA M14 aluminum crankarm fixing bolt	391	434	44	49
FSA M15 steel crankarm fixing bolt	434	521	49	59
FSA chromoly Allen chainring fixing bolt		122		12
FSA aluminum Allen chainring fixing bolt		87		10
FSA aluminum Torx chainring fixing bolt		104		11
FSA aluminum bottom bracket cups	347	434	39	49
Race Face X-Type crankarm fixing bolt	363	602	41	68
Truvativ M8 crank bolts, square taper & PS		372		42
Truvativ M12 crank bolts, ISIS		425		48
Truvativ M15 crank bolts, ISIS		425		48
Truvativ M15 crank bolts, Giga X-Pipe		478		54
Truvativ Giga X-Pipe left crank bolt	363	416	41	47
Truvativ self extractor ring-16mm hex key required	106	133	12	15
Truvativ English BB cup, 1.37"		363		41
Truvativ Giga X-Pipe BB cup	301	363	34	41
Truvativ ISIS Overdrive M48 BB cup		602		68
Bontrager crankarm fixing bolts, M15	370	420	42	48
Bontrager Sport crankarm fixing bolts, M8	320	370	36	42

	inch-lbs		N·m	
BOTTOM BRACKETS (cont.)	min	max	min	max
Bontrager Chainring Fixing Bolt, steel	70	95	8	11
Bontrager Chainring Fixing Bolt, aluminum	50	70	6	8
Trek tandem eccentric	75	100	8	11

BRAKES

Side-pull Calipers

Shimano Caliper Fixing Bolt (to frame)	70	86	8	10
Caliper fixing bolt-carbon seatstays: Trek, Lemond, Klein	55	60	6	7
Shimano Cable Fixing Bolt	53	69	6	8
Shimano Brake-Shoe Fixing Bolt	44	60	5	7
Campagnolo Caliper Fixing Bolt (to frame)		88		10
Campagnolo Cable Fixing Bolt		44		5
Campagnolo Brake-Shoe Fixing Bolt		71		8

Cantilevers and V-brakes

brake lever clamp bolt, M6	50	70	6	8
brake lever clamp — slotted screw	22	26	2	3
brake arm mounting bolt, M6	40	60	5	7
Trek, Fisher, Klein spec for brake arm mounting bolt, M6	70	85	8	10
Avid split-clamp lever mounting bolts	28	36	3	4
brake cable fixing bolt, M5	50	70	6	8
V-brake pad fixing nut	50	70	6	8
cantilever brake pad fixing bolt	70	78	8	9
straddle cable yoke fixing nut	35	43	4	5
Shimano V-brake leverage adjuster bolt	9	13	1	1
Avid Arch Supreme arch-mounting bolt	35	40	4	5

DERAILLEURS AND SHIFTERS

Shimano front-derailleur cable fixing bolt, M5	44	60	5	7
Shimano front-derailleur clamp bolt, M5	44	60	5	7
Shimano front-derailleur braze-on mounting bolt, M5	44	60	5	7
Shimano rear-derailleur cable fixing bolt, M5	35	52	3.9	5.9
Shimano rear-derailleur mounting bolt, M10	70	86	8	10
Shimano rear-derailleur pulley center bolts, M5	27	34	3	4
Campagnolo front-derailleur cable fixing bolt, M5"		44		5

	inch-lbs		N·m	
DERAILLEURS AND SHIFTERS (cont.)	min	max	min	max
Campagnolo front-derailleur clamp bolt, M5		62		7
Campagnolo rear-derailleur cable fixing bolt, M5		53		6
Campagnolo rear-derailleur mounting bolt, M10		133		15
SRAM front-derailleur cable fixing bolt, M5		44		5
SRAM 3.0 front-derailleur clamp bolt, M5		70		8
SRAM X-Gen front-derailleur clamp bolt, M5	44	62	5	7
SRAM rear-derailleur cable fixing bolt, M5	35	45	4	5
SRAM rear-derailleur mounting bolt, M10	70	85	8	10
SRAM rear-derailleur pulley center bolts, M5		22		3
SRAM rear-derailleur cage-stop screw		13		2
SRAM Grip Shift lever-mounting screw		17		2
SRAM trigger lever-mounting bolt		44		5
Trek spec for front-derailleur clamp bolt, M5	25	35	3	4

DUAL CONTROL LEVER

	inch-lbs		N·m	
	min	max	min	max
Shimano STI fixing bolt (to handlebar)	35	43	4	5
Campagnolo Ergopower fixing bolt (to handlebar)		88		10

HUBS, CASSETTES, AND QUICK RELEASE SKEWERS

	inch-lbs		N·m	
	min	max	min	max
Shimano hub quick-release lever closing	79	104	8.8	11.8
bolt-on steel skewer		65		7
bolt-on titanium skewer		85		10
nutted front hub		180		20
nutted rear hub		300		34
quick-release axle locknut	87	217	10	25
Shimano freehub cassette body-fixing bolt	305	434	35	50
Shimano cassette cog lockring	261	434	30	50
Campagnolo cassette cog lockring		442		50
Mavic cassette cog lockring		354		40
Trek spec for front-axle nuts (bolt-on hubs)	180	240	20	27
Trek spec for rear-axle nuts (bolt-on hubs)	240	300	27	34

	inch-lbs		N·m	
MISCELLANEOUS	min	max	min	max
AheadSet bearing preload, M6		22		2
fender to frame bolts, M5	50	60	6	7
Trek spec for rack or fender strut bolts to frame or fork	20	25	2	3
water bottle cage bolts, M5	25	35	3	4
Trek spec for water bottle cage bolts, M5	20	25	2	3
Trek spec for rear-derailleur hanger bolt	50	70	6	8
PEDALS AND SHOES				
Crank Bros. pedal axle to crankarm	301	363	34	41
Shimano pedal axle to crankarm	307		35	
Campagnolo pedal axle to crankarm		354		40
Trek spec for pedal axle to crankarm	350	380	40	43
Time pedal axle to crankarm		310		35
pedal spindle into Truvativ crankarm	186	301	21	34
Crank Bros. shoe-fixing cleat bolt, M5	35	44	4	5
Shimano shoe-fixing cleat bolt, M5	44	51	5	6
Shimano shoe spike, M5		34		4
toeclips to pedals, M5	25	45	3	5
Speedplay Frog spindle nut	35	40	4	5
SEATPOSTS AND SEAT BINDERS				
seatpost saddle rail-clamp bolt, M8	175	345	20	39
cheap steel seatpost band-clamp bolt	175	345	20	39
Campagnolo seatpost saddle rail-clamp bolt, M8		194		22
Campagnolo seatpost binder bolt		88		10
Deda saddle-rail clamp bolt		195		22
Bontrager seatpost with bolt across seatpost head	120	130	14	15
Easton EC90, EC70, EA70 saddle-rail clamp bolts		100		11
Easton EC90 Zero, EC70 Zero saddle-rail clamp bolts		55		6
Easton EA50, EA30 saddle-rail clamp bolts		150		17
ITM K-Sword M6 (for GWS system)	88	97	10	11
ITM K-Sword Special Bolts (saddle-clamp bolt)	88	97	10	11
ITM Forged Lite All series (alu, alu-carbon, carbon) M7	62	71	7	8
Oval Concepts M6 saddle-rail clamp bolts		133		15

	inch-lbs		N·m	
SEATPOSTS AND SEAT BINDERS (cont.)	**min**	**max**	**min**	**max**
Ritchey saddle-rail clamp bolt: Comp, Old Pro, M8		400		45
Ritchey saddle-rail clamp bolt: WCS, New Pro, M6		165		19
Selcof saddle-rail clamp bolt, M6		71		8
Selcof saddle-rail clamp bolt, M8		177		20
Thomson saddle-rail clamp bolt, M6		60		7
Truvativ M6 two bolt		62		7
Truvativ M8 single bolt		80		9
Trek spec for single bolt using 6mm hex key	150	250	17	28
Trek spec for single bolt using 5mm hex key	80	125	10	14
Trek spec for double bolt using 4mm hex key	45	60	5	7
two-piece seat binder bolt, M6	35	60	4	7
seat-tube clamp binder bolt, M6	105	140	12	16
Trek spec for binder bolt for aluminum seatpost	85	125	10	14
Trek spec for binder bolt for carbon fiber seatpost	65	80	7	9
STEMS				
single stem handlebar clamping bolt, M8	145	220	16	25
wedge expander bolt for quill stems, M8	140	175	16	20
bar end M6 bolt	120	140	14	16
3T M5 bolts (front clamp, steerer clamp)		80		9
3T M6 bolts (single steerer clamp)		130		15
3T M6 bolts (two-bolt front clamp plate)		130		15
3T M8 bolts (single steerer clamp; expander bolt for quill)		175		20
3T M8 bolts (single handlebar clamp)		220		25
NOTE: 3T specs also apply to Cinelli stems				
Bontrager M8 steerer tube clamp bolts		200		23
Deda M5 steel bolts (bar clamp, steerer clamp)		90		10
Deda M5 titanium bolts (bar clamp, steerer clamp)		70		8
Deda M6 bolts (bar clamp, steerer clamp)		160		18
Deda M6 old-model hidden steerer clamp bolt		130		15
Deda M8 bolts (quill expander)		160		18
Dimension two-bolt face plate bar clamp, M6	80	90	9	10
Dimension two-bolt steerer tube clamp, M6	80	90	9	10
Dimension one-bolt handlebar clamp, M8 bolt	205	240	23	27

	inch-lbs		N·m	
STEMS (cont.)	**min**	**max**	**min**	**max**
Easton EC70, EA30, EA50, EA70 bar & steerer clamp bolts		70		8
Easton EC90 handlebar clamp bolts		70		8
FSA M5 titanium bolts—use Ti prep!		68		8
FSA M5 chromoly bolts		78		9
FSA M6 chromoly bolts		104		12
FSA M8 chromoly bolts		156		18
ITM K-Sword, Uniko, front/rear clamp		97		11
ITM Millennium, Millennium S.O., front/rear clamp	62	71	7	8
ITM Millennium Carbon, S.O. & White S.O., front/rear clamp	62	71	7	8
ITM Forged Lite Carbon, S.O. & White S.O., front clamp		44		5
ITM Forged Lite Carbon, S.O. & White S.O., rear clamp	62	71	7	8
ITM Millennium 4Ever S.O., Forged Lite Luxe S.O. front clamp		44		5
ITM Millennium 4Ever S.O., Forged Lite Luxe S.O. rear clamp	62	71	7	8
ITM Road Racing, Forged Lite Luxe front clamp	106	124	12	14
ITM Road Racing, Forged Lite Luxe rear clamp		88		10
ITM M8 bolts (single-bolt clamp or expander)	150	160	17	18
ITM M7 bolts	106	120	12	14
ITM M6 bolts (bar clamp, steerer clamp)	88	105	10	12
ITM M5 bolts (bar clamp, steerer clamp), 2 front bolts	62	70	7	8
ITM M5 bolts (bar clamp), 4 front bolts	35	44	4	5
ITM aluminum M6 bolts in magnesium stem	44	53	5	6
LOOK stems, all bolts		44		5
Oval Concepts titanium M5 faceplate bolts for alloy bars		84		10
Oval Concepts titanium M5 faceplate bolts for carbon bars		49		6
Oval Concepts M6 faceplate bolts for alloy bars		93		11
Oval Concepts M6 faceplate bolts for carbon bars		53		6
Oval Concepts titanium M6 clamp bolts for alloy steerers		84		10
Oval Concepts titanium M6 clamp bolts for carbon steerers		53		6
Oval Concepts M6 clamp bolts for alloy steerers		93		11
Oval Concepts M6 clamp bolts for carbon steerers		58		7
Ritchey WCS M5 faceplate bolts for alloy bars	26	52	3	6
Ritchey WCS M5 faceplate bolts for carbon bars		35		4
Ritchey WCS M6 clamp bolts for alloy steerers	52	86	6	10
Ritchey WCS M6 clamp bolts for carbon steerers		78		9

TORQUE TABLE

STEMS (cont.)	inch-lbs		N·m	
	min	max	min	max
Salsa SUL two-bolt face plate bar clamp, M6	120	130	14	15
Salsa one-bolt handlebar clamp, M6 bolt		140		16
Salsa one-bolt steerer tube clamp, M6 bolt	100	110	11	12
Thomson Elite, X2, X4 steerer clamp bolts, M5		48		5
Thomson Elite handlebar clamp bolts, M5		48		5
Thomson X4 handlebar clamp bolts, M5		35		4
Truvativ M5 bolts		50		6
Truvativ M6 bolts-bar		60		7
Truvativ M6 bolts-steerer		80		9
Truvativ M7 bolts		120		14
Trek spec for stem expander	175	260	20	29
Trek spec for handlebar clamp, welded stems	100	120	11	14
Trek spec for handlebar clamp, forged stems	150	180	17	20
Trek spec for handlebar clamp with carbon-fiber handlebar		100		11
Trek spec for stem-steerer clamp	100	120	11	14
Trek spec for stem-angle adjustment	150	170	17	20
Trek spec for tandem-stoker stem extension adjustment	120	140	14	16
Trek spec for tandem-stoker stem seatpost clamp	100	120	11	14

AERO HANDLEBARS

	inch-lbs		N·m	
Oval Concepts A900 extension-clamp bolts, M5		51		6
Oval Concepts A900 base-bar clamp bolts, M5		51		6
Oval Concepts A700 extension clamp bolts, M6		84		10
Oval Concepts SLAM extension clamp bolts, M5		71		8
Oval Concepts SLAM handlebar clamp bolts, M5		71		8
Oval Concepts armrest bolts, carbon bars, M5		62		7
Oval Concepts armrest bolts, aluminum bars, M5		88		10
VisionTech armrest bolts, M5		70		8
VisionTech extension clamp bolts, M6		88		10
Trek spec for armrest bolts, M5		45		5
Trek spec for extension-clamp bolts, M6		60		7
3T extension clamp bolts, all models, M6		133		15
3T New Ahero armrest-offset arm mounting bolt, M5		80		9
3T New Ahero armrest bolts, M6		106		12

STEMS (cont.)	inch-lbs		N·m	
	min	max	min	max
3T Bio Arms handlebar clamp/armrest bolts, M8		177		20
3T Sub-8 and Mini Sub-8 armrest bolts, with riser, M5		71		8
3T Sub-8 and Mini Sub-8 armrest bolts, without riser, M5		44		5

CONVERSION BETWEEN UNITS

The above table is in inch-pounds (in-lbs) and in Newton-meters (N·m) (the latter being the one which I find to be easier to use, since the numbers tend to be nice, round one- or two-digit numbers). Divide in-lb settings by 12 to convert to foot-pounds (ft-lbs). Multiply in-lb settings by 0.113 to convert to Newton-meters (N·m).

BIBLIOGRAPHY

Barnett, John. *Barnett's Manual: Analysis and Procedures for Bicycle Mechanics.* Brattleboro, VT: Vitesse Press, 1989, VeloPress, 1996.

Brandt, Jobst. *The Bicycle Wheel.* Menlo Park, CA: Avocet, 1988.

Compton, Tom. www.analyticcycling.com Web site. 1998.

Dushan, Allan. *Surviving the Trail.* Tumbleweed Films, 1993.

Editors of Bicycling and Mountain Bike magazines. *Bicycling Magazine's Complete Guide to Bicycle Maintenance and Repair.* Emmaus, PA: Rodale Press, 1994

Leslie, David. *The Mountain Bike Book.* London: Ward Lock, 1996.

Lindorf, W. *Mountain Bike Repair and Maintenance.* London: Ward Lock, 1995.

Muir, John and Gregg, Tosh. *How to Keep Your Volkswagen Alive: A Manual of Step-by-Step Procedures for the Complete Idiot.* Santa Fe, NM: John Muir Publications, 1969, 74, 75, 81, 85, 88, 90, 92, 94.

Pirsig, Robert. *Zen and the Art of Motorcycle Maintenance.* New York, NY: William Morrow & Co., 1974.

Schraner, Gerd. *The Art of Wheelbuilding.* Denver, CO: Buonpane, 1999.

Stevenson, John, and Richards, Brant. *Mountain Bikes: Maintenance and Repair.* Mill Valley, CA: Bicycle Books, 1994.

Taylor, Garrett. *Bicycle Wheelbuilding 101, a Video Lesson in the Art of Wheelbuilding.* Westwood, MA: Rexadog, 1994.

Van der Plas, Robert. *The Bicycle Repair Book.* Mill Valley, CA: Bicycle Books, 1993.

Van der Plas, Robert. *Mountain Bike Maintenance.* San Francisco: Bicycle Books, 1994.

Zinn, Lennard. *Zinn & the Art of Mountain Bike Maintenance.* Boulder, CO: VeloPress, 1996, 1997.

Zinn, Lennard. *Mountain Bike Performance Handbook.* Osceola, WI: MBI, 1998.

INDEX

Adams, Douglas, 215
Aerobars, 91, 309, 313
    computers and, 253
    installing, 228
    positioning, 318
    slipping by, 250
    See also Handlebars
Aerodynamics, 105, 228, 286, 309, 317
Air compressors, 17
Anti-chain-drop device, 65, 100–101, 103
Antiseize compound, 16, 32, 176
Art of Wheelbuilding, The (Schraner), 259
Aster, Clyde B., 165
Axle nuts, 24, 26
Axles
    adjusting, 199
    bent/broken, 124
    bottom-bracket, 168, 171, 177, 178, 182, 183, 184
    cleaning, 180
    installing, 126
    ISIS, 176
    Octalink, 176
    overlock dimension, 97, 102
    pedal, 187, 189, 190
    Power Pedal, 195
    removing, 103, 134, 196
    Shimano, 168, 179, 196
    splined, 168, 175, 176, 179
    threading of, 186
    titanium, 168

Barnett, John, 259
Barnett's Manual (Barnett), 247, 259
Barrel adjusters, 70, 82, 84, 141, 143, 145, 147

cable tension and, 74, 160
    turning, 73, 78, 142, 144
Beam suspension, 294, 295
Bearings, 16, 127, 177, 178
    adjusting, 129
    angular-contact, 233, 240, 242, 243
    bottom-bracket, 165, 176
    cleaning, 123-24, 125, 180, 193, 197–198, 200–201, 239, 241–242
    headset, 221, 233, 235, 238, 239, 240, 241–42, 243
    lubricating, 121, 129
    needle, 193, 198, 200, 239, 240
    pedal, 199, 200, 201
    pitted, 235, 242
    removing, 181, 182, 239, 241, 243
    See also Cartridge bearings
Bearing seals, 28, 93, 128
Benchley, Robert, 203
Bench-top organizer, 17
Bicycle Wheel, The (Brandt), 259
Bike pulling, 299
Bike stands, 12, 14, 226
Binding, checking for, 63
Blade assemblies, 85, 86
Blankets, 20, 47
Bolts
    adjusting, 7, 222
    binder, 209, 211, 213
    derailleur, replacing, 95
    cable-fixing, 71, 73, 74, 80, 81, 82, 143, 144, 156, 161
    cage, 293
    chainring, 165, 170, 171, 172, 182
    clamp, 76, 82, 143, 207, 209, 217, 219, 224, 225, 238
    compression, 219, 222, 231, 238

cotter, 168, 169
    crank, 165, 166, 168, 182, 183
    expander, 215, 218
    fixing, 161, 211
    mounting, 67, 71, 148, 153, 158
    pinch, 169, 250
    pivot, 163
    removing, 225
    stem, 218, 219, 221, 225, 239, 241, 250
Bonking, 35, 47
Bosses
    brake, 294
    cantilever, 139, 152, 153, 155, 279
    damaged, 279, 294
    front-derailleur, 75, 76
    riveted, 293
    shift-lever, 286
    water-bottle, 291–292, 293
Bottom brackets, 165, 167, 193, 213, 256, 289
    adjusting, 183
    Campagnolo, 14, 176
    Cannondale, 174
    Cartridge-bearing, 14, 173, 175, 176, 179–180, 182, 183, 184
    chain line and, 103
    cleaning, 28
    cup-and-cone, 173, 176–178, 180–181, 183
    cupless, 180
    derailleurs and, 175
    height of, 285–286, 310, 313
    installing, 175–176
    integrated-spindle, 174, 175, 179, 181
    ISIS, 14, 167, 175

Bottom brackets (continued)
   Loose-ball, 175, 176
   Mavic/Stronglight, 180, 183, 294
   overhauling, 180–182, 183
   Pinarello, 174
   pipespindle, 167
   replacing, 103, 180, 211
   Shimano, 14, 167, 174–175, 176, 182
   Specialized, 174
   Splined-spindle, 14
   troubleshooting, 182–184
   types of, 179-80
Bottom-bracket shells, 168, 174,
   175–176, 177, 178, 182, 183, 313
   damaged in, 184, 294
   Italian, 292
   retapping, 291–292, 293
   unthreaded, 180
Bottom-bracket taps, 16, 293
Bottom-bracket tools, 14
Brake arms, 147, 152, 153, 154
   centering, 158
   loose, 162, 163
   low-profile, 156
   rotating, 158
   slotted, 155
Brake bridges, 161, 289
Brake levers
   Campagnolo, 140, 146, 254
   computers and, 254
   cross-top, 159–60
   installing, 145–146
   lubricating, 145, 159
   maintaining, 21, 145
   movement of, 143
   positioning, 145–146, 159
   problems with, 162
   removing, 145–146, 225
   replacing cable for, 80
   road bike, 152, 161
   Shimano, 80, 146, 254, 315
   squeezing, 143, 148
   top-mount, 159–160
   See also Brake/shift levers
Brake pads, 27, 145
   adjusting, 148, 153–156
   bent rims and, 40, 41
   Campagnolo, 149, 151, 162, 163
   carbon rims and, 149
   checking, 21, 149
   cork, 149
   dirty, 162
   Mavic, 151

Modolo, 151
   mounting bolts for, 148
   replacing, 148, 149, 151, 153
   rubbing, 162–63
   Shimano, 151, 162, 163
   Threaded-post, 154
   V-brake, 161
Brake posts, 156, 158, 292
   damaged, 278, 294
   greasing, 152
   V-brake, 275
Brake/shift levers
   Campagnolo Ergopower, 23, 26, 73,
   78, 80–81, 84, 86, 88–91, 96, 315
   installing, 84, 145–46
   Modolo, 96
   mountain bike, 152
   operating, 83–84
   overhauling, 86, 88–91
   reach on, 146
   removing, 145–146
   Shimano STI, 83–84, 85, 96, 99
Brakes
   adjusting, 21, 156
   Avid, 153
   Campagnolo, 139, 140, 141, 148, 149,
   161, 163
   checking, 22
   Croce d'Aune Delta, 139, 161
   Dia-Compe, 153, 155
   grabbiness of, 148
   Gravity Research Pipe Dreams, 153
   High-end, 161
   hydraulic, 139
   long-reach, 163
   Mavic, 140, 148, 149
   Onza, 153
   reconnecting, 26, 27
   releasing, 23, 26, 14041, 241
   Ritchey, 155
   road bike, 139
   rubbing, 300
   Shimano, 23, 139, 140, 141, 146, 148,
   149, 150, 155, 157, 161, 163
   troubleshooting, 161–163
Brakes, cantilever, 23, 26, 141, 146,
   151–161, 230
   Avid, 153
   barrel adjusters on, 142
   center-pull, 139
   curved-face, 155
   installing, 152–153
   lubricating, 159

Onza, 153
   Shimano, 156
   sidepull, 139
Brakes, center-pull, 23, 26, 230
   Dual-pivot, 139, 140–141
Brakes, sidepull, 23, 160–161
   Campagnolo, 147
   centerpivot, 139, 140, 149–151
   centering, 150
   dualpivot, 139, 147–149
   installing, 147–148, 150
   Mavic, 147, 148
   pad adjustment for, 150
   Shimano, 147
   Single-pivot, 163
Brakes, V-, 23, 26, 139, 146, 153,
   160–161
   opening, 141
Braking
   noise while, 161, 300, 303, 304
   insufficient power for, 162
Brandt, Jobst, 259
Brushes, 12, 28, 30, 31, 129, 181, 198
Bscrews, 70, 71, 75
Bushings, 193, 197, 198, 200, 217
Butting, 287

Cable caps, 16, 79, 80, 81
Cables, brake, 85, 157
   broken, 46
   loosening, 42, 239
   pull on, 161
   Shimano STI, 226
   taping, 226
Cables, derailleur, 71
   attaching, 82
   broken, 45–46
   sticky, 96
Cables, shift, 69, 85
   aerobar, 81–82
   bar-end, 81–82
   Campagnolo, 226
   die-drawn, 83, 144
   disconnecting, 143
   down-tube, 81–82
   frayed, 145, 162
   installing, 143–145, 160
   lubricating, 78–83, 96, 143, 144, 145,
   159
   maintaining, 26, 143
   old-style/aero-style, 86
   replacing, 66, 78–83, 141, 143–145
   sticky, 46, 66

stretched, 162
taping down, 226
thin, 83
Cable stops, 82, 84, 143, 286
Cable tension, 41, 102, 141–143
adjusting, 69, 70, 73–74, 77, 148, 151, 161
barrel adjusters and, 160
on frictional rear shifters, 74
on indexed rear shifters, 73–74
Cage plates, 95
Cage-stop screws, removing/replacing, 94
Calipers, 102, 146–163, 213, 291
Center-pull, 146, 161
removing, 42
sidepull, 161
sticky, 163
testing, 145
Cantilevers, 139, 151, 152, 153, 155, 279
Short-arm, 151
Cartridge bearings, 14, 121–122, 127, 129, 174, 175, 176, 179–180, 182, 183, 184, 193, 198, 199, 241
overhauling, 92–93
sealed, 238, 239, 242, 250
tapping out, 128
Cash, 19
Cassettes, 33, 97–98, 105, 13132
lubricating, 107
Cell phones, 19, 35, 47
Cement
Clément, 116
contact, 14, 115
patch, 109, 110, 114
rim, 14, 115, 116, 117
Vittoria Mastik'One, 116
Chain cleaners, 30–31, 51–52, 134
Chain-dump lever, 78, 80
Chain-elongation gauge, 16, 53, 54, 66
Chain lengths, 55–56, 70
Chain line, 78, 101–102
measuring, 102–103
Chain links, 19
binding of, 40
damaged, 39
stiff, 57, 64, 65
See also Master links
Chain lube, 11, 20, 51, 85, 96, 134, 135
Chainring-nut tool, 12–13, 170
Chainrings, 44, 49, 71, 73, 74, 75, 76, 81, 83, 84
aligning, 101

bent, 171
broken chains and, 39
chain length and, 55
chain line and, 103
chain slipping and, 100
chain suck and, 38, 64
cleaning, 28, 29, 31, 51, 169
clearance for, 172
compatibility issues and, 97
derailleur adjustment and, 75
double, 55, 171
dragging by, 183–184
outer/inner, 172, 174
replacing, 53, 65, 169, 170, 171–172, 174
rubbing, 184
Shimano, 99, 100
spacing between, 98–99
too large, 184
Chainring spiders, 99, 171, 172
Chain rub, 78
Chains
broken, 39–40, 56, 57–58
Campagnolo, 19, 52, 54, 56, 100
checking, 22
cleaning, 21, 28, 29–31, 49, 50, 51–52, 64
connecting, 56–57, 57–58
elongated, 65, 67
jammed, 38–39, 300
jumping, 96
lubricating, 51, 64, 65, 71, 92, 93, 143, 202
replacing, 45,49, 52–53, 54–55, 65, 66, 71
routing, 55–56
rusted, 65
Sachs, 52, 54
Sedis, 97
Shimano, 19, 52, 54, 56, 57, 97, 98, 100
skipping, 5, 65, 69, 96, 100, 300–301
SRAM, 52, 54
Taya, 52, 54
troubleshooting, 64–65
Wippermann, 52, 54, 65, 67
Chainstays, 41, 100, 170, 256, 285, 289, 291
bent, 184
chainrings and, 183–184
chain slapping, 301
chain suck and, 64
checking, 295

clearance of, 102
jamming at, 38, 300
Chain suck, 38, 64–65, 100, 300
Chain tools, 10–11, 19, 45, 54
using, 39, 44, 57, 63, 65
Chain watcher, 78
Chain wax, 143
Chain wear, checking, 53–54
Chain whips, 13, 15, 130, 131
Circlips, 93, 94, 95, 122
Circumference, measuring, 252, 256
Clamps, 215, 220, 226, 227, 236
cable, 157, 161
clip-on, 228
cylindrical, 157
miter, 116
opening, 228
pad, 154
woodworker's miter, 14
worker's band, 116
See also Stem clamps
Cleaning, 4, 27–29, 34
Cleats, 201
adjusting, 188–191
Campagnolo, 202
cleaning/lubricating, 202
Crank Brothers, 188
installing, 188–191
Look, 202
rotational misalignment with, 202
SPD, 187, 188, 189, 191
Speedplay, 187, 190
vertical, 191
Cleat-tightening tools, 191
Clincher tires, 19, 105, 107–113, 117
removing, 107, 108, 110–111
tubular tires and, 113
Clothing, 19, 35, 47
CO_2 cartridges, 18, 38
stuck parts and, 211, 223
Coasting, problems during, 302, 303, 304
Cogs, 26, 39, 49, 51, 55, 64, 72, 75, 76, 129–138
bolt-together, 132
Campagnolo, 98, 99, 100, 136
cassette, 131–132
cleaning, 28, 30, 31, 131, 132
fixed-gear, 130
mountain-bike, 56
removing, 128, 134
replacing, 54, 66, 107, 131–132, 133
Shimano, 100, 132, 138

Cogs (continued)
    spacing of, 64, 97, 100
    worn, 65–66
Cog-wear indicator gauge, 17, 132
Combination wrench and chain tools, 19
Compressed air, 129
Compression rings, 237, 238, 241, 243
Compton, Tom, 305
Computers
    Avocet, 255
    brake levers and, 254
    calibrating, 305
    Campagnolo, 254, 255
    ErgoBrain, 86, 90, 254
    FlightDeck, 86
    information from, 251–252
    installing, 252–256
    problems with, 256–257
    Shimano, 254, 255
    wireless, 253, 256
Cones, 121, 124, 126
    cleaning, 125
    lubricating, 121
ConneX link, 64, 65, 67
Control Tech, 26
Cornering clearance, stability and, 286
Crankarms, 165–172, 174, 181, 184, 206, 256, 311, 316
    Campagnolo, 314
    checking, 22
    drive-side, 178
    length, determining, 314–315
    pedal strokes and, 318
    play in, 183
    replacing, 174
Crank pullers, 12, 166, 167
Cranks
    Campagnolo, 99, 100, 165, 181
    carbon-fiber, 179
    Chorus, 99
    compact-drive double, 99
    components of, 165
    cottered, 166, 168, 169
    double, 181
    French, 165
    FSA, 167, 168, 169, 179, 181
    hard-to-turn, 183
    inexpensive, 174
    installing, 165–169
    integrated-spindle, 165, 167, 168
    ISIS, 166–67, 168
    length of, 315

    mixing parts with, 100
    Race Face, 167
    removing, 165–169, 174
    Shimano, 99, 100, 165, 166–167, 168, 169, 172, 179, 181
    square-taper, 166–167, 168
    steel, 169
    Stronglight, 165
    TA, 165
    triple, 100, 101, 172, 181
    troubleshooting, 182–184
    Truvativ Giga X Pipe, 168, 179
Creaking, 303
    bottom-bracket, 182–183
    crankset, 176
    handlebar, 250
    pedal, 201
    seatpost, 213
Cross gears, 78, 103
Crown race, 246, 247, 249
Crown-race punch, 248, 249
Crown-race remover, 17, 244, 246
Cups, 228, 233, 242, 243, 246
    adjustable, 180, 234, 248
    bottom-bracket, 168, 174, 176, 177, 292
    cleaning, 181
    destroying, 249
    drive-side, 174, 176, 179
    drop-in, 24
    fixed, 177, 178
    installing, 248
    lubricating, 121, 248
    pressing, 249
    removing, 292
    threaded, 230, 234, 235, 236, 239
Cutters, 12, 79, 144, 221, 294
cyclo-cross bikes, 7, 172, 289
    brakes on, 23, 151

Davis, Evan, 275
Deda Dog Fang, 78, 100, 103
Dehydration, 35, 47
Dents, repairing, 294
Derailleurcable guides, 292
Derailleur cages, 44, 73, 76
Derailleur-hanger alignment tool, 17, 66, 290
Derailleur hangers
    checking, 290
    damaged threads in, 293–294
    retapping, 292
    straightening, 290

Derailleurs, front, 45, 69, 183
    adjusting, 43–44, 76–78, 101, 102, 168
    band type, 75
    bottom brackets and, 175
    Campagnolo, 99, 100
    cleaning, 28, 29, 30, 51
    feathering adjustment for, 78
    FSA, 99
    installing, 75–76, 172
    IRD, 99, 181
    Mirage, 99
    routing and, 56
    Shimano, 99, 100
    troubleshooting, 96–103
    V-5, 78
Derailleurs, rear
    adjusting, 55, 66, 71, 75, 301
    bent, 45, 66, 96
    bypassing, 44, 45
    Campagnolo, 96, 99
    cleaning, 28, 29, 30, 93
    compatibility issues for, 96–100
    damaged, 44–45
    described, 69–75
    installing, 71
    long-cage, 55, 56
    loose/worn-out, 66, 96, 301
    maintaining, 92–95
    Mavic, 95
    overhaul of, 93–95
    pulling back, 26
    rusted chains and, 65
    Shimano, 93, 94–95, 96, 99
    troubleshooting, 96–103
    Veloce, 99
Disc wheels, 105, 121
Dishing, 270–272
Dishing gauge, 270, 271
Dishing tool, 16, 120, 271, 274
Distance, measuring, 252, 256
Drills, 17
Drivetrains, 52, 96
    maintaining, 29–30, 182
Dropout-alignment tools, 17, 280, 282, 283
    using, 291, 292
Dropouts, 25, 26, 27, 39, 70, 102, 126
    aligning, 66, 281, 282–283, 290–292, 294
    aluminum, 292
    bent, 291, 292
    derailleur adjustment and, 71, 75
    inspecting, 289

misaligned, 281, 282–283
replaceable, 292
savers, 293
slots, 281
spacing of, 97, 280, 291
steel fork, 279
titanium, 292
Dust caps, 125, 166, 168, 179, 199, 200, 201
    freehub, 136
    Morningstar, 136
    removing, 124

Elastometers, 213
Elbow pads, 228, 317
End caps, 145, 195, 210, 211
Evaporated milk, sealing with, 36

Feathering, 78
Ferrari, Enzo, 139
Ferrules, 16, 79, 80, 81, 82
Files, 12
Finger-lever assembly, 89
Finish Line Threadlock, 32
Finish Line Ti-Prep, 32
Firmly tightened, 34
Fishing line, 16
Fit calculator, 312
Fixed-gear bikes, 186
Flashlights, 47
Flats
    avoiding, 35–36
    fixing, 6, 36–38, 107
    pinch, 112, 117, 118, 302
    riding on, 38
    rim-side, 117
    sealing, 36, 118
    wrench, 293
Food, 35, 47
Ford, Henry, 259
Fore-and-aft position, 285, 318
Fork-crown race, 240
    removing, 244, 245, 246
    setting, 248
Fork-crown-race punch, 15, 248
Fork crowns, 245, 248, 275, 276, 282, 283
    centering under, 278
    clamping, 224
Fork legs, 275, 276, 282
    damaged, 278
Fork rake, 275, 282
Forks, 41, 245, 253
    aligning, 278, 279, 280, 282

aluminum, 278, 279, 282
bent/broken, 275, 276, 282
carbon, 246, 247, 276, 278, 279, 282, 283
clunking from, 303
cyclo-cross, 278, 279
damage to, 223, 278–279
dents in, 278
handlebars and, 217, 275
inspecting, 275–276, 278
installing, 240, 241, 24648
maintaining, 28, 27983
replacing, 223, 239, 278, 279, 283
road, 215, 275, 27983
sensors on, 253
spacing of, 283
steel, 278, 279, 282–283
suspension, 247, 282
threaded, 218–219, 223–224, 278
threadless, 219, 224
titanium, 278, 279, 282
touring, 278, 279
Frames
    aligning, 290–292
    aluminum, 287, 288
    building, 287
    carbon, 287–288
    chain line and, 103
    cleaning, 28, 30, 289
    custom, 312
    damage, 211, 212, 292
    elasticity of, 287
    high-end, 287
    inspecting, 288–289
    long-reach, 163
    materials for, 28687, 288
    preparing, 213, 246–248
    problems with, 211, 212, 285, 288–289, 292
    road bike, 286
    Shimano, 98
    steel, 287, 289
    step-through, 313
    stiffness of, 287
    suspension, 294–295
    titanium, 213, 287, 288
Frame Saver, 210, 289
Frame size, 286, 311
    body measurements and, 312–313
    determining, 315
    finding, 312–313
    measuring, 310
Fraying, 79, 80, 81, 82, 83

Free float, 191, 193
Freehubs, 124, 129–138
    Campagnolo, 98, 138
    cassette, 97–98, 105
    disassembling, 136
    DT-Hügi, 134, 138
    DT Swiss, 138
    Fulcrum, 138
    high-end, 134, 138
    lubricating, 107, 134–38
    Mavic, 98, 134, 136
    Shimano, 97, 98, 122, 133, 134–136
    Suntour, 98
Freewheel removers, 15, 134
Freewheels, 121, 129–138, 186
    cassette, 105
    changing, 133–134
    lubricating, 107, 134, 138
    Suntour, 97
    threaded, 97, 130
French valves. See Presta valves
Front-end geometry, 318

Gear lube, 16, 136
Gears
    checking, 22
    combinations of, 129, 305–307
    wear on, 53
Gel cushions, 203
Gloves, 12, 30, 51, 52, 93, 124, 129
Glue Stick, 226
Grease, 11, 20
    applying, 125
    glaze-hard, 124, 125
    lithium-based, 143
    molybdenum disulfide, 83
    See also Lubricants
Grease guns, 16, 134, 199
Grease injection systems, 129
Growler, 236
G-shaped springs, 86, 89

Hacksaws, 12, 221
Hammers, 218, 248
    Ball-peen, 13, 15
    soft, 16, 128, 210, 238
Handlebars, 84, 215, 222, 224–228
    bent/broken, 46, 223
    carbon, 225, 253
    Cinelli, 215
    drop, 311, 315
    forks and, 217, 275
    height of, 220, 315, 316–317, 318

Handlebars (continued)
    maintaining, 22, 226
    oversized, 159
    overtightening, 225
    positioning, 206, 220, 225, 228, 253, 315
    removing, 225, 226
    reach, 311, 315, 317–318
    road bike, 224
    superlight, 250
    3T, 226
    troubleshooting, 250
    trying, 182
    width, 315
    See also Aerobars
Hangers, 75
    cable, 139, 141, 142, 144, 247, 289
    chain, 28
    derailleur, 290, 292, 293–294
Head angles, 275, 285
Headlights, 20
Headset cup remover, 15, 243, 244
Headset press, 15, 248, 249
Headset "rocket," 243, 244
Headsets, 215, 220, 224, 228, 230–231,
    233–250, 278
    adjusting, 219, 233–238, 240, 243, 250
    Campagnolo, 237, 240, 242, 243, 246
    Cane Creek, 230
    checking, 22, 23334
    Chris King, 238, 239, 240
    cupless integrated, 242, 246
    Dia-Compe, 230, 231, 236, 238, 239,
    240, 249
    DiaTech, 219, 236
    frame/fork preparation for, 246–248
    installing, 247, 248–250
    integrated, 233
    internal, 233
    loose, 234–235, 242
    needle-bearing, 239, 240, 241
    overhauling, 28, 238–243, 278
    pitted, 234, 235
    replacing, 239, 240, 243–246, 250
    Ritchey, 240
    stack height of, 247, 248
    steering tubes and, 233
    threaded, 20, 228, 230, 233, 234–236,
    238–240, 250, 283
    threadless, 219, 220, 233, 236–238,
    240–243, 247
    tight, 234, 235, 250
    troubleshooting, 250
    types of, 228

Head-tube reaming and facing tool,
    16–17
Head tubes, 233, 240, 242, 246, 247, 249
Heart monitors, 251, 256
Helmets, 47
Hemingway, Ernest, 69
Hex keys, 32, 94, 122, 123, 128
    FSA, 169
    using, 33, 34
High gear, adjusting for, 72–73, 77
Housing, 71, 82, 141–145, 147
    compressed, 162
    cutting, 79, 144
    index shift, 79
    installing, 144
    lubricating, 83
    plastic-lined, 144
    replacing, 66, 78, 79, 143
    Teflon-lined, 83
Hubs, 121–129, 193, 260, 282
    adjusting, 119, 123, 126, 127
    Campagnolo, 99, 123, 129, 137
    Cartridge-bearing, 121–122, 127,
    129
    Centaur, 99
    Cup-and-cone, 121, 122–123, 125
    direct-pull, 273
    disassembling, 134
    front, 122
    Fulcrum, 123, 137
    Grease Guard, 129
    lacing, 261, 262, 263, 265, 267, 268,
    272
    maintaining, 28, 122, 124
    Mavic, 127, 128, 129, 129
    overhauling, 107, 121–123, 125,
    127–129, 134
    Power Tap, 256
    rear, 130, 225, 228
    Sanshin, 129
    Shimano, 273
    Specialized, 129
    Suntour, 129
    Wilderness Trail Bikes, 129
Hub shells, 121, 122, 124, 134, 136

Indexed systems, 96
Indexing ratchet, 89, 90
Injuries, 35, 47, 202
Inner tubes, 107
    inflating, 118
    installing, 110–111
    patching, 109

    replacing, 109
    spare, 10, 16, 18, 19, 36–37
Inspections, 21–23

Jockey wheels, 45, 56, 57, 69, 70, 71, 75,
    94, 96
    aligning, 55
    cleaning, 29, 31, 51
    loose, 66
    overhaul of, 92–93
    stiff links and, 65
Jones, F. P., 185

Kahn, Alice, 251
Knee over pedal line, 315
Knee-to-handlebar clearance, 311

Leather-softening compound, 204
Level 1 tasks, 6
Level 1 Tool Kit, 9, 20
    tools in, 10–12
Level 2 tasks, 6
Level 2 Tool Kit, 9
    tools in, 12–14
Level 3 tasks, 6
Level 3 Tool Kit, 9
    tools in, 14–15
Lever hoods, 86, 88, 91, 145, 146, 226,
    255
Limit screws
    adjusting, 72–73, 76–77, 102
    checking, 54, 55, 70, 71
Locknuts, 121, 123, 124, 126, 137, 138
    loosening/tightening, 127, 234, 239
    tightening, 199, 236
Lockring removers, 13, 131, 133, 172
Lockrings, 172, 174, 177, 178, 180, 183,
    184
    cassette, 33
    removing, 130, 131, 133
    threaded, 98, 130
    tightening, 133
Loctite, 32, 66
Low gear, adjusting for, 73, 77
Lubricants, 30
    chain, 49–50
    dry, 49, 50, 143, 202
    freehub, 16, 135
    spray-can, 50
    wax-based, 49, 50, 53, 65
    See also Grease
Lubrication, 21, 34, 53, 86
    bearing, 121, 129

brake lever, 145, 159
cable, 78–83, 96, 143, 144, 145, 159
cassette, 107
chain, 51, 64, 65, 71, 83, 92, 93, 143, 202
cleat, 202
cone, 121
cup, 121, 248
drivetrain, 29, 30
freehub, 107, 134–138
housing, 83
pedal, 202
pivot, 145
shock, 295
threaded part, 32, 154
wet conditions and, 50

Magnets, 255, 256
Maintenance, 5–6, 9, 32-34, 47, 50
    Home-based, 1
    proper, 8
    regular, 30
Mallets, 218, 222, 237
Maslow, Abraham, 9
Master Link (Taya), 31, 52, 54, 56
    connecting/disconnecting, 63–64
Masterson, Portia, 270
Matches, 20, 47
Measurement-multiplying method, 315
Measurements
    bicycle, 102–103, 220, 252, 256, 305,
        310
    body, 310, 312–313, 314
Measuring caliper, 17
Metal-matrix composites, 288
Metric taps, 16
Morningstar Freehub Buddy tool, 16,
    134, 135
Morningstar Freehub Soup syringe, 135
Morningstar J-tool, 16, 134
Morningstar Tooling, 136
Multitools, 18

Needle bearings, 193, 198, 200, 239,
    240
Needles, 16
N'Gear Jump Stop, 78, 101, 103
Nipples, 260, 263, 265, 267
    DT Pro Lock, 261
    loosening, 268, 269, 274
    oiling, 269
    spoke, 119, 120, 121
    tightening, 268, 269

Offset, 275, 282
    forward, 314, 316
    holes, 211, 263, 265, 267
    spokehole, 263

Oil
    linseed, 269
    mineral, 136
    penetrating, 211, 223, 224
    spray, 210
    thread-cutting, 292
O-rings, 135, 136, 167, 200
Orthotics, 202
Overlubrication, 50
Overshifting, 74
Overtightening, 26, 169, 178, 179, 191

Pad height, vertical, 153, 155
Pad mounts, 163
Pad swing, 153, 154
Pad threads, 154
Pad twist, 153, 154
Pain, 202, 301
Paint, repairing, 294
Parallelogram plates, 69, 93, 95
"Parallel-push" linkages, 161
Parker, Dorothy, 49
Park Tool, 221
Parts, frozen, 46, 206, 212, 211,
    223–224, 250
Parts washer, 14
Patching, 38
    with dollar bills, 37, 113
    with energy bar wrappers, 37, 113
    inner tube, 109–110, 111, 112
    sidewall, 112–113
    tubular tire, 117
Patch kits, 10, 18, 3637, 109
Pawls, 123, 136, 137, 138
Pedaling, 183, 185, 318
    efficiency in, 316, 318
    knee/joint pain with, 202
    noise while, 182, 303
    position, 315
    rate, 251
    resistance while, 302
Pedal-release mechanism,
    cleaning/lubricating, 202
Pedals
    adapter plates for, 188
    Bebop, 191
    cage-type, 185
    Campagnolo, 192, 193, 196, 197, 198, 199

cleaning, 28
clip-in, 185, 186, 187–193, 196, 199, 202
Crank Brothers, 191, 193, 195, 196, 199
Diadora, 188, 191, 193, 196, 197, 198,
    199
difficulty entering/releasing,
    301–302
installing, 185, 186–187
Look, 187, 190, 192, 193, 196, 197,
    198, 199
Loose-bearing, 200
mountain bike, 188
noise from, 201–202, 301
overhauling, 193, 195–199, 199–201
overlap of, 311
Power Pedal, 191, 196
quill, 185–186, 199
release/entry with, 202
removing, 186–187, 193, 197
Ritchey, 188, 192, 193, 195, 199–200
road bike, 185, 188
Sampson, 195, 196, 197, 198, 199
Shimano, 187, 188, 191, 192, 193,
    196, 197, 198
SPD, 188, 190, 191, 192, 193, 195,
    199, 202
Speedplay, 188, 191, 193, 199, 200
Time, 187, 188, 190, 191, 193, 196,
    197, 198, 199
troubleshooting, 201–202
Zero, 193, 199, 200
Pins, 49, 52, 56, 63
    lever-pivot, 88
    pushing out, 57
Pivots, 66, 70, 96
    lubricating, 145
    overhaul of, 67, 93–95
Pliers, 10, 71, 107
    channel-lock, 14, 222
    slip-joint, 14
    snapring, 16, 180, 200
    Visegrip, 63
Plugs, 226, 227–228
    expanded support, 220
Plumb lines, 315, 318
Power Link, 54, 63–64
Power meters, 251, 256
Preparations, 46–47
Pressure gauges, 111
Pressure washers, 28
Presta valves, 44, 107, 108, 111, 113
    deep-section, 107
    sealants and, 36, 118

Pumps, 10, 18, 38

Quick-release (QR) levers, 41, 129, 145,
    162, 281, 293, 294
    checking, 21
    tightening, 24–25, 26, 27, 291
    using, 23–24
Quills, 185–186, 199, 215, 217
    greasing, 240
    removing, 218–219
    stuck, 223, 224

Rags, 12
Rain gear, 19
Razor blades, 12
Really tight, 34
Rear-suspension design, 295
Release tension, adjusting, 191–193,
    193, 202
Release-tension adjustment screws,
    191–192
Repairs, 4, 9
    emergency, 20
Retapping, 291–292
Rims, 108, 118–121, 260, 282
    aerodynamic, 105
    aligning, 120
    aluminum, 149
    bent, 40, 107, 118
    blowing tires off, 112
    Bontrager ASYM, 261
    Bora, 107, 113
    brake pads and, 149
    Campagnolo, 107, 113, 261
    carbon, 113, 115, 116, 149
    ceramic-coated, 161, 162
    Cosmic, 107, 113
    C-shaped, 105
    Deep-section, 107, 111, 274
    dirty/oily, 161
    fixing, 42–43
    glue on, 114–115
    Hed, 107, 113
    lacing, 271
    Mavic, 107, 113
    OCR, 261, 262, 274
    replacing, 119
    riding on, 38
    Ritchey, 261, 274
    Rolf, 107, 113
    Spinergy, 107, 113
    tubular tires and, 117
    Vento, 107, 113

Zipp, 107, 113
Rim strips, 37
Rivets, 49, 52, 56, 64, 293
Road bikes, 1, 7
    fitting, 309–318
    sloping-top-tube, 314
    stock-sized, 315
Rollers, 31, 49, 52, 67
Rolling resistance, 112, 117
Roll-out procedure, 305
Rubbing alcohol, 12, 114, 162

Saddle rails, 207, 208, 209
Saddles
    angles of, 285, 316
    Brooks, 204
    comfortable, 203–204, 206
    fore-aft position of, 205–206, 208,
        209, 212
    forward-set, 314
    height of, 202, 205, 210, 315
    Ideale, 204
    installing, 205, 206–209
    positioning of, 203, 205–206, 315,
        316
    setback for, 315–316
    tilt of, 205, 207, 209, 212
    troubleshooting, 212–213
Saddle-to-bar distance, 318
Safety glasses, 12
Sandpaper, 20, 212
Schrader valves, 107
    sealants and, 36, 118
Schraner, Gerd, 259
Screwdrivers, 18, 124, 245
    jammed chains and, 38
    Phillips, 10, 189, 199
    standard, 10, 189, 199
Sealants, 22, 36, 117–118
Seat binders, 46, 109, 213, 292, 294
Seatposts, 203, 208-9, 294
    broken, 46, 206, 212
    Campagnolo, 206
    carbon, 206
    cheap, 206–207
    extension of, 286
    forward-offset, 314, 316
    installing, 209–210, 212, 213
    maintaining, 206
    removing, 211–212, 289
    shock-absorbing, 213
    shortening, 213
    single-bolt, 207

slipping, 213
    stuck, 206, 212
    suspension, 206
    troubleshooting, 212–213
    two-bolt, 207
Seat rails, 46, 212
Seatstays, 27, 28, 291
Seat tubes, 289, 291, 310
    checking, 213
    cleaning inside, 212
    draining water from, 210
    length of, 285, 286, 312
    stretching, 213
Seizing, 16, 32, 176, 186, 218
Sensors, installing, 252–256
Setscrews, 86, 94, 95, 122, 123, 127, 147,
    148, 158
Sew-ups. See Tubular tires
Shift-cable guides, 292
Shifting, 100
    checking, 22
    hesitation in, 73
    improving, 74, 78, 83
    problems with, 78, 302
Shifting ramps, 169
Shift levers, 69, 81, 83–86, 88–92
    adjusting, 71, 76-78
    Campagnolo, 96, 99
    compatibility between, 96, 99–100
    down-tube, 74
    frictional, 74, 77, 91–92
    increasing/decreasing speeds in, 90
    indexed, 73, 96
    overhauling, 91–92
    rehabilitating, 84-86
    replacing, 84-86, 91–92
    Shimano, 73, 74, 78, 80, 91, 92
    troubleshooting, 96–103
    See also Brake/shift levers
Shimano Pedaling Dynamics (SPD),
    187
Shimmying, 299–300
Shims, 213, 220, 238, 250
Shocks, lubricating, 295
Shoes, 182, 188
Shop apron, 12
Shops
    setting up, 17
    well-stocked, 16–17
Sidewalls, 37
    patching, 112–113, 115, 117, 118
Skewers, 127
    Bolt-on, 23, 24, 26

Quick-release, 122, 133
  removing, 131, 134
  tightening, 26, 289
Slime, 36, 118
Snake bites, 112, 118
Snaprings, 180, 193, 200
Soap, 27, 28, 125
Softride beam, 203, 294, 295
  installing, 210–211
Solvents, 92, 94, 124, 131, 162, 198
  bearings in, 125
  citrus-based, 30, 51, 52, 93, 129,
    181, 272
  cleaning chains with, 30–31
  cog-cleaning, 134
  petroleum-based, 51
Spacers, 124, 219, 221, 248
  adding, 236, 243
  hubs and, 123
  steering tubes and, 220
Spanners
  lockring, 33, 130, 178, 180
  pin, 16, 33, 178, 180
Spare parts, 16, 20
SPD. See Shimano Pedaling Dynamics
Speed, measuring, 252, 256
Speedplay "Speedy Luber" grease-
  injection fitting, 199
Spindles. See Axles
Splined tools, 14, 169, 176, 179, 196, 199
Splines, 98, 133
Spoke-length calculators, 7
Spoke prep compound, 261
Spokes, 118–121, 260
  adjusting, 120
  aerodynamic, 105, 255, 273
  broken, 40–41, 107, 119, 120–121, 274
  converging parallel, 267
  diverging parallel, 263
  double-butted, 274
  drive-side, 261, 262, 273
  dynamic, 272
  heavy, 274
  Kevlar, 40, 41
  lacing, 121, 261, 262, 263, 265,
    267–268
  loosening/tightening, 40, 119, 271
  nail-head, 273
  pulling, 272, 274
  radial, 273
  rear wheel, 268
  replacing, 4041, 120–121
  spare, 20

static, 272, 274
Spoke-tension gauge, 17
Spoking patterns
  radial, 259, 261, 262, 272, 274
  three-cross, 259, 260, 267, 274
Spring tension, 94, 95
  adjusting, 78, 148, 150, 157–159
Squeaks, 5, 303
  brake, 148, 161–162
  chain, 52, 65
  handlebar, 225
  saddle, 212
Stability, cornering clearance and, 286
Standover clearance, 286, 309–311,
    313, 315
Star Fangled Nut, 231
Star-nut installation tool, 15, 222
Star nuts, 221, 222, 230, 231, 238
Stationary trainers, 226
Steering, 215
  angles, 246
  axis, 275
  stiff, 302
Steering systems, 215
Steering tubes, 218, 219, 224, 234–238,
    240, 241, 243, 245–250
  aluminum, 221, 222
  broken, 276
  carbon, 220, 221, 222, 231, 238
  cleaning, 242
  cutting, 221
  diameter of, 222, 230
  headsets and, 233
  inspecting, 278
  length of, 220–221, 247
  spacers with, 220
  steel, 221, 222
  stuck stems and, 223–224, 250
  threaded, 278
  threadless, 215–216, 217, 219–220
  thickness of, 222
Stem caps, 225, 250
Stem clamps, 220, 221, 222, 224, 225
  cracked/stretched, 250
  greasing under, 250
Stems, 215, 217–224, 228
  adjusting, 218–220, 250, 317
  aluminum, 222
  carbon, 253
  clamp-type, 219
  front-opening, 225
  installing, 218–220
  length of, 314

light, 225
  maintaining, 22, 222–223
  quill-type, 218–219
  reaming out, 224
  removing, 219, 224, 241
  replacing, 222–223, 226
  road bike, 218
  stuck, 223–224, 250
  threaded, 215
  threadless, 215
  3T, 223
  titanium, 222
  track bike, 218
  troubleshooting, 250
Stiffness, lateral/vertical, 274
Straddle cables, 139, 153
  adjusting, 156–157
Super Link, 52, 54, 63–64
Sutherland's Manual, 247
Swingarms, 294

Taillight, clip-on, 19
Talcum powder, 10, 111
Tandem bikes, brakes on, 151
Tape
  base, 114, 115, 117
  double-sided, 114
  duct, 20
  electrical, 12, 226, 227, 253
  handlebar, 226–228
  rim, 111
  strapping, 111, 226
  Teflon pipe thread, 107, 111
Taya Master Link. See Master Link
Teflon, 83, 107, 111, 114, 144, 202
Telander, Todd, 5
Tensile strength, 28788
Tensioning, 158, 192–193, 261
  wheel, 268, 270, 272, 273, 274
Third Eye Chain Watcher, 78, 100, 103
Threadless saw guide, Park Tool, 221
Threadlock compound, 16, 32, 66, 86,
    88, 168
Threads, 32, 261, 292–294
Thumb levers, 81
Tightness, 34
Time trials, 7, 316, 317
Tire bead, 108, 112
Tire levers, 10, 18, 108, 109
Tire liners, 36
Tire pressure, 22
  rolling resistance and, 112

Tires
　bulged, 302
　checking, 22
　diameter, measuring, 305
　seating, 38
　spare, 16
　suspension/grip and, 105
　See also Clincher tires; Inner
　tubes; Tubular tires
Toeclips, 185, 186, 202
　overlap, 285
Toe-in, 148, 154–155
Toe-out, 154–155, 161, 162
Tool cups, 292
Tools, 1
　for all rides, 18–20, 35
　bike-specific, 9
　required, 6
Top caps, 221, 222, 231, 238, 241
Top tubes, length of, 285, 286, 313–314
Torque, 7, 26, 33-34, 179, 236
TORX screws, 200
Touring bikes, 7, 289
　brakes for, 23, 151
Track bikes, 7, 130
　stems for, 217
Triathlons, 7, 317
Truing, 40, 41, 118–120, 121, 182, 268,
　272, 274
　lateral, 269–270
　radial, 270
Truing stands, 16, 119, 269, 270, 271
Tubes
　carbon, 288
　materials for, 288
　wing-shaped, 286
　See also Inner tubes

Tubular tires, 10, 18, 105, 113–118
　clincher tires and, 113
　Continental, 114
　gluing, 113–116
　handmade, 112
　rims and, 117
　rolling resistance and, 117
　safety with, 113
　stretching, 114
Turning
　problems with, 250
　radius, 286
Twain, Mark, 105

Valve extenders, 107, 111, 113
Valve holes, 263, 267, 281
Valve stems, 108, 111, 115, 302
Velcro, 228
Vent holes, taping over, 29
Vises, 13, 15, 224
Von Braun, Werner, 21

Water, carrying, 46
Wedges, 168, 218, 250
　cylindrical, 215
　loosening, 223
Weight distribution, 314
Wheel base, 286
Wheel-retention tabs, 23, 24
Wheels
　aerodynamic, 105
　bent, 40, 299
　for big riders, 274
　building, 7, 259, 261, 272
　centering, 278
　checking, 21–23
　cleaning, 28

composite, 105
deep-section, 113
installing, 24, 27
lateral strength of, 272
parts for, 260–261
prestressed, 272
radially spoked, 273–274
removing, 23–24, 26–27, 140–141, 224
skewed, 278
tensioning, 268
three-cross, 274
Wheels Manufacturing, 236, 293
Wheelsmith Spoke-Prep, 32
White Lightning, 202
Wires, 20, 78
Wobbles, 171
　checking, 21–22, 120, 281
　fixing, 118, 119, 163
Wrenches
　adjustable, 10, 123, 131, 133, 178
　Allen, 10, 18, 24, 42, 43, 44
　Box-end, 32–33, 196
　cone, 14, 123, 127
　Crescent, 170
　Fixed-cup, 181
　headset, 13, 20, 239
　open-end, 10, 32–33, 131
　pedal, 10, 19, 20, 186, 197, 199
　socket, 12, 3233, 165, 199
　splined, 16, 33
　spoke, 11, 16, 19, 40, 41–42, 119
　torque, 16, 168, 191, 238
　TORX, 32, 170, 171, 172

Zipp beams, 294
Zip-ties, 253–254, 255
Zwanzig, Carl, 285

ILLUSTRATION INDEX

Aerobars
    installing, 228
    positioning, 317
Air compressors, 17
Axle nuts, 25
Axles
    installing, 126
    Mavic Ksyrium, 137
    removing, 137
    Shimano, 196

Barrel adjusters, 71, 75
    turning, 142
Batteries, replacing, 256
Bearings, 122, 131
    installing, 201
    needle, 233
Bike stands, 12, 15
Blankets, 19
Bolts
    cable-fixing, 142
    compression, 237
    crank, 167
    expander, 216
    fixing, 154
    mounting, 75, 154
Bosses
    front-derailleur, 75
    shift-lever, 75
Bottom brackets, 172
    adjusting, 174
    height of, 310
    integrated-spindle, 174

ISIS, 174
    Mavic/Stronglight, 174
    Shimano, 174
    square-taper, 173
    types of, 173
Bottom-bracket shells, assembling, 176
Bottom-bracket taps, 17
Bottom-bracket tools, 13, 33
Brake arms, 152
Brake levers
    Campagnolo, 141
    replacing cable for, 145
    top-mount, 160
Brake pads
    adjusting, 148
    mounting bolts for, 154
Brake/shift levers, 253
    Campagnolo Ergopower, 87
    installing, 145
    Shimano STI, 85, 145
Brakes
    Campagnolo, 22
    Mavic, 140
    releasing, 22
    Shimano, 140
Brakes, cantilever, 151, 152, 153
    ball-joint (Campagnolo), 155
    center-pull, 141
    curved-face (Ritchey), 155
    sidepull, 161
    threaded-post, 153
Brakes, center-pull: dual-pivot, 140
Brakes, sidepull

barrel adjuster on, 142
    center-pivot, 140, 150
    dual-pivot, 140
Brakes, V-, 161
    opening, 141

Cable angles, straddled,
    opened/closed, 156
Cables, brake, 15
    loosening, 42
    taping, 226, 227
    tightening, 157
Cables, derailleur, 15
    attaching, 82
    broken, 46
Cables, shift
    Campagnolo, 81
    crimping, 80
    down-tube, 81
    Shimano STI, 81
    types of, 79
Cage plates, 96
Cage-stop screws,
    removing/replacing, 95
Calipers, 17
    tightening, 147
Cartridge bearings, 122, 130, 232, 233
    tapping out, 128
Cartridge bottom-bracket tool, 13, 33
Cash, 18
Cassettes, 130
Cell phones, 18
Cement, 13, 110

Chain-elongation gauge, 15, 53
Chain lengths
    doubles and, 54
     proper, 54
    triples and, 55
Chain line, measuring, 101
Chain links, 19
    complete, 53
    stiff, 57
Chain lube, 10, 19
Chainring-nut tool, 12
Chainrings
    aligning, 170
    outer/inner, 170
    removing/installing, 170
    shifting ramps/asymmetrical
    teeth of, 169
    third, 166
Chainring spiders, 171
Chains
    broken, 39
    cleaning, 28, 31, 50
    jammed, 38
    lubricating, 31, 50
Chain tools, 10, 19
    using, 56, 57
Chain wear, checking, 53
Chain whips, 13, 14
Circumference, measuring, 252
Clamps, woodworker's miter, 13
Cleats
    centering, 189
    Look, 188, 190
    SPD, 189
    Time, 188
    Clincher tires, 15, 106
    installing, 111
    removing, 108
CO_2 cartridges, 18
Cogs
    cassette, 130
    cleaning, 30, 131
Cog-wear-indicator gauge, 17
Combination wrench and chain
    tools, 19
Computers
    installing, 253
    Shimano, 253
ConneX link, 65
Crank pullers, 13, 167
Cranks, triple, 166
Crown-race remover, 17, 245
Cups

Bottom-bracket, 175
Drive-side, 175
    pressing, 230, 249
    removing, 244
    threadless, 217
Cutters, 13
Cyclo-cross bikes, 7

Derailleur-hanger alignment tool, 17
Derailleur hangers, checking, 289
Derailleurs, front
    adjusting, 43, 77
    band type, 75
    vertical clearance for, 76
Derailleurs, rear, 70, 72
    adjusting, 45, 46
    bypassing, 44
    housing length for, 80
    overhaul of, 94
    pulling back, 27
    Shimano, 94, 95
Dishing, 271
Dishing gauge, 271
Dishing tool, 14, 271
Drills, 17
Drivetrains, parts for, 15
Dropout-alignment tools, 17, 280
    using, 279, 291
Dropouts, 71
    aligning, 280, 291
    bent, 279
    savers, 293
    spacing of, 279
    width, measuring, 290
Dust caps, 195
    removing, 124

Files, 13
Fishing line, 14
Flats, 109
Fork-crown race
    removing, 245, 246
    setting, 248
Fork-crown-race punch, 15
Fork crowns, clamping, 223
Fork rake, 276
Forks
    aligning, 281, 282
    carbon, 231
    cyclo-cross, 277
    damage to, 277
    installing, 241
    rigid, 276

    valve hole alignment and, 281
Frames
    aligning, 290
    dimensions of, 287
    parts of, 286
Freehubs, 130
    disassembling, 137
    lubricating, 137
    Mavic, 137
    Shimano, 135
Freewheel removers, 15
Freewheels, 131

Grease, 19
Grease guns, 15

Hacksaws
    ball-peen, 12
    soft, 14
Handlebars, 160
Hangers
    cable, 142
    derailleur, 289
Headset-cup remover, 15, 244
Headset press, 15, 249
Headset "rocket," 244
Headsets
    Campagnolo, 231, 237
    Cane Creek, 230, 232
    cartridge-bearing, 232, 233
    Chris King, 239
    internal, 232
    needle-bearing, 233
    threaded, 217, 229
    threadless, 217, 229, 237
Head-tube reaming and facing tool, 17
Head tubes, 241
Hex keys, 145, 147
High gear, adjusting for, 72
Housing
    for derailleurs, 80
    types of, 79
Hubs
    building, 126, 127
    cartridge-bearing, 122
    cup-and-cone, 122
    front, 122
    lacing, 262, 263, 264, 265, 266, 267,
    268
    threaded, 131

Inner tubes
    installing, 112

replacing, 109
spare, 10, 18, 19
Integrated-spindle external bracket
tool, 12, 33

J-tool, 15, 135
Jockey wheels, 92, 95
cleaning, 29

Knee-to-handlebar clearance, 311
Knives, 13

Level 1 Tool Kit, tools in, 10–11
Level 2 Tool Kit, tools in, 12–13
Level 3 Tool Kit, tools in, 14–15
Limit screws, 45, 71, 77
Locknuts
loosening/tightening, 123, 127, 235
tightening, 235
Lockring removers, 13, 33
Lockrings, 132, 177
Low gear, adjusting for, 72
Lubrication
chain, 31, 50
freehub, 137
pawl, 137
pedal, 201

Magnets, 254, 255
Master links, Taya, 63–64
Matches, 19
Measurements
bicycle, 101, 252, 290
body, 312
Metric taps, 14
Morningstar Freehub Buddy tool, 15, 135
Morningstar J-tool, 15, 135

Needle bearings, 233
Needles, 14
Nipples, 260

Offset, 154
pad, 154
spoke-hole, 264

Pad height, vertical, 154
Pad swing, 154
Pad twist, 154
Parts, frozen, 224
Parts washer, 14
Patching, 110

with energy bar wrappers, 37
Patch kits, 10, 18
Pawls, 137
Pedal-axle removal tool, 192
Pedals
Campagnolo, 192
clip-in, 186, 194, 195
Crank Brothers, 194
installing, 187
Look, 191
loose-bearing, 197
lubricating, 201
removing, 187
Ritchey, 191, 195
Shimano, 191, 192
Speedplay, 195
Pins
installing, 56
pushing out, 54
Pivots, overhaul of, 94, 95
Pliers
channel-lock, 12
needle-nose, 11
snapring, 15
Plugs
binding by, 217
expanded support, 231
Power Link, 63
Presta valves, 11, 107, 111
Pumps, 11, 18

Quick-release (QR) levers, 24
Quills, 216

Racing bike, 2–3
Rags, 11
Rain gear, 19
Razor blades, 13
Release-tension adjustment screws, 191
Rims
aligning, 271
fixing, 42
lacing, 262, 263, 264, 265, 266, 267, 268
OCR, 262
Rivets
installing, 56
pushing out, 54
Road bikes
dimensions on, 313
exploded view of, viii–ix
sloping-top-tube, 313
Rubbing alcohol, 11

Saddles
Brooks, 204
installing, 208
lightweight, 204
perineum and, 204
positioning of, 314, 316
with Softride beam, 210
Schrader valves, 11, 107
Screwdrivers, 18, 246
Phillips, 11
standard, 11
Seat bag, 18
Seatposts
installing, 209
single-bolt, 207, 208
two-bolt, 207, 208
Sensors, 253
Setscrews, tightening, 147
Shifting ramps, 169
Shift levers, 91
Shop apron, 13
Shops, well-stocked, 17
Skewers, bolt-on, 24
Softride beam, 210
Spanners
lockring, 13, 33
pin, 13, 14, 33
Spare parts, 15, 19
Splined tools, 13
Splines, 132
Spokes, 260
adjusting, 269, 270
broken, 41
converging parallel, 269
diverging parallel, 265
Kevlar, 19
lacing, 121, 262, 263, 264, 265, 266, 267, 268
loosening/tightening, 40, 120
spare, 19
wrapping, 41
Spoke-tension gauge, 17
Spoking patterns
radial, 273
three-cross, 260, 273
Spring tension, adjusting, 158, 159
Stand-over clearance, 310
Star-nut installation tool, 15
Steering systems, 216
Steering tubes, 217
carbon, 231
cutting, 247
measuring at, 220

Steering tubes (continued)
    sighting through, 281
Stem clamps, 220, 224
Stems
    positioning, 314, 316
    road bike, 216
    stuck, 224
    threadless, 217
Straddle cables, 156, 157, 158

Taillight, clip-on, 18
Talcum powder, 11
Tape
    base, 115
    duct, 19
    electrical, 10
    handlebar, 224, 227
Taya Master Link. *See* Master Link
Tensioning, wheel, 271
Third Eye Chain Watcher, 101
Time-trial bikes, 4

Tire levers, 10, 18, 108
Toeclips, 186
Toe-in, 154
Tools
    for all rides, 18
    for extended trips, 19
Touring bikes, 5
Track bikes, 6
Triathlon bikes, 4
Truing
    lateral, 119, 269
    radial, 270
Truing stands, 14
Tubular tires, 18, 19, 106
    stretching, 114

Ultegra, 174

Valve holes, 281
Vises, 13, 15

Wedges
    cylindrical, 216
    loosening, 218
Wheels, 106
    building, 260
    installing, 27
    radially spoked, 273
    removing, 27
Wires, 19
Wrenches
    adjustable, 11
Allen, 11, 33
    box-end metric, 11, 33, 123
    cone, 12, 33, 123, 150
    headset, 13, 19, 235
    open-end metric, 11, 18, 33, 123
    pedal, 10, 19
    socket, 13, 33
    splined, 16
    spoke, 11, 18
    torque, 33

ABOUT THE AUTHOR

Lennard Zinn is a bike racer, frame builder, and technical writer. He grew up cycling, skiing, white-water rafting and kayaking, and tinkering with mechanical devices in Los Alamos, New Mexico. After receiving a physics degree from Colorado College, he became a member of the U.S. Olympic Development (road) Cycling Team. He went on to work in Tom Ritchey's frame-building shop and has been producing custom road and mountain frames at Zinn Cycles since 1982.

Zinn has been writing for *VeloNews* since 1989 and is currently the senior technical writer for *VeloNews* and *Inside Triathlon* magazines. Other books by Zinn are: *Zinn & the Art of Mountain Bike Maintenance* (VeloPress, 2005), *Zinn's Cycling Primer* (VeloPress, 2004), *Mountain Bike Performance Handbook* (MBI, 1998), and *Mountain Bike Owner's Manual* (VeloPress, 1998).

ABOUT THE ILLUSTRATOR

A former mechanic and bike racer, Todd Telander devotes most of his time now to artistic endeavors. In addition to drawing mountain bike parts, he paints and draws wildlife for publishers, museums, design companies, and individuals. Birds are his favorite subject, so he has included a little house sparrow.